Assignment China

AN ORAL HISTORY OF AMERICAN JOURNALISTS
IN THE PEOPLE'S REPUBLIC

Mike Chinoy

Columbia University Press
New York

Columbia University Press
Publishers Since 1893
New York   Chichester, West Sussex
cup.columbia.edu
Copyright © 2023 Michael Chinoy
Published in cooperation with the USC U.S.-China Institute

Library of Congress Cataloging-in-Publication Data
Names: Chinoy, Mike, author.
Title: Assignment China : an oral history of American journalists in the People's Republic /
by Mike Chinoy.
Description: New York : Columbia University Press, 2023. | Includes bibliographical
references and index.
Identifiers: LCCN 2022023842 (print) | LCCN 2022023843 (ebook) | ISBN 9780231207980
(hardback) | ISBN 9780231207997 (trade paperback) | ISBN 9780231557214 (ebook)
Subjects: LCSH: Foreign correspondents—United States—Biography. | China—Press coverage—
United States. | China—Foreign public opinion, American. | Foreign news—United States—
History—20th century. | Foreign news—United States—History—21st century.
Classification: LCC PN4871 .C45 2022 (print) | LCC PN4871 (ebook) | DDC 070.922 [B]—
dc23/eng/20220901
LC record available at https://lccn.loc.gov/2022023842
LC ebook record available at https://lccn.loc.gov/2022023843

Columbia University Press books are printed on permanent and durable acid-free paper.
Printed in the United States of America

Cover design: Milenda Nan Ok Lee
Cover photo: Robin Moyer

ASSIGNMENT CHINA

To all my family

CONTENTS

CONTENTS

Photo gallery follows page 240

ACKNOWLEDGMENTS

I am deeply grateful to my fellow China hands who agreed to share with me their experiences, insights, and feelings about covering the country. Their stories are the heart of this book.

Assignment China would not have been possible without the support, encouragement, and efforts of Clayton Dube, the director of the U.S.-China Institute at the University of California, which has provided an intellectual home for me for more than a decade. Thanks as well to my fellow Institute colleagues Craig Stubing, Venus Saensradi, Catherine Gao, and Linda Truong.

I owe particular thanks to those who read all or parts of the manuscript: my sons Dan and Ben Chinoy; my sister Clara Mora Chinoy; my cousin, the writer John Krich; Dan Lynch; Phil Revzin; and Leon Sigal. The book is far better because of their insights, suggestions, and corrections.

I am especially grateful to Stephen MacKinnon for our brainstorming sessions as I began this project many years ago, and to Jim Laurie and Sandy Gilmour for their enthusiasm and the many photos and videos they provided.

My agents, Nick Wallwork and Chris Newson, were strong supporters of the project from the very beginning. They were a constant source of encouragement and advice. Caelyn Cobb, Monique Briones, Susan Pensak, Peter Barrett, and their colleagues at Columbia University Press brought the book to life.

ACKNOWLEDGMENTS

Many others have offered help, both on *Assignment China* and more broadly over the years: Nolan Barkhouse, Richard Baum, Neil Bennett, Lyn Boyd Judson, Tony Brackett, Richard Buangan, Jade Chien, Marsha Cooke, John DeLury, Ric Dispienseri, Mark Erder, Tomas Etzler, Marvin Farkas, Mitchell Farkas, John Foarde, Tom Grunfeld, Humphrey Hawksley, Justin Higgins, Thomas Hodges, Ming Hsu, Daniela Jurisova, Eric and Nora Kalkhurst, Stephen Lesser, Kenneth Lieberthal, Chuck Lustig, Michael Malaghan, Linda Mason, Carolyn McGoldrick, Mark Michelson, Nate Rich, Stanley Rosen, Robert Ross, Erica Schwartz, Tim Schwarz, Giff Searls, Glenn Shive, Clement So, Stephen Young, Susan Stevenson, James Thompson, Glenn Tiffert, Caroline Van, Carolyn Wakeman, Kathi Zellweger.

For help with translations, and for transcribing hundreds of hours of interviews and conducting other research, I would like to thank Ariel Adler, Shuang An, Andrew Arnold, Sam Ashworth, Caroline Chen, Kailin Chen, Alexis Dale-Huang, Kayla Foster, Chapin Gregor, Tracy Hanamura, Johannes Hano, Xu Hao, Rui Huang, Yingjia Huang, Grace Huang, Michelle Hsu, Kathryn Jacobsen-Majer, Xin Jiang, Ruru Li, Sarah Kirby, Archey Lee, Paul Lee, Amelia Lee, Erin Limlingan, Sophie Liu, Su Liu, Kevin Lu, Lu Lu, Len Ly, Jennifer McCorkle, Jaime Mendoza, Kelsey Quan, Jennifer Wang, Peter Winter, Rao Xing, Zhao Xueyan, Gao Yangjing, Vicki Yang, Gu Jun, Korey Martin, Anthony Vasquez, Kiki Zeng, Su Zitong, and Yuan Zeng.

This has been a long and arduous journey. My sons Dan and Ben, sister Clara, cousin John Krich, and Woodrow and Unit Two have provided crucial intellectual and emotional support. Finally, my biggest thanks go to my wife, Inez Ho, who has understood and supported this labor of love during the many years it has taken to complete it.

CAST OF CHARACTERS
(IN ORDER OF APPEARANCE)

All interviewees are identified by the organization where they worked at the time.

Seymour Topping, International News Service, Associated Press, *New York Times*
John Roderick, Associated Press
Henry Lieberman, *New York Times*
Audrey Ronning Topping, Photojournalist
Roy Rowan, UN Relief and Rehabilitation Administration, *Life*
Murray Fromson, CBS News
Robert Cohen, Freelance Journalist
Bernard Kalb, *New York Times*, CBS News
Stanley Karnow, *Time*, *Washington Post*
Richard Solomon, China Scholar, Assistant Secretary of State for East Asia
Nicholas Platt, State Department
Robert Elegant, *Newsweek*, *Los Angeles Times*
Henry Bradsher, *Washington Star*
Robert Keatley, *Wall Street Journal*
Ted Koppel, ABC News
Jerrold Schecter, *Time*
John Hamilton, Biographer of Edgar Snow
Yao Wei, Chinese Foreign Ministry
Theodore White, Writer

Morley Safer, CBS News

Winston Lord, Assistant to Henry Kissinger, U.S. Ambassador to China

Judy Hoarfrost, member of U.S. ping-pong team

Liang Geliang, Chinese ping-pong Player

Max Frankel, *New York Times*

Dan Rather, CBS News

Dwight Chapin, Nixon Appointments Secretary

Ron Walker, Nixon White House Media Advance Man

Dirck Halstead, United Press International

Tom Jarriel, ABC News

Robert Seigenthaler, ABC News

Barbara Walters, NBC News, ABC News

Ed Fouhy, CBS News

Steve Bell, ABC News

Bruce Dunning, CBS News

Irv Drasnin, CBS News

Richard Bernstein, *Time*

Joseph Lelyveld, *New York Times*

Raymond Burghardt, State Department

John Burns, *Toronto Globe and Mail*, *New York Times*

Orville Schell, *New Yorker*

Fox Butterfield, *New York Times*

Ron Nessen, Ford Press Secretary

Tom Brokaw, NBC News

J. Stapleton Roy, U.S. Ambassador to China

Mike Chinoy, CBS News, CNN

Frank Ching, *Wall Street Journal*

Liu Heung-shing, *Time*, Associated Press

Jay Mathews, *Washington Post*

Jim Laurie, ABC News

Linda Mathews, *Los Angeles Times*

Melinda Liu, *Newsweek*

Sandy Gilmour, NBC News

Graham Earnshaw, Reuters

Jaime FlorCruz, *Time*, CNN

Eric Baculinao, NBC News

Chito Sta Romana, ABC News

CAST OF CHARACTERS

Liu Qing, Chinese Dissident
Barry Lando, CBS News
Michael Parks, *Los Angeles Times*
Richard Hornik, *Time*
Michael Weisskopf, *Washington Post*
James Mann, *Los Angeles Times*
Daniel Southerland, *Washington Post*
John Sheahan, CBS News
Edward Gargan, *New York Times*
Dorinda Elliott, *Newsweek*
Adi Ignatius, *Wall Street Journal*
Cynde Strand, CNN
Kathy Wilhelm, Associated Press
Scott Savitt, United Press International
Terril Jones, Associated Press
John Pomfret, Associated Press, *Washington Post*
Nicholas Kristof, *New York Times*
Sheryl WuDunn, *New York Times*
James Baker, Secretary of State
Bernard Shaw, CNN
Alec Miran, CNN
James Lilley, U.S. Ambassador
Al Pessin, Voice of America
Larry Wortzel, U.S. Embassy Defense Attaché
Jonathan Schaer, CNN
Jeff Widener, Associated Press
Richard Roth, CBS News
James McGregor, *Wall Street Journal*
Lena Sun, *Washington Post*
Kenneth Lieberthal, China Scholar, National Security Council
Andrew Browne, Reuters, *Wall Street Journal*
Marcus Brauchli, *Wall St. Journal*, *Washington Post*
Joseph Kahn, *Wall Street Journal*, *New York Times*
Kathy Chen, *Wall Street Journal*
Wen-chun Fan, CNN
Ian Johnson, *Wall Street Journal*, *New York Times*
Charles Hutzler, Associated Press

Keith Richburg, *Washington Post*
Rebecca MacKinnon, CNN
Elizabeth Rosenthal, *New York Times*
Craig Smith, *Wall Street Journal*, *New York Times*
Ching-Ching Ni, *Los Angeles Times*
Hannah Beech, *Time*
Louisa Lim, NPR
Michael Forsythe, Bloomberg News, *New York Times*
Peter Hessler, *New Yorker*
Barry Petersen, CBS News
David Barboza, *New York Times*
Philip Pan, *Washington Post*
Peter Ford, *Christian Science Monitor*
Stan Grant, CNN
Evan Osnos, *Chicago Tribune*, *New Yorker*
Melissa Chan, Al Jazeera English
Tomas Etzler, Czech TV, CNN
Edward Wong, *New York Times*
Barbara Demick, *Los Angeles Times*
Austin Ramzy, *Time*, *New York Times*
Eunice Yoon, CNN, CNBC
Rob Schmitz, *Marketplace*
Jeremy Page, *Wall Street Journal*
Chris Buckley, Reuters, *New York Times*
Ben Richardson, Bloomberg News
Leta Hong Fincher, China Scholar
Josh Chin, *Wall Street Journal*
Paul Mozur, *New York Times*
Shan Li, *Wall Street Journal*
Gerry Shih, Associated Press, *Washington Post*
Chao Deng, *Wall Street Journal*
Amy Qin, *New York Times*
Megha Rajagopalan, Reuters, *Buzzfeed*
Steven Lee Myers, *New York Times*
Jane Perlez, *New York Times*
Anna Fifield, *Washington Post*
Alice Su, *Los Angeles Times*

CAST OF CHARACTERS

Alison Killing, Architect
Natasha Khan, *Wall Street Journal*
Ramy Inocencio, CBS News
David Culver, CNN
Jonathan Cheng, *Wall Street Journal*

ASSIGNMENT CHINA

INTRODUCTION

In the summer of 1973, I made my first visit to China, joining a group of left-wing American students. At the Wusan People's Commune outside Shenyang, we met model Maoist peasant Yu Kexin. Yu had a broad, weather-beaten face and thick, calloused hands and was wearing a Mao cap. He sat quietly as officials regaled us with statistics to show the commune's achievements, but in his small brick home, he and his wife, Li Lianfang, turned out to be the warmest of hosts. They brought out dish after dish—stir-fried eggs with scallions, chicken, vegetables, noodles with black bean sauce, corn on the cob, and an endless supply of rice and melons. The food was the best I had in China. As I wrote in my journal afterward, "The attitude of the family was so friendly and positive" that it became the highlight of my trip.

Twenty years later, I discovered it was all a lie.

In 1993, as CNN's Beijing bureau chief, I retraced that 1973 journey. My goal was to learn what had happened to the places I had visited and the people I had met for a series of TV reports on the social and economic transformation underway in China. By then, because I had been based in Beijing for six years and had covered the Chinese army crackdown on protesting students in Tiananmen Square in 1989, my illusions about the great Chinese political experiment, which had sparked my initial interest in the country, had long been shattered. But even under these circumstances, my reunion with Yu Kexin was an eye-opening moment.

With the help of the local Foreign Affairs Office, or *waiban*, through which all foreign correspondents then had to route requests for travel and coverage, I was able to track Yu down and get permission to return to his village and speak with him. No longer living in the simple brick dwelling where we first met, he now had a nicely furnished flat with a TV. A beneficiary of the market-oriented reforms introduced by Deng Xiaoping in the 1980s, he had given up working in the fields and was now running a tractor repair shop. His life had clearly improved. As soon as the local officials were out of earshot, however, Yu confessed that almost everything I had experienced during my first visit twenty years before had been an illusion. "I told you then that things were good," he said. "But when you foreigners came, conditions were terrible. Our income was tiny. They didn't let us raise animals or grow anything for ourselves. We got that meal only because you came. It was trucked in from the city the day before. Back then, we were lucky to have a good meal once a week, or even once a month." Even after two decades of experience following China, I was sobered by what Yu said.

When I look back, the episode underscores the central theme that emerges in any discussion about the history and experiences of the foreign correspondents who have covered China—the challenge of finding the truth in a vast, complicated country with a long history of distrust of outsiders, a secretive and authoritarian political system deeply suspicious of journalists, and no qualms about deliberately lying or twisting reality to suit the political needs of the Chinese Communist Party.

The stakes could not be higher. As Sino-American relations have swung from World War II ally, to Cold War enemy, to common foe of the Soviet Union, to "cuddly communists" embracing the market, to emerging economic superpower and strategic rival, how to deal with the country has consistently been a crucial, and contentious, issue in the United States. Reporters for the American media have played a critical role, profoundly influencing U.S. views of the country as well as the policies of successive American governments. Moreover, because of the reach of U.S. news organizations such as the *New York Times*, the major TV networks, and the wire services, such coverage has also shaped perceptions of China around the world.

For many consumers of news, however, the way the information they read in newspapers, in magazines, or online, listen to on the radio, or watch on television actually reaches them remains a mystery. In my more than thirty years as a foreign correspondent, it became clear that an enormous gap existed between the actual dynamic of reporting, writing, and transmitting the news and the final product seen by readers and viewers. Yet the nature of that process, and of the people engaged in it, remains the crucial foundation of any news report—and how the sophisticated news consumer can make sense of it. This is true of coverage all over the world, but is especially relevant for China, where journalists have struggled to report on a complex society with an opaque political system while being buffeted by pressure from the authorities in both Beijing and Washington, not to mention pressure from editors and the remorseless demands of their profession. Understanding the people who have reported on China and how they have done so is, therefore, a crucial step in understanding the news people watch and read. Providing that understanding is the central goal of this book.

Over the years, many of those who have covered the country have written their own memoirs or assisted other scholars and authors of books about China. Nevertheless, there has been no systematic effort to assemble a collective history of these colorful journalists with the focus on how they understood and reported the remarkable events they witnessed.

Assignment China is intended to offer a fresh perspective—a self-portrait of several generations of American China correspondents from 1945 to the present day. Their stories, never before collected into a comprehensive history, can serve a primer on nearly eighty years of dramatic political, social, and economic change as seen through the eyes of journalists who covered those developments.

This book is the outgrowth of a twelve-part documentary film series produced by the U.S.-China Institute at the University of Southern California. The series, which I started working on in 2008, was based on more than one hundred videotaped interviews with journalists who covered China, diplomats and others who interacted with them, and scholars who have studied both China and the media. As in most film projects, the limitations of time and format meant that many fascinating comments and stories were left on the cutting-room floor. Yet the experience of these China hands provides significant insights about China, Sino-American relations, and the craft of journalism—hence this book, which incorporates not only material included in the twelve episodes, but much more that was left out, as well as nearly two dozen additional interviews. All of them have been lightly edited and condensed for clarity.

When we began the project in 2008, we decided that it would be based on interviews we ourselves would conduct. In a few cases, we also included especially valuable excerpts of other interviews or memoirs, which are cited in the footnotes. For example, John Roderick, the great Associated Press China correspondent, who covered the civil war in the 1940s, was a "China watcher" in the 1950s and 1960s, returned to China to report on the visit of the U.S. ping-pong team in 1971, and then reopened the AP Beijing bureau in 1978, died in 2008. However, upon his retirement from the AP, the organization did a long interview with him, and the AP archives kindly gave us permission to use it. Sadly, a number of those we were able to interview have passed away in more recent years. Not all of them wrote books or memoirs. In many cases, their interviews for *Assignment China* constitute the only record of what they did, how they did it, and what they felt or thought about it.

We also made a conscious decision not to look in detail at American coverage of Taiwan and Hong Kong. Unquestionably, both are hugely important. Taiwan has been one of the most sensitive issues in Sino-American relations and remains an economic powerhouse, a remarkable example of how an authoritarian system can transition to a vibrant democracy, and a flashpoint that could conceivably lead to an armed conflict. Hong Kong, from its role after the Communist revolution as the listening post for covering China, to the handover in 1997 and Beijing's more recent imposition of a draconian national security law, has also been of central importance. Developments in both places have frequently been covered by the same correspondents who were reporting on mainland China, and both locations do feature in this book. But Taiwan and Hong Kong have such distinct, rich, and complex histories that it was simply not possible to do full justice here to the story of the journalists who reported about these two remarkable societies over so many decades.

Equally, there was no way to include all members of the multiple generations of reporters who have covered China over the past eight decades. But the people whose accounts do feature here represent a rich and representative cross-section of the American media—newspapers, magazines, the wire services, radio, television, and online—as well as diplomats and scholars who interacted with or studied them. One significant omission concerns the local Chinese drivers, fixers, and interpreters who worked in American news bureaus. Correspondents were virtually unanimous in emphasizing how important such people were to their coverage. But as Chinese nationals, local staff have always been in a sensitive, and often risky, position, frequently pressured to act as informants by the Chinese authorities, often intimidated, and sometimes forced to quit their jobs. Under these circumstances, a deliberate decision was made, for their own safety, not to reach out to those who worked as local staff to speak on the record for this project.

In this project, we seek to answer questions at the heart of the way foreign correspondents operate:

Who were the people who covered China for the American media?

How did they collect, understand, and transmit the news?

What sort of mental baggage did they bring?

What kind of dealings did they have with a Chinese government that was usually hostile, suspicious, and uncooperative?

How did they cope with language and cultural differences, and manage relationships with ordinary Chinese citizens with whom they came into contact?

What kind of interactions did they have with their editors and bosses?

To what extent were they influenced by the policy priorities of the U.S. government?

How did the dramatic changes in media technology—from print and radio to television, satellites, the twenty-four-hour news cycle, the Internet, and social media—shape the way they covered China?

How accurate was the picture of China they presented?

What were some of the consequences of how the country was reported?

Over the course of the interviews, one common thread became clear. For many of the journalists who have covered China for the U.S. media, myself included, the country was not so much an assignment as an abiding passion. The China beat shaped and defined our careers. We studied the language, culture, and history, and found in journalism what we believed was the best way to get access to, and dig beneath the surface of, a vast, fascinating, often poorly understood but enormously consequential nation.

Like the documentary series, this story begins in 1945, the year that World War II ended and the final phase of the Chinese civil war began. When China was at war, the obstacles to coverage were primarily logistical—how to get around in a backward, chaotic country with severed road and rail lines, primitive communications, and territory divided between areas controlled by Chiang Kai-shek's Kuomintang and those controlled by Mao Zedong's Communists.

After the Communist triumph in 1949, reporting on China faced a different challenge. American journalists, like those from most Western countries, were no longer allowed to operate in the newly established People's Republic.

For more than two decades, apart from very occasional visitors, most coverage was done by "China watchers" from places like Hong Kong. Reporters were forced to make sense of China without being able to go there and see for themselves.

With the visit of President Richard Nixon in 1972, the door began—slowly—to open. But it was not until the normalization of Sino-American relations in 1979 that Beijing agreed to allow correspondents for U.S. news organizations to be stationed again in the Chinese capital.

Since then, American journalists based in China have witnessed the country's astonishing transformation from a poor, isolated nation devastated by Mao's Great Leap Forward and Cultural Revolution, to an emerging economic and diplomatic powerhouse now challenging the United States for global supremacy. There have been many ups and downs, both in China's journey and in reporters' experiences covering it, but during all these years one theme stands out—the near-constant struggle of American journalists to test the boundaries, challenge the restrictions on coverage at the heart of the communist system, and explore parts of Chinese society that had long been off-limits. All the while, the Communist Party sought to discourage or prevent them from doing so. This tension, which I encountered during my visits with model peasant Yu Kexin, dates back to the founding of the People's Republic. Even reporters like Edgar Snow, whose book *Red Star Over China* made him Beijing's preferred Western journalist, struggled with restrictions when visiting the country in the 1960s. For others less trusted by the regime, the constraints have been even tighter.

How successful the Party has been in this effort has largely reflected China's domestic political climate. In the 1980s, arguably the most liberal period in the history of the People's Republic, the ability to travel and talk freely with ordinary Chinese increased significantly. The repression following the Tiananmen Square crackdown in 1989 imposed new obstacles on foreign reporters, but as the Chinese economy began to liberalize and grow in the 1990s and early 2000s, so too did the ability of resident correspondents to dig deeper into Chinese society. There was still much official resistance, but especially with the approach of the 2008 summer Olympic games in Beijing—whose official slogan, crafted by the Communist Party, was "a more open Beijing awaits the Olympics"—the authorities dramatically relaxed the rules governing foreign reporters.

In the wake of the Olympics, however, and after Xi Jinping became the country's leader in 2012, the pendulum swung sharply in the other direction.

In a society that had itself become much more open to increased engagement with the rest of the world, with the rise of a Chinese middle class, the emergence of the Internet, and a more modern economy, it was no longer possible for the authorities in Beijing simply to keep foreign journalists confined to the capital. But as Xi Jinping has tightened central control and reversed even the mild political and intellectual relaxation of previous years, the Communist Party's effort to control the narrative of China around the world by targeting foreign correspondents has intensified. China-based reporters venturing into the field have faced increasing harassment and intimidation, often of a physical nature, as well as threats to cancel their visas and expel them. The steadily shrinking number of Chinese people willing to speak with foreign reporters often face severe consequences, including imprisonment. As China's relations with the U.S. deteriorated, the targeting of the American press intensified, climaxing in 2020 when Beijing expelled nearly twenty reporters working for leading U.S. media outlets like the *New York Times*, *Washington Post*, and *Wall Street Journal*.

Yet even as access within the country has been curtailed and journalists have increasingly been used as pawns in China's diplomatic battles with the United States, Beijing's growing international role has meant that, in an ironic twist on the 1950s and 1960s, when "China watchers" covered the country from outside its borders, some journalists today have developed new ways to report on China without setting foot in the People's Republic—focusing on everything from China's global economic ties, investment deals, and growing international footprint to the shady foreign dealings of its corrupt new elite. Still, in such a huge, important, and, in many ways, still-undercovered country, Beijing's moves to reduce the size of the U.S. press corps are deeply troubling. This development is particularly worrisome at a time when the label "fake news" is being used by politicians and others in the West to discredit journalism with which they disagree. The Chinese government has also adopted the term to target foreign media coverage that challenges the narrative Beijing wants to impose not only at home but, increasingly, abroad.

A central theme that emerged in virtually all the interviews done for this project was the curiosity, passion, courage, and cunning journalists must display to get their story. From Morley Safer of CBS pretending to be a travel agent to get a tourist visit to China at the height of the Cultural Revolution in 1967, to Jeff Widener of the AP finding a foreign student to hide the film in his underwear so the historic shot of the man in front of the tank could be smuggled past Chinese security following the Tiananmen crackdown in

1989, to David Barboza of the *New York Times* spending months poring through dense corporate records to document the corruption of a top Chinese leader, the reporters whose stories are told here managed to overcome countless obstacles to present their best understanding of China to their readers, viewers, and listeners. With the benefit of hindsight, what is surprising is not how much they missed or got wrong but, given the conditions under which they have been forced to work, how much they got right.

There's an old saying that journalists write the first rough draft of history. As the United States and the rest of the world struggle to deal with a more authoritarian and assertive China, the story of those who had front-row seats for every twist and turn in its modern history, told in their own words, can add much to our understanding of one of the world's most complicated and important countries.

1

THE CHINESE CIVIL WAR

With the surrender of Japan in August 1945, World War II came to an end. But the struggle between Chiang Kai-shek's Chinese Nationalists (the Kuomintang, or KMT) and the Chinese Communist Party, led by Mao Zedong, which dated back to the 1920s, was about to resume. Their conflict had been placed on hold since the late 1930s as both parties entered an uneasy alliance to combat the Japanese. But while most of the world recognized Chiang as China's legitimate ruler, poverty, corruption, and the upheavals of war left his government severely weakened. Mao, meanwhile, had used the war to build a powerful force that, from his base in the remote northwest, controlled nearly ninety million people, a quarter of the population. China now had two rival governments. With American support the KMT took control of China's major cities, while the Communists gained support in much of the countryside, assisted by Soviet forces that had occupied Manchuria (northeast China) in the waning days of the war.

The United States attempted to broker a political settlement, promoting direct talks between Mao and Chiang in the autumn of 1945, and then sending America's most distinguished general, George Marshall, to mediate. But as Marshall discovered, neither the Communists nor Nationalists were serious about a compromise. There was too much distrust and too many irreconcilable goals.

As civil war loomed, twenty-four-year-old New York native Seymour Topping, who had served as an infantry officer in the Pacific, met the Asian editor of the International News Service wire agency in the Philippines.

Seymour Topping, International News Service

I ran into Frank Robertson, who was in charge of INS in Asia. He offered me a job as a stringer, a part-time correspondent, in Peking. I got on an airplane. My title at that point was Chief Correspondent for North China and Manchuria, and my salary was fifty dollars a month.

Maine native John Roderick had worked for the Associated Press in Washington before the war. Drafted in 1943, he was sent to southwest China. As soon as he left the military, he rejoined the AP in Chongqing, Chiang Kaishek's wartime capital. There, he got to know Zhou Enlai, who had served as the Communist Party's liaison with American officials and journalists during the war.

John Roderick, Associated Press

Zhou was a star, the darling of the press. He had a great charisma. When you were with him, he always concentrated on you. Made you feel important. He made the Communists popular at a time when they might not have been.[1]

Henry Lieberman, who had studied Chinese at Columbia, joined the Foreign News Bureau of the Office of War Information in Washington in 1942, and later went to China as chief news editor of the agency's China branch. At the end of the war, he was appointed the *New York Times* China correspondent. He was equally impressed with Zhou, but at a conference of China hands nearly forty years later concluded Zhou's charm was just a show to win over Western reporters.

Henry Lieberman, *New York Times*

Zhou Enlai was one of the greatest people I ever encountered, in terms of his charisma, his mental ability, his skills. And he was one of the world's greatest actors. I spent hour after hour with him trying to get his story. He had a trick that he'd pull. Zhou spoke poor English, so far as I could make out. The interpreter would go on translating, and then at some strategic point in the interview Zhou would stop the interpreter, and say to him in English, "No, not that word, this word."[2]

YAN'AN

Although no significant agreements were reached during Marshall's yearlong mission, while it continued, the Communists allowed American reporters to visit their headquarters in Yan'an in the remote northwest, the endpoint of the famous Long March in the 1930s. Zhou Enlai arranged for John Roderick to go. Between 1945 and 1947, Roderick spent seven months there.

John Roderick, Associated Press

We arrived after a trip which looked like a voyage over the moon. We were met at the airport by Huang Hua. He spoke perfect English, and later became foreign minister. He took us into town. Yan'an was extraordinary. It was a city of ten thousand caves. The Japanese had bombarded the old walled city and driven the Communists to dig into this soft loess soil. They created cave hospitals, cave universities, cave printing groups, that sort of thing.[3]

During his visits, Roderick had frequent contact with Mao and other Communist leaders.

John Roderick, Associated Press

I saw Mao practically every day in the small downtown area, or at dinners or dances. The leading communists were dressed in their padded woolen clothes because it was wintertime, and they danced around rather awkwardly. Mao was there, and he danced. It was Western music. It was very lighthearted. You saw them in a very unguarded moment. They were much more human. Mao had a price on his head by the Chinese Nationalists for two hundred thousand dollars, yet he walked around, often alone or with one single bodyguard. I'd stroll along with him.

We'd go to the Chinese opera and sit around in a large building, freezing cold in the wintertime. Small braziers would warm your feet. There, for an hour or two, you lost the impression that you were in a remote part of China. On the stage were actors and actresses in the Peking Opera, dressed in their colorful silks and in high falsetto voice, telling the stories of courtesans and emperors. Mao loved it.

He received me for dinner one night. We shook hands and [he] asked how I was. He had a very good sense of humor. We had a sumptuous meal, and

Mao explained that the fish had come from a stream fifty miles away. I couldn't resist saying, "Chairman Mao, this astonishes me. I expected you to be living in poverty, not to eating banquets like this." He says, "Oh, Mr. Roderick, you must remember, you're a guest, and nothing's too good for a guest." Then, he said, "We may be Communists, but we're also Chinese, and we like good food."

As I talked to him during the evening, I had a feeling that this was a man very different from any I'd ever met before. Mao was aloof, lost in thought much of the time. Dressed in patched clothes, he was somebody who, if you were in a cocktail party with a hundred people, everyone dressed alike, you would gravitate to him. There was an inner strength, a stubbornness, a kind of a superior intelligence.

He asked me—Did I think that after the peace was consummated, would somebody like Montgomery Ward, Sears [at the time the two leading American retailers] be willing to come to China to start a mail order business? China was so big and the communication so bad that it'd be a wonderful thing. I was astonished.[4]

Seymour Topping, International News Service

That was one of Mao's most important and revealing interviews. Mao was eager to come to an understanding with the United States. [But] by that time, there was so much anticommunist feeling in the United States that Roderick's interview did not get the attention that it deserved.

John Roderick, Associated Press

I left in 1947 for Peking. When I did, Mao was at the airport. He said to me, "Lo De Li," that was my Chinese name, "I invite you to visit me in Peking two years from now." And, in fact, in less than two years, he was in Peking.[5]

THE CITIES

Most American reporters, however, were not able to go to Yan'an, but remained in Beijing or Shanghai. In his memoirs, Topping recalled Beijing as "a beguiling walled city. On its narrow cobblestoned streets, overburdened camels and peasant carts mingled with American-made trucks of the Nationalist garrison and polished limousines of the foreign consulates."[6] As a rookie reporter, Topping discovered that not all his time was taken up with the big story.

Seymour Topping, International News Service

There was Reynolds Packard of the United Press, a famous character who had worked in Italy and covered Mussolini and had a reputation as a correspondent who had flights of imagination. At one point, he did a story [picked up from the notoriously unreliable local Chinese press] about the discovery of a human headed spider. When this story appeared, I got a cable from the International News Service saying, "Okay, but don't file unless you can find a spider with two human heads." It was a famous story, and eventually was one of the reasons Packard was fired by the UP.

After six months in Beijing, INS transferred Topping to Nanjing, which Chiang Kai-shek in 1927 had made the Nationalists' capital, and to which Chiang returned after the defeat of the Japanese. There, Topping took a better-paying job with the AP. He also met his future wife, Audrey Ronning, the daughter of Chester Ronning, a senior official at the Canadian embassy who had been born in China of missionary parents. Audrey was studying at Nanjing University.

Audrey Ronning Topping, Photojournalist

The city was full of refugees from the North. I went to school in a rickshaw. Every morning you'd see corpses lying on the roads. In the winter, they froze to death. There were beggars all over.

The homeless and starving filling the streets, hyperinflation, and rampant corruption undercut Chiang's support in the countryside and the cities.

John Roderick, Associated Press

I was in Shanghai, reporting on the poverty and the contrasts of life, how we lived in the Broadway Mansions, [a high-rise overlooking Soochow Creek and the location of the Foreign Correspondents Club] and below us in the sampans were the poor, drinking the water from the muddy canals and living in extreme poverty.[7]

Getting out of the army, twenty-five-year-old New York native Roy Rowan went to China hoping to become a journalist, only to end up working with the UN Relief and Rehabilitation Administration, or UNRRA, in Shanghai.

Fed up with corruption in the relief effort, he quit his job and decided to return to the United States. Before leaving, he went for a drink at Shanghai's famous Cathay Hotel.

Roy Rowan, UNRRA

I didn't know what the hell I was going to do. I was standing next to Bill Grey, [the Time-Life Bureau chief in China] and we got talking. He asked what I'd been doing. I told him working for UNRRA and freelancing. He bought me a couple of drinks and asked me about the military situation up there [in Henan] because they [Time] didn't have anyone in the area. I turned out a situation report on the war in Central China. He liked it. He filed it as a part of his story, and it appeared in Time.

A month later, Rowan was the *Life* magazine China correspondent. He teamed up with Jack Birns, a photographer who had been previously based in Los Angeles, and who had spent 1946 freelancing for *Life* in the United States. From his UNRRA days, Rowan had connections with the American pilots working for Chiang Kai-shek's Civil Air Transport (CAT) flying food, medicine, arms, and ammunition to parts of China where railways, roads, and bridges had been destroyed.

Roy Rowan, *Life*

When I went back as a correspondent, the first thing I did was to go to Long-hua Airport [in Shanghai] where the China Air Transport headquarters was and see my old pilot buddies. You couldn't telephone to Taiyuan or Suzhou or even Beijing. The only way you could find out what was going on was to fly around with these guys with no particular destination in mind other than somewhere there was war going on.

THE NATIONALISTS

Seymour Topping, Associated Press

There was a great deal of admiration among the correspondents for the Communists. We had such close acquaintance with Nationalist forces, and we'd seen the extent to which they were infected by corruption. We were looking at the Chinese Communist forces essentially as reformers.

Audrey Ronning Topping, Photojournalist

Anybody that was well informed in Nanking realized the Communist victory was inevitable. There we were, the diplomats and Nationalists, living like Maharajas—great parties every night. People were starving in the streets. I was driving home one night from a party with a Nationalist officer, and the people in the streets were eating grass. I said, "This is such a terrible situation. I can't stand it. And it must be worse for you as a Chinese." And he said, "We don't consider them people." And I thought, "No wonder there's a revolution."

Henry Lieberman, *New York Times*

In retrospect, I think that a lot of the criticism of the Kuomintang was based on the fact that people were living in Kuomintang areas and could see what was going on. What was happening in the Communist areas we didn't know anything about.[8]

Roy Rowan, *Life*

I was positive by this time the Nationalists could not prevail—so much corruption, so many generals going into combat selling arms and taking the payrolls and depositing it back into their own bank accounts in Shanghai.

As Communist forces continued to advance, Rowan, with the help of *Time-Life* publisher Henry Luce, was granted an interview with Chiang Kai-shek.

Roy Rowan, *Life*

Chiang Kai-shek did not grant interviews to the press, but because of Henry Luce, he agreed to see us. He was very nervous. I think he couldn't wait for us to get the hell out of there. The Madame served as the interpreter. [Chiang's wife, American-educated Song Meiling, was her husband's closest advisor. A key interlocutor in Chiang's dealings with Westerners, her opulent lifestyle became a symbol of the Nationalists' corruption.] She was very nice, the smiling friend of America. He tried to convince us that he had things well in hand. They had big wall maps and pointers, showing where the Nationalists were in Manchuria [Northeast China] and where the Communists were, and how they had a very good defense set up.

Jack and I had been to Manchuria before, and we knew things weren't that good. From that meeting, we hopped one of those CAT [China Air Transport] planes and went up there [to Mukden, present-day Shenyang]. As soon as we landed, we could see everybody was trying to get the hell out of town. Chiang Kai-shek had lied to Jack and me. Anybody with any money was gone. The troop trains were going south, Nationalist soldiers hanging all over the engines. We could see the Nationalists were abandoning all their weapons. There were howitzers laying in the field. We went into Mukden, took photographs everywhere we could.

The Communists were at the city gates. In downtown Mukden, at the U.S. Consulate, they found American diplomat Angus Ward, a larger-than life figure who'd been ordered by Washington to stay on and establish contact with the triumphant Communist forces.

Roy Rowan, *Life*

The epitome of an international spy, fluent in several languages—Chinese, Russian—very imposing. We took pictures of him. Talked to him for an hour. He knew the Communists were coming, it wouldn't be long, and he was prepared. He had had his orders to try to make contact with them. He was willing to stay. He was very eager to see what he could do. Around him in the office were sacks of flour, canned soup—a year's supply of provisions. You could hear gunfire. He finally said, "You better get your asses out to the airport." Luckily, CAT always kept one plane at the airport where there was fighting going on to get their last guys out.

Rowan and Birns managed to board the final flight from Mukden. They realized they had an exclusive. No other journalists knew the city had fallen. It was a story even Henry Luce's *Life* couldn't ignore. "Mukden is a ghost city," his cable to *Time* began. "No preparation had been made for a last-stand defense. Most of the government troops were encamped near rail sidings awaiting evacuation. In the city itself, freezing blasts of wind whistled down the broad, empty thoroughfares. The capital of China's richest industrial area looked as cold and desolate as the ragged, half-frozen refugees picking their way through the debris."[9] Rowan and Birns got a five-page spread.

Angus Ward, meanwhile, was imprisoned in the U.S. consulate by the victorious Communist troops and held hostage for eighteen months before being allowed to return home.

THE COMMUNIST TRIUMPH

With the Communists in control of the North, the battle for Central China began.

Seymour Topping, Associated Press

I made a decision to cover this battle. Harold Milks, [the AP's Nanjing bureau chief] drove me up to a town called Bengpu, on the Huai River one hundred miles north of Nanjing. My plan was to stay in a Jesuit Mission, wait until the Communist forces occupied Bengpu, and then emerge and say, "Here I am, Seymour Topping! Where's Mao Zedong? I want to interview him!" It didn't happen exactly that way because the Communist advance was not that rapid. So I celebrated Christmas Eve 1948 in the mission. After I had filed one of my last reports, Milks wrote a brief story saying, "Seymour Topping is the loneliest man in the Associated Press this Christmas Eve."

The previous month, Topping had married Audrey Ronning. Although her father, Chester, remained the senior Canadian diplomat in Nanjing, Audrey had been evacuated to Canada.

Audrey Ronning Topping, Photojournalist

I was walking down the street one rainy night, and I kicked over a newspaper that was on the street. I picked it up. It was the Vancouver Sun. On the front page was a little box that said, "Perhaps the loneliest man in the world this Christmas Eve was Seymour Topping who was in a monastery in Bengpu." I thought, "Oh my. I'd better answer his letters."

The Huaihai campaign lasted sixty-five days. It involved a million men—the biggest land battle since World War II. Topping set forth from Bengpu to cover it.

Seymour Topping, Associated Press

On New Years' Day, I crossed into the Communist areas. At a roadblock, we encountered Communist guerrillas. One of them was pointing a machine gun. I could see his fingers on the trigger. He didn't understand my Chinese. At that point, several regular Chinese Communist army soldiers took over. I showed them my credentials. They weren't too impressed. They took me prisoner and we began to walk. At one point, I was put on a horse, and we traveled to a place called Xiuxian, on the edge of where one of the last battles of the Huaihai campaign was taking place. There were 130,000 Nationalist troops surrounded by 300,000 Communist troops.

I was put into a peasant hut and was interviewed by a Communist commissar. I told him I was there to tell their story and wished to interview Mao. Probably the single most memorable event in my three years covering came the morning of January 7, 1949. I'd been listening all night to the artillery fire. Some of the fire stopped at dawn. I got up and tried to leave the hut to see what was going on. I was blocked by soldiers who pointed guns at me. I went back in, and then the commissar came in and said, "You will have to return. This is a dangerous area. We can't take responsibility for you. The horses are outside waiting." Then I learned that the Communist forces had overrun the Nationalist positions. That was the end of the battle. There were still dead lying on the battlefield. The Communist forces killed or captured a half a million Nationalist troops. That was a decisive battle of the civil war. That morning on the battlefield of the Huaihai, I knew it was all over for Chiang Kai-shek.

For Henry Luce, the publisher of *Time* and *Life*, who had been born in China of missionary parents and was fanatically anticommunist and a committed supporter of Chiang Kai-shek, it was a bitter blow.

Roy Rowan, *Life*

Not too long before it was over, Luce called me back [to New York] for lunch, and I went all the way back. It's a long way to go for lunch, especially when you're flying in prop planes. I told him what was happening. I told him it was gone. This was very upsetting to him. He was deeply hurt and unhappy by what I had told him. There's no question about that.

In early 1949, Chiang Kai-shek fled to Taiwan, which he would rule until his death in 1975, always proclaiming his intent to reconquer the mainland. On April 24, the Communists occupied his capital, Nanjing.

Seymour Topping, Associated Press

I decided to cover the taking of the city. I picked up a friend, a Chinese correspondent named Bill Kwan of the French news agency Agence France Presse.

Bill and I were in my jeep. We decided to meet the Communists coming in from the northwest gate. They were exhausted. They'd been fighting. We took off and went to a telegraph office. Bill and I quickly wrote some things and flipped a coin as to who would file first. Bill won. I wrote a short, detailed dispatch. When Bill's three-word dispatch "Reds Take Shanghai" reached the desk of the AFP in Paris, they waited for the rest of the material. And my dispatch was imme-diately put out by the AP. It gave me a world beat on the fall of the city.

The next Communist target was Shanghai.

Roy Rowan, *Life*

We wanted to do a big essay on the last days of Shanghai. We worked like crazy and got wonderful stuff. The French Club people ignoring the war, going on with their cocktails, their tennis, their lawn bowls in middle of the racecourse with the Brits. We shot all of this—nightclubs and little whorehouse bars down on the waterfront. The execution of the black marketers and the suspected agents. I saw the Nationalists retreating down Nanking Road, and a lot of them discarding their uniforms in the Huangpu River and trying to buy civilian clothes. We did what I thought was a big, wonderful essay. We called it "The Last Days of Shanghai." Life never used it.

Rowan got out on one of the last flights to leave the city.

Roy Rowan, *Life*

I had this feeling—here is this great, wonderful, wild, crazy city. I remember looking down on the river and thinking, you know, I'll never be able to come back here again.

2

CHINA WATCHING

On October 1, 1949, standing on the rostrum of Beijing's Gate of Heavenly Peace with hundreds of thousands gathered in Tiananmen Square below, a triumphant Mao Zedong declared the establishment of the People's Republic of China. After decades of war, upheaval, and oppression, a new era beckoned. But no American journalists witnessed the moment. With the Communist victory, the American press corps had been forced to leave China. The British colony of Hong Kong became the primary base for those who continued to follow the country.

John Roderick, Associated Press

There in Hong Kong was a kind of curious breed of reporter called the "China watcher." Our job was to report on China from outside of China, in this case Hong Kong.[1]

Roy Rowan, *Life*

We set up office in the Peninsula Hotel, in the bridal suite, three hundred bucks a month. And we did the best we could. It was very frustrating being a China watcher, because you're relying on other people's reporting. I had to do a lot of writing of stories based on this secondary material. I didn't find it very satisfying.

Soon after, in June 1950, Soviet-backed North Korea invaded pro-Western South Korea. Various countries under UN auspices, with the United States the principal participant, joined the war on the side of the South. After U.S. forces neared the Chinese border with North Korea in late 1950, Beijing intervened on the side of the North. For nearly three years, U.S. and Chinese forces were engaged in bloody combat before a truce in 1953 left the Korean peninsula still divided into two hostile states.

Roy Rowan was one of many China hands who covered the Korean War.

Roy Rowan, *Life*

We were under fire from the North Koreans. We were retreating along this road. A lot of small arms fire. We took cover behind this big boulder. And these two medics came crashing in behind this boulder right with us. One of these medics stops and says, "If I had your job, I'd quit!"

The Korean War inflamed anticommunist sentiment in the United States. Murray Fromson, who later became a correspondent in Asia for CBS, covered the Korean conflict for the U.S. military paper *Stars and Stripes*.

Murray Fromson, CBS News

American journalists bought into the Cold War psychology. I don't deny it, I was one of those, like everybody else. We looked at China through Cold War eyes. We looked at them as the enemy.

In the United States, the 1950s was the era of McCarthyism, a fevered effort to expose supposed Communist infiltration of the government, media, education, entertainment, and other parts of American society spearheaded by Republican senator Joseph McCarthy. Mao's triumph in China heightened the hysteria, fueling a witch hunt for those whom McCarthy and his supporters blamed for "losing China" to the Communists.

Seymour Topping, Associated Press

It was absolutely unbelievable that there was such a debate. I knew what the diplomats had reported about corruption, weakness, and inefficiency in the Nationalist government. Then there were reporters like myself who had been reporting what was going on. The failed leadership of Chiang Kai-shek, the corruption of Kuomintang officials, and the mistreatment of the peasantry was the reason for the Nationalist defeat. It was Chiang Kai-shek and the Kuomintang party that lost China. But nevertheless, it was exploited by McCarthy.

Washington's hostility to the Chinese communist regime was symbolized by the refusal of President Eisenhower's secretary of state, John Foster Dulles, to shake Zhou Enlai's hand at an international conference in Geneva on the future of Indochina in 1954. A year later, that attitude torpedoed a Chinese overture to the U.S. press made by Zhou at a meeting of nonaligned nations in Indonesia.

John Roderick, Associated Press

Zhou Enlai announced that American correspondents could return to Peking. There was great joy and excitement in the press corps in America. We made plans to go back. In fact, Frank Starzel [the AP's general manager] named me chief of bureau in Peking. Then John Foster Dulles intruded. He said, "Under no circumstances will you go to Peking. If you do, $10,000 fine, five years in jail." That damped everything.[2]

Undeterred by U.S. government threats, Roderick tried going on his own.

John Roderick, Associated Press

I thought about this conversation at the airport years before with Mao, when he said, "I invite you to visit me in Peking two years from now." I sent a telegram to Mao. I said, "I've been away for a while, and haven't been able to take up your invitation, but now I'm in Hong Kong. I'd like to go." In two days, I got back a message saying, "Report to Ulan Bator in Mongolia. Get your visa." I sent this glad tiding to Frank Starzel in New York, thinking he'd jump for joy. Starzel was a very cautious man. He said, "Don't go. I'm trying to get a British AP man in so that you won't have to go to jail and pay a $10,000 fine." I said, "Frank, I'll take the chance. Let's go." "No, no, no. Let's wait." We waited two weeks. At the end of the two weeks he [Starzel] gave up on the British AP man, he couldn't get in. Starzel said, "OK, now you can try it." I sent another message, *but the time had passed. This was a moment in history which escaped us, and I wasn't able to go.*[3]

A very few reporters, however, defied the ban. Among them was Robert Cohen, a freelance filmmaker with a film degree from UCLA. On a trip to the Soviet Union in 1957 with an American student group to participate in the sixth World Democratic Youth Day, he and several of his traveling companions were offered visas for China. The State Department strongly objected.

Robert Cohen, Freelance Journalist

The representatives of the State Department came to our hotel. "The secretary of state doesn't want you to go." The policy was to maintain China as the faceless enemy. But everyone still wanted to go. I had a camera, film, and a letter of support as an NBC special correspondent.

Cohen became the first representative of a U.S. broadcast network to enter China after the revolution. His group visited eight cities—Beijing, Dalian, Changchun, Wuhan, Shanghai, Nanjing, Hangzhou, and Guangzhou. He shot dozens of hours of footage and produced a handful of short pieces that aired on NBC News, seeking to counter the clichés about China and show a country struggling to rebuild after years of war and revolution.

Robert Cohen, Freelance Journalist

The mass media presentation of China is—it's the evil empire. It's worse than Fu Manchu. You can't understand them. They're inscrutable Orientals. [Fu Manchu was a fictional villain. Depicted as inscrutable, cunning, and cruel, he became a symbol of the stereotypical "Yellow Peril" mindset that had shaped attitudes in the United States.] People in the U.S. have no idea about China. If I could shed a bit of light on this, people would benefit. Eleven one-minute spots were run on NBC's Today *show. But what they showed was the story as NBC saw it. That story was—American youths defy travel ban. It was not what was going on in China. The lives, industry, military, everything that was going on in China, was not shown to people in the United States.*

Cohen and the others in his group were also granted an audience with Premier Zhou Enlai.

Robert Cohen, Freelance Journalist

I had my own question for Zhou, which was, "China has stated support for newly independent, formerly colonialist regions, yet some of these countries oppose domestic communism. How do you rationalize supporting a country that is anticommunist?" His answer was, "At this time, our policy was to support these nations and not be concerned with their domestic policies." This was important to me, as it demonstrated pragmatism. The Chinese were ready to deal with whoever they needed to deal with, regardless of their political sentiments.

In a reflection of the atmosphere in the United States, after returning home, Cohen was questioned from the FBI, and harassed by the government.

Robert Cohen, Freelance Journalist

My passport expired, and I applied for a new one, and renewal was refused.

It took a court case for Cohen to get his passport back. But for virtually all American journalists, China remained inaccessible. The Communists' sweeping restructuring of Chinese society in the early and mid-1950s—wiping out social vices such as opium addiction and prostitution, increasing life expectancy, confiscating land from landlords and redistributing it to foreigners, early steps toward collectivization of agriculture, boosting industrial production—took place out of view of American reporters.

HONG KONG

By the late 1950s and early 1960s, Hong Kong had become home to a new generation of China watchers. A four-hundred-square-mile area populated largely by refugees from Mao's revolution, described by some as a capitalist parasite on the skin of communist China, the British colony seethed with energy and intrigue. For the Communists, who maintained a network of agents and sympathizers, Hong Kong was a bridge to the rest of the world, and Beijing's primary source of foreign exchange. For American and other journalists, as well as diplomats, it was as close as was possible to get to the People's Republic.

Bernard Kalb covered Asia for the *New York Times* from 1956 to 1961 based in Indonesia, and for CBS News from 1962 to 1970, operating from Hong Kong.

Bernard Kalb, *New York Times*, CBS News

Chasing China was the obsession that we reporters had. How do we get information about China? We read everything we could. We put the mosaic of pieces together and tried to extract some narrative about what was happening, but this was bits and pieces journalism.

Stanley Karnow, who had served in the U.S. army in the mountains between India and China during the Second World War, had been working for seven years as a correspondent in Paris for *Time* magazine when he was assigned to Hong Kong.

Stanley Karnow, *Time*

It's very peculiar. Here you are sitting in Hong Kong, covering these vast places, like sitting in Bermuda covering the United States.

In the 1960s, Richard Solomon was a young China scholar. Later, he worked for Henry Kissinger at the National Security Council during the Nixon administration and eventually became assistant secretary of state for East Asian and Pacific affairs during the George H. W. Bush administration.

Richard Solomon, State Department

Hong Kong was a hodgepodge of foreign service people from many governments, a journalist community, and academics. Even though we had our different institutional affiliations, we were basically doing the same thing—trying to figure out what was going on in China. We were sharing our information with the journalists and others, all trying to peer over the bamboo curtain.

Nicholas Platt served in the U.S. Consulate in Hong Kong from 1964 to 1968.

Nicholas Platt, State Department

We had very good relations with the press. Some of the reporters were quite learned, and also had sources of their own. Gatherings were usually held at restaurants. It was a way to share information. You had to sort of pay at the door with a contact, or an insight, or a report or something like that, or some visitor that you dragged in. It was a pretty vibrant community.

Robert Elegant had started with *Newsweek* and eventually moved to the *Los Angeles Times*.

Robert Elegant, *Newsweek, Los Angeles Times*

Scholars, diplomats, spooks of various sorts, and so on. Everybody knew who everybody was. We did share. We would kick things around and ideas would come out, subjects would come out.

A Chinese speaker, Elegant was among the more knowledgeable reporters.

Robert Elegant, *Newsweek/Los Angeles Times*

When I was an undergraduate, I got interested in Chinese. And then I joined the army and helped set up the Chinese language department at the army language school. I took an MA at Columbia in Chinese and Japanese, so that I developed "some" understanding, not "an" understanding, but some understanding of Chinese history and Chinese psychology, which I think are absolutely essential. The language is, of course, very important too. By the time I got to Asia, my Chinese was pretty good.

American journalists tried every conceivable approach to get visas to China—without success.

Berhard Kalb, *New York Times*, CBS News

We got absolutely nowhere. I lived in Hong Kong, on the edge of China. We could see China out our window, but that didn't make us experts. I was a young, barely literate New York Times *reporter then, and I wanted to get as close to China as I could. The China I could chase was the Chinese ambassador to Indonesia, Huang Chen. He was a survivor of the Long March, a retired general who had gone into diplomacy. I would always try to see him at diplomatic functions. I would sidle up to him and he would just as quickly sidle away from me. To say he was practicing for the Olympics would be to understate the spurt he took.*

Barred from the country they were covering, the China watchers looked for other sources of information. One resource was the government-controlled Chinese media. Henry Bradsher, who had previously been based in Moscow and New Delhi for the AP, arrived in Hong Kong for the now-defunct *Washington Star*.

Henry Bradsher, *Washington Star*

There were two primary tools. One was Xinhua, the New China News Agency. Second was transcripts of Chinese radio broadcasts, which were jointly done by the BBC and the U.S. Foreign Broadcast Information Services (FBIS). A serious job of China watching required going through that material every day, not only seeing what was being said, but what was not being said. Having spent that time in Moscow, I had learned some of the skills of Kremlin-watching, when you are reading Pravda, Izvestia—*what you have to look for, what was being said differently today from the way it was said three months earlier. I brought those principles to Hong Kong. I had a messenger bring me up every day this pile of stuff. I would wade through it.*

Robert Elegant, *Newsweek, Los Angeles Times*

We had a big house full of men with radio sets, scribbling handwritten Chinese from the local broadcasts. I'd walk into my office in the morning, and I'd find a stack of handwritten Chinese. It was painstaking work, intense examination of sources. Sometimes we missed them, sometimes we got them.

Robert Keatley, who had previously worked as a *Wall Street Journal* correspondent in San Francisco, New York, and London, was assigned to Hong Kong in 1964.

Robert Keatley, *Wall Street Journal*

Reading the People's Daily *could drive you crazy because you had to try to figure where's the phrase that means something in all this drivel.*

John Roderick, Associated Press

The reports coming out of Peking during all those years were stuffed with sort of a verbiage and gobbledygook. But if you read it carefully, between the lines, you discovered something important was happening in China. Some man was mentioned in third place instead of second place. He'd been demoted, or executed, or whatever. It was that sort of thing. It was a kind of a detective work.[4]

Many of the reporters came to rely on Father László Ladány, a tall, bespectacled Jesuit priest from Hungary who had lived in Beijing and Shanghai from 1936 to 1949, and then moved to Hong Kong. The *China News Analysis*, which Ladány published from 1953 to 1982, became a crucial resource.

Nicholas Platt, State Department

Ladány was the doyen of the China watchers. He was vastly respected. He put out a little publication every week, which matched in intensity and depth the analysis of staff that were ten to fifteen times the size. I remember calling on him in his office, and he would pull a drawer out and there would be a tape recorder attached to a radio. He had his different radio stations all organized and he was very systematic. He was highly respected.

Ladány's great skill was his uncanny ability to look beyond what the official Chinese press—national and provincial newspapers and radio stations— was saying and decipher what they actually meant.

Robert Elegant, *Newsweek, Los Angeles Times*

Father Ladány was a great, great China watcher. He had an instinctive feeling [about China] and put together what was happening. We relied on that. He used to say, "You have to understand if they say 'a bumper harvest' that means they almost met their target. If they said, 'it was a satisfactory harvest,' it means they only got halfway to their target."

REFUGEES

Another key source was the continuing flow of refugees from China, mostly from Guangdong or other southern provinces. Ted Koppel was ABC's Hong Kong correspondent in the late 1960s.

Ted Koppel, ABC News

The most accurate information that they were getting out of China tended to come from the waves of refugees who came out. And of course, that began in the late forties and went on into the fifties and sixties.

Stanley Karnow, *Time*

I used to go to Macau. In Macau you had hospices run by religious groups, and they would pick up refugees and take care of them, and they would let me interview the refugees. I got a lot of good stories out of them.

Relying on refugees, however, had its drawbacks. Most refugee insights were limited to what was happening in their own villages and communities—the food situation, what Communist Party cadres were saying and doing, the kind of social and political controls they faced.

Robert Keatley, *Wall Street Journal*

That wasn't a main source. It was good for anecdotes and quotes. They could describe what they saw around them and that was very useful, but this was not a source of policy, an explanation of policy.

Not only were refugee accounts often incomplete, but coming from people whose desperation had prompted them to flee, many stories were biased or tailored to provide what refugees thought interviewers wanted to hear.

Robert Elegant, *Newsweek, Los Angeles Times*

One came out and announced he'd been a photographer at the Chinese nuclear sites. We took him over a few jumps, and it wasn't true. He hadn't been a photographer, and he hadn't been to the Chinese nuclear sites. He later sold that story to somebody who was working for the Daily Telegraph *in London, who bought it.*

Other accounts were deliberately designed to manipulate reporters.

Robert Elegant, *Newsweek, Los Angeles Times*

You had to be very careful with them. Some were planted by the Nationalists on Taiwan, or the Communists. But it often paid off. You'd find that different accounts substantiated each other. People who as far as you knew did not know each other.

HENRY LUCE AND CHIANG KAI-SHEK

As a correspondent for *Time*, Stanley Karnow had to contend with his publisher, the ardent Chiang Kai-shek supporter Henry Luce.

Stanley Karnow, *Time*

To cover China for the Luce publications was a challenge, because Luce was a guy with particular ideas, having been born there and being fiercely anticommunist.

From Taiwan, Chiang Kai-shek continued to declare his intention to retake the mainland. Soon after Karnow began his Hong Kong assignment, he accompanied Luce to meet Chiang in Taipei.

Stanley Karnow, *Time*

Chiang Kai-shek is his great hero. He put Chiang Kai-shek on the cover of Time *magazine a number of times. We go to Taiwan. We have an appointment to have dinner with Chiang. We go to the Grand Hotel, and the baggage has not arrived. The reason, of course, is we flew in and some handlers took us in a limo to the hotel. We didn't know where the baggage was. Luce is fretting. He says to me, "Do you think they lost the baggage?" To which I said, "Well they lost the mainland didn't they?" He growled at me.*

We went and listened to Chiang Kai-shek's usual litany about retaking China. Chiang would talk in these elliptical terms, so Luce would say, "What do you think about the future, Generalissimo?" Chiang says, "Dangerous days ahead, dangerous days ahead," like some sort of an oracle. Luce came out of it and said, "Gotta be careful, gotta be careful these days." It was absolutely idiotic. You could not have a serious conversation with Luce about China. Then we would go to dinner. Chiang would sit at the head of the table. Madam Chiang would come, all dressed up in her fancy cheongsam, with her jade necklace. She would nag Luce. She'd say, "Harry, we've got to do something about the Commies in Washington"—that sort of stuff. She'd go on and on.

Shortly after, Karnow left *Time*, and soon become the Hong Kong correspondent for the *Washington Post*.

THE U.S. CONSULATE IN HONG KONG

The U.S. Consulate had by now emerged as a crucial center of China watching in the territory.

Nicholas Platt, State Department

There were agents operating in China. There were people counting all the pigs that were imported into Hong Kong, people that took photographs of railroad car serial numbers, and a variety of other things. There was also satellite imagery of harvests and stuff like that. We regularly received all of the intelligence reports and wove them into our analysis.

After leaving China, Seymour Topping spent most of the 1950s based in Saigon, London, and West Berlin for the AP. In 1959, he joined the *New York Times*, which posted him to Moscow for three years, and then to Hong Kong.

Seymour Topping, *New York Times*

The American consulate there was a larger mission than most American embassies. They were interviewing refugees. They had managed to arrange for the smuggling out of provincial newspapers. They had an arrangement whereby Nationalists planes were overflying China from Taiwan and reporting their observations, anything that leaked out of China. I as a correspondent had to a large extent access to that information.

The daily routine for reporters was like trying to assemble pieces of a jigsaw puzzle. Jerrold Schecter arrived in Hong Kong in 1960 for *Time*.

Jerrold Schecter, *Time*

You'd read in. Then you'd go to the Consulate, talk to your buddies there. Talk to foreign diplomats. Then you'd try to get a peg [for a story]. A couple of refugees who'd come over—you could send someone from the office who spoke Chinese to interview them and put all that together.

There were often sharp differences of opinion among the journalists and the diplomats about what was happening.

Richard Solomon, State Department

The U.S. Consulate had differing views about what was going on. And some officials were feeding the press their particular perspectives. Someone like Stanley Karnow would publish an article in the Washington Post *making one point or interpretation. It would be read by senior State Department officials who would then say, "Hey, what's going on?" or "We hadn't seen this particular point of view." The press became a vehicle for this internal debate within the government about what was in fact happening in China.*

Stanley Karnow, *Washington Post*

One time Jim Lilley [a longtime CIA China expert who later became U.S. ambassador to China during the Tiananmen Square crisis in 1989] called me on the telephone. He says, "Listen, I've got a story for you." And he tells me something. He's on Garden Road, and I'm on Kennedy Terrace. We were only about five steps away from each other. He's obviously trying to plant something with me. This is the attitude of CIA guys. I'm working for the Washington Post. *The president of the United States is going to pick up the* Washington Post *and read it at breakfast. If he sends it back through channels, it's like putting a message in a bottle and throwing it into the sea. If he leaks it to a reporter, the president is going to read it at breakfast the next morning. Now the reporter has to be very careful. He doesn't want to end up being a conduit for the CIA guy, but on the other hand, he knows that the CIA guy has a lot of information that is very valuable.*

Thrown together, the correspondents, diplomats, and spooks lived and breathed China.

Robert Elegant, *Newsweek, Los Angeles Times*

We had a little group who were known to my wife as "Little Boys Club." We met every month—people from various consulates, various news organizations, and various intelligence organizations. You kicked things around, and you compared notes, and you put it together.

Nicholas Platt, State Department

I knew them all. Elegant was very elegant and very grand in his presentation. Karnow was totally cozy, funny, also made his points by asking questions. Bob

Keatley was always very bland, but that bland appearance belied a keen analytical mind, and he always had some smart conclusion to draw. They were all friends. We did things together.

Stanley Karnow, *Washington Post*

The wives knew each other. The kids knew each other. You know you went to the beach with everybody, dinners with everybody. We were all a part of the family, the China-watching family.

3

"A STRUGGLE OF SEA MONSTERS"

Starting in the late 1950s, China entered a period of upheaval. From 1958 to 1962, the Great Leap Forward, Chairman Mao's wildly unrealistic drive to transform China from an agrarian economy to into a modern industrial society, led instead to economic collapse and a disastrous famine in which up to forty-five million people died.

John Roderick, Associated Press

Mao knew nothing about economics but thought by sheer enthusiasm that they could raise China into the upper reaches of capitalism, as it were. It failed miserably. Countless millions of people died of starvation. It was a great calamity.[1]

During the Great Leap, nearly seven hundred million people were placed into more than twenty-five thousand communes, where the population was pushed to make steel in backyard furnaces in an effort to catch up with the West. Pots and pans were confiscated, and farm work was stopped, so desperately needed food was not harvested. With ideological fervor taking precedence over common sense, provinces reported record grain hauls—exaggerating their figures and resulting in bloated procurement targets, which left nothing for peasants to eat. Tens of millions starved to death.

Stanley Karnow, *Washington Post*

We have the bodies floating into Hong Kong after the Great Leap Forward.

Robert Elegant, *Los Angeles Times*, *Newsweek*

One of the worst famines—with cannibalism.

Still, details remained sketchy. The Chinese government of course said nothing. And at the time, reporters didn't really understand the enormous scale of the catastrophe. In 1960, for example, Richard Hughes, a flamboyant Australian correspondent who covered Asia and China for Australian and British publications for many years, observed in a broadcast: "We used to talk in the old days of famines in which millions of Chinese died. Now at least, whatever terrible tyrannies are happening inside China, nobody is dying on that scale of hunger or hardship."[2]

Jerrold Schecter, *Time*

Looking back on it, the numbers were so enormous that we never had a grip. We knew it was a bad famine, but it was hard to get quantitative reliable information. We didn't know the extent of it. And it was not possible to get firsthand reporting. What came out was a pale shadow of what was really happening.

EDGAR SNOW

The only American journalist allowed to visit the People's Republic during those years was Edgar Snow, who had interviewed Mao and other Communist leaders in Yan'an in the 1930s. In 1960, 1964, and 1965, he was allowed to spend several months in China, and was given unusual access, including meetings with Mao and Premier Zhou Enlai.

John Hamilton, Author, *Edgar Snow: A Biography*

The leadership in China—if they were going to have an American come in and write about them, Snow was the obvious one to do it. They knew and trusted him, and they thought he would do a fair job of reporting on them, just as he had done in the 1930s.

Yao Wei was then a young Chinese Foreign Ministry official who worked as an interpreter on Snow's visits.

Yao Wei, Chinese Foreign Ministry Official

Most of the Chinese leaders took him as an old friend. They gathered all those old Yan'an people, to talk about old times.

Following a five-month stay in 1960, Snow did a series of reports, which were criticized in the West for underplaying the impact of the famine caused by the Great Leap Forward.

John Hamilton, Author, *Edgar Snow: A Biography*

People look back and say, "Oh, he didn't know all these people had died." Actually, he'd ask people. He'd say, "I hear people are dying." People who were old friends of his, some of them didn't know, but if they did know they weren't telling him. His job was difficult. He didn't have the freedom. He couldn't just go where he wanted. He couldn't travel by himself. People weren't going to tell him things. They were going to be saying what they thought he should be hearing. It was hard for him to get an unblinkered view of the country.

But Yao Wei remembered that Snow was willing to challenge Chairman Mao.

Yao Wei, Chinese Foreign Ministry Official

I know as a fact that he asked Mao three different times, "Aren't you bothered by all this personality cult?" Ed Snow was dead serious. Mao didn't answer in a direct fashion, only by asking, "Don't you have a lot of cities named after George Washington in the U.S.?"

By the time of his visits in 1964 and 1965, Snow's primary goal was to produce a sympathetic depiction of China to counter the long-standing demonization of the country and increase the chances of a rapprochement with the United States.

John Hamilton, Author, *Edgar Snow: A Biography*

He realized that if he were to say just negative things, and he did say some nega-tive things—people don't remember he could be negative in what he wrote—but if he dwelled on these things, he was merely fueling the fires of people who didn't want any relations with the Chinese Communists.

In fact, Zhou Enlai told Snow that Beijing was still open to better relations with Washington, saying in an on-camera interview that "agreement should be reached between China and the United States on peaceful coexistence." Although Snow produced both a book, *The Other Side of the River,* and a doc-umentary film, *One Fourth of Humanity,* in the Cold War atmosphere of the mid-1960s, he had trouble finding outlets in the United States. For all his remarkable access, Snow's reports had little impact.

THE CULTURAL REVOLUTION BEGINS

Soon after Snow left China, reporters in Hong Kong began to detect signs that something big was beginning to happen. Following the failure of the Great Leap Forward, Mao had been forced to step back from active rule and allow more pragmatic leaders—state president Liu Shaoqi, Zhou Enlai, and Deng Xiaoping—to guide the country toward a modest recovery. But by the latter part of 1965, Mao and his radical allies, including his wife, Jiang Qing, convinced the reforms introduced after the Great Leap For-ward represented a betrayal of his revolutionary vision, started prepara-tions for what would become the Cultural Revolution. The goal was to topple the pragmatists and revive what Mao worried was China's waning revolutionary spirit.

Robert Elegant, *Newsweek, Los Angeles Times*

By 1965, Mao was even more megalomaniacal then previously. He felt that he had been betrayed by his closest associates because his grand measures, the ideas that he had advanced in the Great Leap Forward, were not put into action. He started a movement which sought to destroy the government of China, and the Communist Party of China, both of which were his creations. That's how it began, and it got worse and worse.

Nicholas Platt, State Department

There was an article that in the Shanghai Liberation Daily *[in November 1965] fiercely criticizing the play* Hai Rui Resigns from Office. *It was about the legendary story of an official who criticized the emperor and resigned from office. All of the old Chinese translators, they said immediately: "This is something big. We have to watch this very, very carefully." It turned out to be something that Madame Mao and her people were aiming at ultimately the Beijing Party committee. It was the opening shot.*

By mid-1966, Mao began to mobilize his chief weapon, the Red Guards, groups of militant high school and university students whom the Chairman encouraged to attack political adversaries he deemed to be insufficiently "revolutionary."

Nicholas Platt, State Department

The campaign didn't really get underway till the spring of 1966, and then all hell broke loose. You had wall posters going up, and Red Guard newspapers after the Red Guards emerged in June of 1966. You began to get refugees leaving who were the casualties of factional fighting, so we had a lot more material.

Stanley Karnow, *Washington Post*

So here's the Cultural Revolution starting off, and the Red Guard papers start coming in. The consulate is translating the Red Guard papers, giving me copies of the translations. And the classified stuff was very good. I was trained as a cryptographer during the Second World War, so I was kind of accustomed to puzzles. They fascinated me.

In scouring the Chinese media, reporters found clues coming from many places.

Nicholas Platt, State Department

We put Seymour Topping onto a story about the great Beijing Opera Festival on Socialist Subjects. The pièce de résistance was a one-act opera called The Bucket, *about the good guys and the bad guys—the good guys being the women in the family and the bad guys being the men—struggling over a bucket full of night soil, trying to figure out whether it should be placed on the private plot or the collective plot. This was considered hilarious, even though it was deadly serious and something that Madame Mao felt very personally strongly about. Topping did a story on this after I brought it to his attention.*

As throngs of Red Guards paid homage to Mao in Tiananmen Square, turmoil spread across the country.

Robert Elegant, *Newsweek, Los Angeles Times*

There were things happening that couldn't happen if Mao had not lost control. There were battles going on.

Sitting in Hong Kong, the reporters tried to piece the details together.

Robert Keatley, *Wall Street Journal*

It was chaos but what we knew was very limited. The translations of provincial papers and Red Guard papers and manifestos—lengthy descriptions of group X attacking group Y—who knew how true they were? But obviously, something had to be going on. It would give you some sense that there really was a lot of trouble, even if you didn't know the details. I think I had the basic concept of what Mao thought he was doing, and the results were chaos and damage.

Murray Fromson, CBS News

I did radio pieces in which I talked about the madness of the Cultural Revolution, but could I prove what I wrote? No. I could only say, "It appears that . . ." That's what we were always saying. "According to informed sources" being the people at the Consulate General.

In a famous documentary in the mid-1960s called *China: The Roots of Madness*, Theodore White, who, as a *Time* correspondent, had become known for his reporting from China during World War II, spelled out the frustrations of the China watchers.

Theodore White, Writer

At the American consulate in Hong Kong there are cascades, piles, mountains of translations that come in from the Chinese. And these are sandy, gritty, gravelly bits of information that are meaningless, because we don't know who does what to who in Peking. We don't know how they think or how they make up their mind. Because no matter how hard we study China, we cannot predict such a thing as the Great Leap Forward of 1958. We can't predict such a thing as the Red Guard purge of 1966. It is as if there was a struggle of sea monsters going on, deep, deep beneath our vision. Only these bubbles come to the surface to tell us that there are terrible struggles, but we don't know what they are struggling about.[3]

Richard Solomon, State Department

Our attitudes during the sixties had been shaped by the reporting about the Cultural Revolution and the turmoil, the Red Guard rampages. And there was a movie that Theodore White had produced called China: The Roots of Madness. *The basic point was that this internal political struggle represented a kind of insanity or political madness on the part of the Chinese.*

SNEAKING IN

With Americans barred from China, Audrey Topping, who was now a professional photographer, somehow managed to get a tourist visa in the summer of 1966.

Audrey Ronning Topping, Photographer

I went in as a Canadian housewife. I walked into a tourist bureau in Hong Kong and said, "I'd like a tourist visa." Two weeks later, I got a call saying, "Your visa's been approved." I packed my bags, took the train from Kowloon through the New Territories to Lowu, and walked over the bridge. As I walked in, there were huge propaganda pictures. When I got to Nanjing, I was met by a fellow student I had gone to school with. I was so happy to see somebody that I knew. He said, "I want to meet when everybody else is sleeping after lunch and the guards aren't there." We went around to the places we used to go to in Nanjing, and where I'd lived. Then he said, "Audrey, don't go to Beijing." I said, "Why not?" He said, "It's too dangerous. Things are happening. People are demonstrating. Do not go." But he wouldn't tell me why. So I went.

She arrived in Beijing to find the city in chaos.

Audrey Ronning Topping, Photographer

The Red Guards were all around. And opposite was the International Club. I was standing on the fence taking pictures. One Chinese student said, "I want your camera." He started coming toward me. I said, "You're not getting my camera!" Then across a street I heard a voice saying, "Audrey! Audrey!" I turned and there was Jacques Guillermaz on the steps of the International Club. He was the French military attaché and he said, "Run! Run!" He told me this was a serious demonstration, hostile students. He didn't really know what was going on, but his read was to get me out of there as soon as possible. And he got me tickets on the train. We get to Canton, and I think, "Uh, oh. They're going to get all my film." They didn't. They just said, "Go. Go." I got all my pictures, and it was a cover story for the Times.

"SOME PRETTY GOOD STUFF"

For American TV reporters in Hong Kong, however, covering the upheaval was virtually impossible.

Ted Koppel, ABC News

It was an enormously difficult story to cover, both in terms of content, but most especially in terms of pictures. We resorted to extraordinary means to get pictures. We would drive out to the border in the New Territories. We would set up a large antenna, put a film camera and shoot the output of a black-and-white television set, which was hooked to the automobile battery. And with the help of that big antenna, we'd pick up Guangdong television. Every once in a while, you'd get some pretty good stuff.

With so little information, rumors ran wild.

Ted Koppel, ABC News

I would get a phone call at three in the morning, which of course was two in the afternoon back in New York. And some idiot on the [ABC News] Foreign Desk had just seen a wire story quoting a Hong Kong newspaper. And there were some real crap papers in Hong Kong. And these would always be the real crap papers which had reported that Mao had died. So the call would come saying, "We have a wire service report that Mao is dead." I'd say, "It's three o'clock in the morning here. What do you think I'm going to do about that?" "Well, I don't know, but see if you can confirm it."

By the summer of 1967, the violence unleashed by the Cultural Revolution had led to virtual civil war. In the midst of it, Canadian Morley Safer, a correspondent for CBS News, and Johnny Peters, a British CBS cameraman, secured tourists visas by pretending not to be journalists.

Morley Safer, CBS News

There was a Paris travel agency offering visas to academics and the like. I applied claiming to be an amateur archeologist. The cameraman said he was a London travel agent looking to arrange tours of China. We waited for some months. Out of the blue the visas were approved.

Off we went and spent the best part of a month during the Cultural Revolution. It was quite honestly like Alice falling down the rabbit hole. It was just another world. When we got off the plane, we were handed the Red Book, the thoughts of Mao Zedong, and we stood in the airport reception area reciting the first couple of quotations together with this gentleman from the tourist bureau. Then we got on a minibus to the hotel.

Johnny Peters, the cameraman, had a 16mm camera that was converted to look like an 8mm tourist camera. I was also rigged for sound, so was able to do one or two stand-ups while no one was looking, which was very difficult because there were always people looking. We were just winging it.

We had to begin every day with reciting these morning prayers from the thoughts of Chairman Mao. It was a religious catechism. You would see people in the street doing it and you would hear it coming over the loudspeakers and people would stop and read out loud.

It didn't take long for Safer to get into trouble. Visiting an agricultural museum near Shanghai where the guides declared, as Safer recalled, that "all of the equipment in the museum was made and designed by local people because the capitalists and their running dogs and the Russians had boycotted China in terms of industrial and agricultural equipment," the CBS correspondent quietly observed to cameraman Peters that not all the farm machinery had in fact been made in China.

Morley Safer, CBS News

One of them heard me. I was arrested for "insulting the people's machinery." Literally that was the charge. We were frog-marched out of the museum, taken to a hotel lobby where a makeshift court was set up, with a very, very angry young woman as judge sitting behind this desk. She spoke English, and she read the charge of "insulting the people's ingenuity and machinery." I said, "Well, let me explain." Every time I said, "Let me explain," she said, "Shut up!" Our guide, the man who met us at the airport, was a lovely man. He whispered in my ear, "Don't explain anything. Just apologize. Just apologize." So she asked me some question, and I said, "I wish to apologize." She said, "Let me hear your apology." I said, winging it as I went, that "as a victim of Western propaganda and the United States and their running dogs, I have been led to believe that the Chinese people were not up to this that and the other, and, of course, my experience in China has shown me the truth, and I want to apologize for these mistakes, which were the result of a bad education." Whereupon this angry young woman beamed like a Cheshire cat and said, "that was beautiful." The court broke up. Tea was brought out and everyone laughed and had a good time, and off we went.

Safer's documentary was virtually the only firsthand report on the Cultural Revolution to air on American TV.

Morley Safer, CBS News

The Alice in Wonderland analogy is the only thing I can really think of. It was a different world, another reality. It was as if we were in some kind of play or opera. Everything was a stage set, including the people, and it was all being run by the Lords of the Flies. It was very, very strange.

CBS executives made no effort to control how he presented China. But even Safer couldn't avoid some of the political sensitivities of the time.

Morley Safer, CBS News

They decided to call this CBS Reports: Morley Safer's China Diary. The day we were taping the studio parts of it, Richard Salant, the president of CBS News, terrific guy, great believer in the First Amendment, said, "We're going to change the title." I said, "Why? What are we calling it?" He said, "You've got to call it

Morley Safer's Red China Diary." *Clearly Dick had been told, perhaps—I don't know—or just fearful himself that if we did not call it "Red China" that we would be accused of being soft on Communist China, so it was called* Morley Safer's Red China Diary.

THE RUSSIANS, THE CHINESE, AND NIXON

As the Cultural Revolution continued, tensions between China and the Soviet Union intensified. Once close allies, differences had been growing since the late 1950s. Mao bitterly opposed Moscow's policy of "peaceful coexistence" with the West, denouncing the Soviets as "revisionists" who abandoned their revolutionary principles. For their part, the Russians saw Mao as an ideological extremist challenging Moscow's leadership of the Communist movement. The two sides had been trading increasingly shrill insults and threats for years.

Henry Bradsher, *Washington Star*

This became very open, very hostile—the Chinese publishing their version of what Marxism really said, the Soviets trying to defend their position. Things went steadily downhill.

In 1969, armed clashes erupted along the Ussuri River, the poorly demarcated border between the Soviet Union and Northeast China. With heavy casualties, both sides staged large military buildups. For once, the Chinese made no attempt to hide what was going on.

Ted Koppel, ABC News

When the Chinese were fighting the Soviets along the Ussuri River, we would get combat footage off Chinese television. And then it was possible to do a story with video, which was a change for us. This notion of a global Communist hegemony really was not true. The Chinese and Soviets had been at one another's throats for a long time.

The Sino-Soviet split was one of the catalysts in Richard Nixon's evolving view of China, one the former vice president, now out of office, had begun to spell out in private meetings with journalists. Morley Safer had lunch with Nixon in Hong Kong.

Morley Safer, CBS News

It was an off-the-record lunch. We were talking to him about Vietnam and Nixon just waved it aside. He said, "Vietnam is a sideshow. The important player here is China and the most important thing we can do is recognize China, and the only person who will be able to achieve that is a Republican president." It was clearly on Nixon's mind long before he became a candidate. I think he probably considered that it was the most important foreign policy move an American president could make, and he was the one who could pull it off, and he happened to be right.

Nixon also sought out Robert Elegant.

Robert Elegant, *Newsweek, Los Angeles Times*

He wanted to know what the Chinese were like. He was told I knew about China. He called me. I was curious. I saw him at the Mandarin Hotel. It was four hours. I was very impressed. He was asking questions about China. He kept asking for more and more detail, and more and more searching questions. I was talking most of the time. This was a very penetrating mind.

The Sino-Soviet dispute and China's domestic weakness, even if self-inflicted, also led Mao to rethink his long-standing hostility to the United States. In 1970, he invited Edgar Snow to join him in Tiananmen Square for Chinese National Day. And in an interview, Mao told Snow Nixon would be welcome to visit China.

Yao Wei, Chinese Foreign Ministry

The leadership took seriously . . . that interview. They wanted every word to be exact. Ed was supposed to give it to a magazine or newspaper intact. Nothing should be changed. I was curious. Why all the fuss? And that was the interview where Mao said welcome Nixon to come, even as a tourist.

But the Nixon administration missed the signal.

Winston Lord, Assistant to Henry Kissinger

This was a very significant interview, and either lower-level people in the government were aware of it and did not understand its significance and pass it up to the policymakers or it was missed completely. But there's no question that Mao never did things casually with sending signals.

PING-PONG DIPLOMACY

It took an even more dramatic signal for the message to become clear. In April 1971, an American ping-pong team attending a tournament in Japan was invited to visit Beijing.

Judy Hoarfrost, Member of U.S. Ping-Pong Team

It was absolutely out of the blue. We weren't expecting it. I didn't know much about China. There were signs all over the place, some in English—for example, "People around the world unite and defeat the U.S.'s aggressors and all their running dogs!" But the people treated us kindly. I remember at one point asking someone about that. They said that "We make a distinction. We are friends with the American people, but this is about the U.S. government."

Liang Geliang was the world table tennis champion then and played against the visiting Americans.

Liang Geliang, Chinese Ping-Pong Player

We were happy to have this contact, because we hoped through ping-pong we could boost mutual understanding. It was friendship first, and competition second.

Judy Hoarfrost, Member of U.S. Ping-Pong Team

The biggest thing about our trip was how it changed perceptions of the American people for the Chinese. We were a people-to-people exchange. When we came out, we talked about all the good things that we experienced and that these were real people like us. Table tennis and sport is a unifying language, and it transcends politics and divisions.

To ensure the message from this conciliatory overture was not missed, in an unprecedented move, three American reporters were allowed to cover the trip. One of them was the AP's John Roderick.

John Roderick, Associated Press

There were only two other Americans invited, John Rich and Jack Reynolds of NBC. We flew from Canton to Peking and joined the ping-pong team. Zhou Enlai, whom I hadn't seen since the caves of Yan'an, met me at the Great Hall of the People. He shook hands and said, "Mr. Roderick, it's been a long time, hasn't it?" He gestured around the Hall and says, "How does this compare with the caves of Yan'an?" I said, "Well, it's somewhat of an improvement." I said to him, "We were allowed to come to China, and we hoped it would be just a beginning." He leaned forward and said through his interpreter, "Mr. Roderick, you have opened the door." And what he meant was that China was opening up. He said, "We've been at odds for many years, the United States and China, but we now have a period where we must be friends. We want more Americans to come."[4]

Winston Lord, Assistant to Henry Kissinger

What was clever about the Chinese move was it made clear to the world, and to their own domestic audience which had been living with hostility toward the U.S. for twenty years, that the policy was changing, but it was done in a strictly people-to-people cultural way, so it was not directly a government breakthrough. But anybody watching could see that more concrete diplomatic changes could now take place.

OPENING THE DOOR

In May 1971, Audrey Topping was visiting Beijing with her father, Canadian diplomat Chester Ronning, who had long maintained a cordial relationship with Zhou Enlai dating back to Ronning's years with the Canadian Embassy in Nanjing in the late 1940s.

Audrey Ronning Topping, Photojournalist

We were having dinner, and he asked Zhou if Top [her husband Seymour Topping] could have a visa. Zhou gave permission, and Top got his visa. Zhou arranged for Top to arrive in China on my birthday. We were in Hangzhou, and I didn't know Top was coming. Our Chinese friend said, "Get in the car, we have to go to the airport." I said, "Go to the airport?" He takes me to the airport and Top gets off the plane. That's my surprise present from Zhou Enlai.

Just days after Topping arrived came invitations for the *Wall Street Journal*'s Robert Keatley and William Atwood, the publisher of the Long Island newspaper *Newsday*. The journalists were invited to dinner by Zhou, who used the occasion to indicate a desire for better relations with the United States. Following the dinner, Chinese officials made clear to the three reporters the significance of the signal Zhou was trying to send.

Seymour Topping, *New York Times*

Chinese officials told us, "You must understand what was said at this dinner was very important." We filed our stories and we found that the stories had been held up until Zhou Enlai had seen them. Then they went out.

Although the reporters were not aware, the groundwork was already being laid for a secret visit in July by Henry Kissinger. Indeed, at a dinner with Chester and Audrey Ronning a few days before his meeting with the journalists, Zhou asked Chester Ronning to stay behind.

Audrey Ronning Topping, Photojournalist

He said to Dad, "Will you stay afterward?" My sister and I went back to the hotel, and Dad had a secret meeting. I didn't learn until a year later that Zhou Enlai had asked him, "Can I trust Henry Kissinger?" Dad was very anti-Kissinger because of the Vietnam War. But he said, "Any communication with the Americans will be good for both China and the United States."

On July 9, 1971, Henry Kissinger and three colleagues secretly flew into Beijing. Winston Lord was by that time Kissinger's special assistant.

Winston Lord, Assistant to Henry Kissinger

We were entering uncharted waters. We hadn't had any contact with the Chinese for two decades. We'd had constant propaganda exchanges and mutual isolation. There was a chance this would not be successful. We were very concerned about keeping it secret. If word had got out in advance, in the U.S., those who were fiercely against any rapprochement with the Chinese, and the pro-Taiwan lobby, would be invading the White House and pressuring us either to call it off or constraining what we could do.

We were there forty-eight hours. There were hours of discussions with Zhou Enlai and others on various international issues, to set up the agenda for the president's trip, not to mention a roadmap for moving forward with U.S.-China relations. This involved negotiating a mutual announcement of Kissinger's trip, and the fact that the president was going to China. The public perceptions were an important part of this. The Chinese wanted to make it look like Nixon was eager to come to China, and they were gracious hosts and inviting him. We wanted to make it look like the Chinese in their own interests were inviting Nixon and we were happy to go. So there were tricky negotiations.

Kissinger's mission remained secret until Nixon's stunning announcement that he would visit China.

Bernard Kalb, CBS News

This represented an extraordinary breakthrough with a great diplomatic gamble—to play the China card against the Soviet Union and give the Soviet Union a case of the jitters.

From the start, though, Nixon was obsessed that the press, with which he had a famously hostile relationship, would sabotage his initiative. Even during Kissinger's secret visit, Nixon was furious at the *New York Times*. Following Seymour Topping's trip, the *Times*' influential columnist James Reston had been given a visa and was in Beijing at the same time as Kissinger. Reston was granted an interview with Zhou Enlai. Zhou said nothing about Kissinger's presence, but an angry Nixon ordered a White House freeze on all contact with the *Times*.

Max Frankel was then the *Times*' Washington bureau chief.

Max Frankel, *New York Times*

When they published the interview with Zhou Enlai, Reston had dared to ask how the Chinese felt about having this classic Red-baiter now becoming their negotiating partner. Nixon read that, and decided, in his particularly paranoid manner, that they [the Times] are going to sabotage my new relationship with China by calling me a Red-baiter.

In China, Mao's decision to welcome Nixon had generated opposition, especially from his designated heir, Lin Biao, an important general in the civil war who had been instrumental in promoting Mao's personality cult. In September 1971 China watchers in Hong Kong detected clues that something serious was happening in the leadership.

Henry Bradsher, *Washington Star*

There was a reception in Hanoi for a visiting Chinese delegation. The usual toasts were to "Chairman Mao Zedong and his loyal deputy, Marshal Lin Biao." That was standard. About three days later, there was another reception in Hanoi for another Chinese delegation. At that reception, the toast was to "Chairman Mao Zedong"—period. Oh boy. Lin had suddenly been dropped from the leadership. So I wrote that Lin had fallen from power but we didn't know yet what had happened exactly. Then, several days later, the Russian media announced that a Chinese plane had crashed in Mongolia.

Soon came more detailed reports that Lin had died in a plane crash after allegedly trying to overthrow Mao.

Stanley Karnow, *Washington Post*

One day, I go to the Yenching Palace restaurant on Connecticut Avenue in Washington, DC. It's run by a guy called Van Lung. He was the son of Long Yun [a Chinese warlord who threw in his lot with the Communists in 1949 and held several largely ceremonial positions in the Chinese government]. Van Lung had been in China recently and seen documents about Lin Biao and the plane crashing in Mongolia. I did a story on page one of the Washington Post. *The Nixon administration went berserk. They thought that anything that came out that the Chinese didn't like was going to cancel the trip.*

By now, Richard Solomon was working for Henry Kissinger at the National Security Council.

Richard Solomon, Kissinger Aide

Nixon and Kissinger were concerned that if negative stories appeared in the press about instability in China, you would get questioning. How can we have this opening to China if they're tearing themselves apart with their internal conflicts? Henry was not happy when the Lin Biao business broke out, because it made it look as if China was politically unstable—which it was—and would put in jeopardy this strategic maneuver of trying to normalize with China as a counterweight to the Soviet Union. All of us working on his staff were basically interdicted from talking openly to the press about what we really saw going on in China.

But for most American reporters and their audiences, internal politics in Beijing were much less important than the fact that, with the Nixon visit, a country almost inaccessible for more than two decades appeared ready to open its doors.

4

THE WEEK THAT CHANGED THE WORLD

On a chilly day in February 1972, Richard Nixon left Washington for Beijing. Before departing, he spoke to reporters.

Richard Nixon

The government of the People's Republic of China and the government of the United States have had great differences. We will have differences in the future. But what we must do is find a way to see that we can have differences without being enemies in war.

For the president—and the journalists accompanying him—the China trip was a journey into the unknown. Dan Rather, who later became the anchor of the *CBS Evening News*, was then the network's White House correspondent.

Dan Rather, CBS News

I found myself thinking, "What is President Nixon getting into? What is the United States getting into? And what are we journalists getting into?" That was the atmosphere.

As Nixon talked to the press, White House staffers, including Dwight Chapin, who had been working for Nixon since his failed campaign for governor of California in 1962, and who was then managing the president's schedule, had set up a TV on *Air Force One* to watch the live coverage. They well understood how important the press was to the success of this trip.

Dwight Chapin, Nixon Appointments Secretary

At the White House, we would figure out what we wanted to be the headline, the picture, the story, and the caption on a given event. We took the days that we were going to be in China, broke it into what you would call media sections, and we figured out the headline, picture caption, and story for each one of the segments that we were going to be doing, and how we wanted to have that unfold. That was the art form.

Nixon's China visit—which he called "the week that changed the world"— would reshape the global geopolitical map, alter the balance of power in the Cold War, and open the door to the establishment of relations between the People's Republic and the United States. It also became a milestone in the history of journalism. After more than two decades during which virtually all American reporters had been banned, Beijing agreed to issue visas to nearly one hundred U.S. journalists plus technical staff, and allow the most dramatic events—the president's arrival in Beijing, Premier Zhou Enlai's welcoming banquet, Nixon's visits to the Great Wall and the Forbidden City—to be televised live.

The coverage was arguably almost as important as the details of the diplomacy. It profoundly transformed American and international perceptions of China, generated the public support Nixon needed to change U.S. policy, and laid the groundwork for the Chinese government's gradual moves to open the country to greater coverage by the American media.

THE PRESS ARRANGEMENTS

Initially, Beijing was less than enthusiastic about allowing scores of American journalists to come with Nixon.

Yao Wei, Chinese Foreign Ministry

We had the Korean War between the U.S. and China, and animosity of the Cold War. China of course was suspicious of everything in the U.S. A lot of people were still skeptical, suspicious.

Winston Lord, Assistant to Henry Kissinger

For the president and Kissinger, they wanted this dramatic event to be covered as widely as possible. The Chinese of course had been incredibly paranoiac and secretive and controlling the press completely. So you had these two cultural and political giants clashing here. There were semihumorous exchanges in which Kissinger would joke about how we're invading them with a media army. But Kissinger was very good at explaining why it was in the Chinese interest to have this covered, so we got more than the Chinese had ever agreed to before.

Ron Walker was the thirty-four-year-old chief of the White House advance office, responsible for setting up all presidential events. In the weeks before Nixon's departure, he made two trips to China to work out every detail—security arrangements, motorcade routes, banquet arrangements, planning the president's tour of the Great Wall—as well as how to deal with the press.

Ron Walker, Nixon White House Media Advance Man

I don't think they had any idea what was about to fall on them. We told them they're going to be obnoxious. They're going to want to cover that, want to do that. You've got to set the ground rules. We'll help you enforce it. But you've got to help accommodate us as we accommodate you.

Meanwhile, among news organizations across America, there was intense jockeying among reporters desperate to get on the trip. Dirck Halstead, who had headed the United Press International photo desk in Saigon during the Vietnam War, was the wire service's White House photographer.

Dirck Halstead, United Press International

The warfare started among all these companies as everyone was jockeying to go. We are talking about people [who] would do anything, people who would very happily push their own mothers under the wheels of a plane to get on the trip.

Tom Jarriel, who'd previously been based in Atlanta and had covered the assassination of the Rev. Martin Luther King for ABC News, was now the network's White House correspondent.

Tom Jarriel, ABC News

They had limited numbers of places for the news media. As the trip got closer and the interest built in New York, suddenly there are nontechnicians, vice presidents, presidents, executive producers, all jumping on the bandwagon and signing on as soundmen, electricians.

Richard Solomon, Kissinger Aide

The American press and media officials were crawling over themselves. One young lady approached someone in the administration and said only half-jokingly, "Who do I have to sleep with to get on the Nixon China trip?"

NIXON'S "ENEMIES"

For his part, Nixon vowed to exclude reporters from the newspapers he most disliked—the *New York Times* and the *Washington Post.*

Max Frankel, *New York Times*

Nixon had said, "Nobody from the Times.*" Somebody on his staff said, "You can't do that. This is the international newspaper etcetera." He reluctantly allowed one seat for China. I used my seniority* [as Washington bureau chief] *to leave the White House correspondent at home and took the trip myself. But imagine my shock when I get on the plane, and I find at least a half a dozen tourists from the vice presidents of networks that were along with no function at all. I could understand the networks getting multiple seats for technicians and cameramen, but there were hangers-on for each of the networks. It became very clear this whole trip was being set up for television. I was quite enraged.*

Stanley Karnow, who had been the *Washington Post*'s chief Asia correspondent, had by now returned to Washington.

Stanley Karnow, *Washington Post*

Nixon doesn't want me on the trip, because I'm working for the Washington Post, *and he doesn't like the* Washington Post. *I'll show you the list with Nixon's handwriting running through my name—"absolutely not." I'm also on the enemies list from my reporting from Vietnam, so that's another reason for me not to go. [The "enemies list" included more than five hundred people, among them members of Congress, labor unions, think tanks, academics, celebrities, and journalists. Its existence was revealed during the Watergate hearings in 1973.]*

Eventually, Nixon's press secretary, Ron Ziegler, and his chief of staff, H. R. Haldeman, convinced the president he could not keep Karnow off the China trip.

Dwight Chapin, Nixon Appointments Secretary

It would not be unlike him to say, "Damn it. We're not going to let him go on that trip to China." Ziegler would wait a couple of days, go back to Haldeman, and say, "You know we really can't do that. This is not right." And Haldeman would go back in and raise it with President Nixon, and he would say, "Well, that's how I felt, but if he's got to go, he's got to go."

LOGISTICS

With less than a month before Nixon's departure, however, the White House and the Chinese had still not been able to agree on key questions concerning the press—including how the army of reporters would file their stories.

Ron Walker, Nixon White House Media Advance Man

We took in three scenarios. The first was bringing in three 747s where the networks and wires could file, and photos could be moved. The next was to bring in three transmission trucks. The third one was a model of a transmission center.

For reasons of national pride, the Chinese rejected Walker's first two ideas. But in just three weeks, they built their own transmission center, which the U.S. TV network pool then equipped.

ABC News producer Robert Siegenthaler was the pool coordinator.

Robert Siegenthaler, ABC News

They built to our specifications a television station, totally unfurnished, and the U.S. pool took a 707 full of television equipment. Half the technicians and

*the equipment in the chartered 707 and the two mobile units were airlifted by
the same air force plane that airlifted the president's vehicles. The People's
Republic folks built the broadcast center, and we did the innards, and that
worked out fine.*

Yao Wei, Chinese Foreign Ministry

*At that time, you didn't have any digital. You had to film everything in 35mm
or 16mm. They had to be developed. The place close to the old Beijing airport
was set up as a U.S. center where all those networks would come to develop
those films and send it to the "bird." I was quite amused by the word "bird,"
that's the satellite.*

There were other problems that emerged when the TV equipment was
unloaded ahead of Nixon's arrival.

Robert Siegenthaler, ABC News

*When they arrived, the first mobile unit was sent to Tiananmen Square to have
a look at what they have to deal with. They were training the camera on the
picture of Chairman Mao on the Forbidden City. In those olden days of color
television, they were going through the sequential registering of the camera in
red, green, and blue, the primary colors. Later in the day, I had a meeting with
my counterpart. Someone had reported that the crew was disrespectful to
Chairman Mao because they were filming him in blue [because in the registering of the camera colors, Mao had appeared in blue]. It was a big sticking
point until we got it sorted out that it was a misunderstanding.*

NIHAO ONE AND *NIHAO TWO*

As Nixon set out for China, a half-dozen reporters made up the White House
pool traveling with him on Air Force One.

Tom Jarriel, ABC News

*We had two other newspaper guys and a camera crew. The accommodations on
pool on Air Force One were strictly coach. We had a desk, a table in front, and
four seats facing each other, and no place to sleep, the technicians sat in a couple*

of seats in the back. You really didn't want to be pool on Air Force One, *it was a chore—except when* Air Force One *is heading to Shanghai and then on to Peking. Then we thought, holy cow, we're going to be among the first ones there.*

The rest of the press corps traveled on two specially chartered planes.

Dirck Halstead, United Press International

They had two 707s. One was a TWA 707, and that was named Nihao 1, *which was Chinese for "hello." The second one was a Pan Am clipper, and that was named* Nihao 2. *Then they had to worry about who is going to be on which plane. Of course, the reporters all wanted to be on* Nihao 1, *together. And the photographers were put on the Pan Am clipper. So there was that stratification.*

While crossing the Pacific, the mood on board was almost giddy.

Dan Rather, CBS News

It was pretty much a party atmosphere of, "Wow, I'm finally aboard the plane and I'm going to China." It was a little of the feeling we were leaving Earth and going deep into the cosmos of some distant planet.

Few of the reporters were experienced China hands.

Stanley Karnow, *Washington Post*

Most of the reporters on the trip, they knew nothing about China. They knew nothing.

Barbara Walters of NBC's *Today Show* was typical.

Barbara Walters, NBC News

I knew nothing about China. Nobody had any idea what it was going to be like. It really was like going on the moon. What are we going to see? We had no idea what to expect.

Walters had her own anxieties. Her role had initially been as the "Today Girl," a job traditionally involving little more than looking attractive, making small talk, and reading commercials. Yet, through her skillful interviewing techniques and on-camera presence, she had risen to become one of the net-work's most popular personalities. Nonetheless, she was one of only three women reporters making the trip and had little experience covering foreign affairs.

Barbara Walters, NBC News

When I was asked to cover it for NBC, I was scared, because I never been at the level with the big guys, with the Eric Sevareids, Teddy Whites, Walter Cronkites, and so on. But I had one advantage, and that is I knew Henry Kissinger.

Cronkite was the anchor of the *CBS Evening News*. Sevareid was one of CBS's most famous correspondents and commentators. And White had covered China in the 1940s for *Time* magazine. But White was the rare exception. Most of the reporters knew little of China. Their perceptions had been shaped by nearly a quarter-century of isolation and hostility.

Bernard Kalb, CBS News

Until then the idea was—Mao Zedong ate babies for breakfast, so to speak. There had been this exaggerated characterization of the way the Chinese were, and the Communist system had been basically dehumanized.

Max Frankel, *New York Times*

It was the dark period. It was closed to us and yet we knew there was this huge society, ancient and revered, and the largest population on Earth. The fascination was tremendous, but it was all frozen in ice and we were steeped in ignorance.

TOUCHDOWN

The press planes—*Nihao 1* and *Nihao 2*—stopped first in Shanghai.

Dirck Halstead, United Press International

From the minute we passed over the coast everybody was gawking out at the windows for their first look at China. And of course, to say these are well-seasoned travelers is an understatement. They were like kids. Everybody was leaning out trying to see stuff.

Dwight Chapin, Nixon Appointments Secretary

The enthusiasm quotient was off the charts. Everybody was excited and everybody felt privileged to go. I don't care if you're talking about Walter Cronkite and Barbara Walters or the guy from the Des Moines Register. *I mean, everybody was excited.*

Dan Rather, CBS News

The very first time we stepped foot in China was exhilaration. We had made it. This is a story of a lifetime. There was this sense that this was literally history in the making, a story for the history books. From the very second the plane door opened there was this feeling of setting foot on some distant planet. Everything looks strange, everything sounds strange.

Then it was on to Beijing so the press would be in a position to cover Nixon's arrival.

Dirck Halstead, United Press International

We got to Beijing the day before Nixon was to arrive. We all loaded in our buses and drove into town and there were no cars. That was the first enormous surprise. Just bicycles.

The president also stopped first in Shanghai to take on board some protocol officials, translators, and a Chinese navigator for the final leg of the trip to Beijing. In a report he filed for ABC, Tom Jarriel described the scene.

Tom Jarriel, ABC News

He, Mrs. Nixon and the official party were met at the base of the stairs of Air Force One *by three high Communist Party officials and local officials. There were broad smiles as handshakes were exchanged as the American delegation walked along a red-carpet receiving line. At the head of the Chinese delegation*

was Qiao Guanhua, Vice Minister of Foreign Affairs, who led the China del-
egation to the United Nations last fall. There was no public crowd outside or
inside the terminal building. The day is cloudy and cool, but not uncomfort-
able. Both the United States flag and the flag of the People's Republic of China
are flying in a light breeze.[1]

ARRIVAL IN BEIJING

Air Force One then took off for Beijing. As the plane descended toward the
Chinese capital, Nixon and his staff were well aware of how crucial the first
TV images would be in setting the tone for the entire trip.

Ron Walker, Nixon White House Media Advance Man

Central. Number one. We knew the world was going to see this event and it
was going to be huge because we were opening a door to a billion people that
had been isolated, so everything we did was for that camera.

Boston native Ed Fouhy was the Washington producer for the *CBS Eve-*
ning News with Walter Cronkite.

Ed Fouhy, CBS News

They were stage managing everything. Haldeman, who was one of Nixon's clos-
est aides, had been an advertising man, and right from the first time I covered
any Nixon campaign, it was clear that Haldeman was an expert at and a great
devotee of television, and so he was constantly thinking about setting up
pictures.

Dwight Chapin, Nixon Appointments Secretary

It was very clear upon arrival that we would have the president and Mrs. Nixon
down that stairs and that that picture with Zhou Enlai would be an incredibly
important picture. That was the establishing shot in virtually every newspaper
the next morning.

Waiting at Beijing airport, the reporters, too, wondered about the
moment.

Dan Rather, CBS News

When President Nixon got off the aircraft, it was very clear to me that he had thought about what he would do at the bottom of the ramp in terms of the order of the handshaking and that·sort of thing.

Max Frankel, *New York Times*

I had in mind John Foster Dulles's refusal in the 1954 Vietnam Conference to shake Zhou Enlai's hand. I was straining to see Nixon shaking Zhou Enlai's hand at the airport. I remember having to struggle to get the right view of it because I was going to make a point of it in my story.

The arrival was broadcast live by all the American networks.

Dirck Halstead, United Press International

We had six still photographers, and one cameraman and soundman from the networks. There was a flatbed that was in position to photograph Nixon coming down the ramp and being met by the Chinese, and of course the normal White House pool scurried around to the front of the plane to get close-ups of the greeting.

Robert Siegenthaler, ABC News

I felt what I always felt at a time like that—great relief that it [the transmission] was working. I don't think that I had a view that this was [a] wonderful historical event. But I was grateful that the plane stopped where we asked it to stop. Once that was achieved, the U.S. traveling press got a sense that they were going to be able to report from China.

What the reporters didn't know was that even the choice of the color for Pat Nixon's coat had been made with the cameras in mind.

Dwight Chapin, Nixon Appointments Secretary

We knew that everything was all in that muted grays and browns and greens. The only things in red were the propaganda signs that said "running capitalist pigs" or something that was anti-American. So the idea came. Mrs. Nixon needed a heavy coat because it's February. And a red coat might really set her apart and make a statement, and it did.

Apart from Premier Zhou, a handful of other officials, a Chinese army band, and a guard of honor, the welcome was decidedly low-key. And it remained so as Nixon, his entourage, and the press corps headed into Beijing.

Max Frankel, *New York Times*

We were herded off on a bus. It was quite remarkable because it was dead silence. Normally when you're with a presidential party, the host government had arranged for cheering crowds on the sides. Here we were gliding into Beijing and hardly anybody taking notice of us.

Dirck Halstead, United Press International

This was an airport ceremony unlike any I had ever experienced in a foreign country. There were no "Welcome Nixon" signs. There were no people lining the streets to see him come in. It was like sliding in the back door in the middle of the night.

Max Frankel, *New York Times*

The single most profound impression that I came away with was—wow, what a poor country. The degree of poverty and backwardness that we were able to glean from a bus window I found just startling.

For a president used to pomp, pageantry, and crowds, the austere reception left Nixon's aides—and a skeptical press—wondering about the prospects for the visit.

Ted Koppel, ABC News

When the Nixon motorcade came into Tiananmen Square, there were several hundred Chinese in the Square. But nobody paid any attention to the motorcade. People were wheeling their bicycles, wheeling prams with children, walking through the Square. You would have expected that the sight of a big American limousine, and all the escort vehicles going by with the American flag flying from the fender, would have attracted some attention. It did not.

The press was housed in the Soviet-style Nationalities Hotel, with a filing center nearby.

Max Frankel, *New York Times*

Just as they had set up a satellite to serve the TV networks, they had a well-lit, vast pressroom where we could each leave our typewriters. Off to the side were telephone booths. Almost without fail, I got immediate connections to New York, and I could dictate my stories. That was a pleasant surprise.

MEETING MAO

Nixon was taken to the Diaoyutai state guesthouse. The official schedule called for a rest, followed by a formal meeting and then a banquet with Zhou Enlai.

Winston Lord, Assistant to Henry Kissinger

An hour after we landed and got to the guesthouse, Zhou Enlai came and said to Kissinger, "The Chairman would like to see the president right away." This caught us off-guard. We thought, given his usual pattern, that we'd be seeing him at the end of the trip, not at the beginning. We were delighted it was at the beginning.

The invitation was for Nixon, Kissinger and one note-taker. Kissinger brought his assistant Winston Lord. William Rogers, Nixon's secretary of state, was excluded from the meeting, as he had been throughout the negotiations that had led to the visit—part of an ongoing power struggle between Kissinger and the State Department for control of U.S. foreign policy.

The meeting with Mao lasted an hour, with the two leaders talking mostly in generalities. Yet the mere fact it took place meant Mao had given his blessing to a new relationship with the United States.

Winston Lord, Assistant to Henry Kissinger

We were delighted it was at the beginning, because this was saying to the Chinese audiences and the cadres and the people, and the world, that even not knowing how the negotiations on the communiqué and everything else on the trip was going to come out, he was putting his positive stamp on it.

But Lord's participation in the meeting and the exclusion of Secretary of State Rogers had created an embarrassing problem for Nixon and Kissinger.

Winston Lord, Assistant to Henry Kissinger

After it's finished, the Chinese come in with a communiqué about who was there including myself and pictures of all of us. Nixon and Kissinger said to Zhou Enlai and Mao—"Mr. Lord was never in this meeting. Take him out of the communiqué, out of all the press releases, all the pictures." Because they figured if it was just Kissinger and Nixon and Rogers wasn't there, that was humiliating enough, but to have a third person who was Kissinger's personal assistant instead of Rogers was too much. And I understood this. The Chinese, I think, didn't really understand what was going on.

Lord was cropped out of all the pictures. Years later, the Chinese gave him the originals. The episode highlighted the internal tensions on the U.S. side that would soon come to a head, even as Nixon's entourage struggled to keep the press in the dark.

That no American journalist was allowed to cover the meeting left the reporters furious.

Dan Rather, CBS News

It was announced the president had gone to see Chairman Mao, and it was— well, what press is with him? There's no press with him. I would say the discontent in the press corps, including myself, was very high. Were there ever complaints, saying, "How could you do this? We come all this way, halfway around the world. And this is a case of you are manipulating the news. You're controlling the news."

For Nixon, it didn't matter. He had the image he wanted—the first meeting between Mao and an American leader.

Ron Walker, Nixon White House Media Advance Man

Then Zhou Enlai takes him from there to the first plenary session at the Great Hall of the People and we don't have any press there. All the sudden we get the word, they're at the Great Hall. Well, we hauled ass and got there as fast as we could, got the pool in there immediately.

THE WELCOME BANQUET

As the Nixon-Zhou meeting ended, the press corps was assembled on the steps of the Great Hall of the People to watch the president arrive for a welcoming banquet, another set-piece event designed for American TV.

Richard Solomon, Kissinger Aide

They timed events so that because of the twelve-hour time difference between events in Washington and Beijing there would be evening events that would be timed for the morning television shows. Americans would be having their breakfast coffee watching Nixon and Zhou Enlai toasting at an evening banquet in Beijing. All that was very carefully organized.

In the United States breakfast viewers saw Nixon and Zhou exchange toasts and talk about a new relationship. The obvious—and surprising—warmth was evident on TV. It was exactly what the White House wanted.

Dwight Chapin, Nixon Appointments Secretary

We knew that there were going to be toasts and the clicking of the glass and that was what we were after. That was the shot.

Indeed, in his opening toast in Beijing, Nixon boasted that "more people are seeing and hearing what we say here than on any other occasion in the whole history of the world."

The next day, after a brief photo opportunity, Nixon and Kissinger began negotiations with Zhou on a communiqué to form the basis of a new U.S.-China relationship. Both sides agreed on the need for secrecy. But Zhou had ensured that the official *People's Daily* highlighted the Mao meeting and Nixon's presence in Beijing, as Tom Jarriel noted in a report for ABC News.

Tom Jarriel, ABC News Report

Today's edition of the Communist Party–controlled newspaper People's Daily *removed the question mark by coming out with full front-page coverage including three photographs and two banner headlines on the Nixon visit. The Chinese are telling their people through these papers, which are circulated to millions on the streets, about as much as the Nixon White House is telling American newsmen about the substance of his private talks. This paper has about the same line as the White House—that the two met with frank and serious talks. No more substance about details of the talks is given here than the American press in being told.*

SCRATCHING THE SURFACE

With the real business of the summit taking place behind closed doors, the reporters were offered carefully controlled visits to various Chinese work units.

Dan Rather, CBS News

You have to follow the script. If you don't go, all you will be doing is sitting back in the press center or your hotel room, and your competition will beat you. We all recognized how heavily we were being manipulated, but none of us could do anything about it.

Ted Koppel, ABC News

We would each be given a menu of events first thing in the morning. You can pick, quite literally, one from Column A and one from Column B. You can go to the Chinese– [North] Korean People's Friendship Commune. Or you could go to such and such a hospital.

Barbara Walters, NBC News

We went where the Chinese told us to go, in cars the Chinese provided for us. There were events every day for Mrs. Nixon. There was a visit to the school where we could see how advanced they were, where they would know one song, "Home on the Range." These were the things that didn't have to do with politics but had to do with the way a society lives that were brand new to us.

On the second night, the President and his party were taken to see *The Red Detachment of Women*, a "revolutionary ballet" that told the story of a peasant girl who escapes from an evil landlord and finds refuge with a Red Army unit on Hainan Island, entirely comprised of women. The ballet, one of just eight model theatrical pieces allowed to be performed in China during the Cultural Revolution, was a favorite of Chairman Mao's wife, Jiang

Qing, a former actress, who was more radical than Mao or Zhou, and opposed to any accommodation with the West.

Barbara Walters, NBC News

She was in charge of the Cultural Revolution. She said, "This is what you are going to listen to, what you are going to be watching, what you are going to be taught in the schools." When it had to do with culture, Madame Mao probably played a more important role than her husband.

The ballet was broadcast live by the U.S. networks.

Robert Siegenthaler, ABC News

This was much harder than all the other events. The director from CBS had never seen the performance.

Nixon watched the rifle-wielding ballerinas in military garb and stirring odes to Chairman Mao, flanked by Zhou Enlai on one side and Jiang Qing, Zhou's bitter political rival, on the other. At the end, he clapped politely. Later, when asked his opinion by reporters, he struggled to find something positive to say. After multiple stumbles, Nixon told reporters: "The ballet was . . . of course, as you all know, it had its message. And that was one of its purposes. But also, while it was a powerful message it was also very dramatic and excellent theater."

Max Frankel, *New York Times*

The red detachment triumphing over the capitalist dogs. Nixon in his most deferential manner sitting through this insulting performance. I thought that was a great synopsis of this entire trip that they were rubbing it in, and Nixon for his own reasons was taking it.

MINDERS

All the reporters accompanying Nixon were assigned government minders. They served as translators and guides—but were also there to keep the press in line.

Ed Fouhy, CBS News

The Cultural Revolution was going on, so it was very difficult to get the minder to be anything but an animated robot. As the week went on and we got to know him a little better, he loosened up a little bit, but there was a real sense that this guy was not just a translator and a minder, but really was an intelligence agent.

Dan Rather, CBS News

The minders were all very uptight. Their instructions were—don't let them go anywhere they are not supposed to go.

Ted Koppel, ABC News

I remember the one thing of interest I got out of our interpreters was, I said, "Do me a favor. Every place I go, I'd like to hear what the local humor is. Tell me a Chinese joke." And I would get these vacant stares. I'd say, "You know, a joke, something to make you laugh." The answer I got over and over was, "I don't know any jokes." It was really chilling. I think people during the Cultural Revolution were so thoroughly terrorized and so afraid of saying or doing the wrong thing that humor would have been far too risky.

Photographers and technicians had their own minders, who struggled to make sense of the complex technology being used to cover the visit.

Dirck Halstead, United Press International

The day that Nixon arrived at the airport, the Chinese minder was just amazed as the director went "Cut to camera one, let's have camera three" . . . bang, bang, bang. At the end of that transmitting session, the minder turned to the director in the van, and he says, "Well I think I understand almost everything. I understand about the feed, about the bird, but there's one thing that you kept saying that I don't understand. Can you please tell me, what is this 'fucking audio'?"

As Nixon's visit progressed, the reporters became increasingly frustrated at their inability to get beyond staged events.

Dan Rather, CBS News

If you complained, and we did complain, the White House press representatives would shrug their shoulders and say we are in China and we have to do things the Chinese way.

Max Frankel, *New York Times*

A few of us badgered the hell out of our minders that we were getting sick and tired of these laid-on events, and was there no chance at all to engage some real people?

The result: the Chinese laid on a visit to a people's commune.

Ed Fouhy, CBS News

I think we saw a Potemkin village that was carefully stage-managed, probably a joint effort between the Chinese and the White House.

A few journalists, including the *Washington Post*'s Stanley Karnow and Robert Keatley of the *Wall Street Journal*, were taken to Peking University.

Robert Keatley, *Wall Street Journal*

We met [Zhou Peiyuan] the vice chairman of the Revolutionary Committee, a physicist who had gotten his degree at the University of Chicago. This was an intelligent, accomplished man, well known in his field. He sat there and described how thanks to the thoughts of Chairman Mao they had reorganized the university and let workers and peasants in. It was just all nonsense, and you felt sorry for him because you know he couldn't believe a word he said, but he was a captive.

Stanley Karnow asked about the fate of Nie Yuanzi, a Communist Party functionary who soared to prominence early in the Cultural Revolution after she put up a poster in May 1966 denouncing the university's top officials, but who was herself later purged and imprisoned.

Stanley Karnow, *Washington Post*

I wondered what had happened to her. You're at the table with them and you start asking questions. "What ever happened to Nie Yuanzi?" "Mr. Karnow have you tried this squab?" They kept ducking every question.

Some reporters decided to elude their minders and strike out on their own.

Max Frankel, *New York Times*

I remember walking down one alley all alone. Every time I came to a hole in the wall, I realized there was a gang of kids on the other side of the wall following me. The most vivid thing was how scared the kids were. They'd never seen anybody with a long nose or a lot of hair on their skin. These kids would stare in fascination, and then suddenly burst into tears. It was just startling.

Dan Rather, CBS News

I managed to shake the minders for just a couple of minutes and got around what couldn't have been more than three-quarters of a block into a small shop. The camera crew joined me. The Chinese in the shop were shocked to see us. The minders came in as the camera started rolling. The minders were clearly looking at one another, saying we don't want to be on camera intruding. On the other hand, this is not supposed to be happening. The minders made it very clear that we were not supposed to be there, you have to get back to the hotel.

But Rather kept trying.

Dan Rather, CBS News

I went out the front door of the hotel just in time to catch a bus. The minders were trying to catch up with the bus, saying, "what the hell is that Western idiot doing on the bus?" I rode for twenty-five or thirty minutes with no interpreter. The bus seemed to get to what was the end of the line. I did not speak Chinese. The driver was trying to tell me you have to get off. I was trying to tell him, "If you don't mind, I'll stay on the bus until you turn around and go back the other way." It was an awkward moment but in terms of breaking away from minders, it was the one and only time that I was able to break away.

MADE FOR TV

Tensions also began to emerge between the print reporters and their TV counterparts.

Max Frankel, *New York Times*

We became factionalized. The print people wanted some real contact, to talk to some Chinese people as per the episode at the university, and some sense of the real diplomacy going on, whereas the TV people were transmitting pictures that were in themselves sufficient novelty to satisfy their curiosity and their needs.

Barbara Walters, NBC News

The print people were very put out with us. The whole New York Times *team headed by Max Frankel, Teddy White, who had written definitive stories about China, and here were we, on before they were. And they were very resentful.*

At the heart of the tension was the fact that the White House, recognizing the power of television, had explicitly designed the trip with TV coverage as a top priority.

Dwight Chapin, Nixon Appointments Secretary

We knew daily how the trip was covered. We knew hourly how the trip was covered. We would get reports from back from our media operation in the White House. It was like what goes on with the Olympics or something. I mean, it was nonstop.

Stanley Karnow, *Washington Post*

What Nixon really wanted was a television extravaganza. He didn't want print reporters. He didn't care about print reporters. He cared about television. He wanted a television extravaganza.

Winston Lord, Assistant to Henry Kissinger

I think the basic grumbling of the print press versus the TV press is probably fair but in terms of the U.S. national interest, too bad for them.

THE GREAT WALL

Nowhere was the impact of television more evident than when Nixon visited the Great Wall.

Tom Jarriel, ABC News

It looked like the picture postcards. It was higher than anyone thought, so the cameramen, with their heavy gear, were breathing hard. But there were photo ops, and they had the best possible camera positions, and it was a must.

Ed Fouhy, CBS News

There was a bus that took us there. The president came an hour later, after we'd had time to set up. He paraded around with Mrs. Nixon and a whole group of Chinese and American officials. CBS had issued us very nice coats and hats and long underwear because it was going to be so cold. Walter Cronkite, in anticipation of the really cold weather, had a pair of electric socks like a duck hunter would wear. The socks kept shorting out on him. I think he finally took the batteries out of his socks.

Max Frankel, *New York Times*

My memory is the positioning of everybody for the pictures of Nixon and Mrs. Nixon. The TV people were most concerned about where they were positioned so they could get their canisters of film to the couriers in a competitive way back to the transmission center in Beijing. And it was Cronkite and the others behaving in this really childish way about where they could be positioned, and how their couriers could get out of there, whereas we were all hemmed in. It was the one time I felt the television people were suffering in the same manner that the print people had suffered.

As Frankel wrote in his report for the *New York Times*: "The American Commander in Chief . . . moved confidently past the firing slits in the wall for several hundred yards, showing by his gaze that he knew the position of every major camera emplacement."

After completing his tour at the U.S. consulate in Hong Kong, Nicholas Platt had become director of the China Desk at the State Department, and then head of the department's secretariat staff. He was on the China trip as an aide to Secretary of State William Rogers.

Nicholas Platt, State Department

The most memorable sight of the trip was not Nixon on the Wall, but the big multimedia trailer truck parked next to the wall with wires snaking out of it, and the reporters connected to the rest of the world via satellite. That was the main point of the trip. The White House was choreographing it, and the Chinese understood exactly what they were trying to do and were very supportive of their efforts.

The images were in fact spectacular. Nixon was left almost at a loss for words, pausing for several seconds before telling reporters: "I think you would have to conclude that this is a Great Wall."

THE MING TOMBS

From the Wall, Nixon headed for another famous site, the Ming Tombs, the burial place of thirteen emperors from the Ming Dynasty, which ruled China from 1368 to 1644.

Ted Koppel, ABC News

This was late February. Damn cold out there! And here were all these Chinese, taking photographs of one another, listening to the radio, having a picnic. I thought to myself, "This is really dumb." So I told my crew, "When the bus comes to pick us up, we're not getting on. Just go hide behind that building over there and we'll come out. I want to see what happens to the crowd." Sure enough, as soon as the reporters left, trucks came. A cadre came by with baskets. They picked up all the tape recorders. They picked up all the cameras. They picked up all the portable radios. Put them in the baskets. They loaded the people on the trucks, and off they went.

Yao Wei, Chinese Foreign Ministry Official

You can tell, it's a staged thing. I felt so embarrassed, as well as my colleagues.

Ted Koppel, ABC News

Henry Kissinger told me later that after our piece aired, he received an apology from Zhou Enlai, who said, "That was really kind of 'ham-fisted' of us, and I'm sorry that we did that."

With a U.S. presidential election scheduled for November 1972, some correspondents began to feel they were little more than props in a giant Nixon campaign commercial.

Max Frankel, *New York Times*

It was an election year, and the fact that all this was happening at the beginning of 1972 was hardly lost on us. To that extent, we're part of a partisan propaganda effort.

Dan Rather, CBS News

This had all the trappings and all the inner core of a campaign trip. No doubt, we were on a reelect President Nixon campaign trip.

"TOTALLY, TOTALLY FOREIGN"

In contrast to the carefully stage-managed public events, reporters were told virtually nothing about the closed-door diplomacy between Nixon and the Chinese. That only compounded their frustration.

Tom Jarriel, ABC News

There was nothing at all. We wanted to know—Did they discuss Taiwan? Did they discuss the Soviet Union? Did they discuss military matters? Did they discuss future trade?

But as they left Beijing to cover Nixon's next stops, the scenic resort of Hangzhou and then Shanghai, the press remained in the dark—preoccupied instead with the quirks of the Chinese system.

Barbara Walters, NBC News

It was so totally, totally foreign. And I remember I had asked for hot water, because in those days I was boiling my contact lens, and every time I asked for hot water, they sent me tea.

It was also impossible to throw anything out. There was a particularly embarrassing incident involving a young aide to Nixon's press secretary, Ron Ziegler, named Diane Sawyer—later the evening news anchor at ABC.

Ed Fouhy, CBS News

We were on the bus. Just as it was ready to leave, a Chinese guy came running out of the hotel. He had pantyhose, and he was clearly agitated. He thought someone had left this behind. Well, it was Diane Sawyer who came forward on the bus to claim that. I guess she had just thrown them away. In those dark days in China, a poverty-stricken country, the notion that somebody would throw away a perfectly good pair of pantyhose didn't cross this guy's radar screen.

By this point, the reporters had been working around the clock for days. As the only correspondent for the *New York Times*, Max Frankel was struggling.

Max Frankel, *New York Times*

Most days there were three articles. There would be a news article, a news analysis, and then the notebook, and that took most of the night. I was living on aspirins. I discovered that aftershave lotion was very good for waking you up. I had this bottle of aftershave lotion that I would wipe on my face and wake up.

Dirck Halstead, United Press International

The poor minder had to be up as long as I was. About the third night of this, about five o'clock in the morning, I came out from the dark room and the minder was sprawled out on the floor and said, "Please Mr. Halstead, you must get some rest. You are going to die soon if you don't get some rest!"

NBC's Barbara Walters was having a particularly tough time, resented and shunned by many of her male colleagues.

Barbara Walters, NBC News

I knew Henry Kissinger socially, and there was one incident where he had asked me to buy some presents for his lady friends, and the press thought he was giving me secret information. But what he was doing was giving me a list.

Ed Fouhy, CBS News

Barbara Walters was always very tough competition, and frankly I remember being very concerned that she was going to get something that the rest of us were not. She was on pretty good terms with both the president and the first lady, and she probably had other sources as well. We kept a close eye on her.

Barbara Walters, NBC News

I sort of aggravated them. The fact that I was a woman, that I hadn't paid my dues in the Associated Press, the United Press, the way they did. The fact they thought I was getting special treatment. The most difficult part was at night when we weren't working. No one asked me to come and have dinner with them. Nobody said, "Do you want to have a beer?" I found it very important trip, but I was very lonely. When I got home, I realized that I had done a really good job. It was probably the most important experience I would ever have, though I didn't feel it at that time.

THE SHANGHAI COMMUNIQUÉ

In their private meetings, Nixon and Kissinger had reached agreement with the Chinese on a communiqué. The sticking point had been Taiwan, with which Washington still maintained formal diplomatic relations and a security treaty. The two sides found a formula to acknowledge Beijing's claim to the island while stressing the U.S. commitment to resolving the issue peacefully. But the text of the communiqué was not shared with Secretary of State William Rogers.

Stanley Karnow, *Washington Post*

I thought that there was difficulty in drafting the Shanghai Communiqué between the American delegation and the Chinese. What I didn't realize is that the problem was within the American delegation.

The issue was that the Chinese would not accept any reference to the U.S.-Taiwan defense treaty, so the draft communiqué made no mention of it.

Nicholas Platt, State Department

We got on the plane to Hangzhou, and Marshall Green [assistant secretary of state for East Asian affairs and the State Department's top Asia expert] and Secretary Rogers got their first look at the Shanghai Communiqué. They had not seen a draft. It had not been shared with them. It had already been approved by the Chinese Communist Party Central Committee. They looked at it analytically and said there were some mistakes here. There are some issues that really need to be raised. The security arrangements were left out. Kissinger was furious, Nixon was furious. But you know, if you don't show the pros what you're doing, there is a chance maybe you got something wrong.

Nixon knew he risked the anger of conservative supporters at home if it appeared he was abandoning U.S. commitments to Taiwan. And there was the danger of bad publicity if the story leaked. The result was that he was forced to insist on a return to the negotiating table.

Dwight Chapin, Nixon Appointments Secretary

There was significant concern and there was a lot of tension. There was tension with the president. There was tension with the staff. There was tension in terms of how it was going to be interpreted back home among conservatives. It was a very, very delicate several hours.

Several hours of difficult negotiations followed. The Chinese would not budge. Eventually, Kissinger and Zhou Enlai agreed to simply eliminate all references to U.S. security commitments in Asia.

Dan Rather, CBS News

Our information was not very good about what was happening with negotiations, but the dominant feeling in the press corps was they were having much more trouble than had been anticipated. Nobody thought they were shouting matches, but it was clear that they were running into trouble. Everybody had their eye on the Taiwan situation. They had a great deal of difficulty with it.

The Shanghai Communiqué was unveiled on February 27 in Shanghai, Nixon's last stop. The key passage read, "The U.S. side declared: The United States acknowledges that all Chinese on either side of the Taiwan Strait maintain there is but one China and that Taiwan is a part of China. The United States Government does not challenge that position. It reaffirms its interest in a peaceful settlement of the Taiwan question by the Chinese themselves." Conservative critics were still bitterly opposed. A headline in the *Detroit Free Press* on February 28 blared, "They Got Taiwan. We Got Eggrolls."[2] But that was a minority view.

Nicholas Platt, State Department

Immensely skillful because it finessed the whole issue. It allowed us to sidestep Taiwan and get on with the business of forming a relationship with the mainland.

Moreover, Nixon calculated—correctly—that for most Americans, the pomp, pageantry, and excitement conveyed by the television coverage were much more important than the details of the communiqué.

Tom Jarriel, ABC News

Nixon knew he was going to get this political windfall beyond his greatest wishes. Whether they had a communiqué at the end of the talks was important for the diplomats and foreign affairs reporters, but for the generalists like me, he had already hit the home run.

Winston Lord, Assistant to Henry Kissinger

This was one of the three or four biggest events in the last half of the last century. But clearly it was Nixon at the Great Wall. It's toasting each other. It's going to a ballet, the Forbidden City, and the visuals with the leaders that clearly were going to carry the day, and that's what did happen.

Nicholas Platt, State Department

I think that you could argue that in that one week the groundwork was laid for U.S.-China relations amongst the American public. It was a great awakening. They became aware of China, and that was a huge shift.

"THE HIDDEN KINGDOM"

Like their viewers, the reporters were captivated by what they saw in China.

Bernard Kalb, CBS News

It was China, the mystery, the dragon, the hidden kingdom, the secret country. And the television was a wow, because in China, wherever you put your camera you got exotic pictures. We didn't get a chance to go to the reeducation camps. We saw none of that. We were given staged affairs to cover.

Robert Keatley, *Wall Street Journal*

It was kind of a love affair with an earlier China that didn't really exist anymore. You know, the exotic China, Marco Polo, all of that stuff.

Nixon and his entourage said their farewells to Zhou Enlai at the Shanghai airport. There was also another banquet, this one laid on for the exhausted reporters.

Max Frankel, *New York Times*

I literally fell asleep on my plate. I conked over the table, and somebody had to revive me. It was pretty exhausting. I counted it up later. It was thirty-five thousand words in eight days.

Ed Fouhy waited for the food on the press plane.

Ed Fouhy, CBS News

The Pan Am press charter served us hamburgers and hot dogs on the way out of Shanghai, and a hot dog never tasted better.

From old China hands to the vast majority who'd never been there or covered the country, the reporters' heads were spinning as they tried to process what they'd seen.

Stanley Karnow, *Washington Post*

Nixon called it "the week that changed the world," and it was. You had to hand it to Nixon. Nixon was a smart guy. And I think people were ready for that. It was useful in playing China against the Soviet Union. I think it was useful in dramatizing that Communism was not a monolith. It was playing triangular diplomacy, get the Russians worried.

Barbara Walters, NBC News

This is what is important. It changed our views of China, but it also changed China's view of the U.S.

Bernard Kalb, CBS News

The impact of television on an American audience was extraordinary. China had suddenly come alive [for American audiences], and all the rest is just commentary.

Dirck Halstead, United Press International

The Nixon trip to China was without any doubt the most important presidential trip ever. With the exception of a president going to Mars, nobody is going to be able to do a trip like that again.

5

END OF AN ERA

American journalists got a tantalizing glimpse of China during the Nixon visit. But after his departure, the power struggle intensified between moderates like Zhou Enlai and radical ideologues led by Chairman Mao's wife Jiang Qing, who became known as the "Gang of Four." U.S. reporters were again stuck on the outside, forced to decipher China's complex politics from Hong Kong.

Steve Bell, an Iowa native who had covered the Vietnam War in the late 1960s, was ABC's Hong Kong correspondent from 1972 to 1974.

Steve Bell, ABC News

All you could do when you were a China watcher in Hong Kong was get these very broken-up TV broadcasts from Canton TV, throw in anything people were saying after they came out of China, and talk to the China experts. But it was like a Ouija board. You were always searching for a reality, and there were a lot of conflicting signals.

Bruce Dunning, who had also covered Vietnam, was then a correspondent for CBS operating from Tokyo.

Bruce Dunning, CBS News

We would send a cameraman with a special film camera with a special lens to go up to the border where you could bring in a signal from the Canton TV station. He would set up a portable TV set and tune it and film off the screen. The images were black and white, and terrible quality, but usually that was all the picture we had out of China.

But in the spring of 1973, the United States and China agreed to open liaison offices. It was a step short of full diplomatic relations, but both offices functioned virtually as embassies—staffed by diplomats and focusing on promoting better political and trade ties. It was a way to lay the basis for future cooperation while acknowledging continuing disagreements over Taiwan. Beijing agreed to this step on the assumption that Nixon, after his reelection in 1972, would soon move to break diplomatic relations with Taiwan. While China insisted that no U.S. news organization would be allowed to open a full-fledged bureau in Beijing until normalization, with the establishment of the liaison offices, the three American TV networks were invited in 1973 to send crews for extended visits.

Irv Drasnin, CBS News

This is the first time they have let American television journalists come to China except to cover Nixon's visit. They let each of the networks in to make one documentary.

CBS News producer Irv Drasnin, who had studied Chinese at Harvard, had been trying, unsuccessfully, to get into China for years. At the time of the Nixon visit, he had produced a controversial documentary called *Misunderstanding China*, narrated by veteran CBS News correspondent Charles Kuralt. It was an exploration of popular American attitudes, and stereotypes, about China—what Kuralt called a "chop suey of prejudices"—fed by movies, pulp magazines, and decades of sharply differing images, linked only by a lack of appreciation for the immensely complex reality of China.

Irv Drasnin, CBS News

I spent weeks and weeks in the darkroom watching all this material. It was a process of discovery. Who thought about the Charlie Chan films? Or about the

Fu Manchu films? We didn't really think about things in those terms. [Charlie Chan, the hero of six novels and numerous Hollywood movies from the 1920s to the 1940s, was a fictional detective who, while benevolent, was portrayed with stereotypical features of American images of Asians—elaborate politeness, his habit of dropping articles and the first-person pronoun, as in "May ask question please?"] My original title for Misunderstanding China *was* The Yellow Peril and Other Things We Think We Know About China. *Cooler heads prevailed, and it became* Misunderstanding China—*which worked perfectly because into each commercial break during the broadcast the announcer would say,* "Misunderstanding China *will continue after this message," which was certainly true. We did misunderstand it because we are basically ignorant of it. Your tendency is to believe the worst about a place we can't even visit.*

Now, though, in the wake of the Nixon visit, America attitudes, shaped by the media, were shifting again.

Steve Bell, ABC News

If you ever want to see the influence of the media, just look at America-China relations between '72 and '73. The Nixon trip was pure television, and it had enormous impact on Americans. In a way it went from [the Chinese] being mindless hordes coming over snow-capped mountains in Korea killing Americans, to almost a warm cuddly picture of Chinese civilians and the Chinese people in general. It was a huge shift.

Yet the gulf between Americans and Chinese remained enormous, as Drasnin and his team discovered while shooting their documentary in the city of Shanghai, in 1973.

Irv Drasnin, CBS News

We were curiosities in China. Here are these Americans. We would go out on the street and be surrounded. People would just press in on us. We literally couldn't move. Of course, the Chinese solution is—trying to help us—to clear the streets. So we set up a shot, and in Shanghai, one of the biggest, most crowded cities in the world, the streets would be devoid of humanity. I had to explain how this wouldn't really work. We are not here to see Shanghai as a stage set. Finally, the cameraman persuaded the Chinese to give us a canvas covered pickup truck. We put the camera in the back, and we could part the canvas wide enough to put the camera through and drive around Shanghai to get pictures of everyday ordinary life. That limited us somewhat, but it worked.

Drasnin and his crew found themselves constantly at odds with their Chinese minders.

Irv Drasnin, CBS News

It comes down to this. It's their country, but it's my film, in the sense that it has to live up to the expectations of an American audience. We have to do this our way. We can't do it their way. This came up, time and time again. We believe in spontaneity. The Chinese believe in planning. We want to discover reality, get as close to it as we can. The Chinese want control, and, if necessary, staging. There was this constant tug of war. The frustrations of trying to penetrate these cultural differences, these political differences, just kept mounting. We kept asking for official interviews, and the answer was, "It is not our custom to give interviews." I wanted to get the story, and I also wanted Chinese to speak for themselves. I wanted to be respectful of how they did things. Getting past the surface of things was very, very difficult. It was hot, it was humid, you were exhausted all the time, and before you know it, no matter how well you've trained and no matter how much you know or think you know, you are becoming frustrated, impatient, bad-tempered. It was pretty tense just trying to get a story.

After two months in China, and shooting seventy thousand feet of film, Drasnin produced a one-hour documentary. It included on-camera interviews he had convinced reluctant Shanghai officials to grant, as well as visits to the homes of local residents, where Drasnin was occasionally able to elicit comments beyond the standard party-line boilerplate, offering a somewhat more nuanced picture of Chinese society than most Americans had seen.

As the CBS team left, ABC News correspondents Ted Koppel and Steve Bell arrived for a ten-week stay to do their own documentary.

Ted Koppel, ABC News

What we proposed was to look at different categories of people—the military category, the student category, the worker-peasant category. During the Cultural Revolution, everybody was a worker-peasant, a soldier-peasant. It was always this hyphenated kind of person. So we spent some time at a university outside Shanghai. We spent some time in Wuhan. We spent some time with a military outfit outside Tianjin. It wasn't bad, but we were very carefully watched. They had preselected the people that we would be allowed to talk to.

The most shattering image was the relationship between the students and the professor. They let us go into an English class at the university. The professor was a woman in her late thirties, early forties. She was clearly terrified of her students. And they were quite openly delivering little political lectures to her. They had been selected not because of their academic ability but on the basis of ideological purity, and then sent to university.

In one revealing interview, Koppel asked the teacher, "Does it make it more difficult for you as a teacher to know that if you make mistakes, the students will severely criticize you?" She replied, "Sometimes I felt ashamed and would blush, and I felt I had lost my face at the very beginning. But gradually I found that the students criticized me only for the sake of helping me."[1]

Ted Koppel, ABC News

We came back about a month or six weeks later. They were all out participating in the cotton harvest. The teacher was there with this big sack over her shoulders, plucking the cotton. I asked her, "Don't you feel a little awkward doing this? You're an academic, you're an intellectual." [She replied,] "Oh, no, no, no. This is very useful. This helps me to identify with the student-worker, and the student-peasant, and the student-soldier. I'm so grateful to be here." She was scared out of her mind. And that comes across.

In 2005, Steve Bell went back to China and found three of the students he and Koppel had interviewed in 1973, as well as the teacher.

Steve Bell, ABC News

The goal was to find out exactly how straight they had been with us in 1973. I first pulled the teacher aside. She told me that she came from a prominent prerevolutionary family that had been accused of bourgeois ideas during the Cultural Revolution. She was extremely fearful. She said, "We would wake up every morning and I would look out the window to see if there were posters criticizing me. I was scared to death." The students had no knowledge of that. The irony is they were now adult educators in their own right. They had completely missed the tension of their own teacher when they had been in college. It was just extraordinary. I then did an interview with all of them together and she retold that story. They were completely flabbergasted. When the interview ended, the young woman who had been a student, who was sitting right next to her, put her hand on the teacher's knee and said, "We are so sorry. We didn't know." The former students said, "We were so naïve. We had no idea what was really going on." As someone sitting there watching this, I think it was genuine. They literally didn't know what their teacher had been going through. She had never shared it with them. When I saw the former student put her hand on the teacher's knee and say, "I'm sorry" at the end of the interview, the first thing I did was turn to make sure the cameraman was still rolling because that was THE moment, the most enlightening moment that I've ever had in China.

The ABC documentary, called *The People of People's China*, aired in December 1973. But the program infuriated the radicals in the Chinese leadership. Koppel and Bell's interpreter, Li Dan, paid the price.

Steve Bell, ABC News

The Gang of Four was still very much a reality in China when we were there, and the closing section of the documentary was on the political reality. There were pictures of Mao with this ominous music as we tried to put the Cultural Revolution into perspective. That was heavily criticized by the Gang of Four. That's what led our interpreter, Li Dan, to be sent to the reeducation camp.

It was more than a year before Li Dan was freed.

THE POWER STRUGGLE

At the same time, the power struggle within the leadership was intensifying. With Chairman Mao's health failing, his wife Jiang Qing and her radical allies targeted Premier Zhou Enlai and Deng Xiaoping for putting economic productivity over ideological purity. In 1973, Deng, a pragmatist who had been purged during the Cultural Revolution, had been rehabilitated and made vice premier, with responsibility for reviving the country's floundering economy.

Henry Bradsher was still the Hong Kong correspondent for the *Washington Star*.

Henry Bradsher, *Washington Star*

*I could see there was tension and disagreement over policies. I wrote a series
for my newspaper saying the logical understanding of this has to be that Mao
is not happy with the way Zhou Enlai is running the government. Although
you couldn't see it directly, and Mao didn't say much about it publicly himself,
there seemed to be tensions.*

With normalization talks between the United States and China deadlocked
over the issue of American support for Taiwan, Henry Kissinger in particular was upset with articles reporting discord within the Chinese leadership.

Henry Bradsher, *Washington Star*

*Kissinger on a couple of occasions tried to keep my editors from publishing my
articles. He called up the editors at the* Washington Star *and said, "You don't
want to publish this. This isn't right." Kissinger didn't want anybody looking
like his policy was maybe wrong or a misunderstanding in terms of what was
happening in China.*

In Beijing, too, there was anger at Bradsher's reporting.

Henry Bradsher, *Washington Star*

*After writing these articles, in the spring of '74 a couple of non-American jour-
nalists were visiting Beijing, [and at] the Foreign Ministry in Beijing were told
that "Everything was fine here, unity, peaceful. Hong Kong journalists are a
despicable bunch, and Bradsher is the most despicable of them all. He is seeing
things that are not there." Sent down the world. "Bradsher is the most despicable of them all, and that he will never visit China ever again."*

Other journalists, however, were coming to similar conclusions. Richard
Bernstein, who, like so many other China reporters of that period, had studied Chinese at Harvard, had recently become *Time* magazine's Hong Kong
correspondent.

Richard Bernstein, *Time*

*I think in retrospect, we, meaning the China-watcher community, the diplo-
mats and the journalists, more or less got it right. We understood there was a*

power struggle, which the Chinese propaganda machine vigorously denied, and denounced the Western reporters that talked about divisions in the leadership, when in fact there was an absolute vicious power struggle going on—the divisions between Zhou Enlai and Deng Xiaoping on the one side, and the Maoists on the other side.

HONG KONG LISTENING POST

With access to China still restricted, the reporters and diplomats continued to rely on the techniques of China watching developed over the preceding two decades. Joseph Lelyveld, who had been the *New York Times* correspondent in South Africa and India, moved to Hong Kong in 1973, expecting to be able soon to open the paper's bureau in Beijing.

Joseph Lelyveld, *New York Times*

I figured because Nixon had gone and after the election China would open, right? But it did not. So that's how I ended up in Hong Kong China watching.

Stuck in the British colony, Lelyveld relied heavily on sources at the U.S. consulate. Raymond Burghardt was then a young Foreign Service officer based in Hong Kong.

Raymond Burghardt, State Department

There was a lot of classic Sinology and tea leaf reading. We had a Chinese employee named Vincent Lo who was famous because he and some his colleagues in the China watching business could look at a photograph or a list of names of the Central Committee and tell you immediately, "Oh, this guy served in the Third Field Army with him, so of course he's there. The location of the two people in the photograph reflects the fact they were together in 1928 in Hunan," and they were right. This stuff tended to bear out in terms of who was up and down, and how people related to each other.

Joseph Lelyveld, *New York Times*

Vincent and I would meet twice a week for lunch in the Clipper Lounge of Mandarin Hotel. Vincent was a very brilliant analyst. It was quite enjoyable because I liked his mind. I liked the game. I had expected to hate China watching, and it turned out I did not. There were little mysteries you could get into. The real question was the status of Zhou Enlai. It was clear that he was coming under attack, and that was the story we followed.

THE *TORONTO GLOBE AND MAIL*

There was one important exception to the blanket ban on North American journalists in Beijing. Since the late 1950s, the Chinese government had allowed the *Toronto Globe and Mail* to station one correspondent. In 1971, the paper gave the assignment to twenty-six-year-old John Burns, who had been born and raised in Britain but moved to Canada as a teenager.

John Burns, *Toronto Globe And Mail*

When I was the Globe and Mail *correspondent, I was also de facto the* New York Times *correspondent, because, the* Times *having no correspondent, there was a syndication agreement. From the moment I landed in China, if there was something about mainland China in the* New York Times, *it was going to appear under my byline.*

Arriving in China in May 1971, Burns had a less-than-auspicious start to his assignment.

John Burns, *Toronto Globe And Mail*

I crossed the covered wooden bridge leading from Hong Kong's New Territories into the People's Republic of China. Midway across the bridge, I met a dispirited fellow who identified himself as a German correspondent based in China, then one of a tiny crew of Western reporters in Peking. The sad-eyed German fellow had some ominous advice. "Turn around!" he said. "Go back! It's crazy where you're going! Save yourself now!" With that, he lumbered off toward Hong Kong.[2]

Burns soon devised an approach to handle the propaganda he was fed during his few carefully controlled encounters with Chinese officials.

John Burns, *Toronto Globe And Mail*

I learned very early on a lesson about being a foreign correspondent. Every offi-cial untruth, and God knows there were many, tells a truth. An interview with a Chinese official, which others might judge to be very unrevealing, to me became very revealing. You could learn a great deal notwithstanding all of their efforts to conceal.

I decided I have two eyes, two ears, two feet, two hands, that I'm in a really remarkable position as a correspondent to work out what the truth is. The tale most often told about covering China during the Cultural Revolution was how restricted we were. But I discovered the bicycle. I could go out in the evenings and cycle, either down the hutongs, the old alleyways of the city, or out into the countryside to a village—and I felt I had all of China spread out before me.

People were extraordinarily friendly, something which has remained for me the principal characteristic of life and work in China. They were willing to talk to me about almost anything. There was another element, which was that peo-ple in distress—and the people of China were in distress in those years—are very keen to tell their story, much keener than is good for their health, actu-ally. I think that a responsible correspondent is always going to be careful in how far they lead these people into terrain that could be dangerous. But the fact of the matter was, for all the efforts the government and the Communist Party made to obscure the realities of the Cultural Revolution from reporters like me, it was all unavailing.

It was also accessible to someone who was a runner. I started running in the early morning or late at night, not to beat the surveillance, but because the traffic was, even then, so dangerous—mostly bicycle traffic—that it was much safer to run at night. I learned an extraordinary amount, because there would be others running at night, Chinese. Everywhere in the world there is a great fraternity amongst runners. You could team up with somebody and run for an hour, and learn a lot about the city, but also about the society, because there is this basic sense of trust.

I can remember running early one morning past the State Security Minis-try headquarters, and hearing volleys of gunfire. I was sure I was listening to executions. Six o'clock in the morning, just a volley, sometimes followed by a single pistol shot. And I would say to my interpreter, who was of course sup-plied to me by the Chinese state, "I think they are carrying out executions there." "No, no, no," he said, "just rifle practice." When Mao died, we began to learn the truth. Of course, it turned out that they were executing people. It was just one of many examples of how all efforts to conceal the truth about what was going on in China had been unavailing.

Being in China gave Burns the opportunity to decipher clues about the leadership struggle not available to his colleagues in Hong Kong.

John Burns, *Toronto Globe And Mail*

You could go to the airport for heads of state arrivals. The Politburo would turn out if it was an important head of state. But it was visibly divided. There were two groups. There was the gang of four, Jiang Qing and the other three. Then there was the other group, most of them much more venerated in the history of the Communist Party. Between them, there would be somebody commuting, physically, on the airport apron. And that person was Zhou Enlai. You didn't have to be a Sinologist of fifty years standing to understand what was going on there.

But Burns found his reporting often angered the Chinese government.

John Burns, *Toronto Globe And Mail*

I got used to the phone calls at three, four in the morning from a very chilly voice saying, "You will be in the Foreign Ministry." I would drive through utterly deserted streets and park my Volkswagen Beetle in the Foreign Ministry compound and go to [a] room empty save for a portrait of Mao. In would come the reproving officers of the state. The address, shouted at me by somebody in a Mao suit in a shrill voice, was almost always the same: "You have insulted the leadership of the People's Republic of China. You have abused the hospitality of the People of the People's Republic of China, and these are most grave matters. Do you have anything to say?"

I learned quickly that what was known in the nineteenth century as a kow-tow is what was required. It didn't matter if it was insincere. If you gave them some sort of apology, you'd be off the hook. I would say, "I have tried to report honestly about what is happening here in China. But I have limited access to Chinese life and to Chinese officials. I try and do my best to understand what is going on. But sometimes perhaps I get it wrong. If that's the case, I apologize." This would immediately be followed by a very relieved riposte saying, "We accept this." And immediately the atmosphere would then change.

"Would you like a cup of tea?" And this occurred on numerous occasions. And you learned from this what the really sensitive issues were.

TRAVELING WITH KISSINGER

In August 1974, Richard Nixon had been forced to resign because of the Watergate scandal. Gerald Ford became president. Ford retained Henry Kissinger as secretary of state and pledged to continue Nixon's policy of rapprochement with China. In November, Kissinger flew to Beijing. Rebuffed in all previous China visa requests, Joseph Lelyveld managed to switch places with the *New York Times* State Department correspondent when Kissinger's plane refueled in Tokyo.

Joseph Lelyveld, *New York Times*

When he got to Tokyo, we'd arranged for Bernie Gwertzman, who was the State Department correspondent, to get off the plane, and I got on the plane as the faux State Department correspondent of New York Times. *We'd outmaneuvered them. They could not do anything about it without stopping Kissinger, because it was Kissinger's plane. And the Americans have agreed to it. So I went in.*

This was Kissinger's seventh trip to China. But the prospects of a breakthrough seemed slim. Beijing was eager to normalize relations, but insisted that Washington must first sever diplomatic relations with Taiwan. This was a serious problem for President Ford because of the strong support that Taiwan enjoyed in the United States, especially from conservatives in the Republican Party. Moreover, Zhou Enlai, Kissinger's longtime interlocutor, was suffering from cancer. Kissinger began his trip with a courtesy call on Zhou at the hospital, but it was clear that other officials, especially Vice Premier Deng Xiaoping and Foreign Minister Qiao Guanhua, would now be taking the lead in negotiations.

Joseph Lelyveld, *New York Times*

Zhou Enlai was in the hospital, where he had a very showy bandage around his head. It looked like he had brain surgery or something. Deng Xiaoping appeared out of nowhere and took his place at the Great Hall of People on that first night. That was pretty dramatic.

Deng, to whom Zhou Enlai had given day-to-day responsibility for foreign affairs, was blunt and tough. He criticized Kissinger for pursuing detente with the Soviet Union and failing to deliver on promises to break ties with Taiwan. As Lelyveld noted in his report about the banquet concluding Kissinger's final day in Beijing, "The Chinese toast at the banquet, given by the new Foreign Minister, Chiao Kuan-hua [Qiao Guanhua], seemed unusually terse and understated. Unlike Mr. Kissinger's it made no mention of any progress."[3]

Joseph Lelyveld, *New York Times*

They took us to Suzhou at the end. We went to those great gardens. There was a young girl skipping rope and singing songs. Foreign minister Qiao Guanhua was down in the garden with Kissinger, and I went up to see the girls skipping rope and listening. Of course, within three minutes, Qiao Guanhua was leading Kissinger up in the hill and Kissinger said, "What a sweet little girl. What is she singing?" Whereupon the man who was standing there said: "She is singing we must not give up Taiwan."

The only concrete result of the Kissinger trip was an invitation for President Ford to visit the following year.

A NEW GENERATION

In the spring of 1975, Orville Schell, a young Harvard-trained Sinologist, was invited to participate in a trip to China with a group of twenty American left-wing activists. Schell, though, was writing for the *New Yorker*.

Orville Schell, *New Yorker*

It was a very interesting and confusing trip. I spoke some Chinese, and had spent a few years around Chinese, and thought I knew how to interact and avoid some of the cultural pitfalls. But no amount of understanding could bridge the gap between foreigners and Chinese at that point. That was 1975. Mao was still alive. The Cultural Revolution was far from over. All the rhetoric of friendship was not backed up by much actual friendly sentiment. When they learned I was writing for the New Yorker, *this created an immense amount of static. At one point, when we were working at Dazhai, a model agricultural brigade in Shanxi Province, they became exercised about the fact that I was a writer. They told me I will be spending a few days in my cave. We all lived in caves, in the Shanxi loess hills. It was my first intimation of what it was like in China to run afoul of "The Man" for crimes you're not quite sure what they are you committed. You're ostracized. And then few days later they decided to let me out.*

I remember we flew on the very first Boeing 707 the Chinese had bought to Beijing. Driving into the city, I remember an old two-lane road. It was pitch dark. You felt a little like going into North Korea in contemporary times.

Schell was part of a new generation of China reporters that emerged in the mid-1970s. Most were based in Hong Kong. Fox Butterfield, who had studied Chinese at Harvard, covered the Vietnam War, and been part of the *New York Times* team that had published the Pentagon Papers, took over the *Times* Hong Kong bureau. He replaced a frustrated Joseph Lelyveld, who had given up waiting for the Chinese authorities to allow the opening of a Beijing bureau and returned to New York.

Fox Butterfield, *New York Times*

I was almost scared the first few months when I was writing these stories—this is going to blow up in my face and I am going to be completely wrong, because we are speculating based on a few people's understanding of what is going on, and we are hypothesizing. We're not able to go there. We're not able to see it. We're not able to touch it. We are not able to do what reporters normally do. But story after story turned out to be basically right, I began to develop more confidence and be a little less quaking in my boots.

Others arrived, including Jay and Linda Mathews, a young couple who had also both studied at Harvard. She was working for the newly established Asian edition of the *Wall Street Journal*, he for the *Washington Post*, following in the footsteps of the Post's veteran Asia correspondent Stanley Karnow. To do so had been Mathews's goal since college.

Frank Ching, who'd been born in Hong Kong, had been editing China stories in New York for the *New York Times* since 1967. His official title was "area specialist," a position created by Seymour Topping, who by now had become the *Times* foreign editor. In 1974, however, Ching left the *Times* and returned to Hong Kong, where, like Linda Mathews, he joined the Asian *Wall Street Journal*.

In late 1975, I arrived to freelance for CBS News after having studied Chinese at Yale, gotten a journalism degree from Columbia, and made my 1973 visit with a left-wing American student group.

Meanwhile, Robert Elegant, who had been following China since the 1950s, still lived in Hong Kong. Like Henry Bradsher's, Elegant's reporting had long angered the Chinese authorities, and both men remained on Beijing's blacklist. As in the case of Joseph Lelyveld, it took help from Henry Kissinger for Elegant to finally get to China in October 1975, when Kissinger returned to Beijing to lay the groundwork for a planned December trip by President Ford.

Robert Elegant, *Los Angeles Times*

I didn't get into China until '75, but Kissinger took me, because Kissinger said that he'd asked Zhou to give a visa. "You get on the list the next time I go to China." The Chinese said he can't come. And Kissinger said, "You're not going to tell me who is coming in my press party. No Elegant, No Kissinger." So we went in.

Later, Elegant wrote of a conversation he had with a Chinese Foreign Ministry official during his visit.

Robert Elegant, *Los Angeles Times*

[He] told me I wrote too critically about the People's Republic, even if accurately. That accuracy was evidently his chief objection. He said: "Yes we have crime, but why write about it? Just change your approach and we'll give you visas." I replied: "If you give me a visa, I might change my approach after close observation. But then again I might not." He exploded: "Besides, your Chinese is too damned good!" These testimonials from the Communist regime were bittersweet. I was flattered but frustrated. Clearly it would be some time before I saw China again.[4]

MAO'S FAILING HEALTH AND THE FORD TRIP

Two days before leaving Beijing, Kissinger was granted an audience with Mao Zedong.

Robert Elegant, *Los Angeles Times*

The last night [of Kissinger's trip], we're having dinner. Henry had been to see Mao. And Henry came back. Previously we all knew that he would talk about Mao. He said, "I'm sorry I can't brief you on Mao." And somebody else said afterwards, "If you don't know what he said, I'll tell you what he said." He said, "Mao's in terrible condition and that's why he's not going to talk to us."

Indeed, in a secret memo to President Ford following the trip, Kissinger's assistant Winston Lord, who had been in the meeting, wrote that "Mao is very sick. He looked it, despite his mental agility. He was unable to walk us to the door as on previous occasions. He was just about unable to speak at all, making most of his points on paper or in obscure grunts. He is 'going to heaven' soon. And he described his various ailments."[5]

In early December, President Gerald Ford arrived in Beijing. Ron Nessen, a longtime NBC News correspondent, had been appointed Ford's press secretary in 1974.

Ron Nessen, Ford Press Secretary

It was a difficult time for China, because Mao Zedong, who was the revolutionary hero and founder of Communist China, was very old and sick. Other leaders were moving up to fill in the void.

The pomp and pageantry were the same. But in contrast to Nixon's visit in 1972, Ford's trip was characterized by bad feelings and diplomatic missteps, compounded by the president's own inexperience in foreign affairs.

Tom Brokaw was then NBC's White House correspondent.

Tom Brokaw, NBC News

Foreign policy, and especially China, is not exactly what you called Gerald Ford's strongest suit. He was kind of being led around by Henry Kissinger. After about twenty-four hours in China, we all began to complain because it was one photo op after another. We couldn't tell what was being done, and we didn't know what the president was doing. There was a lot of unhappiness about that. We were being paraded around. We didn't have a lot of information or good briefings. Everything was just routine.

Ron Nessen, Ford Press Secretary

There were very tight restrictions. The Chinese kept total control.

Ted Koppel, ABC News

I got arrested because we had at least enough freedom to go wandering off, but we clearly wandered off into an area they didn't want us to wander to. Some of the local citizens came around. Before I knew it, I was surrounded. Then a couple of cops came by, and they took us back to the station, and we had to wait there for a couple of hours while they made the requisite phone calls and then we were released.

Given Beijing's frustration over Washington's failure to break relations with Taiwan, and China's perception of U.S. weakness in the face of Soviet behavior, as well as Mao's failing health, the Americans were not sure if Ford would see the Chairman.

Ron Nessen, Ford Press Secretary

The Chinese would never tell you what the schedule for the next day was, who Ford was going to get to talk to, especially whether he was going to get to meet Mao Zedong.

Suddenly, on the president's second day in Beijing, the meeting materialized. But Mao could no longer control the symptoms of Parkinson's disease. His speech was slurred. His assistants struggled not only to translate but simply to make sense of his rambling.

Ron Nessen, Ford Press Secretary

Mao was very old and had been sick. What he sounded like to me was "blah blah blah blah blah." Then the translators would translate this into beautiful English sentences.

Later, reporters heard that the rambling, two-hour conversation had ended with a Ford faux pas.

Tom Brokaw, NBC News

Mao was obviously failing. At the end of the meeting, Kissinger said to Mao, "Mr. Chairman, this meeting demonstrated to me that your time is not up, and that you will live and lead your people for a long time." And Mao invoked God and said that "my God is calling me home." And Henry says, "No, no, it's not time for you to go." Ford leaned in and at that moment said, "Mr. Chairman, you do whatever you want to do, Henry is always trying to tell people what to do." He was talking about dying! Everyone was trying to get Ford [out] of there.

The official transcript confirms this account. "Secretary Kissinger said that he was glad that the Chairman obeyed his orders, i.e., not to go to heaven. President Ford said that he hoped to straighten the Secretary out so that the Chairman could go to heaven."[6]

The traveling press corps for the Ford trip had one unusual member— Garry Trudeau, creator of the wildly popular satirical comic strip *Doonesbury*. Trudeau, who started the strip while a student at Yale, had won the Pulitzer Prize earlier in the year.

Ron Nessen, Ford Press Secretary

We had all different kinds of people who would travel. I don't recall another cartoonist. We had columnists and so forth. Garry Trudeau—his cartoons are always focused on current events. It doesn't surprise me that he would have gone on this trip.

Mao's female interpreters, who had so impressed Ron Nessen, became the inspiration for Honey, one of the most famous characters in the Doonesbury strip. And Trudeau's satirical take on China produced some striking insights, such as Honey explaining how she translates for the ailing Chairman Mao.

From *Doonesbury*

Well, he changes his mind a lot, and although his word is absolute law, I have to account for that. For instance, last Monday, he told me to have the Great Wall torn down, since it's a symbol of ancient tyranny. On Tuesday, I reported that all 1,500 miles had been dismantled. Then on Thursday, he told me he had second thoughts and that he wanted the wall rebuilt at once. Friday night, I told him that I had personally directed the mobilization of 20 million workers, and that the entire wall had been restored to its former condition. Actually, I spent the whole week watching TV, but he thinks I'm a genius.[7]

Ford's visit ended with no breakthrough—the two sides unable to agree on how to move forward. J. Stapleton Roy, who had been born of missionary parents in China in the 1930s and would in the early 1990s serve as U.S. ambassador, was then deputy director of the State Department's China desk.

J. Stapleton Roy, State Department

The main essence of the trip was to convey to the Chinese that President Ford was not going to complete the normalization process until after his reelection, which he hoped would take place in 1976. This, of course, was a big disappointment to the Chinese, because they had been led to believe by President Nixon that he intended to complete the normalization process within his two terms. Of course, he wasn't able to finish his second term. So the Ford visit to China was a tense one. If Ford wasn't planning to move ahead on the normalization process, then in Deng Xiaoping's view, there wasn't much to talk about.

Tom Brokaw, NBC News

We knew the Chinese weren't happy. And that was manifested in many ways. At one point President Ford made a terrible decision. He took his crew out on the Air Force One *for a steak dinner because after two days he was tired of Chinese food. And there was this meeting scheduled and the Chinese made him sit through four courses of dinner later in the evening. It was not a very successful trip.*

THE YEAR OF THE DRAGON

A month later, on January 8, 1976, Zhou Enlai died of cancer at the age of seventy-eight. Widely beloved within China and seen by many at the time as a voice for restraint who sought to moderate Mao's most extreme policies, his passing triggered an outpouring of national grief, compounded by fear that the resurgent radicals around Jiang Qing would seize power. Although under attack, Deng Xiaoping was allowed to deliver the eulogy, in which he praised Zhou in terms that were clearly intended to offer oblique criticism of the radicals. Significantly, Chairman Mao did not attend.

For me, having just arrived in Hong Kong, Zhou Enlai's death was the first big story I had been involved in. By this time, it was possible to monitor Canton TV in the Cable and Wireless Building in downtown Hong Kong and was no longer necessary to go to the border and set up a small TV set the way journalists had done in previous years. Instead, every evening, my colleagues and I would gather on the sixth floor of the Cable and Wireless Building to watch extraordinary scenes of public mourning. Finally, the pictures broadcast by China Central Television (CCTV) were dramatic enough to be able to produce a television story.

But once the funeral was over, Mao appointed not Deng Xiaoping but Hua Guofeng, the colorless, politically reliable former party secretary of Hunan province, to succeed Zhou as premier. And the power struggled continued.

Soon after Zhou's death, the radicals escalated their campaign against Deng. Wall posters appeared on university campuses denouncing him by name for taking the "capitalist road." On the weekend of the Qing Ming festival in early April, when the Chinese honor their dead, several hundred thousand people gathered in Tiananmen Square. They laid wreaths to commemorate Zhou Enlai, but their action was also a clear—although indirect— protest against Jiang Qing and the radicals.

Richard Bernstein, *Time*

The Qing Ming demonstrations for me [were] probably the first time that I saw a crack on the surface. I remember thinking—this is amazing that people would even be able to demonstrate. We certainly sensed there were divisions within the leadership. But more important was that there was a large, maybe even a majority of the Chinese people who had not been brainwashed, who did have some sense of what they wanted and that they were being deprived of it by this leadership. Maybe even Mao wasn't quite as revered and as worshiped as we supposed.

The radicals correctly saw the popular expression of pent-up resentment at the harshness of the Cultural Revolution as a threat. On April 5, they sent in police to remove the wreaths and disperse the crowds. A brief but violent skirmish followed, resulting in vehicles and buildings being torched. Hundreds of people were detained.

For those of us based in Hong Kong, it was an enormously difficult event to cover. There was no footage, so at CBS and the other broadcast networks, it was basically a radio story. It took hours to get phone calls through to foreign embassies and the small number of other foreigners in Beijing who were willing to talk to reporters.

Fox Butterfield, *New York Times*

I was really heavily dependent on a lot of diplomats in Hong Kong, British, American, sort of the basic sources. And the handful of China watchers we had contact with.

Frank Ching recalled speaking about the protests with Father László Ladány, the Hungarian Jesuit priest whose weekly *China News Analysis* remained a crucial source of insights for those following the country from outside.

Frank Ching, *Wall Street Journal*

The demonstrators were taking flowers to Tiananmen Square to honor Zhou Enlai, and overnight, they disappeared. I remembered talking to Father Ladány about this. He said it has to be organized. It cannot be purely spontaneous. Where did they get these flowers from? In China, you need a supplier, you need permission to buy anything. It cannot be just individual people who are going out and getting flowers. It had to be factional fighting. That's what he was thinking.

That subtle inference was validated when, the day after the protests were crushed, Deng Xiaoping was removed from his government positions, with the radicals blaming him for the disorder. It was the second time Deng had been purged in less than a decade.

Later in the spring, Chairman Mao made what turned out to be his last public appearances, greeting Singapore's Prime Minister Lee Kwan Yew and then Pakistan's Zulfikar All Bhutto. As Fox Butterfield described him in the *New York Times*, Mao was "a weak old man, fragile as a piece of translucent porcelain."[8] It was clear the Chairman would not live much longer. The reporters intensified preparations to cover his death.

Fox Butterfield, *New York Times*

The New York Times *had a tradition of writing advance obituaries. For Mao, they were going to do four full pages, the longest obituary they had ever written. They said, "We'd like you to do it." I said, "Well, it will take me some time." They said, "Do it in your spare time." I said, "There is no way I can do that. I want to go back and read everything I could find and talk to everybody." They finally gave me a week. Four full pages of the* New York Times *with no ads is long. It is practically book-length. I worked day and night on that.*

On July 28, a magnitude-7.6 earthquake devastated the city of Tangshan 110 kilometers east of Beijing. Striking in the middle of the night, with almost everyone asleep in their beds, the quake, which leveled almost all of Tangshan's buildings, was especially costly in human life. An estimated quarter of a million people died. It was a massive natural disaster and a huge story but was virtually impossible for journalists to cover. None of the few foreign reporters in Beijing was allowed close to Tangshan. Very little information dribbled out. As was the case during the Tiananmen Square riot in April, all those of us in Hong Kong could do was monitor the official Chinese media and try to reach foreigners in Beijing on the phone. I had become friendly with a young Canadian woman studying there who was able to give me a description of conditions in the capital, because the quake had been felt in Beijing and people were sleeping on the streets. I recall going every day to the Hong Kong train station to meet trains coming from the mainland in a fruitless effort to find a foreign traveler who might have taken some home movies. In the end, despite the Tangshan quake being one of the great natural disasters of the twentieth century, only a handful of still photos emerged, and no film footage at all.

Richard Bernstein, *Time*

What I remember was Hua Guofeng rejecting offers of aid like blankets and things like that. I remember being very shocked. Because by then, we had a pretty clear sense that it was an immense tragedy and China was very, very poor, and that there were tens of thousands of people out on the streets. And they rejected aid on this sort of ideological grounds that China was self-sufficient.

THE DEATH OF CHAIRMAN MAO

Traditionally in China, natural disasters have heralded the end of a dynasty. On September 9, less than two months after the Tangshan quake, Mao Zedong died. It was a huge story.

Tom Brokaw, *NBC News*

In '76 I took over the Today Show. *The* Today Show *was a little different then than it is now in terms of what we put on the air. I got a call at 2 AM saying that Mao has died. We just blew out the show. We didn't know where this was going. We were trying to do the best with informed speculation that you could, but it was throwing snowballs at the moon.*

Bruce Dunning, *CBS News*

The announcement came from Beijing that he had died, and we started filing radio material. Everything had to be with file footage for TV, because nobody could get into China. It was like doing crossword puzzles in the dark.

By sheer coincidence, *Time*'s Jerrold Schecter happened to be in China, covering a visit by James Schlesinger, President Ford's former defense secretary.

Jerrold Schecter, *Time*

We were in Tibet. Late at night, we are told Chairman Mao has died and they're sending a plane to bring you back to Beijing. Former defense secretary Schlesinger is going to be the official American representative at the funeral. All the members of the party will go pay their respects with him. We got to Beijing. As we drove through the city, there were no cars, but people were in the streets wailing. It was a tremendous open expression of emotion, as if the head of the family had died. There was this feeling of being bereft and not knowing what would happen next.

Mao's body lay in state for a week as huge crowds filed past to pay their respects. On September 18, Premier Hua Guofeng, now nominally China's new leader, gave a memorial speech in front of a million people in Tiananmen Square.

Bruce Dunning, CBS News

CCTV put up a signal for hours and hours of material on the funeral. Anyone who wanted it could take it down. That's where we got the images. Everything else we had to do were telephone calls to Beijing if we could get somebody, the wire services, Xinhua, scraping whatever we could together.

But Schecter was there—the only American correspondent in the receiving line.

Jerrold Schecter, *Time*

At the funeral, we all met Madame Mao to pay our respects, and the other three members [of the Gang of Four, the term that came to be used to describe Jiang Qing and her three key allies, Wang Hongwen, Zhang Chunqiao, and Yao Wenyuan]. I looked at them. They seemed self-contented. This was the moment they were waiting for. They could hardly wait for the corpse to be buried. I went back and wrote a file to New York. The next morning, Schlesinger called me and asked me to come to his room. I got there, and he said, "The Chinese have complained bitterly about your copy, in which you said it looked like the Gang of Four was trying to seize power. I told them that I had no control over you, even though you were a guest here in China." He made it clear that it was an embarrassment for him, but it was the American way. You just go and write what you want. Of course, we discussed the fact that since the material had to be filed from the Central Telegraph Office, obviously someone had taken a copy of my file and sent it to the powers that be, and they responded very quickly with their annoyance.

To Schecter's dismay, however, *Time* didn't publish his analysis.

Jerrold Schecter, *Time*

Time *didn't mention anything about the Gang of Four in the story. Why, I never found out. They totally edited out the whole question of internal rivalry. I guess they thought it was unseemly to do that since such a historic figure had died.*

Time had missed a colossal scoop. But it did get some exclusive pictures from Liu Heung-shing, who had been born in Hong Kong to mainland parents but had grown up in the United States. Liu was then a freelance photographer in Hong Kong and managed to get to Guangzhou.

Liu Heung-shing, *Time*

Hong Kong people who come into China just need the reentry permit, which I have. I remember very distinctly that instead of seeing people's face in sadness, what I saw was unusual, extraordinary. I sensed people kind of relieved, even people who were wearing the black armband mourning Mao's death. All the body language was a sense of relief. I remember distinctly. I felt that it was the start of the transition.

THE FALL OF THE GANG OF FOUR

Indeed, behind the scenes, the power struggle was reaching a climax. Jiang Qing and the radicals sought to claim Mao's legacy as their own and, using their continued control of state media, schemed to seize total power. But more moderate figures in the leadership enlisted the support of both Hua Guofeng and key military leaders and, on October 6, effectively staged a coup. Jiang Qing and her three key allies were arrested.

Richard Bernstein, *Time*

We could never have known how fragile the Gang of Four's situation was, and that so quickly after Mao's death that they would be under arrest.

Fox Butterfield, *New York Times*

Clearly these people had been wildly unpopular, even though they had had almost absolute power. When Mao was gone, their big backstage supporter was gone. Their fall was precipitous.

The toppling of the Gang of Four triggered an outpouring of public celebration. Unable to get into China, American reporters relied on accounts and occasional home movies from travelers. At the same time, Jiang Qing and her followers were the targets of a venomous campaign of character assassination, most notably in a series of cartoon-like posters that gave the network news correspondents something visual for their TV reports.

As a radio reporter, I had never done a TV piece before. But Judith Lubman, an American businesswoman friend of mine whose company imported goods from China, and whose husband, Stanley, was a specialist on the Chinese legal system, had been invited to attend the semiannual Canton Trade Fair in mid-October. She returned to Hong Kong with a series of remarkable color photos she had taken of wall posters depicting Jiang Qing as a snake and denouncing the Gang of Four as "wolves with human faces" and "malignant tumors." She gave me copies, and, as the person who had procured the photos, despite my lowly status, CBS allowed me to put together a piece for the *CBS Evening News*. It was my first television story.

Meanwhile, the four were quickly airbrushed out of the official photos of Mao's funeral.

Frank Ching, *Wall Street Journal*

After the overthrow of the Gang of Four, they were cut out of all the tapes at that time, and photographs. And I remember looking and finding a sleeve still on the photograph. They had cut out the person, but they had left the sleeve. They became nonpersons.

By the end of 1976, China had settled into an uneasy calm.

1976 had been the Year of the Dragon. In Chinese mythology, a Dragon Year often heralded upheaval. But no one could have foreseen the multiple shocks that would rock China that year—from a literal earthquake to the deaths of Zhou and Mao, political purges, and a palace coup. As the year drew to an end, I was not alone in feeling exhausted and almost shell-shocked, wondering, along with the rest of my China-watching colleagues, what would come next.

6

OPENING UP

On December 15, 1978, following months of secret negotiations, President Jimmy Carter, the Democrat who had defeated Gerald Ford in the 1976 election, announced the establishment of diplomatic relations between the United States and the People's Republic of China. As part of the deal, Washington agreed to withdraw diplomatic recognition from the Republic of China, the Chinese Nationalist government on Taiwan. In early January 1979, a dozen American reporters based in Hong Kong were granted an unprecedented interview in Beijing with Deng Xiaoping, who was about to embark on a visit to the United States to consolidate the historic diplomatic breakthrough.

Jay Mathews of the *Washington Post* flew up from Hong Kong to cover the event. Like others, he was bowled over by Deng.

Jay Mathews, *Washington Post*

The interview with Deng, he first shook hands with all of us. That was the lead of my piece. I shook hands with Deng Xiaoping. An historic figure was coming in and leading what appeared to be a surge of Westernization in China.

ABC's Hong Kong correspondent was Jim Laurie. He had grown up in Massachusetts, spent 1970 to 1975 covering the wars in Vietnam and Cambodia, and was one of the only American journalists to remain in Saigon after the Communist victory in 1975.

Jim Laurie, *ABC News*

We had about an hour and a half of questions. Much of the discussion was about reform, or the Soviet Union. Nothing was said about human rights. The most amusing part was that Deng Xiaoping had a tendency to spit a lot. He smoked constantly—his Panda cigarettes. And placed to his right was a gigantic spittoon. You would stand up to ask your question, and while you were asking—he was waiting for the translation, of course—he would be getting together this giant wad of spit, which just before the translator began to translate, he would put into the spittoon next to him. One China scholar, when I told him the story, said, "That's not unusual. He used to do that to keep people off-balance. They would get confused when he was doing that." Later the Foreign Ministry spokesperson who had arranged for the interview came to the three American networks and said, "We only have one request. In the interest of friendship and cooperation, would you agree not to use any of the tape of Deng Xiaoping spitting, and not to use the sound?" And in the interest of friendship and cooperation, that first act of self-censorship was carried out.

DENG XIAOPING VISITS THE UNITED STATES

Deng's nine-day U.S. trip in late January and early February was a watershed moment, solidifying in the eyes of the American public a new picture of China, not as an enemy but as a friend and as an ally against the Soviet Union.

John Roderick, Associated Press

Deng Xiaoping was a chirpy little type, brilliant as you could be, always making jokes. He was unlike most Chinese Communists. Most Communists, they have one failing, and that is they lack a sense of humor. They're too grim. But he didn't. He saw all the nuances. As a person, he was very attractive in that sense. So this little man arrives in America and the reaction of the American public and American newspapers was extraordinary. I went to Washington and joined all the other correspondents, and he then set out on an extraordinary odyssey in America.[1]

Jim Laurie, ABC News

It was almost like an American presidential trip, in the sense that the networks and the other news agencies got together and rented a plane, and we flew behind

Deng, as reporters do with the White House, and stopping in every stop. The stops were New York, Washington, Atlanta, Houston, and Seattle.

Longtime Chinese Foreign Ministry official Yao Wei was handling Deng's U.S. press arrangements.

Yao Wei, Chinese Foreign Ministry

Deng was a very deep-thinking person. He well knew of the past years of animosity. He wanted to change it. I was with the advance team, three people, one from protocol, one from security. One of the things, from my point of view, was to have press conferences that would not hurt his image. Of course, CBS, NBC wanted to have their own interviews. I vetoed that. Deng at that time was seventy-something. There would be no end, every network one after the other. If you want to do it, do it pool. Of course, they all agreed.

Jim Laurie, ABC News

The single most interesting stop was the Houston stop. Deng went to the Johnson Space Center. We did stories there of China's aspirations, even then, to become a power in space. Deng, very curious as he was, wanting to know how the astronauts had gone to the moon in the space capsule. "And how," he asked, which was very typical of him, "did they go to the toilet?" That was one of his key questions.

If there was a single moment where Deng captured the imagination of the American public, it came when he donned a cowboy hat and rode in a stagecoach at a rodeo in Houston.

Jim Laurie, ABC News

Getting into that stagecoach and riding around the arena was amazing—a single moment where the Chinese delegation seemed to me to be amazingly loose. They were sitting around, drinking beer, having a grand time, as you would at a rodeo in Texas.

As Laurie noted admiringly in his report for ABC News, "Deng Xiaoping not only went west, but went western."

The symbolism resonated in China as well.

Yao Wei, Chinese Foreign Ministry

That stood out as something very American—a cowboy hat. It was quite spontaneous. There was no plan on the Chinese side of "Mr. Deng, put on a cowboy hat." He did it in a very charming way—unlike a year or so before, when one of our diplomats in Washington, DC, had a picture taken with a cowboy hat and a cowboy shirt and was criticized in China—a diplomat doing that, it's not something he should do, especially a Chinese diplomat. Deng didn't mind.

John Roderick, Associated Press

It was a great, great tour. It is hard to remember today when the relations are not so close, what euphoria there was in 1979 about Deng's visit. It was a milestone in our relationship, and, at a period where we, where we really felt good about each other, much more so than any other time.[2]

Jim Laurie, ABC News

The coverage was amazingly positive. Deng Xiaoping was on cover of Time *magazine. Everywhere on television. This was the great reformer, the cuddly Communist. He was seen almost as a Communist hero in America. All of it was emphasizing reform. Here was the guy for whom it didn't matter if the cat was black or white as long as it caught the mouse.*

OPENING BUREAUS

With the establishment of diplomatic relations, the Chinese government agreed to allow American news organizations to open bureaus in Beijing, and the Carter administration welcomed Chinese journalists to be based in Washington. In addition to a press conference, before leaving Washington, Deng met with the bureau chiefs of the networks and papers planning to send correspondents. The *Washington Post* had appointed Jay Mathews, while the *Los Angeles Times* decided to send his wife, Linda.

Linda Mathews, *Los Angeles Times*

We didn't know whether we would be admitted together. That, we owe to Deng Xiaoping and Jack Nelson of the LA Times *[the Los Angeles Times*

Washington bureau chief]. There was a small meeting Deng held with Washington bureau chiefs. Jack raised his hand and said, "Sir, you may not know this, but the LA Times *correspondent is married to the* Washington Post *correspondent, and we were concerned whether they will get their visas simultaneously." Deng huddled briefly with one of his aides and said, "Of course they will. It would a violation of their human rights if we did not allow that." I was forever grateful to Jack Nelson for raising his hand, and to Deng Xiaoping.*

Time sent its Hong Kong correspondent, Richard Bernstein.

Richard Bernstein, *Time*

There was this tremendous hopefulness among academics, students of China, ordinary people who were charmed by the Chinese culture and civilization, who found something loveable in China they would never have found in the Soviet Union. And also maybe this thrill that comes from a breakthrough with a people that you have had no contact with for such a long time. There was this tremendous wistfulness in the United States for China to be good, to be making progress, for the propaganda image to have some validity.

The *New York Times* sent Fox Butterfield.

Fox Butterfield, *New York Times*

I always considered myself really fortunate, not only because I got to get into China and open the New York Times *bureau there and be with the first wave of American correspondents to open news organizations in Beijing since 1949, but also to have arrived at precisely the moment when China was, for the first time since '49 opening itself up a bit.*

Indeed, at a historic plenum of the Communist Party's Central Committee in late December 1978, Deng Xiaoping had laid out a pragmatic vision of reform. Economic development, symbolized by the call to achieve the "four modernizations"—agriculture, industry, science and technology, and defense—replaced ideological correctness as the Party's top priority. Rejecting the ideological straitjacket of the Mao years, virtually all the late Chairman's purged opponents were reinstated, and Deng called on Party members to "emancipate their minds and seek truth from facts." In place of austerity and perpetual class struggle, the focus shifted to the expanded use of market mechanisms, and sharply increased international economic contact. The plenum was a turning point in the emergence of a new political climate based on "reform and opening," *gaige* and *kaifang*, which, in the following decades, would profoundly transform the Chinese landscape. Establishing ties with the United States was a key part of Deng's strategy, both to create a better international environment, and to make use of American investment, technology, and expertise to spur development.

The newly arrived reporters, and their editors in the United States, were entranced by the prospect of a changing China. Melinda Liu, a Chinese American from Ohio, opened the *Newsweek* bureau.

Melinda Liu, *Newsweek*

The early eighties theme of China was Deng Xiaoping on a roll, isn't it great, China opening up, Sino-U.S. love affair—that sort of a story. The Chinese were the good guys because the Russians were the bad guys. Deng Xiaoping was the cuddly Communist. We did a lot of stories like that.

For Liu, whose parents had moved to the United States before the revolution in 1949, the desire to cover China was deeply personal.

Melinda Liu, *Newsweek*

I was born in the States, but my parents were born in China. Not only that, but my older brother was born in China and didn't come with my parents to the States. I'd been fascinated with China. I'd always wanted to learn the language and know something about the country. For a long time, it wasn't possible, but then came the opening in the late '70s, and so I came. I knew that my parents were very wary of the Communist regime. For me, a lot of the motivation was personal. What is this animal of China that I have some of its genes in me that I don't know too much about? I want to know about it. I had a personal sort of mission there.

Shortly after Deng's U.S. visit, Liu traveled to Beijing and met her older brother for the first time.

Melinda Liu, *Newsweek*

My brother was born ten years before I was. My parents had just been married and wanted to go to the States and study. When World War II war ended, they quickly took advantage of that and went to Minneapolis, leaving my brother behind with my mother's parents, thinking they would study and then go back. What they didn't realize is that the Second World War was followed almost immediately by the civil war in China and then the Communist takeover. And they were never able to go back. So he was raised by my maternal grandparents in Suzhou.

It was strange meeting him. The physical resemblance was there, but we were strangers. We sort of knew each other but we didn't. He was a very warm, very quiet guy. Never went to college because he had overseas connections. Was working in a factory. But he himself at that time was also being treated better than before because his parents were overseas. I bought TV sets, and this and that. He was able to build a little addition to his house in Suzhou. So things were looking up.

The small American press corps quickly discovered that the experience of living in Beijing was very different from visiting China on a short tour where, for all the limitations, they were usually treated as "honored guests." John Roderick returned to reopen the Associated Press China bureau.

John Roderick, Associated Press

The problems that were involved in setting up a bureau were quite extraordinary. The Communists didn't know how to cope with this. They had never had us in there. But it was a big event, so they did what they could to cooperate.[3]

Foreign residents were required to live in foreigners-only compounds. Since there weren't enough apartments available, the Chinese put the reporters in a grimy, Soviet-style building.

Richard Bernstein, *Time*

Most of us lived in the Qianmen, an old Soviet-era hotel. Many of us knew each other from before. We had been in graduate school together—Jay Mathews, Linda Mathews, Fox Butterfield, and I had all been at Harvard. Then we were in Hong Kong at the same time and then we were in Beijing. I think we were a kind of community that had the same experience and a lot of the same attitudes about that experience—the attempts to control us, the attempt to control others. But of course, we were also competitive, as journalists are. I had perfectly cordial relations with Melinda Liu, the Newsweek *correspondent, but she was my competition. I didn't want her to get stories that were better than mine and vice versa.*

Melinda Liu, *Newsweek*

There was competition between us, but there was also a sense of camaraderie.

Bruce Dunning moved from Tokyo to open the CBS News bureau.

Bruce Dunning, CBS News

We lived in the Qianmen commune. We'd meet at breakfast, lunch, and dinner. We would be watching who was coming and going. It was very much a communal type of living, and we would trade stories over lunch or dinner. It was incestuous—a very tightly knit group.

Melinda Liu, *Newsweek*

We definitely felt like pioneers, particularly those that came with kids and family, to be living in this Chinese hotel. It was the kind of hotel where the room boys would literally come into your room to start cleaning, whether your door was locked, whether you were taking a bath, whether you were changing your clothes. They would just come in. My room was infested with bats.

Jim Laurie, ABC News

Access by Chinese to the hotel was virtually impossible. Every Chinese entering any hotel where foreigners lived had to be checked and inspected. Generally, Chinese were kept out of hotels were foreigners lived except those who worked in the hotels.

Melinda Liu, *Newsweek*

I had never run a bureau before, much less opened a bureau. I discovered you had to bring in everything—paperclips, typewriters, typewriter paper, typewriter ribbons. All the normal little things—pens that worked and all that stuff—had to be brought in from Hong Kong, because what was available locally didn't work very well. Staplers. People were still using sewing pins to hold paper together. It was that kind of thing. What is mind-boggling to me today, when you're surrounded by computers and filing instantaneously, is how long the physical act of writing a story took. Not the reporting, because we all know what reporting is like. But I would type it out on an electric typewriter in my hotel room. I would get on my bicycle, because in the early days we hadn't even had time to import cars, and ride to something called the "telegraph building," the dianbao dalou. *There would be this huge, lugubrious hall, very dark. And there'd be this clerk. Sometimes the clerk would do the typing for me on a telex. But most of the time I had to then retype the whole thing on a telex machine, that spewed out this long tape that then had to be run back through the machine during the actual transmission. The whole thing just took hours. And sometimes the clerk wasn't there. Sometimes somebody was in line, so you had to wait for the telex machine. It was literally something out of the Stone Age.*

John Roderick, Associated Press

At the beginning, we had to take our copy down to the telegraph office and send out photos the same way. The bureaucracy in Peking didn't allow us to set up our machines in my office. Finally, we did that. But there were times even then, it was so difficult and so complicated—you had to punch in so many curious numbers and things like that. Sometimes you get a story at nine o'clock at night, it was five o'clock in the morning by the time it got to Tokyo and New York. It was that sort of thing.[4]

Jay and Linda Mathews faced a special problem. They were married—and competitors. Neither of their papers was happy.

Jay Mathews, *Washington Post*

The Washington Post *had a tradition of correspondents signing a letter of understanding before they went overseas. There was a paragraph in my letter which said—don't you dare ever be beaten by your wife on any kind of story, and if you can beat her as often as possible, that's fine. And I signed that very happily. But we've learned, as correspondents go overseas, that they do team up.*

Linda Mathews, *Los Angeles Times*

There was a night when we were at a party where the Boeing representative, another American, got a little drunk and started complaining about the disappearance of one of the Boeing 707s that the Chinese had purchased. We took him aside and said, "Tell us more. That's very fascinating. Where do you think the plane is? Did it crash?" He said, "No, it's in a hanger in Shanghai. They've dismantled it and are trying to design their own aircraft. We at Boeing, call it the 708, because it's so much like the 707." I remember going back to the hotel room and saying to Jay, "We have to write it." Obviously, we have to get comment from Boeing. We just split up the reporting tasks and shared notes. It was the most blatant collaboration of our time there. Then we delivered our separate stories to our desks, and said this has to run tomorrow, because, we explained, this other guy has the story.

The Mathews' partnership was a source of constant frustration for the *New York Times*'s Fox Butterfield, whose hotel room/office was next to theirs.

Fox Butterfield, *New York Times*

In those days we used typewriters, and they made a lot of noise. If she was writing a story, I could hear her typing. If I was writing a story, she could hear me typing. If she got up to take her story to file it at the post office, which is how we sent things, by cable, I knew she was going. And she knew if I was going to file a story. And she and her husband, Jay Mathews of the Washington Post, *often went out together to do stories. I sometimes felt outgunned. It was like they were double-teaming us.*

Linda Mathews, *Los Angeles Times*

That's the only time I remember Fox Butterfield really got angry with us. He sat in the chair, and he said, "You guys are double-teaming me, and I don't like it."

FIGHTING THE SYSTEM

As they covered the dismantling of Mao's radical policies, the reporters found themselves in daily struggles with the Chinese system of control. The Chinese were particularly leery of the network correspondents.

Jim Laurie, ABC News

Chinese officialdom had a tremendous aversion to TV. They feared the medium of TV more than anything else. They felt that Western TV would inevitably portray China as a backward nation. Whatever images would be recorded and played for the world would, in the Chinese view, be negative images as far as China was concerned.

Bruce Dunning, CBS News

They knew how to handle print people, but TV kind of scared them, so they were very cautious. At first, we only got one visa per network, so I went in but had no camera crew and no producer. I had to do my own shooting.

Indeed, Sandy Gilmour, who had been based in Houston for NBC, was offered the Beijing job when a Hong Kong–based correspondent turned the post down because of its many difficulties.

Sandy Gilmour, NBC News

It was quite a shock when I got the call from Bill Small, president of NBC News. He needed a correspondent to go to Beijing. The correspondent who'd been in Hong Kong for many years had refused the assignment. He was very comfortable in Hong Kong and didn't want to live in Beijing.

It was not until 1983 that the U.S. networks were allowed to station cameramen in Beijing. This was just one challenge as the journalists struggled to penetrate the wall the Communist authorities were determined to maintain between the reporters and their own people.

Richard Bernstein, *Time*

I think that the informal restrictions, the ones that weren't written in Chinese law, were the most serious. That is, it was forbidden for ordinary Chinese to talk to you. There's no law, but people were afraid. Everybody there at the time managed to find a few people who were brave enough to talk, and I had my few people like others. That was very, very important. But it was very, very hard to just have friends, and certainly even harder to develop sources. It was just too tightly controlled.

Bruce Dunning, CBS News

You couldn't invite a Chinese friend to your office or hotel or apartment, and it was very difficult to get in touch with people. It was almost impossible to have a real friendship. I remember I was in a park one time with a Chinese friend. We were talking, and there were people looking at us, and a couple came up and said, "what are you doing?" There was great suspicion of a foreigner meeting a Chinese person.

There was never any censorship per se. You didn't have to submit scripts or stories to the authorities, but they made the gathering of news and stories so difficult. And the transmission, we had to order satellites in advance. Before we could move the material on the satellite, they would ask us to play the piece, ostensibly for engineering purposes, but it was obvious they wanted to see what was going out. If there was something they didn't want to go out, there would be "technical difficulties."

Fox Butterfield, *New York Times*

For me, there was the daily challenge of trying to penetrate the official, happy, smiley face of China, and trying to figure out how Chinese were really living. When American correspondents first went there, very few people had been able to penetrate beyond that because China was closed to itself, and Chinese had not been able to talk to each other. So there was very little knowledge of the basic vocabulary of everyday Chinese living.

Yao Wei, Chinese Foreign Ministry

It was because of the past so many years of animosity. I don't think you can blame them [uptight Chinese officials]. They were afraid to make mistakes.

Frank Ching opened the *Wall Street Journal* bureau.

Frank Ching, *Wall Street Journal*

The first thing was to go to the Chinese Foreign Ministry. I saw Yao Wei. He said you can talk to anyone you like to. They don't need permission to talk to you. I was so impressed. But then he didn't tell anyone else. So every time I talked to a Chinese, he would say I don't have permission to talk to you. And

I would say you don't need permission. Of course, nobody would believe it. I got to a point where I would get the press department's phone number, and I would call this number and would say, "Tell this man he doesn't need permission to talk to me!"

Richard Bernstein, *Time*

While I was there, a Chinese American friend came to visit. She introduced me to a relative who was a university student—a bright young man interested in having some sort of a relationship with me. For a lot of Chinese, it was a conflict. They were excited by the opportunity to have contact with foreigners after all these years shut off from the outside world, but they were afraid.

His name was Little Gu, "Xiao Gu." Maybe I met him five or six times during my whole time in China. I would meet him outside the Friendship Store or the International Club. He would get into my car, we'd drive someplace, maybe walk in the park, just talk, or walk in the department store. He never came to my apartment because he had to register with the security people.

Years go by. I came back to the U.S. The phone rings and it's a Mr. Yuan on the phone from Los Angeles. I don't know a Mr. Yuan from Los Angeles. He says, "You know, Xiao Gu." I said, "Oh my God, Xiao Gu." He said he'd come to America, he's in business in LA, he's doing pretty well, he's making an investment in New York, and he's going to be in New York for a few days, and could he take me to lunch?

I said, "Wow! Xiao Gu is going to take me to lunch. This is a reversal of fortunes." We had lunch. He told me that two or three days after I left China, he was arrested and detained for three days and three nights. At the end, he was told to go home to his parents' house. When he arrived, there were three officials from the public security bureau. They told him they wanted him to spy on my successor. They knew that he knew me. He said, well, yes, he met me through his relative once or so, but didn't really have a relationship with me. They played for him a recording of all the times he had called me up and identified himself as Xiao Gu. They had as well a series of photographs showing him getting into my car, walking through the park, walking in the department store. They had kept tabs on our entire innocent relationship, every detail of it, and they had it all recorded.

Of course, I knew that they watched foreign journalists. But I was really surprised to learn the extent of it—this totally innocent relationship. He didn't know any secrets to tell me. There was nothing that he could have told me that would have been forbidden or would've compromised Chinese national security or anything, yet they were watching that closely.

The frustrated reporters did everything they could to break through the barriers.

Fox Butterfield, *New York Times*

I was always trying to think how I could meet some Chinese. I would set out to find places. I would go to parks. I would go into department stores and try to strike up a conversation with people. I had heard that one way to try to talk to a Chinese was to take a train ride. I went to Shanghai. From Shanghai to Beijing was twenty hours by train. I decided I would take the train and sit with a Chinese and get a story. I bought my ticket at the China Travel Service. They hadn't asked me anything about myself. But when I got on the train, a woman conductor said, "Oh, you must be the American correspondent." Clearly, they had been keeping track of me. And she announced to all the passengers in the car, "We have an American on board. He is a foreign correspondent, and he speaks Chinese." Basically warning all the passengers not to talk to me.

Newsweek's Melinda Liu, the *Wall Street Journal*'s Frank Ching, and Liu Heung-shing, now working as a photographer for the AP and *Time*, discovered that as ethnic Chinese, with the right clothing, they could pass for locals.

Melinda Liu, *Newsweek*

I look Chinese. For me, it was much simpler, but I still had to put on a big grey coat with the furry collar and a big hat. Your shoes always gave you away as a foreigner, so you had to wear Chinese shoes, and slip out so that people thought you were a local. Because otherwise, people would follow you, find out who you talked to, find out what you said. Even something small like sneaking out to talk to petitioners, protesters who'd come to the capital to air their grievances. One of my great achievements during that period was being able one evening to slip out, go to a place where these petitioners were living in a ditch with a kind of a tarp over them. I talked to them about wrongs that had not been righted yet going back to the Cultural Revolution. When I came back to the Qianmen Hotel, the guards stopped me and wouldn't let me come in because they thought I was a local. Then I revealed myself. The look of consternation was, "Oh my God! I didn't recognize you," and also, "What have you been doing out there that we didn't know about?"

Frank Ching, *Wall Street Journal*

I had gotten to know Cao Yu, a well-known playwright. I thought, "OK, I'll interview him, since I know him." I asked, "Can I interview you?" He said, "Of course, but you need to get permission." I called the Information Department, and said, "I want to interview Cao Yu. He's already agreed. It's just a formality. He needs your approval." The man said, "OK, we'll see." A couple of days later they called back, and said, "Sorry, Cao Yu is too busy to see you." I said, "That's not possible. He's already agreed to see me. You just talk to him." After he called me back the second time and said, "No, he doesn't have time to see you." I said, "I'm having lunch with him tomorrow. How can you say that he doesn't have time to see me?" So the man said, "Well, if you're having lunch with him tomorrow, then you can interview him."

Liu Heung-shing, *Time*, Associated Press

I was able to call on the writers, artists, go and visit their home, eat with them, photograph them. They would tell me what happened to them, to their lives and so on. I think that period constitutes one of the best experiences for me as a foreign correspondent.

GETTING OUT OF BEIJING

Many of the most interesting developments were taking place outside of Beijing. But the correspondents found that leaving the capital was not easy.

Fox Butterfield, *New York Times*

If you wanted to go to Shanghai, Canton, any cities, you had to get permission, to involve the Information Department of the Foreign Ministry, and often get clearance from the Public Security Bureau if you wanted to go to an area normally closed to foreigners, which was an awful lot of China. In those days, there were just a few cities that were open.

I had seen pictures in some glossy Chinese magazines they circulated abroad of one of China's ski resorts in the Northeast. I thought it would be fun to go there. I put in a request to the Information Department. Several weeks passed, and they came back and said, "We're very sorry to tell you, there is no ski resort in China." I reapplied enclosing copies of the magazine with pictures, saying, "I think there is, and here's the evidence that's printed in your own magazine." After a few more weeks, they came back and said, "Yes, you are right, but we are very sorry to tell you it's in an area closed to foreigners." So I thought, "They're not going to let me go."

Soon after, an American businessman friend of mine and his wife who were staying in the Peking Hotel came through the lobby with skis on their shoulders. I asked them, "Where have you been?" They said, "We've just been to the ski resort," the same one I wanted to go to. They said it was wonderful. I was pretty upset. I reapplied again to the Information Department and described how this American couple had just been. After several more weeks, they said, "Well, yes, you're right, Mr. Butterfield. There is skiing in China, there is this resort, and yes, it has been open to foreigners. But we're very sorry to tell you that now there is no snow." So that ended that. They had many ways of frustrating you.

Melinda Liu, *Newsweek*

In those days you need a travel permit to travel outside of Beijing. So the government would organize journalists to go and cover stories.

Sandy Gilmour, NBC News

Whenever a group trip would come up, we jumped at those opportunities, because you could go out and see a slice of Chinese life which otherwise you would not be able to see.

Jim Laurie, ABC News

In these early days, the Chinese used to love these organized trips. My favorite organized trip story was to the Daqing oilfield for Nightline. *It was freezing cold. Everywhere we went we would pick up a minder. First, we had a minder coming with us from Beijing. We went to Harbin and picked up a minder from Harbin. We went to the next town near Daqing and picked up another two minders. And by the time we got to the oilfields, we had eight people with us.*

Within the Chinese bureaucracy, there were sharp debates over how much access the reporters should be given. In the Foreign Ministry's Information Department, Yao Wei argued for an easing of restrictions.

Yao Wei, Chinese Foreign Ministry

We always wanted the opening of more cities. A lot of cities were not accessible to foreigners. The Information Department was trying our best to do that, "What do you have to fear with people coming in?" In many cases, it was not a fear of people prying into state secrets. More of that was based on, they didn't want to see the poor conditions than anything else.

Liu Heung-shing, *Time*, Associated Press

People would get very upset because they said I photographed backward scenes of China.

The press tours had certain rituals, highlighted by the "brief introduction" from local officials, which often lasted for hours.

Sandy Gilmour, NBC

They were filled with propaganda, briefings that would last to two or three hours at a time. But there were also opportunities to get pictures, to get photographs, and truly, to get some useful information that could be strung together for a story later.

Yao Wei, Chinese Foreign Ministry

You go anywhere, the head of the commune, the head of the factory, would welcome you with a pretty long speech, starting with all of the slogans—under the guidance of the Communist Party of China, under the guidance of the thoughts of Mao Zedong, under and under.

This was a source of particular frustration for the TV reporters.

Jim Laurie, ABC News

They would insist on sitting around and having tea. Cameramen would be driven nuts if you had a cameraman. I was being driven nuts. I wasn't a very good cameraman so I needed as much time as I could have to shoot. And you'd be sitting around having tea. You wanted to get out. You had limited daylight in the wintertime and [were] trying to figure out a way of stopping this endless conversation over tea and getting out and shooting something. That was one of the more frustrating issues in terms of being a television person in China.

CHANGING CHINA

Slowly and painfully, however, the American correspondents began to penetrate beneath the surface, as momentous changes got underway.

Sandy Gilmour, NBC News

Clearly the primary story was the economic opening to the West, China beginning to develop some semblance of private enterprise, to reform this socialist command economy. I tried to do as many stories along those lines as I could. In addition, I tried to focus on religion, to show how they were liberalizing and letting people go back to church. And slice-of-life stories. What was it like living there? What's the traffic like? What's life like back in the back alleys? Those kinds of stories were always very popular.

You could go out on the street, and you could shoot street scenes, bicycles, people walking, the cabbage piled up on the sidewalks in the wintertime for storage, stores, and shops, and so forth. You could go up to people and ask them questions, although many didn't want to answer because they were afraid of the potential consequences, even if it was a nonpolitical question such as "How do you enjoy life?" But to get into a Chinese enterprise, to go to a collective farm, a factory, those kinds of things took weeks and weeks of preparation, of phone calls, of begging and pleading and wheedling with the office in the Foreign Ministry that permitted correspondents to get out and do their business. It was extremely frustrating.

Bruce Dunning, CBS News

A lot of us were trying to counteract the years of "Red China Menace" kind of stories and say, "These are people." It's the largest country in the world. What are they really like? There was generally a lot of good feeling. Early on, you could get almost anything on the air. There was just that novelty, you know—we have a bureau in Beijing. We have a presence in China. They were willing to put almost anything on the air.

Jim Laurie, ABC News

In the early days, the opening of China to the West, there was a "gee whiz" mentality. If you go back and look at the programming on ABC, NBC, and CBS in 1979, that is very much reflected. China opening up. Every little innovation that was part of the reform program that Deng was outlining was seized upon. The first private restaurant. The first private car. It was all a series of firsts. There was an insatiable appetite for slice-of-life stories, particularly if you could get good images. It's hard to understand now, but you've got to realize that in this period, '79 to '83, this was "coming out" for China. Very little had been seen of China, especially by American TV viewers. So almost anything that was visually interesting went.

Bruce Dunning, CBS News

We did stories on private restaurants. People would set up restaurants in their homes and those were some of the first examples of private enterprise. I remember when free markets began to show up on the outskirts of Beijing, just a few farmers setting up primitive benches and selling produce, but it was such an improvement over the state stores and the quality of produce just increased remarkably.

Linda Mathews, *Los Angeles Times*

On Good Friday 1980, some of the churches were just being reopened after being shut down during the Cultural Revolution. We walked into a church, and met this bishop named Moses Xie. There was a choir practicing for Sunday services, and they had hand-lettered hymnals because the real hymnals had been burned during the Cultural Revolution. They were singing in Chinese, "Rise up, you men of God." It was a magical moment to be in a Chinese church, which had been a factory for years and years, and here was a choir and a couple of Jesuits.

As part of his reforms, Deng Xiaoping authorized the establishment of four special zones along the country's southeastern coast as laboratories to experiment with market-style economics, and, he hoped, spearhead economic growth. For the first time since the Communist revolution, capitalist activities such as private enterprise and foreign investment were not only permitted but actively encouraged. The first zone was Shenzhen, at the time just a small fishing community directly across the border from Hong Kong.

Frank Ching, *Wall Street Journal*

Shenzhen was nothing. A little village, very few people. When you first went down, there was nothing to see. They hadn't done anything yet. But they talked about their plans. Now there are millions of people. It's incredible that China could build up a city like this almost overnight.

Liu Heung-shing, *Time*, Associated Press

They were laying out their blueprints and telling us where they're going to build a highway and where they're going to build a Holiday Inn hotel and convention center, where they're going to build the port. And the reaction from my colleagues on that trip was that—"yeah, right."

Richard Bernstein, *Time*

I think what we got wrong was we totally underestimated the ability of China to change rapidly. Nobody could have predicted. We certainly didn't predict the extent to which China would become a country like a lot of others.

Some the most dramatic changes began to unfold in the countryside, where Deng Xiaoping authorized the breakup of that symbol of radical Maoism, the people's communes. The collective farms, set up during the Great Leap Forward in the late 1950s, were replaced by a system of household family farming that sharply boosted rural incomes.

Bruce Dunning, CBS News

We showed how the communes were beginning to break up, and people were beginning to have their own personal parcels of land, and their own flocks of animals, so we were able to show how the cooperative, the commune system was beginning to break down.

Melinda Liu, *Newsweek*

The People's Commune system was such an icon of Maoism. The fact that it was being broken up into family-based farms, which turned out to be much more productive than the big collectives, was very telling. On the group visits, the challenge was, how do you get anything out of it that's not the same as everyone else? There was one of these group visits to Anhui where a People's Commune was being literally parceled out. I kind of infiltrated a family and they were so excited and really happy. One farmer was like, "Yeah, I got such and such a plot, [of land]." They had even divided up the wheelbarrow so that someone had half, and someone had the other half. "My neighbor got the wheel, and I got the rest of it." And I'm like, "How is that going to work?" But they were so happy.

The arrival of the resident U.S. correspondents also coincided with the launch of China's draconian one-child family-planning policy. Authorized by Deng and designed to spur economic growth and curb a population that in 1980 was nearing a billion, the policy included stiff penalties for families having more than one child. It was a traumatic social experiment, characterized by enforced sterilizations and abortions, as well as producing a generation of children who would grow up without knowing what it was like to have a sibling, that left major scars on individuals and Chinese society. For the journalists, it was a major story.

Sandy Gilmour, NBC News

We went to a so-called "family-planning hospital" in Beijing and got exclusive photos of the women there, many of whom had had forced abortions, forced sterilizations, and so on. We went to the neighborhood where the official is keeping track of all the women in the neighborhood and their menstrual cycles with a chart stating who was authorized to have a child and who isn't. It's just extraordinary, and was, I thought, a very important story and showed that, while China was talking about reforming, the power of the state had just such a broad reach that it was formidable indeed.

But, as with so much in China, as they dug deeper, reporters like the Mathews discovered the reality was more complex.

Jay Mathews, *Washington Post*

Both of us were very keen on finding out how people lived in the country, looking at contrast between the way people lived and what the government said about the way people lived, looking for cracks in the façade of certain polices, like the one child per family policy. Early on we did stories about how in the countryside that wasn't operating at all.

Linda Mathews, *Los Angeles Times*

Somebody said once when we were interviewing at a commune where the commune leader's wife was pregnant with her fourth child, "The mountains are tall, and the emperor is far away." They knew very well they were going to get away with violating the one-child rule.

Despite the restrictions, one of the first trips the Foreign Ministry organized for the newly arrived American journalists was to Tibet. The territory, which was occupied by Chinese troops in 1959, and then devastated during the Cultural Revolution, had long been off-limits to reporters.

Frank Ching, *Wall Street Journal*

I remembered them telling us what special treatment we were getting. When we were in Tibet, one of the people asked to see a particular monastery. The Tibetan guy said, "It doesn't exist." "What do you mean it doesn't exist? It's in this book." He said, "It doesn't exist." It turned out that the monastery had been destroyed during the Cultural Revolution. That's what he meant by "it doesn't exist." But it used to exist. And then they talked about the Dalai Lama, they painted him in totally black colors. But it was quite amazing to see people going to the monastery and prostrating themselves on the ground. They were so devout, so religious.

Jim Laurie, *ABC News*

It was very short—four days, and very guided. The usual places—the Jokhang, the Potala palace, one monastery. There were interviews with local officials. It was very much a gee-whiz trip, but your first trip to Tibet has to be a gee-whiz trip because it was an amazing place. But what I am proudest of in the story I did was that we were able to capture the palpable tension between the Chinese and the Tibetans in Lhasa. That was very apparent even in these early days.

BURNOUT

But for every story the foreign correspondents could do in China, many more remained out of reach. Their struggles with their minders and the Communist Party cadres left many reporters weary.

Melinda Liu, *Newsweek*

The personal restrictions that we operated under. The constant surveillance, phones always being tapped, people always listening in on you. Simple things like you couldn't have a normal romantic relationship with a Chinese person. These sorts of things.

Fox Butterfield, *New York Times*

My staff consisted of a Chinese assistant and translator who actually worked for the security people. His main job was to spy on me. I was also given a driver who was charged with spying on me. They had to go every Saturday to report at a meeting on everything I had done for the week.

Bruce Dunning, CBS News

We all felt it would be a good idea to be on good terms with your translator so he wouldn't give you a bad report.

Some of the Americans found an unlikely source of help in getting a better handle on the country—a trio of young Filipinos. Chito Sta Romana, Eric Baculinao, and Jaime (Jimi) FlorCruz had been among a group of left-wing students from Manila on a "friendship tour" of China in 1971, when they learned Philippine strongman Ferdinand Marco had ordered their arrest if they returned.

Jaime FlorCruz, *Newsweek, Time*

I came here originally as an accidental tourist for a three-week tour. During that time, there was an abrupt change in the political situation in the Philippines. I was blacklisted for my radical student activities, so I ended up staying longer than the three weeks.

Eric Baculinao, NBC News

I was at the forefront of the student movement against Marcos. I was part of a delegation of youth leaders invited by the Friendship Association of China as part of people-to-people diplomacy. On the third day of our three-week visit, some bombings took place in Manila. That started the ball rolling leading to martial law. We were on the wanted list, to be arrested on arrival [in Manila] so we decided to wait, thinking that it would be a few months. It turned out to be fifteen years waiting in China.

By the time the American correspondents arrived, all three had graduated from Chinese universities, were fluent in Chinese, and offered the reporters an alternative window into the country.

Jaime FlorCruz, *Newsweek, Time*

Because of my familiarity with Beijing and China in general, I already had a network of friends, former classmates, and former students, because I also taught English part-time. So I had this network of friends that I could turn to for information or to double-check certain news or rumors, people who trusted me because they knew me first as a friend and later as a journalist. That was my big advantage.

Eric Baculinao, NBC News

We were foreign enough to understand what American correspondents would like in the environment of China, and we were acquainted enough with the locals to understand what their concerns were, so that their concerns were properly addressed. We were kind of a bridge. We had that unique position.

Chito Sta Romana, ABC News

Jimi was the first one who did this, because he was working for Melinda of Newsweek, *then eventually for* Time. *And it was through him, other journalists were asking him, "Where can we find people like you?"*

Romana ended up at ABC News, while Sandy Gilmour hired Eric Baculinao at NBC.

Sandy Gilmour, NBC News

He was my right-hand man during my entire stay in China, with me on just about every story. He knew what the standards were. He knew the kinds of information we needed to get. At the same time, he was very attuned to what you could do, what you could get away with, what the authorities would permit and not permit. It was extremely valuable to have this Western oriented, basically American journalist in Beijing working for me and for NBC.

But even with the extra help, China remained a tough assignment.

Jim Laurie, ABC News

I think most of us who came in the '79–'81 period—we had followed China on the outside for so many years. We were very enthusiastic about China. And then it sort of ground us down.

Melinda Liu, *Newsweek*

They actually came with an image of China that did not jibe with reality on the ground. This was not an idealized, beautiful paradise by any means. It was actually a grotty, poor country, with a lot of human rights abuses, and a lot of systemic problems. There was a disconnect. I think some people reacted against it in a very visceral way. They felt betrayed by China, and some of them became very bitter about China.

Richard Bernstein, *Time*

It's kind of standard, no matter where they are, for the foreign press to develop a slightly contemptuous attitude of the host country. Contemptuous might be too strong a word, but yeah, we did have it. We certainly shared our view of the Information Department, which we used to call the "lack of information department."

DISSIDENTS

It was easy to make fun of the system. But the grievances of those victimized by the excesses of Maoism, voiced most dramatically in the posters on what became known as Democracy Wall in Beijing, and by a small group of out-spoken dissidents, were no laughing matter.

Fox Butterfield, *New York Times*

There was this sudden outpouring of posters. For the first time since the Commu-nist revolution, they were able to put up what they really felt and tell stories about what had happened to them. They would find themselves shouted at, criticized politically, accused of being rightists, very often badly beaten, or made to kneel on broken bits of glass, or suspended from the ceiling. There were terrible tortures. I was writing these things for the Times. *There were so many of those stories.*

Butterfield, who had studied Chinese at Harvard, met one man who had gone to Harvard before the Communist revolution.

Fox Butterfield, *New York Times*

In 1949, he could have stayed on [in the United States]. He had a job at Har-vard. But he wanted to be patriotic. He believed the Communists were doing a good thing for China, so he went back, and he immediately fell under suspi-cion because he'd been educated in the West. He'd been labeled a rightist in the Great Leap Forward, and then during the Cultural Revolution was impris-oned again. His son, who was in medical school in Beijing, was thrown out of school because his father was a rightist, and his daughter was thrown out of her job. They'd all been sent to labor camps, or to work on farms. It had taken him fifteen years to get back to his hospital, where nobody wanted to talk to him, because a lot of the people who had accused him were still there. He described how he'd been beaten every day for several years, literally. He'd been kept in a small room in the dark and been given these political lectures to make the same confession, hundreds and hundreds and hundreds of times. His major crime had been that he was Western-educated. And I wrote this for the Times.

Some TV reporters, however, found their bosses so enamored of the romance of China that they weren't interested in the human rights story.

Jim Laurie, ABC News

Whenever I would propose stories that touched on human rights issues or much more critical stories, there wasn't a tremendous enthusiasm in New York. Partly it was being television, you didn't really have pictures to tell the story. There were so many wonderful images in China, which Americans had not seen, that to do a story on a lone dissident, which was not very telegenic, if you will, was a problem.

Sandy Gilmour, NBC News

Even if I found one or two people that I would talk to, they certainly were not going to go on camera. And I was also very leery of getting somebody in trouble, knowing that they would be picked up and interrogated, if not jailed subsequently.

Liu Qing was one of those lone dissidents, a prominent Democracy Wall activist who edited an unofficial magazine called the *April Fifth Forum*. Liu had circulated the transcript of the trial of another leading dissident, Wei Jingsheng, who had been given a fifteen-year jail sentence after posting a long essay at Democracy Wall calling on China to add a "fifth modernization"—democracy—to the four economic goals outlined by Deng Xiaoping. Richard Bernstein went to Liu's home in Beijing and spoke with him. A few weeks later, Liu was arrested and sentenced to three years of "reeducation through labor." While in prison, Liu wrote a two-hundred-page account of his experiences, including the harsh conditions and beatings he endured. Mid-way through his term, his prison journal was smuggled out.

Richard Bernstein, *Time*

He gave it to a fellow inmate, who wrapped it around his leg, underneath his quilted clothes when he was released from prison. And the inmate then gave it to some friends. I think maybe Liu Qing had a brother living in Beijing, so he gave it to his brother.

Eventually, the document came into the hands of sympathizers in Hong Kong. They passed it to Bernstein, who, on a visit to the city, photocopied it and sent it to his editors at *Time*, where a long excerpt was published.

Richard Bernstein, *Time*

It was my big scoop during my time in China. We had this kind of detailed description of the Chinese, the arrest, the interrogation, the imprisonment, the so-called trial, the imprisonment, the terms of imprisonment, everything, the whole story was there written by an extremely intelligent, a very honest guy too.

In an article written some years later for the *New York Times*, where Bernstein worked after leaving *Time*, he wrote:

I realized its importance immediately. It described a part of the vast, secret Chinese gulag that people on the outside knew about only through rumor and second-hand accounts. Liu Qing recounted his experience in vivid detail, describing the "blind fury" of the Public Security Bureau interrogators, the constant cold of the cells, the "infinite flexibility" of "the dictatorship of the proletariat"—a reference to the police being able to do whatever they wanted.[5]

Upon returning to Beijing, Bernstein was called in and interrogated by the police, who accused him of having engaged in "illegal activities."

Richard Bernstein, *Time*

I was grilled for a whole day. There were four, five of these guys and me, and a translator although most of the meeting was in Chinese. They knew about the Liu Qing manuscript, everything. I didn't name any names or anything like that. I was fully prepared to go to prison to not to disclose any names, but it was a kind of silly bravado on my part, because they knew all the names.

In his article for *New York Times*, Bernstein noted that

The meeting at the public security office was farcical in one sense. The chief interrogator declared for my benefit that "the Chinese people enjoy full democratic rights." Then, rather stiffly, he announced something to the effect that if I did not cease my "illegal activities" I would bear all of the consequences. Just before I left, I was told that three of my six rolls of film, which had been processed by the security police, would not be returned to me. "Why?" I asked. "You took those rolls, so you know why yourself," was the reply. I found this answer striking. I knew that one of the basic techniques of serious Chinese interrogations—the kind that lead to imprisonment, rather than just warnings—is to refuse to tell a defendant what he is suspected of. Instead, he is informed that if he confesses to the unspecified crimes he "knows" he has committed, leniency will follow.

"But I don't even remember what was on those rolls," I protested, informing the interrogator they had been taken months earlier during my various travels, none of which had been to unauthorized areas.

"You know what is wrong about them," the agent repeated, "since you took the pictures yourself."

"May I look at them to remind myself of what is on them?" I asked. "That is forbidden," he said.[6]

After *Time* published the excerpts of Liu Qing's diary, Liu was given a secret closed trial and sentenced to a further seven years in prison. In all, he served eleven years before being freed, and, in 1992, he was allowed to leave China for the United States.

Liu Qing, Chinese Dissident

Bernstein getting this out helped expose the Chinese government's behavior to the rest of the world. It was what I hoped to accomplish. I am grateful to him. I am not angry at all.

Still, Liu Qing's fate underscored one of the central dilemmas faced by foreign reporters in China—the danger, in an authoritarian system, of putting your contacts at risk.

Sandy Gilmour, NBC News

If I get to be friendly with this person, are they going to get interrogated? If I put them on camera, are they going to lose their job? How do you weigh that up? I was very leery of trying to involve the sort of average Chinese in any kind of controversial story. I feared they would be picked up and jailed and I didn't feel I could live with that.

Melinda Liu, *Newsweek*

Most of us disguised our sources very, very carefully when we wrote about them. But we saw what happened when it wasn't adequate enough.

Fox Butterfield met a young woman willing to talk about one of the most taboo of all topics—sex.

Fox Butterfield, *New York Times*

Clothes were designed to look sexless. There were no open displays of affection. There was no dancing. Sex was considered "bourgeois." But I soon discovered that Chinese of course had active sex lives and had certain interests. And this woman was, for whatever her personal reasons, very comfortable talking about Chinese sexual mores.

In an article for the *New York Times Magazine* titled "Love and Sex in China," Butterfield did not use the woman's real name, but he described her— "an office worker in her mid-30s, . . . a tall, spare women with prominent cheekbones and a quizzical expression"[7]—and her circumstances.

Fox Butterfield, *New York Times*

We probably got careless, because we met too often, and became too confident that we were able to keep our meetings away from prying eyes. She also was indiscreet. She called me from her workplace. I am sure the calls could be traced. I would never call her because that would be a dead giveaway. But she would call me, and I was getting very worried about it. I thought she was being indiscreet. In the end she did get arrested. I am pretty sure she was sent off to a labor camp. I heard back later that she'd been released. She was in touch with me. But by that time, I was back in the U.S. I felt that sending a letter would only cause her more grief. That's weighed on me a lot. It's weighed on me for years.

But even as reporters and their contacts struggled with the heavy hand of the state, Deng Xiaoping continued to liberalize the economy and dismantle Chairman Mao's radical legacy, a cycle of tightening and opening that became for many years a central feature of China's reform process.

THE TRIAL OF THE GANG OF FOUR

While dissidents came under pressure, Deng put Mao's widow, Jiang Qing, and her key allies—the so-called "Gang of Four"—on trial, blaming them for the excesses of the Cultural Revolution. The trial in 1980 was a big story—a national political catharsis after years of upheaval. But foreign reporters were barred from attending the proceedings.

Jim Laurie, ABC News

This was an amazing event, Mao's widow, the Gang of Four, on trial, in the big courthouse just off Tiananmen square. Yet we as foreign journalists had no access whatsoever.

Fox Butterfield, *New York Times*

When the Gang of Four had their trial, you saw news clips at night. I would write my story after watching the clips. We'd get the New China News Agency report that night and accounts in the People's Daily. *At least we could see on the TV news what the Chinese wanted us to see. The level of bitterness that average Chinese had towards the government and that group of Communist leaders was astronomical, because almost everybody's life had been disrupted or destroyed in some terrible way—whether it was physical injury, death, loss of jobs, loss of education, brothers, sisters, parents, children taken away, regular beatings, humiliations. The humiliation people went through in the Cultural Revolution was incredible. So, it was a catharsis for China.*

The images shown on Chinese television were dramatic, especially the astonishingly defiant attitude of Jiang Qing, who was totally unrepentant, disregarding the instructions of court officials, interrupting prosecution witnesses, and invoking Chairman Mao's name to justify her past behavior. By allowing these scenes to be screened, China's leaders tacitly acknowledged that Mao too bore responsibility for the excesses of the Cultural Revolution—an important message for the country to be able to move forward with the changes Deng Xiaoping had introduced.

Frank Ching, *Wall Street Journal*

She said she just did what Mao told her to. The trial showed that China realized that they had to do something about these people. They were talking about a country ruled by law. They felt that there had to be some legal resolution and so they had the trial.

To cover the trial, the American networks were desperate for footage. The state-run China Central Television was the only source.

Jim Laurie, ABC News

A major battle developed with CCTV over access to footage of the trial. At one point, video came in showing Jiang Qing in her cell. A bidding war began between ABC and CBS on acquiring this video, which we desperately wanted. CBS in this case won the bidding war and I lost.

Bruce Dunning, CBS News

We had a contract with CCTV to provide material and it was a special deal because CBS was providing programming material to CCTV, so in exchange they were very favorable to us and our requests for material.

"SOCIALISM WITH CHINESE CHARACTERISTICS"

CCTV's display of newfound entrepreneurial tendencies was a good metaphor for what was beginning to happen across China, as Deng's model of "socialism with Chinese characteristics," in which markets, competition, foreign investment, and wealth creation were allowed to flourish under the auspices of the Communist Party, took hold. To spearhead his reform drive, Deng Xiaoping promoted two younger officials. Hu Yaobang, a political liberal who had been purged in the Cultural Revolution but rehabilitated after Mao's death, was made general secretary of the Communist Party in 1982. Zhao Ziyang, the Party boss in Sichuan, China's most populous province, was named premier. Zhao had developed a reputation as a bold reformer, promoting market-oriented policies that dramatically boosted economic growth in Sichuan. Deng now asked him to supervise similar changes throughout the country.

In a sign of the changing times, just before taking up his new job, Zhao agreed to talk to Fox Butterfield.

Fox Butterfield, *New York Times*

To my surprise I was told I was going to have a meeting with Zhao. The next thing I knew, this man appeared in my hotel, by himself, which was astonishing, because Chinese Communist officials always have large retinues, lots of security. According to Chinese protocol, the senior Chinese leader would not come to the hotel of a lowly foreign correspondent. I was really stunned. I was very impressed that he was willing to open himself up. We had a frank, engaging talk about the economic reforms he was carrying out, and how optimistic he was, and the big changes he wanted to make. He struck me as being modest, open, and very thoughtful. I was very impressed.

Indeed, that was the big theme as this first generation of American reporters began to wind up their groundbreaking assignments.

Bruce Dunning, CBS News

I would say I was optimistic. I felt that China had an opportunity to head in a positive direction.

Jay Mathews, *Washington Post*

We were fairly hopeful leaving. This very strong culture was coming back, was building businesses, was creating a government that was more responsive to the people's needs, was letting people talk more freely, if not in the public press. That was unleashing all kinds of interesting and hopeful changes in the way Chinese were going about their lives—and producing flashes of humor, creative art, filmmaking, things they hadn't had before and were going in interesting directions. I am an optimist, so I was always looking to see the glass half-full, and I thought the glass was really getting much fuller in that period.

Linda Mathews, *Los Angeles Times*

Clearly the economy was improving, the free markets were functioning, there were some private plots, there were more choices available to individuals about where they worked, there were more people going to college. There were lots of things to indicate China was on an upward trajectory.

Even the government's handling of the media began to improve.

Frank Ching, *Wall Street Journal*

I thought when I left in '83 that China was just beginning to open up to journalists. '83 was when they began to hold a regular press conference. The Foreign Ministry had a weekly press conference. That was when they appointed spokesmen for all the ministries and gave their phone numbers. And before that, none of this was available.

Still, covering China remained a struggle. Some correspondents believed the continuing restrictions obscured even the good news.

Richard Bernstein, *Time*

The Chinese really shoot themselves in the foot. They want to control you so much you feel whatever they tell you was a lie even when it's the truth.

Yet as the Mao years faded into memory, the dominant theme in the China of Deng Xiaoping was hope.

Liu Heung-shing, *Time,* Associated Press

I have a photograph showing this high school student sitting in Tiananmen Square and studying. That was when they first reinstituted the college exam, but they have no electricity at home, [so] they go to Tiananmen Square, and they study under the streetlight. As a photographer, I was very moved.

By the end of the decade, the students would be back on Tiananmen Square—under very different circumstances.

7

"YOU WERE WRITING WHAT WE WERE THINKING"

In September 1986, exactly ten years after Mao's death, Deng Xiaoping spoke with CBS News correspondent Mike Wallace, the lead reporter for *60 Minutes*, America's highest-rated weekly television news magazine show.

WALLACE: I asked Deng Xiaoping whether China would ever go back to the days before his economic reforms.
DENG: So long as the people think the existing policy is correct, whoever wants to change it will be brought down.

Canadian Barry Lando was Mike Wallace's longtime producer.

Barry Lando, CBS News

To meet the man who was the architect of those changes, that was a very important moment.

Deng's references to internal differences and the possibility of leaders being brought down proved prophetic. But the tensions that would produce the Tiananmen Square crisis in 1989, three years after the interview, were still largely bubbling below the surface. For most American reporters, Deng's abandonment of Maoist ideology, his adoption of market-style reforms, and the resulting transformation of Chinese society remained the story.

In 1984, John Burns, who had left the *Toronto Globe and Mail* for the *New York Times*, returned as the *Times* correspondent. He met Ma Yuzhen, a Foreign Ministry official who a decade before had denounced his critical reporting.

John Burns, *New York Times*

I said, "Mr. Ma, I was always puzzled, because you must have warned me eight, nine, ten times. It was a pretty frightening experience sometimes. Why did you never arrest me, put me in prison, or, more simply, throw me out?" I'll never forget his answer. It was a lesson for life for a foreign correspondent. He said, "The reason was that you were writing what we were thinking."

Michael Parks, who had covered the Vietnam War for the *Baltimore Sun* and opened the *Sun*'s Beijing bureau in 1979, joined the *Los Angeles Times* in 1980, replacing Linda Mathews. After a year in China, she and her husband, Jay, had left Beijing to write a book.

Michael Parks, *Los Angeles Times*

It was said that every Chinese husband wanted to give his wife the "three movements"—a watch, a sewing machine, and a bicycle. They were buying more furniture for weddings. I would go into a village, and I would see new or refurbished housing. We also saw in the stores that there were more things on the shelves, and they weren't rationed. I was writing economic stories about a mode of development that I had never seen before, and actually nobody had—how to take a state-run economy and turn it into a market-driven one, how to deal with problems that they had never encountered before.

Richard Hornik, who had a master's degree in Russian studies and had previously been based in Eastern Europe, arrived in Beijing in the mid-eighties for *Time* magazine.

Richard Hornik, *Time*

The big theme was, How were the reforms going? One of my specialties was Soviet economies. I knew a lot about the planned economy, and state ownership.

It struck me early on that in China they had done all the easy reforms. They had stopped doing a lot of stupid things, like telling the peasants to grow rice where they should be growing wheat. They had taken the low-hanging fruit. I was looking for stories about what they were going to do to take it to the next level. Because in these systems, if you don't take it to the next level, you create roadblocks and choke points, where there can be corruption. It's a very, very slippery slope if you don't keep the momentum up. By that point the momentum had begun to slow.

Even as Deng's reform program had gathered steam, the domestic tensions generated by the changes became increasingly evident and were an important theme for American and other foreign journalists. Deng's oblique comment to Mike Wallace about internal political conflict was a clear indication of a battle within the leadership that would last throughout the decade. On one side were the paramount leader's key lieutenants, Communist Party general secretary Hu Yaobang, widely seen as Deng's designated successor, and Premier Zhao Ziyang, supported by many intellectuals, who sought to modify the basic structures of Chinese socialism, decentralize state control, and relax restrictions on private business to raise economic efficiency. Others in the leadership, however, especially some influential Party elders, were uneasy about the pace and consequences of reform, fearing that too much liberalization would threaten the Communist Party's authority. It was left to Deng to play the role of power broker, balancing the rival factions in the Party while keeping his reform program on track.

John Burns, *New York Times*

The policy of the Open Door was not at all secure. Deng was having to manage his position. He was trying to hold together a very shaky coalition in the Politburo and the Central Committee—in consequence of which, there was a lot that had not yet changed, including the system for the management of foreign media. Many of the same people were still there. And it was very frustrating, because we knew that there were seismic changes going on in Chinese society.

Michael Weisskopf, who had studied Chinese in college and had previously worked for the *Baltimore Sun*, took over the *Washington Post* Beijing bureau from Jay Mathews in 1981.

Michael Weisskopf, *Washington Post*

You had this breathing in and breathing out on repression. There would be a breath of fresh air, which people would misinterpret as an opening, which would be quickly closed off with an anti–spiritual pollution campaign.

POTEMKIN VILLAGES

To better understand the story, it was critical to see the country beyond Beijing. Correspondents were still required to get permission ten days in advance to travel outside the capital, and still forced to sit through endless "brief introductions" from local officials, but nonetheless developed strategies to obtain real information and insights.

Richard Hornik, *Time*

A lot of it was you just kept applying for trips. Also, I got pretty good at figuring out what it was they wanted me to see. At that point, they were very big on township-village enterprises, and so I asked to see one. They let me go to this place south of Chengdu in Sichuan. As a Soviet specialist, I have a real affinity for Potemkin villages, and this place was a Potemkin village. They kept telling us how well people were doing. You go to a place like this, you always know they're going to show you the absolute best they've got. So you need to reverse-engineer backward from that to what the middle might be.

But such briefings, usually packed with mind-numbing statistics, occasionally contained fascinating nuggets, as the *Washington Post*'s Michael Weisskopf discovered when he stumbled on a story that would shock the world.

Michael Weisskopf, *Washington Post*

We started talking about births, which was also a statistic. And it was some crazy lopsided number of males born versus females born, like three to one or four to one. I said, "How is it you have this odd statistic?" He said, "Well, people in the village want to have boys and they abort or kill the children at birth if they are daughters." They didn't realize how horrifying this picture was. This was a story that needs to be told. Every reporting trip I took after that, I would have these kinds of interviews. And the interviews became much more sophisticated over time. I was able to enlist many of these commune bosses in being collaborators without them realizing it. I had a lot of anecdotal information from doctors and firsthand sources—doctors who were under orders to kill children, to stick forceps through their brains as they came out of a woman's uterus if it was unplanned. Horror stories of that nature. There was an extraordinary imbalance between the birth of males and females. It could only be explained by extraordinary infanticide.

Fearing expulsion, Weisskopf waited until his China tour ended. In early 1985 the *Washington Post* published his explosive three-part series under the headline "China's Birth Control Policy Drives Some to Kill Baby Girls." Based on a detailed analysis of Chinese statistics, citations from the official Chinese press, and moving accounts from those he managed to interview, Weisskopf wrote: "The frantic push for boys in a one-child society can be charted in official accounts of drowning, suffocation, poisoning and desertion of baby girls. It is seen in the popularity of scientific fetus tests and superstitious rites to forecast the gender of the unborn child—with abortions following for women thought to be carrying a girl."[1]

Michael Weisskopf, *Washington Post*

The Chinese reaction was denial, that this was a horrible stain on their reputation. They condemned the Washington Post, *and me in particular, on the front page of the* People's Daily. *But there was international reaction as well. The UN, which was then financing Chinese family planning, had a fairly large program for which the U.S. was the primary sponsor. I think it was about fifty million dollars that we gave, and this was in the middle of [the] Reagan administration, and he just cut it off.*

The episode was a powerful example of how, with China becoming increasingly open and engaged with the world, the chronicling of its internal behavior by foreign journalists could elicit significant international reactions. Nonetheless, for editors at many U.S. news organizations, the good news about China continued to outweigh the bad. This often led to tension between reporters and their bosses.

THE "GEE-WHIZ" FACTOR

James Mann, who as a young *Washington Post* reporter in the 1970s had helped to cover the Watergate scandal, and later joined the *Los Angeles Times*, covering the U.S. Supreme Court, became the paper's Beijing correspondent in 1984.

James Mann, *Los Angeles Times*

The whole thrust of the eighties was cross-currents. China was opening up, but not as open as people in the United States imagined. Part of the dynamic was a reaction against the "gee-whiz." Living in China, you saw how super-ficial the Westernization was. More and more visitors were coming, and they would stay at places like the Jianguo Hotel or the new Great Wall Hotel. [In the mid-1980s, the Jianguo and the Great Wall were the only two Western-style joint-venture hotels in Beijing.] They would come out with these sort of "whoopee" perceptions. American companies were overly impressed with how much the Chinese wanted genuine joint ventures with them, as opposed to simply wanting Western technology and management tech-niques. If you lived in China, you saw how slow change took place, and how much resistance there was to change, certainly at the political level. I think correspondents in China in any era react against the simple bromides back home in different ways. Certainly, in the eighties there was a reaction against "gee-whiz."

Daniel Southerland, a veteran Asia hand who'd spent years covering the Vietnam War for the *Christian Science Monitor*, replaced Michael Weisskopf as the *Washington Post* correspondent in 1985.

Daniel Southerland, *Washington Post*

China had opened up quite a bit at this time. I didn't expect the political situ-ation to change much, but you had a lot of experiments, not only in the econ-omy, but also in art and music, and people were speaking out a bit more. My tendency was to try not to get carried away with the "first this" and the "first that." China watchers and the general public go through periods of unwonted optimism about China, almost euphoric. "China's going to be a capitalist coun-try. They're buying our stuff." I was trying to guard against the idea that China was going capitalist, because I was a bit skeptical. I could see the state owner-ship component of a lot of things, even if it was hidden, even if township indus-tries might have looked private, a lot of times they were not. They were part of the establishment.

Richard Hornik, *Time*

Unfortunately, the appetite in Time *magazine was that the Chinese are drinking Coca-Cola and driving around in Cadillacs, and isn't it wonderful?* Time *showed up with a group of thirty-five CEOs of Fortune 500 companies on the* Time *News Tour. We got an interview with Deng. Terrific, charismatic, funny, good at answering direct questions, engaged everybody. I was very impressed by him.*

Hornik's colleague at *Time* was Jaime FlorCruz, the onetime Filipino leftist who'd been in China since 1971.

Richard Hornik, *Time*

Jaime had the connections. He knew lots of people. He could make things happen, but also, he had the perspective. As someone who didn't know China, I was reliant on him to tell me when I was going off the rails, and when I was making too much of something.

Jaime FlorCruz, *Time*

Through all those years I had collected a lot of friends, former classmates. It gave me an extra layer of entrée into people's lives and thinking. It was a big advantage being able to put on my so-called Mao suit and wear a hat and just strike up conversations. I would have a little accent here and there, but they would think I was a local Chinese and that made for a more spontaneous and genuine interaction. The problems with reform came out in various kinds of reports that we did. Sometimes I would say to myself—that's really not what I knew or understood to be what's going on. Especially when you hear the "gee whiz" factor. You could tell it is not quite right.

But Deng's charm created a big journalistic problem for Hornik and FlorCruz.

Richard Hornik, *Time*

Jaime and I had done a big cover story for Time *in September of '85 on the reform hitting some tough spots. Because of Deng Xiaoping's charisma and his legendary figure, I think he just bamboozled a lot of the editors who joined that interview. They were all just overwhelmed. They went back to New York and came up with a request—tell us why we should choose Deng Xiaoping as* Time's *Man of the Year? The burden was reversed—give us reasons so we can choose him as the Man of the Year. They fell into that "gee whiz" China, let's do Chinese drinking Coca Cola, Chinese turning capitalist, Chinese turning like us syndrome. He'd already been Man of the Year once, and things [in China] weren't going that great, so it was a real struggle for us to get what they wanted. Things really were starting to go wrong, since you're either moving forward or you're sliding backwards, and they had started to slide backwards. In the meantime,* Time *didn't want to run anything else, so it was a frustrating time.*

No matter. At the end of 1985, for the second time in six years, *Time* named Deng Xiaoping Man of the Year.

DENG XIAOPING AND MIKE WALLACE

Well before the *Time* cover story, Mike Wallace had been trying to land an interview with Deng for *60 Minutes*. The Chinese leader had never done a one-on-one TV interview.

Barry Lando, CBS

We tried for a couple of years, making regular requests in Beijing and through the Chinese embassy in Washington, DC. We were told by the Chinese embassy that we had got the interview, and they wanted us to come down and talk about it. Mike and I flew to Washington and had this big lunch at the embassy. The ambassador was there, and three or four of his assistants, and their press guy. We promised them the moon and told them that this was going to be sensational, the first time he's really spoken out. We told them that the West is going to hear him, and we'll lead the season of 60 Minutes *with it. Who knows, maybe there'll be an hour broadcast. We put all these things out there.*

Wallace had interviewed almost everybody—Egyptian president Anwar Sadat, the Palestine Liberation Organization's Yasser Arafat, Iran's Ayatollah Khomeini, countless other politicians and celebrities. But the Deng interview in September 1986 presented a special challenge.

Barry Lando, CBS News

Our big problem was, How do you make Deng Xiaoping human? For any kind of television interview, he cannot come across as a theoretician. It has got to come across as an interview with a human being, particularly for a wide audience. I've never seen Mike Wallace as scared, in a way, before an interview as before that one with Deng. He really was an unknown quantity on television. We didn't know how he would come across, but we had to get him to respond as a human being. That was a big problem.

When Wallace arrived in Beijing, he met with John Sheahan, a network veteran with years covering the Middle East and Eastern Europe, who had become the CBS China correspondent in 1985.

John Sheahan, CBS News

Mike Wallace and I had worked on previous interviews. In Egypt, I helped arrange his interview with Yasser Arafat and with Anwar Sadat. In both cases, Mike came, and before the interview, he would ask me to suggest questions and give him explanations of why this question might be important. I remember telling him to ask Deng about the joint American/Chinese intelligence unit on the Soviet border—this very sophisticated listening post that was spying on the Russians. To ask about China's violations of intellectual property, with specific examples. I remember suggesting a question about these hordes of jobless, homeless people in China, and what was the government planning to do about that? He wrote down everything. Then I was present in a conversation between Mike and Chinese authorities, including Deng Xiaoping's daughter. The Chinese were impressing on him, "Now Mr. Wallace. We want you to understand that this [is] a unique event in history. That Deng has never done an interview like this, even on Chinese television." And that the historic importance is the interview itself, implying, I guess, that you don't have to ask tough questions.

Barry Lando, CBS News

The interview was in one of the huge government halls. Rather than a normal interview, where it's usually ourselves and the film crew, in this case, there were probably a couple of hundred Chinese officials watching in chairs grouped behind us. That turned it into a totally different kind of interview. It was really a performance by Deng Xiaoping. Also, Chinese television was recording the whole thing. We started the interview with a few questions, and Deng Xiaoping was very, very wooden. He was coming back with ideology, and we tried to get him to open up a bit.

John Sheahan, CBS News

I sat there and listened to Mike softball Deng Xiaoping, and not ask a single hard question. I could hardly believe my ears.

Barry Lando, CBS News

Mike at one point asked how Deng felt about the Cultural Revolution, where he had suffered tremendously, and his son had been thrown out of a window at the university and been crippled for life. Deng refused to talk about that. He said, "That's not important." There's no expression in his face, no anger whatsoever, not even any feeling about his son. He kept throwing us off. Then we got a signal that our time was up. We thought, my God, the time is up, we've traveled halfway across the world, we've got this interview with Deng Xiaoping, yet there's nothing on it.

John Sheahan, CBS News

When the agreed time elapsed, Mike said, "Mr. Chairman, would you consent to letting us run one more twenty-minute cassette?" Deng Xiaoping was very agreeable to it and said, "Sure." I said, "Ah, now. This is where he's going to come in with the real questions." Another twenty minutes went by of softballs, and I don't understand what happened. I don't know why Mike did it the way he did.

Barry Lando, CBS News

The Chinese had a totally different view of it. They thought, of course, that it was a great interview, the "great man" was expressing himself. Many of them had never heard him talk like that before.

But back at CBS headquarters in New York, Lando and Wallace were struggling.

Barry Lando, CBS News

We had to get at least ten or fifteen minutes of decent interview to fill the broadcast. In the end, I cut our interview down to about seven or eight minutes. Once I looked at it, I noticed it was kind of boring. Then I cut it down to six minutes and showed that to executive producer Don Hewitt, and it's like he fell asleep halfway through.

John Sheahan, CBS News

Don said, "This is absolute trash. There is not a shred of news in this. We are not going to broadcast it."

Barry Lando, CBS News

Finally, he agreed to a show, which I think had about four minutes of actual interview in it, plus a number of scenes of China to illustrate what we were talking about. The whole thing was a disaster because we had had this historic moment with Deng Xiaoping and hadn't been able to transfer it into something that was really alive and human. I did a hundred interviews or more with Mike Wallace over the years. This was probably the worst interview that we did.

The Chinese, to whom Wallace had promised massive prime-time TV exposure, were furious. For John Sheahan and the CBS Beijing bureau, the consequences were immediate and severe.

John Sheahan, CBS News

I was summoned to the Foreign Ministry. They sat me down, brought in a high-ranking person. He read a statement. "Mr. Sheahan—as bureau chief of the CBS bureau in Beijing, the Foreign Ministry and the entire government of China declare to you a policy of absolute noncooperation with you personally or with your company."

A "MOST WONDERFUL TRIP"

For the *New York Times*'s John Burns, frustration over the lack of official cooperation led to a fateful decision. Accompanied by Edward McNally, a lawyer who was teaching at Peking University, and Zhang Daxing, who had recently returned to China after studying in the United States, Burns set out to retrace the journey made by Edgar Snow in the 1930s—on a motorcycle.

John Burns, *New York Times*

I decided to break free and see China for myself, defying the travel restrictions.

I chose a Chinese motorcycle, because it was universally available, so you could get spare parts easily. We decided we would retrace the steps of Edgar Snow in the preparation for writing the book Red Star Over China. *We stopped in small villages and towns to seek out the families of the people that Edgar Snow had talked to.*

Burns was secretly encouraged by Foreign Ministry official Ma Yuzhen.

John Burns, *New York Times*

Over dinner, he said, "Tell me where you are going to go." We sketched it out on my notebook. He even said to me, "When you reach Sichuan, don't go by this route. There are too many sensitive installations," including, as it turned out, a base from which China was testing missiles. "Don't go that way, go this way. Don't apply. If you apply, we'll have to turn you down. If you're stopped along the way, simply refer them to me, and [I] will tell them it's OK. He's a friend of China." My purpose was not to conduct espionage, but to find out what the Open Door policy meant to the people of China.

I traveled from northeast China to southwest China and learned a great deal. It turned out that the Communist Party had disappeared. There was in effect no central rule any longer. We were looking at a China similar to what foreigners had last seen in the 1920s. It was fascinating. When we got into the Chinese hinterland and saw the power of entrepreneurship, of initiative, you understood the sleeping giant was stirring. Private coalmines, private motor dealerships, private everything. The instinctive genius that China had for enterprise had been released and it was just bursting forth everywhere we went. As was also the instinct of speaking freely. It was the most wonderful trip.

Eventually, near the border of Shaanxi and Sichuan provinces, Burns and his companions were detained by local police.

John Burns, *New York Times*

We ventured into areas which really had never been seen by foreigners before. We avoided county towns because they have telephones. Eventually we made a mistake. We broke our own rule and decided to overnight in a hotel in a county town. Soon enough, we were effectively under arrest. As I had been counseled, I referred them to Beijing. And within two or three days of rather comfortable confinement, the Party secretary of the county came to us and said they had heard back from Beijing, and all was well. I was a friend of China, and we are going to organize a banquet for you because you are the first foreigners ever to have visited our county. It was a very congenial occasion, and many glasses of mao-tai were downed, and all was well. They put us and our motorcycle on a train and we went back to Peking, and I wrote a magazine piece about it.

Several weeks later, as Burns and his family arrived at the Beijing airport to leave on a vacation, he was suddenly arrested.

John Burns, *New York Times*

As we were sitting in the departure lounge, a man came to me and presented me with a very formal document informing me I was accused of espionage. It was very unpleasant. The penalty for spying in China is [a] bullet to the head. It could potentially become very nasty. Then I was taken off to prison. The prison governor stood in front of me and said, "You shall hope for the best, and prepare for the worst." Then they took me to a cell. They had painted in fresh red characters on the wall of the cell door, "The penalty for spying China is death." Fortunately, I knew enough about China to know that this was a charade, and there was going to be no bullet to my head.

They started their interrogations, which were farcical. They weren't interested in learning anything about my journey, which was the cause of my ostensible arrest. They said I had broken into a Chinese intercontinental missile base and stolen Chinese state secrets. Turned out that there was at that time an intercontinental missile base outside a town which we had stayed overnight [in] in a cave. Why did we stay in a cave? We didn't go into county towns because there are telephones there. But when the Chinese resolved that we had been spying, they said that that night, when we couldn't account for where we stayed, other than this cockamamie story about us sleeping in a cave, was the night that we had broken into this base.

They did bring to these encounters—always at three or four in morning—my notebooks. I had a hieroglyphic scribble. General Wang, the State Security official who had been very charming to me, said, "Start reading." And I said, "Let me explain something to you." I said, "You can't read this. I can barely read it, the scribble. But if there were anything here related to espionage, do you think that I would read it to you? This is a pointless exercise." And he said, "Mr. Burns, read. Please read." We went through this farce a few nights. My reading my notebooks, which I have to say were extremely tedious. Even he gave up after a while and suggested we play board games.

Meanwhile, Winston Lord, who had accompanied Henry Kissinger on his secret trip to China in 1971 and had been present at Richard Nixon's meeting with Chairman Mao in 1972, had been appointed by President Ronald Reagan to be the U.S. ambassador, and was vigorously pushing to resolve the incident.

Winston Lord, U.S. Ambassador

I worked very hard with the Chinese, because the system there, once you're brought to trial, you're guilty, I mean ninety-nine percent. So you have to make sure you don't have a trial. I worked very hard explaining to them the impact of this and made it a very high priority.

In the end, however, it took a personal letter to Deng Xiaoping from Richard Nixon, who hated the *New York Times*, but liked John Burns.

John Burns, *New York Times*

As he told me later, he was leading an American business delegation in the Soviet Union and read about this in the International Herald Tribune. *He had a certain fondness for me because I had written a story about him visiting China as the former president, and the reception he got, whilst he was not being treated at that time with the honor due a former president in the United States. And he did write, addressed to Deng Xiaoping, saying words to the effect of, this is a good guy. He is not employed by the U.S. or any other intelligence agency. I am assured. Basically, let him go.*

I knew nothing of this. Winston Lord delivered the letter at two o'clock in the morning to the Foreign Ministry. And at 5 AM, they rustled me from my cell, stood me in front of a video camera with a denunciation of the sins I had committee against the Chinese state. I kept interrupting them. This is all in Chinese, of course, saying, this is a pack of lies. I didn't spy, etc. They kept saying to me, "You have no right to speak." And I said, "I don't care whether I have a right or not." Eventually, after about fifteen minutes of this farce, they gave up. Gave me my own clothes back. Put me into the paddy wagon manacled, shackled, and drove me to the airport.

Burns was put on a plane to Hong Kong. His Chinese fellow traveler, Zhang Daxing, was imprisoned for several months before being freed, and, in the 1990s, was allowed to move to the United States. For the rest of the press corps in Beijing, the message from the Burns episode seemed clear.

James Mann, *Los Angeles Times*

This was not a simple case of John Burns goes to forbidden territory to a neibu [restricted] area and is kicked out. This was meant as a warning to other correspondents not to travel too much, not to get too close.

John Burns, *New York Times*

When I got to Hong Kong, I was met on the tarmac at Kai Tak Airport by the American consul general and another man whom I knew, because he had served an assignment in Peking, to be CIA. He was in fact the CIA station chief in Hong Kong. Although we were several hundred yards from the terminal building, I could see television cameras along the fence. And I remember saying to them, "You are convicting me. Just the fact you are here convicts me."

Only later did Burns learn the real reason for his detention.

John Burns, *New York Times*

The circumstance which we were not aware of had to do with a dispute between the intelligence agencies of the United States and China involving the defection to the U.S. in Hong Kong of a very senior Chinese State Security official. The Chinese demanded the defector back. The U.S. said no.

It turned out that, because of his prominence as a *New York Times* correspondent, Burns had been seized by Chinese intelligence as a bargaining chip. The U.S. officials in Hong Kong were desperate to learn what the Chinese had asked him. When Burns said they hadn't asked about the defector, the Americans lost interest. But Burns was worried he'd been tarnished and held a press conference to proclaim he wasn't a spy. Two years later, a senior Chinese official visiting the United Nations met with the editors of the *New York Times* and acknowledged that Burns was not guilty—that what he called "bad elements" in the State Security Ministry were responsible—and said Burns was welcome to return to China. But by then, Burns was based in Canada and the *Times* had replaced him with Edward Gargan, a Chinese-speaking correspondent who'd previously been covering Africa.

Edward Gargan, *New York Times*

My sense of China was established when I arrived, and it took four hours to get the luggage off the plane. It was not an efficiently run country. I remember standing around with my office manager and just waited, and waited, and waited, and waited. That was my introduction to China.

REFORM AND CORRUPTION

Gargan found that, despite the bureaucracy and the restrictions, he was able to move around much more easily than his predecessor. With the help of a surprisingly friendly official in the *waiban*—the Foreign Affairs Office—of Guangdong province, he was given permission to spend more than a week in a small village called Lolam.

Edward Gargan, *New York Times*

I wanted to see how rural China was transforming under the agricultural reform policies of Deng and Zhao Ziyang. I spent nine days in this little village in far western Guangdong. It was great. It was interesting to see, for example, the effort to bring back ancestor worship. They were trying to reconstruct the genealogy of the village, because the Red Guards came in and destroyed everything, the ancestor hall, the books with the genealogy. The feng shui master had returned—the man who determined which way houses were oriented, where graves should be positioned on the hillside, what's a good day for people to get married. The rise of moneylenders—a wealthy person in the village who became the sort of de facto mayor of the village, even though he was not a Party guy. It was a way of looking at how a tiny bit of rural China was beginning to undergo some really rapid changes. The Times ran a full-page account.

Further testing the limits, Gargan and Stefan Simons, the Beijing correspondent for the German magazine *Der Speigel*, decided to hitchhike from Shanghai to Hong Kong.

Edward Gargan, *New York Times*

We had no trouble whatsoever. One of the places we hitchhiked to was Wenzhou [a coastal city in Zhejiang province]. It was doing things so far in advance of what the rest of China was. There were private banks. You'd go into the bank, and talk to the bank manager—so what does the Party say about this? They'd point at the wall and say, "See those plaques there? Those are issued by the Party secretary of Wenzhou saying what a wonderful job we are doing providing capital to the businesses of Wenzhou."

But the inefficiencies, the dislocations, the inequities, and, especially, the corruption produced by the process of change were fueling popular discontent.

Daniel Southerland, *Washington Post*

You had this talk about corruption, the cadres who were making money, or their relatives were making money, the sons and daughters of officials who were making out well. I got to know a private businessman who became a friend. He was basically paying bribes to keep the electricity running because there were electrical problems with factories. He had his own private enterprise, but he had to pay the local authorities to keep the business going.

The mode of corruption causing the most anger was known as *guandao*—officials buying goods at low, state-fixed prices and then selling them on the open market with huge profits.

Dorinda Elliott, who had an East Asian studies degree from Harvard and had been working as the Hong Kong correspondent for *Business Week*, was hired by *Newsweek* and sent to Beijing in 1986. She noticed the same issues as Southerland.

Dorinda Elliott, *Newsweek*

There was this thing called guandao. It was kind of arbitraging prices. They sort of partially relaxed prices. If you were a smart Chinese entrepreneur, you could play the cheap prices there and sell at a higher rate. People were getting screwed all over the place. Farmers who were getting screwed because they were being underpaid for their crops, which were then being sold at a higher price elsewhere and kinds of stuff. Tremendous corruption emerged.

Soon, the people would no longer be silent.

8

TESTING THE LIMITS

In December 1986, student demonstrations broke out in Shanghai and several other cities. Thousands of young people took to the streets demanding an end to corruption, greater freedom, and a more open political system. It was the largest expression of popular protest since the start of Deng's reforms.

Edward Gargan, *New York Times*

I flew to Shanghai. There were students marching in the street. Very jubilant. Kids with no sense of even the possibility of danger toward them in any respect. They felt they had command of the story, command of their lives or their futures, of where China should go. There was an absolute explosion of confidence that they were going to change China.

John Sheahan, CBS News

It started with the students, but it wasn't too long before some of the workers who were very sympathetic to the students were supporting them. It was an incipient movement, and it was unpredictable. Unless they [the Communist Party] found some way to choke it off at the beginning, it was sure to grow.

Many of the students had been inspired by Fang Lizhi, an astrophysicist who was vice president of the prestigious University of Science and

Technology in Hefei in Anhui province. An outspoken advocate of human rights and intellectual freedom, Fang had been sent to a reeducation camp during the Cultural Revolution, an experience that sharpened his doubts about the Communist system. As he began to write and lecture about its shortcomings, he gained an increasingly large following. A month before the protests broke out, he gave a speech at Shanghai's Jiaotong University, where he declared: "The core problem is, if China's reforms depend completely on the moves of our top leaders, China will not become a developed nation. . . . Democracy granted by leaders is not true democracy. . . . Democracy means that each human being has his own rights."[1]

Dorinda Elliott, *Newsweek*

We first knew about Fang when he was at the University of Science and Technology at Hefei. He was having these "salons" with the students, and the students were in love with him. I first encountered him at Peking University. I saw him speaking to students. The students were incredibly excited. He was this remarkable phenomenon—an astrophysicist who based his ideas on science. He pursued a democratic political vision of what China could be. And had dissected Marxism based on his scientific theories. He was incredibly courageous. He had nothing to gain personally from what he was doing. He was just one of these intellectuals who believed there was a higher calling, which was the pursuit of the truth. It was a moment where he captured the imaginations and idealism of these kids at the universities. It was kind of "We want China to be great. How do we make China great? How can we learn the best of the best from around the world and how can we make our country, that we love so much, into a great country?"

In a society where so many people remained afraid to talk with foreign journalists, Elliot and other reporters were thrilled at how accessible Fang and other critical intellectuals were.

Dorinda Elliott, *Newsweek*

The intellectuals, economists, theorists, writers, artists—the ones that were exploring change—tended to be the ones that we got to know. That was one of the thrilling things for journalists. They wanted to know us. So we started getting to know them, especially if you spoke Chinese. They gave us a window onto what was going on. They knew they were taking chances. They had lived through the Cultural Revolution, knew just how bad and scary things could get. But there was this feeling in Beijing at the time of incredible excitement, intellectual ferment.

On New Year's Eve, the demonstrations spread to the capital, especially Peking University—Beida.

Edward Gargan, *New York Times*

A group of us decided to have a New Year's party. That was thrown into complete chaos because of the protests at Beida. I brought a bottle of champagne, because I thought, everyone had been working around the clock, it would be fun. We sat around after we'd done a lot of interviews as the clock ticked towards midnight. We went to the car after freezing ourselves to death and had a little bit of champagne and went back to work.

The Party leadership was sharply divided over how to respond to the protests. Despite pressure from Deng and other Party elders to crack down, General Secretary Hu Yaobang refused to denounce the demonstrators or their intellectual mentors, or to retreat from the political reform agenda. Instead, he continued to support political liberalization. But Party conservatives gained the upper hand.

James Mann, *Los Angeles Times*

The Party responded by kicking out of the Party Fang Lizhi and Liu Binyan, a dissident journalist. [Liu had been expelled from the Party for his critical writing once before, in 1957, but had been rehabilitated after the Cultural Revolution and in the 1980s had continued to write about greed, corruption, and the abuse of power.] I heard this as a rumor and called a friend working at the People's Daily *compound. I said, "Would you have time for tea later today?" She said, "I'm busy late in the afternoon." "Would you have time maybe for lunch?" She said, "Can't do it then." "Dinner?" She said, "Just ask what you want over the phone. You foreigners, you're always so paranoid." And I told her I heard that Fang Lizhi and Liu Binyan had just been kicked out of the Party. She said, "I haven't heard that." About a half-hour later the phone rings and she said, "What you heard was true," which is what I needed to report the story as I did. The next time I saw her, she said, "You were right about the telephones. I was called in and admonished for talking to you.*

The same week, Hu Yaobang was removed as Communist Party chief. Although Deng had long promoted and protected Hu, he finally decided to sack his protégé after Party elders convinced him that Hu's ideological laxity was responsible for the upsurge of dissent. At the same time, a new campaign was started against "bourgeois liberalization," seeking to discredit Western political concepts and emphasize the importance of Party control. The campaign became the way the conservatives sought to undermine Deng's reforms.

Edward Gargan, *New York Times*

Without any doubt, it marked a moment at which the brakes were being applied very strenuously to any drift toward political liberalization. It wasn't clear what the consequences were going to be for economic policy.

Dorinda Elliott, *Newsweek*

They launched this antibourgeois liberalization campaign. I decided to see how this was being received in a village. As a journalist this was no easy thing. You had to go through the Foreign Affairs Office of the province and then the township level. By the time I got to the village, I probably had twenty Party officials following me. I remember going into this farmer's house, trying to have a conversation with this farmer. Twenty government officials come into this house with me. The entire village is basically looking through the window. These farmers are totally terrified. They have no idea what's going on. I turn to this woman, and I say, "So tell me, what do you think about the bourgeois liberalization campaign?" She looks absolutely terrified, doesn't know what to say— and she says, "Well, the reason we are supposed to support bourgeois liberalization is because"—and you could see the official saying, "No, no, no—you're supposed to be opposing bourgeois liberalization." And I felt like, "oh my God, what have I done to this poor farmer?"

REFORM CONTINUES

Despite Hu Yaobang's ouster and the conservatives' growing clout, Deng was determined that economic reforms would continue. He nominated the pragmatic Zhao Ziyang to replace Hu as Party general secretary.

Edward Gargan, *New York Times*

Zhao was not only a reformist. He was the leader of the reformists. Deng may have set the overall course. Zhao Ziyang is the guy who did it. Zhao Ziyang is the guy who went out and did the reforms in the countryside.

Although Zhao was forced to share some authority with the conservative Li Peng, a Soviet-trained engineer who was named premier, economic and social liberalization continued. Moreover, Deng Xiaoping signaled that reform of the political system to make it more efficient and responsive was now also on the agenda.

Adi Ignatius, who was married to *Newsweek*'s Dorinda Elliott, arrived for the *Wall Street Journal* in early 1987.

Adi Ignatius, *Wall Street Journal*

From that period until June 4, 1989, there were two main themes. One was an economy that was in trouble. China had begun the first significant economic reforms. They were obviously leading to an opening up in the economy. They were also leading to problems a state-led economy had never really dealt with before, including price rises. You had that as one undercurrent. The other was a gradual liberalization on the political side, the social side. You had people really testing the limits in terms of free expression, in terms of calling for change. Those two currents were kind of interrelated, because as the government was obsessed with dealing with the economic challenges, I think there were people who saw that as an opening to then take some chances on the political side, knowing that the government was preoccupied.

In mid-1987, I opened the CNN Beijing bureau after nearly five years as a roving correspondent for the fledgling network based in London. I found the mood upbeat. Deng Xiaoping and the reformers appeared to have gained the upper hand and, at least on the surface, the political tensions of late 1986 and early 1987 seemed to have eased. There was a sense that the society was opening up, and state control over people's lives was easing. My crew and I did stories about the earliest discos, about foreign businesspeople coming to China, about a growing curiosity about connecting with the outside world.

My team consisted of soundman/editor Mitch Farkas, a Korean American whose father, Marvin, had been a cameraman in Asia since the 1950s, and camerawoman Cynde Strand. Cynde was an intrepid CNN veteran whom I had first worked with in Beirut during the height of the Lebanese civil war in 1983. Subsequently, she had traveled throughout the Middle East and Africa, and had just finished a year's leave studying Chinese in Nanjing.

Cynde Strand, CNN

One of the first stories we covered was the first-ever makeup exhibition in China. This was held in an exhibition center. The young women, mostly still then in pigtails and a lot of them in Mao suits, broke down the doors to get in, because they wanted a different kind of face. They wanted to experiment with makeup. They wanted to look pretty and wanted to have what people in the West had. It was amazing.

In October 1987, just as the first Kentucky Fried Chicken outlet was preparing to open in Beijing within view of Chairman Mao's mausoleum in Tiananmen Square, the government allowed NBC News to send anchor Tom Brokaw to the country for a week of live programming. The theme was "Changing China."

Tom Brokaw, NBC News

So things were changing. I would like to say I could see the scope of the change. But no one could have imagined it.

The highlight of NBC's broadcasts was an interview Brokaw was granted with Zhao Ziyang for NBC's Sunday talk show *Meet the Press*. It was the first time a Chinese leader had ever agreed to an interview with one of the hugely influential U.S. network Sunday morning shows. The new Party general secretary was blunt about his desire to accelerate change, telling Brokaw, "We will criticize those thinking which are conservative, ossified, and which do not favor reform in China."

Tom Brokaw, NBC News

In that interview, he was talking about how we have to provide economic opportunity for young people. It was not the theology of Maoism.

China scholar and journalist Orville Schell and his well-connected Chinese wife, Baifang, had helped NBC arrange the Zhao interview.

Orville Schell, *New Yorker*

He talked for an hour, totally unscripted. Not only did he talk for an hour, but he was drinking beer the whole time. He had a couple bottles of beer beside him.

Tom Brokaw, NBC News

When the camera would cut to me, they knew that. He would have a drink and they would replace it. I think he drank two quarts of beer during the interview. But he was very candid and not pandering to the American audience. I was very impressed with him. He had this quiet intellectual confidence and was very articulate.

Orville Schell, *New Yorker*

It was this moment you could see this belief that maybe China would join the world as we knew it, politically as well as economically.

TIBET ERUPTS

Yet at almost the same time, violent protests against Chinese rule broke out in Tibet.

Adi Ignatius, *Wall Street Journal*

Monks were protesting and rioting, and a lot of us got out there. We violated a very clear rule that we weren't supposed to go to Tibet without official permission. But there were loopholes in the system. We went to Chengdu in Sichuan and then got plane tickets to Lhasa from there. There were more than a dozen of us. We checked into the joint venture hotel, rented bicycles, and went out every day to the monasteries, and were able to witness what was going on and talk to the monks who were protesting.

Edward Gargan, *New York Times*

They tried to keep control of us, but we spread out very quickly throughout the city. We stayed—in those days, there was really one hotel where they could eavesdrop on us—called the Holiday Inn. We went out and interviewed monks

who were extremely unhappy. Monks had been shot. There were enormous pro-
tests by the Tibetans against Chinese occupation for several days.

Adi Ignatius's wife, Dorinda Elliott, was not among those who rushed to
Lhasa.

Dorinda Elliott, *Newsweek*

I'm sitting in Beijing and I'm the Newsweek *bureau chief and we get word on*
a Tuesday that the monks in Tibet are protesting. The reason this is important
for me is because I work for a weekly magazine, and the weekly cycle is the end
of the week, Saturday. Tuesday is very much towards the beginning the week.
I get in touch with my editors and say, "This is incredible. This is a big story.
I've got to go." They say, "Well, I don't know. It's early in the week. Let's see how
the story develops and we'll see." I have to say, with a tiny bit of bitterness, that
it was kind of like when we read about it in the New York Times *it becomes*
real, and they hadn't read about it in the New York Times *yet. They were hear-*
ing it from me instead. I sit there in Beijing. My husband is the Wall Street
Journal *bureau chief, and we have tons of friends who are journalists, and*
they're all jumping on planes going to Lhasa.

One of those who did make it to Tibet that week was Raymond Burghardt,
the political counselor at the U.S. embassy in Beijing, along with a colleague
from the American consulate in Chengdu.

Raymond Burghardt, State Department

At the airport, there were no hotel buses, so we had to take the regular bus,
which was a good break, because the regular bus first came into the center of
the city, and that's where everything was happening. We actually saw demon-
strators throwing rocks at the police. We didn't see any firing at that point, but
definitely a lot of rocks being thrown.

The continued trouble finally piqued the interest of Dorinda Elliot's bosses
at *Newsweek*.

Dorinda Elliott, *Newsweek*

They read about it in the New York Times, *and they start saying to me, "Oh*
my God, Dorinda, get yourself to Lhasa."

Meanwhile, as the protests continued, the Chinese authorities ordered the American reporters in Lhasa to leave.

Edward Gargan, *New York Times*

The Chinese brought in the military. Then they decided to throw all of us out so we wouldn't report on what they were going to do to the Tibetans.

Raymond Burghardt, State Department

There was a very memorable occasion in which the press was all summoned to a meeting. We said this was a consular issue, so we had to be there. We were able to witness them telling the press how wrong it was for them to be there because they hadn't followed the rules in terms of applying ten days ahead of time. It was a loud and contentious session. I remember speaking up on behalf of the press, without accomplishing a thing of course.

Meanwhile, Dorinda Elliott had made her way to Chengdu in Sichuan, where she bumped into the *Washington Post's* Dan Southerland, who was also trying to get to Lhasa.

Dorinda Elliott, *Newsweek*

I go to the China Travel Service office in Chengdu. It's a Thursday. They have just declared martial law in Tibet and have stopped selling tickets to Lhasa. I'm thinking, "Holy shit." I have to get to Lhasa. I'm standing at the window, and I see these two kind of hippies right in front of me, who've just gotten tickets to Lhasa, just before they stopped selling them. I said to them, "I'll pay you three times what you just paid for these tickets if you give them to me." And I swear to God, they said to each other, "Well, I guess we could go to Greece instead." So they went off to Greece. I get these two tickets, which mind you do not have my name on them, or Dan Southerland's name on them.

That night, the journalists being expelled from Lhasa were confined to the Holiday Inn.

Edward Gargan, *New York Times*

When you are confined to a hotel there is not much you can do except have a party. So I had a big party in my room. Ray Burghardt came. A guy who was in the consulate in Chengdu showed up, and the reporters. You opened the door down the hall and all along were scattered these Chinese plainclothes security guys.

Raymond Burghardt, State Department

I remember people had a good time that night. There was a lot of drinking and revelry, and something happened with Eddie Gargan.

Edward Gargan, New York Times

The security guys tried to come into the room. In those days, there was just yak to eat. We had yak snacks, and yak burgers, beer and whatever we could get our hands on at the Holiday Inn. These security guys tried to break into the room, and we pushed them out. I was regarded as having instigated the "unpleasant moment." I was taken away and interrogated for a couple of hours.

Raymond Burghardt, State Department

I was summoned by a high-ranking official of the Tibeta, so-called Autonomous Region, to a meeting in order to protest to me [as an American diplomat] the behavior of my citizen, Mr. Gargan. I took that on board—sort of—without giving any promises or anything.

The next morning, as the reporters waited at Lhasa Airport to leave, the plane from Chengdu with Dorinda Elliott and Dan Southerland on board arrived.

Dorinda Elliott, Newsweek

The tickets were for Friday morning at six AM. I didn't know how I was going to file. I was just going to get to Lhasa. At that point, we didn't realize that the journalists who were in Lhasa were being expelled. Dan and I go to the airport trying to look like hippy backpackers. The rest of the people getting on the plane are Chinese, and then there's us. I remember getting to the front of the line and this guy looks at passports, looks at the tickets upside-down. For some reason—I have no idea why—we got through and onto the plane. We arrive in Lhasa, and, literally, the journalists who have been expelled the night before are *getting on the same plane to leave. I could see the journalists across the tar-mac. Somebody had said to Dan and me, "Don't go to the Holiday Inn because you will be expelled immediately." So Dan and I found some hippies and went to a place called the Yak Hotel, where we shared a room. My memory was that it was two or three stories up. It had a hole in the floor and that was basically the toilet.*

Elliott spent one day in Lhasa interviewing dissident monks.

Dorinda Elliott, *Newsweek*

Dan and I get two bicycles and we ride out to the Drepung monastery. I don't know why we succeeded. The whole security apparatus must have been watch-ing us. It's so laughable, these two foreigners on bicycles, huffing and puffing trying to get to this monastery. We left our bikes halfway there, walked up to the back of the monastery, snuck in, and found a couple monks who spoke Man-darin. We stayed long enough till we got the story of what happened and how the police had come in. The roads were lined with Chinese security people. I don't know why or how we got through, but we did. We then went to the Jokhang Temple in the center of Lhasa and talked to some monks. Got back to our hotel. At this point I felt my head was going to explode because of altitude sickness. There was a flight out the next morning. So we were in Lhasa for one day and we flew to Chengdu and I managed to get the story to these jerks in New York who had said to me, "This story doesn't look that interesting," but then said, "Get yourself to Lhasa."

Shortly before the protests in Lhasa erupted, NBC's Tom Brokaw had been allowed to visit Tibet to do a piece to be aired during the network's China week.

Tom Brokaw, NBC News

I had taken into Tibet postcards of the Dalai Lama. They had said he has no standing here anymore. And I walk around counterclockwise—the pilgrims go clockwise—and I had a camera crew behind me, and I held up a postcard [of the Dalai Lama] in front of me and they would fall on their knees and [get] emotional and weep. They caught on to that quickly and we got thrown out.

Then Brokaw went to India to interview the Dalai Lama before returning to China for NBC's planned week of programming.

Tom Brokaw, NBC News

All hell broke loose. They said I had got it all wrong. I violated the arrangement, wasn't playing by the rules. Even after I got back to the U.S., I was called into the embassy in Washington. The ambassador's wife took my wife aside and said, "Tom got that all wrong." My wife said, "Have you been to Tibet?" The ambassador's wife said, "I never have." My wife said, "I was there with him. I don't think he got it wrong."

THE WIRE SERVICES

As many reporters managed to travel, despite all the obstacles, the American wire services—the Associated Press and United Press International—faced different pressures. Kathy Wilhem, who'd earned a journalism degree from Columbia and an MA in East Asian studies from Harvard, joined the AP Beijing bureau in 1987.

Kathy Wilhem, Associated Press

The AP itself made it difficult. There was a fear of leaving the Xinhua machine unattended. Oh my gosh. Are we going to actually unstaff the office and all go out and commit news and leave the Xinhua wire unattended? What if it comes up with the announcement that Deng Xiaoping has died? He did not actually die until '97. But the whole time I was there, there is the idea was to have had somebody in that office watching the Xinhua machine for news of Deng's death. So that made it hard to get out.

Scott Savitt, who had first come to China as a language student in 1983 at age nineteen, was a young reporter for United Press International.

Scott Savitt, United Press International

I lived in the UPI office. My apartment was in the office. I never left the UPI office. When you opened those offices, the first thing you do is pull the wires—so that's Xinhua, Reuters, and the UPI wire. And that was my job. Pull it off the old telex machine.

Terril Jones, whose mother was Chinese, was based in the AP's Tokyo bureau but spent much of his time in Beijing.

Terril Jones, Associated Press

The AP was kind of a vacuum cleaner for the news of the day, going through all the local papers, watching the evening newscast, and then writing up stories from these sources and ministry declarations that were not things that others might do on their own. But our work definitely appeared in a lot of other people's eventual stories. I think the AP was very much a general reference to a lot of the foreign reporters. I know a lot of reporters would call up and say, "Are you translating that People's Daily editorial thing, because we don't have the staff," or "I can't get to it," and they'd want to wait for our story.

Daniel Southerland, *Washington Post*

I had a couple of friends who worked for the wires, and fortunately I would keep in touch with them, because they were often getting stuff that we couldn't get right away. They were sort of the frontline troops slogging it out.

THE THIRTEENTH PARTY CONGRESS

From October 25 to November 1, 1987, the Chinese Communist Party held its thirteenth Party Congress. For the first time, some of the proceedings were open to the foreign press. It was a dramatic sign of how much had changed since my first visit to China, In August 1973, I had been in Beijing with my student group during the tenth Party Congress. No one even knew it had taken place until a communiqué was released at its conclusion. This time, a foreign press center was set up, regular media briefings were held, and journalists were allowed into the Great Hall of the People to witness the opening and closing ceremonies and other key moments.

After the political upheavals earlier in the year, the reformers now appeared to have the upper hand. Half the members of the old Politburo, including Deng Xiaoping and a number of prominent conservatives, announced their retirement. Hu Yaobang, despite his ouster as Party general secretary in January, retained his Politburo seat.

Kathy Wilhelm, Associated Press

It was huge because Deng resigned from his official positions. He stepped back. It was the first peaceful transition since Hua Guofeng, by which Deng's faction came to power. This was a big change for Chinese politics.

Deng did retain his position as head of the Central Military Commission, which controlled the Chinese armed forces, and it was evident he remained the country's paramount leader. But Zhao Ziyang appeared to be setting a clear course for accelerated change.

Kathy Wilhelm, Associated Press

In Zhao's work report, he had called for political reforms to match the economic reforms. It was a huge boost to reform, and it came against the backdrop the prior winter of them having put down—obviously not so violently—student protests and calls for reforms. It flipped people's perceptions of where China was going.

Telling the nearly two thousand delegates that China was still in the "primary stage of socialism," Zhao broke sharply with Party ideologues by declaring that virtually any economic policies were acceptable if they spurred modernization. He pledged to minimize Party interference in government and called for greater "consultation and dialogue" between the government and the people. While details remained sketchy, Zhao's effort to carve a fresh path was clear, highlighted by his extraordinary exchange with foreign reporters at the end of the Congress.

Jaime FlorCruz, *Time*

The press conference when he became the Party chief was memorable. He came out and walked around this table lined with snacks, and we on the other side of the table pushed our mics in front. He walked very slowly and answered probably a dozen questions from the Chinese and foreign press corps. It was quite a break from the past.

Wearing a stylish, double-breasted pin-stripe suit, Zhao took numerous questions, none of them vetted in advance. With Tibet having recently been in the headlines, I asked him about the extremely sensitive subject of human rights. He stuck to the party line, denouncing American critics of Chinese policy there, but it was fascinating to observe the kind of give-and-take that is normal for Western politicians, but almost never seen with top Chinese leaders.

Adi Ignatius, *Wall Street Journal*

A lot of us were struck by how different this felt. We knew a little bit about Zhao and his reputation as a relative liberal, as an economic reformer, but here he was with this kind of ease in this international spotlight. It was hard not to think, based on these atmospherics, that maybe this was a new group that was in place to change China significantly.

1988: THE MOST OPEN YEAR

In 1988, John Pomfret, who had majored in East Asian studies at Stanford and, in 1980, become one of the first Americans to study in China, attending Nanjing University, joined the Beijing bureau of the Associated Press.

John Pomfret, Associated Press

1988 was an incredibly exciting time. You had the first nude art exhibition at the Central Academy of Fine Arts. There is this sense of unlimited possibility. There were a series of bizarre events. Pretty much every week, something would just happen. The Chinese would call them a shi—just a "thing" would happen, There's this palpable feeling that some type of change was going to happen very quickly.

Daniel Southerland, *Washington Post*

'88 was the most open year—really exciting. I did stories on art and music and things changing. People talking about sex more than they ever were able to before. People trying out jobs. Experiments going on. And some opening in the media.

Cynde Strand, CNN

They didn't want to do art in the traditional ways. They didn't want to do the giant mountains with the fog and the pagodas and the temples. They wanted to do a funny picture of Chairman Mao like Andy Warhol would have done. The West was coming in in art and music, and it was just a whole different thing that was going on. This was a different kind of generation. They're curious about art and music and sexuality and they don't want to be denied.

Adi Ignatius, *Wall Street Journal*

An art exhibition took place that to me summed up everything that was happening, which was basically that people felt like they could do stuff they could never do before. The government gave permission for these wacky young artists to take over one of the primary art galleries in the capital, and have this insane display of new, provocative, politically challenging and weird performance art. The police knew it was a potentially weird scene, but it was happening. I remember some of this art became really popular, showing Mao in Warhol-esque ways. There was performance art, and on the second day, there was a telephone booth with a mirror in it. A young Chinese artist, who I think herself was the daughter of a Chinese official, her performance art was to take out a gun, an actual pistol, and shoot the mirror inside, shattering the thing. It was wild.

In this fevered atmosphere, Bette Bao Lord, the Chinese-born wife of U.S. Ambassador Winston Lord and a successful novelist, became an important link between the American journalists and China's increasingly disaffected artists and intellectuals.

Winston Lord, U.S. Ambassador

There was more discussion of reform and opening, and we did a lot of that at our embassy, particularly my wife, who had great access as a writer to the cultural and academic and reform communities.

Daniel Southerland, *Washington Post*

Bette Bao Lord was very helpful because she had this sort of salon where she was inviting writers and artists to come in. Through her I met a number of really top-notch intellectuals and artists.

Dorinda Elliott, *Newsweek*

I give the Lords a lot of credit for the way in which they were connected and kind of had their finger on the pulse of what was going. Especially Bette Lord. She knew these artists and intellectuals. They would have these events at the embassy. She was a connector. She would go out of the way, if she liked you, to introduce you to interesting Chinese intellectuals. That's a pretty amazing thing for an ambassador's wife to do.

United Press International's Scott Savitt had a special connection with the Lords.

Scott Savitt, United Press International

My girlfriend Dede Huang was Bette Lord's secretary. I played tennis with Ambassador Lord and Mrs. Lord pretty much every day. Those were my sources of information. We got treated like their children. We hung out at their residence. It was a salon. They would have everyone from Minister of Culture Ying Ruocheng to Cao Yu the playwright. I attended all of them.

In the summer of 1988, China Central television aired a six-part documentary called *River Elegy*. Written and produced by six young intellectuals, the series argued that China had to replace its stifling, inward-looking culture—symbolized by the slow-moving waters of the Yellow River, long a symbol of China's ancient civilization—with one open to science, democracy, free markets, and the outside world. The provocative critique of China's isolation and backwardness, and, although unspoken, the role of the Communist Party, created a sensation. Nearly two hundred million people watched the program, which was endorsed by Zhao Ziyang and the reformers but sharply criticized by Party conservatives, although the behind-the-scenes politics were much less clear at the time.

Dorinda Elliott, *Newsweek*

Suddenly everybody was talking about it. It was basically this group of cutting-edge, almost underground intellectuals, led by a guy named Su Xiaokang, who studied Chinese culture and Chinese civilization and determined that it was all based on feudalism. The Communist Party was an extension of what had been a very feudal society, and essentially needed to be smashed, to be broken open, and the solutions are in the West. We need to basically follow what they're doing in the West, what we had before in China is garbage and needs to be thrown away. Obviously, this was dynamite. It was incredibly amazing that it was shown on Chinese television. That was a sign of something. We journalists couldn't figure out what it meant, which faction or who had it appear on Chinese television.

The controversy over *River Elegy* erupted at a time when discontent over the state of the economy was growing, triggered by moves to eliminate long-standing price controls, which set off panic buying and bank runs.

Adi Ignatius, *Wall Street Journal*

As the economy started to go sour, that was something you could report. You could go to stores, you could see the prices, you could talk to people who were shopping, and they were willing to talk to you in a straightforward way about how they felt and what was happening in the economy. On that level you could get relatively straightforward information. What you couldn't really under-stand was the debate happening behind the scenes.

In late 1988, Nicholas Kristof, who had studied government at Harvard and then obtained a law degree, arrived to take over the *New York Times* bureau. He was accompanied by his wife, Sheryl WuDunn, a third-generation Chinese American and the first Asian American reporter hired by the *Times*.

Nicholas Kristof, *New York Times*

I had a great interest in Africa and had studied Arabic, so you know there was always this expectation that the New York Times *was going to send me to either West Africa because I had French or to the Arab world because I had Arabic. So I got a call out of the blue asking if I wanted to study Chinese and go to China.*

Sheryl WuDunn, *New York Times*

For me, partly because I am Chinese American, going to China was a real adventure. It was very easy for us to meet lots of people. We were extremely lucky. There really were no restrictions at the time. Things were very open, and we met people in all walks of life.

Nicholas Kristof, *New York Times*

Sheryl and I both tried to spend a lot of time with ordinary Chinese. We had a lot of Chinese friends. We spent a lot of time trying to talk to people about larger social issues, about attitudes. We were there really at a golden time, because before Tiananmen, you could have a lot of really good contacts with elite people. We had a period where we could really build these connections. And because Sheryl was Chinese American, there was some sense that she was kind of a "friend of the country" and that people could get away with being our friends where they would not have been able to do that if we were just two Caucasians.

Meanwhile, social and economic tension mounted, intensifying the struggle between Party reformers and conservatives. Although expelled from the Communist Party, Fang Lizhi continued to speak out for reform, and became a favorite of many journalists.

Nicholas Kristof, *New York Times*

We knew Fang Lizhi. He was one of the first people we met. I liked him a lot, so we wrote about that extensively.

Adi Ignatius, *Wall St. Journal*

I adored Fang Lizhi. He came out of this tradition of physicists and astrophysicists who just saw the world with certain clarity and felt empowered as individuals to speak the truth. I thought he was amazing, and he obviously helped inspire students at various universities to test the limits.

As 1988 drew to a close, Dorinda Elliott and Adi Ignatius organized a big Christmas party.

Dorinda Elliott, *Newsweek*

We lived in this foreign compound where Chinese who came to visit had to pass through guards. It was for a lot of Chinese a pretty scary experience. The guards often would take their names and ask who they were. We were astounded that all these Chinese friends and contacts came. Most exciting was that Fang Lizhi and his wife, Li Shuxian, came.

Adi Ignatius, *Wall Street Journal*

We had avant-garde artists, we had Fang Lizhi, all singing Christmas carols. Honestly, 1988 was probably the best year of my and my wife's professional life because there was so much sense of hope, so much of a sense that China's future direction was really up for grabs in profound ways, and that everything was on the table in terms of economic direction, in terms of political direction.

Dorinda Elliott, *Newsweek*

The whole crowd started singing Christmas carols, these Chinese and Westerners. It sort of touched on this moment where everything was possible and everything was doable, and everything was optimistic.

The bloody crackdown in Tiananmen Square was just six months away.

9

BEIJING SPRING

In early February 1989, China and the Soviet Union announced that Soviet president Mikhail Gorbachev, the architect of controversial political and economic reforms at home and more benign Soviet behavior internationally, would visit Beijing from May 15 to May 18 for a summit meeting with Deng Xiaoping. The summit would end animosity between the world's two Communist giants dating back more than three decades, and, which, in the late 1960s, brought them to the brink of war. For Deng, having orchestrated the normalization of relations with the United States, it would be the crowning diplomatic achievement of his career, marking the emergence of China as a major actor on the world stage, no longer a card to be played in superpower diplomacy but a force in its own right. For journalists in Beijing, it promised to be the biggest China story in years

Later in February, the new American president, George Bush, who had served as head of the U.S. diplomatic mission in China in the 1970s, visited Beijing. For Bush, the idea was to consolidate ties with Deng, whom the American president considered an old friend.

Winston Lord, U.S. Ambassador

A new president was returning to where he'd been Liaison Office chief. It was going to be a very friendly reception. People now forget that in the late eighties, we were selling considerable arms to China. We'd cooperated with them to

send arms for the Mujahedeen in Afghanistan to use against the Russians. We had secret radar installations along the Sino-Soviet border that we jointly operated, and which I visited, to spy on the Russians. This was a high-water mark where we were expanding our relations. Bush would for the first time for a U.S. president go on live national television to talk to the Chinese people. We had the Chinese agree to a photo op in Tiananmen Square, where the crowds would rush out and he would say hello. We also had the challenge of—you can't avoid the human rights issue. We debated how to do this, both to send signals to the Chinese and to reformers in China, but also to the American audience and Congress and human rights groups. We didn't want to expose the president to doing nothing, although we didn't feel that that should dominate the trip.

When Bush's predecessor, Ronald Reagan, had visited the Soviet Union in 1988, he'd met with Soviet dissidents and human rights activists at the residence of the U.S. ambassador in Moscow. For China, Lord's solution was to invite dissident scientist Fang Lizhi to a banquet Bush would host for hundreds of Chinese dignitaries at the Great Wall Sheraton Hotel.

Winston Lord, U.S. Ambassador

We were asked by the White House to put together an invitation list, about five hundred people. The overwhelming majority were Chinese government and political figures, but we figured this would be a chance to invite a few reformers as a gesture—safe political reformers and academics, one of whom was Fang Lizhi and his wife. We knew he was controversial, but he was also a renowned astrophysicist and was still technically working for the Chinese government. In terms of face, we put him on the list as an astrophysicist. We figured Bush had to do something, but this would not be controversial. We sent the list into Washington for clearance. We highlighted that this guy could cause controversy, but for the reasons I've mentioned we should do it. The State Department and the White House approved the list.

The move infuriated the Chinese authorities.

Winston Lord, U.S. Ambassador

Just before the president arrives, the Chinese start complaining, and then they say their leaders wouldn't attend the banquet if Fang Lizhi was there. Finally, to save face, the Chinese agreed to attend the banquet as long as Fang was not at the head table, and he didn't have a press conference.

But the Chinese authorities went back on their word. En route to the Great Wall Sheraton Hotel, Chinese police stopped Fang's car and prevented him from reaching the banquet. It was the ugliest moment in nearly two decades of American presidential visits.

Dorinda Elliott, *Newsweek*

I heard that Fang was going to have a press conference. He appears and there are tons of undercover police. And Fang just came out and told what happened.

Adi Ignatius, *Wall Street Journal*

Chinese officialdom's stated goal was that Fang was not going to be at that dinner, and they succeeded. They did not succeed in keeping this out of the world spotlight, though, because suddenly it became this big issue. It blew up in ways that I think are typical of how Chinese officials handle things. They did so with such a heavy hand in terms of the PR effect and world opinion that it always seemed to backfire.

James Baker, a Texan who had been Bush's lawyer and close friend for decades, was now secretary of state.

James Baker, Secretary of State

The president wasn't happy about it because it was the first trip, and that incident overshadowed the trip, as far as the press was concerned. He was not the least bit happy about it. There was a big kerfuffle internally about how Fang Lizhi got on the guest list.

Instead of blaming the Chinese, however, Bush's national security advisor, Brent Scowcroft, hoping to smooth relations with Beijing, held a background briefing for reporters from the *New York Times* and *Washington Post* and—identified only as a "senior administration official"—blamed Winston Lord.

Winston Lord, U.S. Ambassador

Scowcroft gives a backgrounder which basically says the president's trip was screwed up because the embassy invited this guy, didn't check it with us, and now we've had a disaster. To have your own White House blame you instead of the Chinese was one of the more frustrating episodes in my life. I sent a secret message to Scowcroft and said, "You look very weak to the Chinese. They behaved outrageously and you're blaming your own team. This is not a good signal for a new president to send to China in how tough you're going to be in dealing with them. You discouraged the other reformers in China by backing down from the one human rights gesture you were making. And you've totally destroyed my credibility. I can't be effective here."

In less than two months, Lord would be out as U.S. ambassador, to be replaced by James Lilley, a longtime CIA China specialist who'd served as CIA station chief at the U.S. Liaison Office in Beijing when Bush was the American envoy there. But Beijing's heavy-handed treatment of Fang underscored the nervousness of China's leaders.

Dorinda Elliott, *Newsweek*

We sort of realized, wow, China doesn't care whether this is going to create a story in the States. We learned that there are people in the Party who will say "enough is enough" and that we will not let this happen even though it will be internationally embarrassing. And that was a moment that was important.

THE FUSE IS LIT

The Chinese leadership had good reason to be nervous. Even before the Bush visit, at the beginning of the year, Fang Lizhi had written an open letter to Deng Xiaoping calling for the release of political prisoners. And he had become the inspiration for what became known as "democracy salons," which were being held on college campuses that winter.

Dorinda Elliott, *Newsweek*

I remember going to a couple of these salons. It might have been a hundred people in the room, and those intellectuals in the front. They would be talking about political change and economic reform. It was too much. The Party hard-liners, they weren't going to stand for this anymore, and you knew that.

Scott Savitt, United Press International

I remember Fang Lizhi said it in front of me, "Shei dou bu pa shei"—Nobody is afraid of anyone. And you know that the fuse is lit.

THE DEATH OF HU YAOBANG

On April 15, Hu Yaobang, who, although ousted as Party chief in 1987, had remained a Politburo member, died after suffering a heart attack a week earlier at a heated Politburo meeting. United Press International's Scott Savitt, whose girlfriend was the secretary to Bette Lord, got the first tipoff and told his boss, bureau chief Dave Schweisberg.

Scott Savitt, United Press International

I got a call from Dede. That's how I knew. Dave knew that my source of this information was the U.S. ambassador. Nobody else knew. It was coming directly from the highest source at the Embassy.

Schweisberg, a Long Island native and Boston University graduate, had worked for United Press International since 1979. Bearded, chain-smoking, hard drinking, he was one of the most colorful members of the Beijing press corps, but his contacts, understanding of China, and reporting skills were widely respected.

Scott Savitt, United Press International

Dave—he liked to have a drink, definitely. But if a story ever happened, I would watch him come in. He wouldn't have passed a Breathalyzer test, and he could sit down and bang out a one-thousand-word story that was just crystal-clear prose. I've never seen that before or since.

Based on Savitt's information, Schweisberg filed the first report about Hu Yaobang's death. Over that weekend, wall posters went up on campuses to mourn the passing of the former Party chief, who, to many students, had become a symbol of efforts to liberalize the Communist Party and Chinese society.

Nicholas Kristof, *New York Times*

It was already clear way before Hu Yaobang died that there were major ten-sions between Li Peng and Zhao Ziyang. I think the students were aware of that. That was one reason why they protested. They took advantage of this paralysis that arose from the leadership split. One of our best Chinese friends was at Peking University. That friend called after Hu's death had been announced and said that there are a few Dazibao *[big character posters] going up at Beida* [Peking University]. *We drove over and there were just a tiny number of peo-ple there. We didn't have any inclination that it was going to grow the way it did.*

On the night of Monday, April 17, several thousand students marched to Tiananmen Square, calling on Party leaders to follow Hu's more liberal exam-ple. I learned about the march when Dave Schweisberg of United Press International called me at 2 AM. He had become one of my closest friends. We had created a kind of informal alliance between United Press Interna-tional and CNN—both underfunded, struggling, underdog news organiza-tions, and helped each other wherever we could. I immediately woke up cam-erawoman Cynde Strand and soundman Mitch Farkas. We grabbed our equipment and headed off to Tiananmen.

Chanting *"Hu Yaobang wansui"* (Long Live Hu Yaobang), *"Minzhu wan-sui"* (Long live democracy), and *"Ziyou wansui"* (long live freedom), the crowd, several thousand strong, surged into the square. A dozen students car-ried a huge white banner with three black characters in a tribute to Hu: THE SOUL OF CHINA. While the crowd sang the communist anthem, *The Inter-nationale*, the students draped the banner on the Monument to the Heroes of the Revolution in the center of the square. It was the moment when mourn-ing turned into overt political protest.

Cynde Strand, CNN

They were putting up wreaths and banners. It was quite clever because they were mourning Hu Yaobang and using that legitimate mourning to start pro-testing for more freedom and democracy.

Back at the bureau, I called CNN headquarters in Atlanta, told them we had an amazing story, and begged them to book a satellite feed. In 1989, a ten-minute satellite feed cost about $2,000, and CNN hated to book a unilateral feed, preferring to join other networks so that the cost could be shared. But I convinced them this was an important enough story to merit a unilateral feed. It became the first piece to air on American television about the protests in Beijing that spring. But for all our excitement I was already worrying about how it might play out. Indeed, at the end of my report, I did on on-camera stand-up asking the question "How much longer will the government wait before moving to crush this challenge to its authority?"

PREPARING FOR GORBACHEV

But at CNN and the headquarters of other U.S. news organizations, the focus was not on Tiananmen Square. It was on the impending China visit of Soviet leader Gorbachev. Bernard Shaw, who had spent almost a decade as a correspondent for ABC News before joining CNN the year it began broadcasting, anchored CNN's primetime newscast.

Bernard Shaw, CNN

These two great powers in the communist world finally deciding to meet in Beijing and settle this decades-long dispute. Very historic. And because CNN was a global network on the air twenty-four hours a day, seven days a week, we had to be there. So the planning started months before this summit. CNN did not have a lot of money in those days, but we knew it would take a lot of money and a lot of personnel.

Alec Miran was a senior producer for CNN's Special Events unit. For years he had handled presidential debates, summits, and other major live events.

Alec Miran, CNN

We had this audacious idea. I talked to Mike Chinoy and said, "We'd like to bring in our own satellite dish. We want to broadcast from the Gate of Heavenly Peace," which overlooks Tiananmen Square, which to my knowledge had never been done live. An engineer and I went [to Beijing]. Mike had set up meetings with the Foreign Ministry and we said, "Please, we would like to transmit." And we will show live coverage of the crowd to see Mikhail Gorbachev.

We laid it out for them. You could see this gentleman's face and he asked thought, "This is that big a story for you?" We said, "Yes. It is an important

moment for China. It's an important moment for Russia. It's an impor-
tant moment for the world." That's when we also made the request for the
microwave transmitter. We thought that was rather audacious—bring a little
microwave transmitter, a unit that is not very much bigger than a book, which
would transmit our signal of Mike and Bernie Shaw, our anchor, back to our
Beijing headquarters.

To CNN's surprise, the Chinese agreed to let them bring in the dish, or
flyaway, as well as microwave links, but insisted the dish be set up at the Great
Wall Sheraton Hotel, five miles from Tiananmen. But the Chinese authorities seemed less concerned about the media logistics than they were with the
steadily intensifying protests in the streets.

MOURNING AND PROTEST

Saturday, April 22, was the state funeral for Hu Yaobang. As Deng Xiaoping
and other top Party officials gathered in the Great Hall of the People, outside
in Tiananmen Square, tens of thousands of students held their own memorial, laying wreaths at the foot of the Monument to the Heroes of the Revolution and singing China's national anthem. Although blocked from the steps
of the Great Hall by columns of police, the protestors remained peaceful,
shouting, "We demand dialogue" and "Li Peng come out," as they watched a
long line of elderly officials shuffling into the hall for the official ceremony.

Adi Ignatius, *Wall Street Journal*

Given what had happened in 1976 when Zhou Enlai had died, we should have
realized that this might not be a one-off, that something important may be
happening. Given the general sense of testing the limits that we'd seen since
'88, I remember having a feeling this might be something that had staying
power.

The authorities had the same concern. On April 26, the *People's Daily* carried a strongly worded editorial denouncing the protests as "counterrevolutionary turmoil" intended to "plunge the entire country into chaos." The next
day, the students responded by defying the authorities and marching ten
miles, from Peking University all the way to Tiananmen Square. For the first
time, significant numbers of nonstudents joined the protest, and many Beijing residents lined the streets to offer encouragement, food, and drink.

Nicholas Kristof, *New York Times*

April 27 was my thirtieth birthday. A small number of students came out of Beida and began marching, and all these other students came in and we walked all the way to Tiananmen Square, and it was an extraordinary sight. And the fact that it was my thirtieth birthday—wow, what a party!

John Pomfret, Associated Press

The sense of freedom you had being amongst people—it was intoxicating.

Adi Ignatius, *Wall Street Journal*

My wife, Newsweek correspondent Dorinda Elliott, was eight months pregnant, but so devoted to this story. She was marching all the way with the students. Chinese citizens were locking their arms around her to help her push through the crowd safely, and there were mothers who were saying to us, "Thank you for being here, for bearing witness to this." I remember being on the front lines of that, and just being so moved and surprised and shocked and secretly thrilled at what I was seeing. It was a moment that you felt all of Beijing was out there in solidarity. And I was thrilled that foreign correspondents were there so the world could see what was happening.

Dorinda Elliott, *Newsweek*

There was this feeling of optimism. Like for the first time you felt nothing can go wrong. And we just basically figured, well, if they believe that this is OK, it must mean that change is really underway.

Two days before arriving in Beijing as the new U.S. ambassador in early May, former CIA officer James Lilley met in Washington with Winston Lord.

James Lilley, U.S. Ambassador

We were having dinner together. On the TV screen were those demonstrations in Tiananmen Square. I said to Win, "Is this for real? This is not being manipulated, is it?" And Winston said, "Yes, it is for real. This is a genuine populist movement. You must pay attention to this."

Two days before Gorbachev's scheduled arrival on May 15, the students dramatically escalated their protest by starting a hunger strike in the square. Initially only a few hundred, their ranks quickly swelled to nearly three thousand. In a country where food was an obsession, where many people were old enough to remember when millions starved to death, and where a common greeting was "Have you eaten?," the hunger strike stirred powerful emotions and generated enormous public sympathy.

Terril Jones, a Chinese speaker based in Tokyo, joined his colleagues at the Associated Press.

Terril Jones, Associated Press

On May 13 the students began a hunger strike, which I remember was met by some exasperation in the bureau because it was something else we have to find out what's going on and spend time on.

Jones was one of many journalists not based in Beijing who'd been given a visa by the Chinese to cover the Gorbachev visit—including scores of people for the networks.

John Sheahan, CBS News

You apply officially to bring in all manner of equipment and people for this event. We wound up with fifty-seven people from outside China, with several camera crews, multiple correspondents, producers, editors, everything you would want.

GORBACHEV ARRIVES

Despite the protests, CNN received permission from the government to do live broadcasts from the rostrum of the Gate of Heavenly Peace. It had a spectacular view of Tiananmen and was a perfect vantage point for covering Gorbachev's arrival ceremony on Monday, May 15. The network's engineers set up a microwave link on the rostrum to beam a signal to the dish set up in the garden of the Great Wall Sheraton Hotel, from where it was beamed via satellite to the United States. But what CNN Moscow correspondent Steve

Hurst and I—and millions of CNN viewers around the world—saw that morning was that the students had literally occupied the stage where Chinese leaders were to welcome Gorbachev.

Alec Miran, CNN

We had these amazing reports showing Mike. Behind him was Tiananmen Square and on the edge of Tiananmen was the Great Hall of People. And suddenly Gorbachev was not there. We waited and waited. Finally, there was word that they were canceling the arrival ceremony. Mike said: "Oh my God, this is a tremendous loss of face for the Chinese." Our Russian Bureau chief, Steve Hurst, said, "This is unprecedented that the Russians and the Chinese have been outmaneuvered by the students."

Jim Laurie, who'd opened the ABC News Beijing bureau in the early eighties, was now based in Moscow, and had returned to China for the Gorbachev visit.

Jim Laurie, ABC News

They couldn't use the area just outside of the Great Hall of the People for official events. That was the place where they would greet their state visitors. They did it at the airport and had to bring Gorbachev in through a back door of the Great Hall of the People. It struck us at the time as quite a humiliation for the Chinese leadership.

The embarrassment was compounded by the fact that it was all being broadcast live.

Dan Rather, CBS

This spoke to the rapid changes in technology. In 1989 you could do what you could not do in 1979. You could take your whole evening news broadcast and get up from anywhere in the world at any hour of the day or night. We were broadcasting live not just for our evening news broadcast. We were taking up large chunks of airtime during the day. It was almost unthinkable.

On the day after Gorbachev's arrival, my CNN colleagues and I arrived to continue our live broadcasts from the rostrum, only to find that the Chinese authorities had rescinded permission.

Alec Miran, CNN

They were telling us—no more Gate of Heavenly Peace. We said we have to keep a presence there. This is some of the most compelling video any of us had ever seen. So we established a spot at the edge of Tiananmen Square.

A CNN engineer figured out that a microwave link in the square could send a signal to China Central Television, which would then relay it across Beijing to the dish in the CNN workspace at the Great Wall Sheraton Hotel. From there, it was sent up to the satellite, down to CNN headquarters in Atlanta, and put on the air. Somehow, the process worked. Interestingly, the engineers at CCTV made no attempt to interfere. It was clear they, like so many other ordinary Chinese, sympathized with the protestors.

Cynde Strand, CNN

We were live from the square. For us, as a journalist, it doesn't get any better. I mean, you're live from Tiananmen Square! These days, you can be live with an iPhone anywhere. But that was an extraordinary moment.

THE END OF THE DYNASTY?

In the following days, the number of protestors swelled, sometimes to more than a million, inspired in part by Gorbachev's efforts to change the Soviet Union.

Jim Laurie, ABC News

Most of the interviews I had dealt with the positive feelings they had towards Gorbachev the reformer—and we need a generation of reformers in China.

Longtime China scholar Orville Schell was also in Beijing.

Orville Schell, *New Yorker*

Tiananmen Square was like a great sound stage. Any journalist could go down to Tiananmen Square and there was a cast of thousands ready to perform for them. There were fabulous stories. It just went on and on and on. It was like a serial on television that never stops. And reaffirming the narrative of the

American version of history—that everybody wants to become more like us. It was very seductive.

Alec Miran, CNN

There's always the question of whether American audiences had an appetite for international news. This proved that we did. The feedback from people around the United States and the world was "Give us more. These are amazing pictures. These are amazing stories." You know, every time Mike Chinoy would come on the air, it seemed that he had some new tidbit that was just fascinating. It was a tremendously liberating time for the Chinese people. The American audience was flabbergasted, as we all were.

It wasn't just American audiences. The Voice of America's coverage was making independent news of the protests available to Chinese audiences. Al Pessin had served multiple VOA foreign assignments before becoming the correspondent in Beijing.

Al Pessin, Voice of America

The impact that foreign broadcasters had during that time was really incredible. Shortwave radio was still in its heyday when you're talking about its impact on a closed society like China. It was a very big deal. People would transcribe our Chinese newscasts by hand and copy them on mimeograph machines and post them on telephone poles around the city.

Like CNN, other news organizations were now staffing Tiananmen Square twenty-four hours a day.

Cynde Strand, CNN

The feeling was a little Woodstock at first. These kids are misbehaving for the first time in their lives. Imagine that feeling, to suddenly express yourself in that way. They had a printing press and a medical clinic, and they had people bringing in food. It was like a city within Tiananmen Square.

Terril Jones, Associated Press

It was a twenty-four-hour party scene early on. There were people with guitars, and people awake at all hours. Even on an overnight shift, it was still buzzing—just an incredible sense of something is happening, and we don't know what the outcome is, but the outcome is probably going to be positive, probably going to be good because there weren't riot police coming in.

With fewer staff and resources, United Press International, which was already in financial trouble, fought to keep up with the competition.

Scott Savitt, United Press International

UPI at that point was very beleaguered. Our competition was AP, Reuters, AFP [Agence France Press]. They were all much better resourced, but Dave evened the competition.

Cynde Strand, CNN

Oh my God, Dave, Dave. He was funny and cynical, and he loved China and he hated China and he used his humor to get him over those humps of the frustrations of covering China. Always curious, always wanted to be in the middle of it.

By this point, CNN and UPI were basically operating as one organization. Schweisberg and I both felt like underdogs—CNN was competing with the big three networks, and UPI with the other wire services. We shared everything and helped each other however we could, meeting or speaking several times a day, and trading insights from our respective sources.

ON THE SIDE OF THE PROTESTORS?

Reporters worked hard to develop relationships with the student leaders. For the AP's John Pomfret, this led to a decision to take one of them, Beijing Normal University student Wu'er Kaixi, to dinner at the height of the hunger strike—and not report about it.

John Pomfret, Associated Press

He took a page right out of the U.S. news media by saying, "Can we go off the record?" I would say, "Yes." He would say, "Well, I'm kind of hungry, so can we go get noodles?" It was interesting that he grasped that idea. It was one of these funny moments. What do you do? Do you write that "Wu'er Kaixi breaks hunger strike and goes to get noodles with beer"? My decision was not to write about it, because I felt this guy was a very useful source, and he turned out to be a good source. You have to protect him, and so I did. Later on, there were people who criticized me for doing that, but in the heat of the moment, I feel I did the right thing.

This was just one illustration of the degree to which many reporters openly sympathized with the students.

Terril Jones, Associated Press

The media were on the side of the protesters. It just seemed that there couldn't be a bad, and certainly not a tragic, end to what was happening. There was definitely a sense of exhilaration on the part of the protesters who were there on the square, the citizens of Beijing who came to see what the fuss was about, and the media.

Adi Ignatius, *Wall Street Journal*

To see the idealism, to see the bravery, to see the kind of raw excitement, it was, to be honest, very hard not to get wrapped up in that.

The pressure of deadlines, space limitations, and audiences unfamiliar with China also led many journalists to oversimplify what the students were demanding.

Nicholas Kristof, *New York Times*

It was definitely complicated. People were motivated by many different things. Some of it was economic. There was a lot of resentment of corruption. Often our shorthand was "prodemocracy" protests. We did try to regularly explain what that was shorthand for, and I'm not sure how good a job we did at that.

Dan Southerland, *Washington Post*

The students were concerned about corruption, accountability, freedom of speech and press, expos[ing] the wealth of the government and Party officials. They wanted to be recognized as patriotic, a legitimate opposition movement. We probably had a tendency to make it sound too much like a made-in-America kind of democratic movement.

Adi Ignatius, *Wall Street Journal*

But that doesn't invalidate this as a popular movement for reform. Maybe "democracy" is an easy catchall. Maybe that confuses Western-style democracy or U.S.-led democracy. But it was clearly a movement that was driven by some really powerful sense of the injustices in society. It was a popular protest against a government that was not even remotely responsive to the people, against a government that wouldn't share authority and that was totalitarian.

Bernard Shaw, CNN

I think what people have to remember is that these protesters didn't have concepts of Jeffersonian democracy in mind. What they wanted was, first, respect. They wanted freedom of expression. They wanted to be able to trust their newspapers and other media. They wanted an end to corruption. And when you think about their pleas, which were officially put into formal demands, what they wanted threatened the power structure, the Communist Party, and that's what the elders would not tolerate.

James Lilley, U.S. Ambassador

The media coverage of the students, of the hunger strike, of the demands they were making, which all seemed so reasonable to us, were played up in the press. This word was getting out, and the students looked good. They looked pure. There was a perception in Washington until right before it happened that it wasn't going to be nasty. People were looking through rose-colored glasses about the capability of the Chinese Communist Party and the army to crush these people.

Even some seasoned China watchers were swept away by the euphoria.

Orville Schell, *New Yorker*

It was very difficult not to believe it's over. The system is going to change. It wasn't just us. I think most Chinese had that sense that maybe we have come to the end of this dynasty. The Western media coverage of 1989 conveyed a sense that we were already predisposed to follow—Chinese history heading in the direction of greater openness and democracy. Reaffirming the narrative of

the American version of history that everybody wants to be more like us. It
was very seductive. I think I was very much a prisoner of the Western view—
even among those of us who had spent a lot of time in China, our naïvete
about understanding that things don't change that quickly.

"NO GOOD OUTCOME"

But not everyone shared the optimism. Melinda Liu, who'd opened the *News-*
week Beijing bureau nearly a decade before, flew in to replace Dorinda
Elliott, who had gone to Hong Kong to have her baby.

Melinda Liu, *Newsweek*

I had been in Rangoon in 1988, where there was also this outpouring of student-
led demonstrations and then this really bloody crackdown. I was convinced
pretty early on that there was going to be a bad ending to this.

Dan Southerland, *Washington Post*

I thought it might end badly, but I didn't think it would end with weapons being
fired.

Scott Savitt, United Press International

I remember a saying in Chinese, "meiyou hao xiachang." My Chinese friends
would say too—no good outcome. But I don't pretend, even until the night of
the massacre, to have believed what was going to take place would take place.

From the very beginning, I had worried about a crackdown. I simply could
not imagine the Communist Party tolerating this kind of protest movement.
Yet at each moment when I thought the Party would strike—the funeral of
Hu Yaobang, the first big march from the campuses to Tiananmen, the occupation of the square as Gorbachev arrived—the authorities held back. That,
however, only made me more nervous. Midway through Gorbachev's visit, I
remember asking for an urgent meeting with an American diplomat friend.
Over coffee at the Beijing Hotel. I poured out my fears about blood in the
streets. He kept saying there had to be other ways, that Deng Xiaoping
wouldn't jeopardize all his reforms. But I remained unconvinced.

For most of the media, the demonstrators had turned the Sino-Soviet summit into a side story. But the humiliation of the Gorbachev visit brought the power struggle within the leadership to a head. Hardliners led by Premier Li Peng—with the support of Deng Xiaoping—accused Zhao Ziyang of supporting the students and demanded a crackdown.

Orville Schell, *New Yorker*

I think I inadequately appreciated the degree to which the humiliation of this whole demonstration had been absorbed by the leaders who were being humiliated. Subsequently I think I have been able to appreciate much more how important this question of face is in China. The harder you push these guys, and the more in public you humiliate them, the less likely they are to yield.

10

CRACKDOWN IN TIANANMEN SQUARE

On the night of May 17, at an emergency meeting of the Politburo, the decision was made to impose martial law. Just before dawn on Friday, May 19, the reformist Communist Party general secretary Zhao Ziyang, looking haggard and pale, came to Tiananmen Square and addressed the students.

Bernard Shaw, CNN

I remember that utterly sad moment when Zhao went to the Square. He goes among these young people, and says, with tears in his eyes, "I've come too late." His physical presence was a statement to these students. "I lost the fight, and soon, you will feel the wrath of our government." And I found myself breathing harder and harder and getting tense, because in effect he had the appearance of the Grim Reaper. Here was Mr. Bad News. That to me was the flashing red light signal that things were about to change.

It was the last time Zhao Ziyang would be seen in public.

MARTIAL LAW

Throughout the day, rumors of a coming crackdown swirled through Beijing. At an earlier demonstration, John Pomfret had befriended a young army officer. Late in the afternoon of May 19, the two held a furtive meeting, where the officer read Pomfret the text of a speech given by the Beijing Party boss saying that martial law would be declared that night.

John Pomfret, Associated Press

I sat in his car, and he read the speech and basically said there was going to be martial law. So I knew five hours before that there was going to be martial law. My problem was that I was so tired I never filed.

Late that evening, Premier Li Peng appeared on television and announced the imposition of martial law. The army was on the outskirts of Beijing. Reporters feared the worst. I had been doing live shots from Tiananmen Square throughout the day and was on the air as Li Peng spoke. We were deeply concerned the soldiers would move in. The CNN live shot location was next to a giant flagpole at the north end of the square, surrounded by a three-foot-high concrete wall. My camera crew and I agreed that if shooting started, lying down next to the wall might provide a little safety.

Kathy Wilhelm, Associated Press

I was shooting pictures and I was watching. And I started to cry because it suddenly hit me what this meant. They were going to come in and put this down. It was definitely going to be violent. It was not going to be good.

Scott Savitt, United Press International

When they finally declared martial law, Dave said—and his Chinese wasn't very good—he said, "Wo yao tanke" (I want tanks). We went out and got the first story and the first photographic evidence. I drove all the way to the Marco Polo Bridge [ten miles southwest of Beijing's city center] and there was a line of T-72 battle tanks. I had never seen anything like that in my life.

Larry Wortzel, a longtime China analyst for American military intelligence, was the U.S. embassy's assistant defense attaché.

Larry Wortzel, U.S. Embassy Defense Attaché

The education from the intelligence community was to avoid the press. But I thought of the press as allies. If they were ethical, it was a two-way street.

Somebody might come to me and say, "I saw or heard this, does it make sense?" And I'd say, "Yes," or "No," or "Yeah, it does, but here's a place you could go to check it out." Or I would suggest to them that there was something going on and they may want to be at such-and-such place, or look at this, it's the type of story they'd like to cover.

Wortzel became an important source for a few trusted reporters—including Dave Schweisberg and Scott Savitt at United Press International—and my team at CNN. It was the kind of give-and-take that often develops between reporters and intelligence sources, especially in moments of crisis. For Schweisberg, Scott Savitt, and those of us at CNN, the relationship with Wortzel proved invaluable.

Scott Savitt, United Press International

I would take photos and write down all the identifying information on these armored vehicles. That was gold to the embassy. They reciprocated. I remember seeing—now we all see these satellite images—but at that time it was top, top secret classified. And Larry showed me what it looks like when a quarter-million armed troops converge on a national capital. It looked like a giant donut. He pointed to the center and said, "This is us." And they are coming from all sides.

Larry Wortzel, U.S. Embassy Defense Attaché

We watched this buildup. It was very clear at one point that there were around twelve to fourteen divisions of PLA. That's somewhere around 150,000 to 160,000 soldiers from outside the area, with tanks and heavily armed, sequestered around Beijing, and essentially being told that this is a counterrevolutionary crisis, and their loyalty to the Communist Party was at a test.

But in the outskirts of the capital, troops were met by crowds of citizens, who blocked their way. To the astonishment of almost everyone, the soldiers halted their advance.

Bernard Shaw, CNN

As an anchor, I always strove to maintain calmness. The more intense the story, the more I ratchet down. When you show emotion on television, it's exaggerated, and I knew the whole world was watching our coverage. But I almost lost it. When I learned that martial law had been declared, I could feel rage. I was fighting myself, trying to control that rage, so it wouldn't be shown on camera. I had an emotion thermometer in my head, and as the day dawned that thermometer started rising. The emotion of reporting civilians swarming around army trucks loaded with troops who were armed to the teeth, stopping them in their tracks, and telling them, "You are us. Don't go to the Square. Don't beat us. Don't shoot us. You are our brothers. We are your children." I didn't want anyone to accuse CNN of being biased, of being pro–hunger strikers or progovernment. But I became emotional. There were a couple times when I had to take a break. But to me, the dagger in the chest was when the Chinese government said, "CNN, stop what you have been doing."

PULLING THE PLUG

At 9 AM on Saturday, May 20, two grim-faced Chinese officials came into the CNN workspace at the Great Wall Sheraton Hotel and ordered the network to stop its live transmissions.

Alec Miran, CNN

They were saying, "What you are showing now has nothing to do with Gorbachev. Your license was only for Gorbachev." My direction from the CNN president in Atlanta was we had a lease. "You have to let us stay on the air. If you want to shut us down, you have to write it." Suddenly, we were the story, because shutting down American media was a big deal. I was thinking, "We've got to get this on air. This will be amazing television." Suddenly, a cameraman from ABC came in and said, "Hey, mate. I hear you're being shut down. My folks sent me here to get some pictures." And I'm thinking, "Do I really want him to shoot my control room?" But we had no cameras. All of our cameras are out, watching the troops, watching the square. I said, "How about I run a line from your camera into our transmission and you gave me permission to use your pictures?" He said, "Well, I have to call New York." Then he said, "Hell. They sent me here to get pictures. Just do it."

What followed became one of the most memorable moments in the history of television news. CNN managed to hook up the camera—and suddenly the standoff was being shown on live TV around the world.

Bernard Shaw, CNN

To have a government official walk into your control room and say, "Stop what you are doing." I just felt raging resentment. I couldn't show it on the air, but my hand literally was shaking.

Alec Miran, CNN

The way it ended was, Mike Chinoy, Tokyo bureau chief John Lewis, Steve Hurst, our Moscow bureau chief, and Bernie Shaw were standing in this garden. They were looking at the monitor, seeing what was playing out upstairs, seeing what was playing out at Tiananmen Square, and they are all offering their expertise. Mike, as a longtime China hand, was saying, "This is not good. Surely it could end in violence," foreshadowing June 4. These gentlemen came back in, and they said, "OK. We have permission to write you a letter." I gave him my pen and notebook and he leaned over, and you see the camera zooming in as he is writing in Chinese characters. He wrote in English as well. Bernie Shaw said the most quotable thing. "We came to cover a summit and walked into a revolution. Goodbye, from Beijing." Our director dissolved to a shot of a lone person standing on a bus with a flag fluttering on the top of the bus on Tiananmen Square and we went to black and that was it.

Bernard Shaw, CNN

At one point, Atlanta sent word to Beijing that President Bush was watching. So here was one capital reacting to another capital, not through diplomatic channels, but solely on what was seen and heard in live CNN coverage. Extraordinary. I think you could say that was the beginning of the "CNN effect," whereby time is truncated, and reactions and decisions are made based on events as they're happening in real time, which puts a lot of pressure on foreign capitals.

James Baker, Secretary of State

Tiananmen was the first example of the power of the global technological revolution, the power of the media to drive policy.

James Lilley, U.S. Ambassador

It was a hell of a story. It was breaking all over American TV, because the leading people were there, and what they said mattered. There is no question I was really introduced to the power of the media for the first time.

Bernard Shaw, CNN

That night, when I got back to the hotel, I wept. Why was I crying? I was angry that no longer could we do our jobs. And I also thought about being a citizen of the United States of America. I'm a child of democracy. Freedom is all I've known. And after those days of protest, of high emotion, of pleading for recognition and respect, and knowing, not specifically, but generally knowing that eventually these aged Chinese leaders are going to crack down on these young people.

"WORSE THAN TRYING TO GET INTO PARTY HEADQUARTERS"

But the anticipated crackdown still did not come, despite almost daily rumors that troops and tanks were on the move. Instead, the square remained occupied by protesters.

Terril Jones, Associated Press

There were people taking things into their own hands. There were random checkpoints around town. The people in the square tried to form their own little city. They were asking journalists for press passes to let them in to the inner sanctum of the Heroes' Monument. I remember watching some Canadian tourists show them a credit card and get waved through. It was very haphazard and unorganized.

Scott Savitt, United Press International

These Chinese students re-created a hierarchical order. They'd been through Communist youth leagues. They had been trained to do this their whole lives.

Dan Southerland, *Washington Post*

The student security system—I had to pass through eleven checkpoints to get to the leaders, and it ended with a kind of shoving match with me and the bodyguards. I remember thinking this is worse than trying to get into Party headquarters.

Jaime FlorCruz, *Time*

I remember going to Tiananmen Square and seeing the sorry state of the square. It was dirty. The organizers had started to lose control.

Cynde Strand, CNN

As the days went on, the mood did start to change. It started to get quite trashy, and the kind of festival feeling started to be replaced by people who were getting sick. It wasn't just students anymore. But I had my ladder, and it was my place on the monument, and that's where I'd sit every day.

EXHAUSTION AND REINFORCEMENTS

With exhaustion taking its toll, news organizations brought fresh staffers who got tourist visas by pretending they weren't journalists. Jeff Widener, the AP photographer in Bangkok, flew to Hong Kong, told the U.S. consulate he'd lost his old passport, which had China journalist visa stamps, got a new one, and secured a tourist visa from a local travel agent. Jonathan Schaer, a cameraman with international experience based at CNN headquarters in Atlanta, got a tourist visa in the United States.

Jonathan Schaer, CNN

When I first got there, I was put on the overnight shift, just to take pictures of the students sleeping, the people spraying some kind of antibacterial spray to keep the vermin down, and just in case something happened.

CNN's Tokyo bureau chief, John Lewis, was able to rent a room at the Beijing Hotel with a balcony that had a clear view down to Tiananmen Square—both for a high vantage point and for a place where exhausted staffers could take a break and recharge their equipment.

By now, the protestors at Tiananmen were divided and weary.

Melinda Liu, *Newsweek*

They were becoming as factionalized as the Politburo was. They were fighting for influence and power among themselves, not agreeing in terms of tactics. They had prima donnas all over the place.

The big division was whether to remain in the square or, in effect, declare victory and leave.

John Pomfret, Associated Press

I remember trying to talk to as many of these student leaders as possible, because I felt they had to go home. As a journalist, I guess I was going outside my ethical boundaries, but I just thought this is not going to end well.

Terril Jones, Associated Press

There was a vote taken and there was a split. Some people thought that the point had been made. They could declare victory and return to their dorms. Others said we must continue because we have momentum on our side, and history will be on our side.

Orville Schell, *New Yorker*

When they decided not to declare victory and go home, that was a big mistake. But this wasn't a creature with a central nervous system. It wasn't like the Communist Party, which could make a decision and execute. By that time, students from all the provinces had poured in, and there was no way to control it. It was not a question of good decision, bad decision. It was out of control.

As protestors dug in on the square, news organizations continued to bring in fresh blood. CBS sent Richard Roth, a correspondent from New York, and the AP brought in photographer Liu Heung-shing, who was based in Seoul, but who'd covered China years earlier. Others, however, began to scale back.

Jaime FlorCruz, *Time*

I remember the week before June 4, people thought it was over.

Melinda Liu, *Newsweek*

Everyone is human, and you get exhausted. Basically, only half the Newsweek *team was in Beijing because the other half wanted to go on R & R to Hong Kong. Many journalists left before the climax because they were really tired.*

On May 30, the mood in the square changed dramatically with the arrival of the Goddess of Democracy, a thirty-seven-foot-high statue made of plaster and wood by students at the Central Academy of Fine Arts. It was positioned directly in front of the Tiananmen gate, standing almost eye to eye with the portrait of Chairman Mao. It was a brilliant piece of political theatre, a brazen act of defiance against the Chinese Communist Party.

The arrival of the statue revived the students' flagging spirits. Large crowds flocked to the square. For China's hardline leaders, already alarmed the rising groundswell of popular sympathy for the protest movement, especially from the emergence of militant workers' organizations, it was the last straw.

THE CRACKDOWN BEGINS

Terril Jones, Associated Press

On the night of June 2, I was late duty at the office. I remember hearing noises outside—huffing and shuffling. I looked out onto Chang An Avenue. I saw hundreds of soldiers jogging towards the square. I got in the car and drove in the same direction. They weren't armed. They got toward the square, and were turned back by angry citizens who were scolding these seventeen-, eighteen-year-old foot soldiers, saying, "What are you doing? You are supposed to protect the people."

If it was intended as a show of force by the military to convince people to leave the square, it didn't work.

The next night it would be different.

John Pomfret, Associated Press

I was eating dinner near Muxudi [west of Tiananmen Square]. There had already been announcements telling people to get off the street. Buses had blocked the small bridge coming towards the center of the city where we were. People began to throw stones at the military. The military approached the buses and got off the trucks. At that point they began to fire. I saw people either fall-ing or who had been shot. I had a cellphone, so I called [bureau chief] Jim Abrams and told him they were beginning to shoot. Then people lit the buses on fire, and the army brought an armored personnel carrier, and they rammed through those buses, and began going east on Chang An Avenue towards the center of town. I got on my bike and biked through alleyways. I would drop down at some intersections to see what was happening. People had thrown Molotov cocktails in the tanks, and there was bloodshed on the military side as well. I then biked around Zhongnanhai [the leadership compound located just northwest of the square] and entered the square from the east.

United Press International's Scott Savitt was at Muxudi as well.

Scott Savitt, United Press International

I can hear it right in my mind like I am reliving it—"pa pa pa pa pa." And those are AK-47 [rifles] firing on semiautomatic.

THE ASSAULT ON THE SQUARE

On the balcony of CNN's room at the Beijing Hotel, I had a clear view a few hundred meters down Chang An Avenue to the north end of the square. We managed to keep a phone line open to CNN headquarters in Atlanta. I could see red tracer bullets, and hear the occasional crackle of gunfire, as I broadcast live, telling viewers, "The assault on Tiananmen Square is now underway."

Nicholas Kristof, *New York Times*

I hopped on my bicycle and hurtled toward Tiananmen Square. You could hear the gunfire and the crowds were rushing the other way. And I keep thinking this is a crazy job where there's gunfire, everyone in their right mind is going the other way, and you're going towards it.

Melinda Liu, *Newsweek*

Going into the square with all this shooting was really foolish. Even if they weren't intending to kill people, there was just people shooting in the darkness. A lot of people were getting hit by accident. The bullets are so close that you not only hear the percussion of the shot, you hear the "zing." There were armored vehicles all over the place. In my mind there are a lot of vignettes of individual things that I could see—people being shot, bloody bodies being put onto these three-wheel ambulance things, people shouting all kinds of stuff at soldiers, and just total fear and chaos. Occasionally, you'd see some kind of vehicle on fire.

Cynde Strand, CNN

Then the most extraordinary thing happens. An APC comes in front of Chairman Mao's portrait and is set on fire. It was shocking and incredible, and you couldn't actually believe that it was happening. Bodies were starting to be carried into the square. Bullets would fly past us and you'd hear crying and screaming, and this APC [armored personnel carrier] was on fire. I think many soldiers died in that APC that night.

Jeff Widener, Associated Press

The protestors crawled on top of the armored personnel carrier I was photographing. I'd brought just a small amount of film and batteries because I didn't want to be obvious as a journalist. I was starting to run out of film. I was running out of batteries, but I had great shots. I'm looking down the street, and there's this other armored car completely ablaze. I'm literally walking in front of this burning armored car, and I'm worried that if I flash a picture, they're going to shoot me.

I don't know what to expect. These protestors are going crazy. They're putting the barricades into the tank treads. I come around the backside and I'm taking a few pictures. Then somebody grabs me. They're grabbing my cameras. I thought they were going to tear me apart. They're screaming and yelling at me. I pull my passport out and say, "American, American!" One of the leaders comes over and he grabs my passport and looks at it. Then he calms the crowd down and he says, "You photo, you photo."

They point to the ground, and there's a soldier who's dead curled up on the ground. I took one photo. I couldn't take more because I had no battery power, hardly. At this point I'm thinking to myself, this is comical. I have one of the biggest stories of the twentieth century, and I can only take a picture every sixty seconds. People are throwing rocks. They're going crazy. They're running around. There's one guy who's on fire. He's rolling around on the ground, and there's people trying to put him out. I'm looking down at my camera, and I'm waiting for the flash to get the ready light on. I put the camera up to take a picture, and boom! My head jerks back. I look down. There's blood all over me. The camera is completely ripped off, the lens is ripped off. Massive concussion. Somebody had just thrown this rock. I don't think it was intentional. It was just a rock thrown by a protester, and it just nailed me in the face. Fortunately, the camera saved my life. I was already sick as a dog from a bad case of the flu. Now I've got a concussion. Then I look in front of me. There's an armored car. Door opens up. Another soldier comes out. I can still remember how pristine and ironed his uniform was. The crowd just moved in on him with clubs and knives, and at that point I realized that I had to get out of there.

I pedal my bicycle back to the AP office, and it seemed like it took an eternity, because there were burning buses, exploding vehicles, and there were red tracers flying over the Great Hall of the People. Everything was like in slow motion. It was almost like a scene out of Apocalypse Now. *I got back to the AP office and the photographer had to pry the film open with a pair of pliers in the darkroom.*

Jonathan Schaer, CNN

It was chaos, just chaos. There was a tank that was coming right at us. People were coming around, and we heard some gunshots and we said, "We're getting out of here. This is not a safe place to be." And we went to the Beijing Hotel.

Cynde Strand and United Press International's Dave Schweisberg decided to stay in the square.

Cynde Strand, CNN

There were moments of fear. There were moments of—what the hell are we doing here? But this is what you are a journalist for. This is right where we need to be. We are witnessing history. This is what makes a difference. There is no real record unless you are standing there. And that's what Dave was about. Dave was about being there and watching this moment unfold. We had no cellphone. Nobody knows where we are, but I'm sure Mike Chinoy knows that I'm not coming back until it's over.

GOING LIVE

CBS correspondent Richard Roth, cameraman Derek Williams, and sound-man Dexter Leung found a vantage point on the western edge of the square. Roth was reporting live over a large and clumsy cellphone.

Richard Roth, CBS News

We could film right into the square. We had a good view of the action but were not at its center. We were immediately noticed. A squad broke off from this column of troops and headed directly towards us. An officer came up to the group and he looked at me for a second and he just threw a punch and knocked me down. The phone went spinning. I went down to the ground.

As Roth described the advance of helmeted troops with rifles on their shoulders, the soldiers came for the CBS team. Viewers in the United States heard Roth shouting over the phone, "They're coming for us. We're trying to move back and move away. I'll go. I'll go. I'll go. I'll go. I'll go!"

Richard Roth, CBS News

So the sequence heard by listeners was, "I'll go, I'll go," which to some sounded like "Oh no, Oh no," a phone dropping, gunfire, and the line goes dead.

Dan Rather, CBS News

Give Roth some credit. He was on a cellphone broadcasting live as the soldiers were in the process of arresting him, and he was at least roughed up in the process, but he kept his cool and kept broadcasting for as long as he could. The Chinese government wanted to stop the messengers. People like Richard Roth, correspondents on the scene, were the messengers. After we received the final communication from Roth, we didn't know where he was for a long time. We knew he'd been at least roughed up. We didn't know how badly he'd been injured.

Nicholas Kristof, New York Times

In the excitement and fear of that evening, I'd forgotten that it was a Saturday night so I had early deadline, and so that hugely complicated things, and I ended up staying out later than I should have, and that left the foreign desk and Sheryl really terrified that something had gone wrong when I didn't turn up.

Sheryl WuDunn, *New York Times*

It turned out to be really scary. We were recently married, and here we were in this scary place. I just remember calling my foreign editor and almost like really having a fit. He's trying to calm me down, and he said, "Just do me a favor. The one thing you need to start doing is keeping a tab." I said, "What do you mean by keeping a tab?" He said, "You know—trying to track the number of people who get killed."

Nicholas Kristof, *New York Times*

I was pretty shaken and scared. On the square itself, I tried to keep a layer of people between me and the troops, but I remember realizing after a bit that I was a few inches taller than most of the Chinese, so it was a pretty critical part of my real estate that was exposed. There were people in the crowd who were getting shot. My notebook from that evening was damp with sweat just from fear. I ran to the Xiehe Hospital. There were lots of bloody people in the hallways and everywhere. One of the ambulance drivers showed me bullet holes in his ambulance. I then ran home from there, so very hurriedly filed, much later than I should have. New York was right on deadline.

While all of this was happening, I continued my live reporting over the phone. At mid-afternoon Washington time—around 2 AM in Beijing—Secretary of State James Baker appeared on CNN, having been previously scheduled for a weekend talk show. I did a quick update, talking about seeing bullets and bodies, and then White House correspondent Charles Bierbauer, who hosted the show, turned to Baker and said, "Mr. Secretary, does the U.S. government now take a stronger demarche against the Chinese government? Do you do something more?"

James Baker, Secretary of State

It caught me by surprise because I was on the air at the time it began to happen. I was very much caught on the spot. I do remember vividly being caught and thinking to myself, "How do I handle this one?" I remember being caught flat-footed. There's no doubt this was the first example of this phenomenon.

Richard Roth and Derek Williams were now prisoners of the Chinese army, although soundman Dexter Leung had escaped with their video.

Richard Roth, CBS News

My face below my eye was bleeding. My shirt was bloody, and two soldiers carted me off. They marched Derek and me up a ramp to the Great Hall of the People.

Melinda Liu, *Newsweek*

I was in the north edge sort of between the Forbidden City and the square because I wanted to have a clear shot back to the Beijing Hotel if I had to. There are some bushes and streetlights and things you could sort of hide behind. I actually did not get into the Monument of the Martyrs. It was just too dangerous.

Cynde Strand, CNN

It was just a surreal scene because bodies would be coming in from the outlying streets where the real crackdown was happening. It was happening around the square, not yet in the square. We decided to get off the Monument. We were playing cat and mouse all night. There was a line of spectators around the square. We would be hiding behind the spectators and would go in and try to film, and then we'd drop back. You could hear bullets and gunfire.

For many reporters, deadline pressure and filing requirements kept them away from the square at critical moments.

Dan Southerland remained in the *Washington Post* bureau.

Dan Southerland, *Washington Post*

I was getting calls from the Beijing Hotel, which was still working, but my constant concern was that they were going to cut off communication. They don't want this to reach the outside world. I'm the bureau chief. I have to be the guy that gets everything out that I could, almost like a wire service, having to call Washington to let them know what was going on.

Jaime FlorCruz stayed in the *Time* office. As with *Newsweek*, the final deadline for the weekly was Saturday.

Jaime FlorCruz, *Time*

We had already closed the magazine. The cover was not about China, because the conventional wisdom was, it's probably over. I reached a New York editor, and he decided we are going to change our cover. They held the press basically to switch covers.

John Sheahan, CBS News

I mostly sat in a studio. We had moved our whole operation into the Shangri La Hotel, and I just did constant stream reporting. We had open lines to New York. All you had to do was pick up a microphone and say, "Hello New York, this is Beijing" and you're ready to go. And make little forays out to gather material with a camera crew and come right back in immediately.

"MY HEART WEPT"

Cynde Strand, CNN

In the actual square, some of the students had their arms linked around the monument, and they were still singing. The kids were frightened, but they were resolute.

Scott Savitt, United Press International

We would congregate at the Monument because the students still had a radio system set up, so they were broadcasting until the final assault. One of the first things they did was shoot out those loudspeakers on the monument. I thought they were going to kill them all.

But as dawn approached, four liberal intellectuals who'd been staging a hunger strike negotiated with the army to let the remaining students leave the square.

John Pomfret, Associated Press

I stayed in the center of the square with the remaining students until they conducted their negotiations with the military, and I walked out with them. I was phoning the AP the entire time. You were involved with the simple logistics of doing your job, which is to describe what you see. Going through my mind was that it was hard to get the story out, and what's happening, and what's going to happen next. But it was the most incredible experience I've ever had in my life.

Cynde Strand, CNN

We came off the square with them. Some of them were dejected, bandaged, crying, some of them are a little bit bloody, so defeated. But some of them were still singing. Then there was the dilemma. We've got great tape. How are we going to get it back? This old man in an old Mao cap and old Mao jacket was driving one of those bicycles with a flat panel. He let us lay on that, and the students gave us blankets, and we covered everything over us, and he rode us back to the Beijing hotel.

Worried about Chinese security officers in the lobby, Strand hid the tapes in Dave Schweisberg's car parked outside the Beijing Hotel and came up to the CNN workspace. Until then, I had no idea where she or Dave had been, or whether they were OK. I remember being almost near tears and giving her a big hug. Then she went and grabbed a packet of cheese balls, put them on a plate, and said, "Happy birthday, Mike," because June 4, ironically, was my birthday.

Even among normally hard-bitten journalists, the shock of the crackdown was intense. Dan Rather was by now back in New York anchoring the *CBS Evening News.*

Dan Rather, CBS News

Watching the climactic moment in Tiananmen Square when the army moved in, my job as a broadcaster is to keep my own emotions in. But it was clear the army was moving in with violent force. It may strike some as corny or sophomoric, but my heart wept. Once I got off the air, I took a long walk home because I wanted to think about it, because I'd been in Tiananmen Square, made the

*acquaintance, even, I would say, the friendship of some of the young people—
and I thought of what might have been.*

Nicholas Kristof, *New York Times*

*China for us had been kind of a honeymoon, literally. We'd just gotten mar-
ried as we'd moved there, and it had been tremendously exciting to run around
the country, to feel this openness. We had so many ties with people in the Zhao
Ziyang camp who envisioned a more open country. Those forces for openness
were real, they were exhilarating. When the other camp won and our friends
started going to jail and we saw the troops open fire, there really was a sense of
betrayal and bitterness.*

THE DEATH TOLL

Richard Roth, CBS News

*Dawn was just breaking. The light was soft and grey and suffused with smoke
from what was left of the protestors' encampment. We were hustled into two
jeeps. There was a driver in front and an officer in the passenger seat in front.
I remember he stood up and held on to a bar as we were driving though the
square. There were workers bulldozing rubble. But there were no bodies. There
was no smell of tear gas. I don't remember seeing an ambulance. There was
certainly no sign there had been any mass killing in the square.*

But as the army moved to consolidate its control, shooting continued in
other parts of Beijing.

Terril Jones, Associated Press

*Sometimes there would be people lying in the street. I saw a girl who was in a
white shirt and a navy dress. Her chest was red. People put her on one of those
tricycles and peddled off to a hospital.*

Jim Laurie, ABC News

*We got into an ambulance. We rode with the ambulance for an hour and picked
up more people and went back to the hospital. It was pretty gruesome. I had*

been through Vietnam and Cambodia. But it was tough to see as much blood as we saw that night.

Nicholas Kristof, *New York Times*

One of the things that shook me then was there was a young man, I think roughly my age, who had been shot in the back who was fighting for his life, and you know he hadn't done anything riskier than I had. His luck has just run out.

Sheryl WuDunn, *New York Times*

We were calling some of the hospitals. Some we had been able to get to before they were being told not to talk to outsiders.

Dan Southerland, *Washington Post*

We wanted to find out how many people were killed. We started checking every hospital we could find. We got turned away at several. Suddenly, the whole psychological atmosphere went from openness to people really afraid. I decided I had to see one of the hospitals myself. I got to a hospital and some people outside were saying, "Don't let the foreigner in." A very brave doctor came out and said, "I'm taking him in." We went to a makeshift morgue where there was a pile of bodies riddled with bullets. The doctor later called me and said, "I've been disciplined." The point was, don't come back again. I then tried a kind of trick. I tried to get into a hospital pretending I was sick. I said I have something wrong with my stomach, to which the guy behind the desk said, "Sir, are you really sick, and who are you?" And I said, "OK, I'm a journalist and I am trying to find out more about what happened," and he threw me out.

It didn't take long for a controversy to erupt—which continues to this day—over how many people died.

Terril Jones, Associated Press

One of our reporters was talking to a Red Cross person. He said, yeah, at least five hundred people were killed, without any real verification. We went with that number for at least a cycle, a day.

Scott Savitt, United Press International

I spoke to the Chinese Red Cross, and they said we have an accurate record of more than two thousand deaths.

Al Pessin, Voice of America

At VOA, we settled on a phrase "perhaps thousands."

Dan Southerland, Washington Post

We knew it was in the hundreds because people had witnessed the shootings. A dozen here and a dozen there and it started to add up. If it had been over two thousand people, we would have seen more bodies. I also felt for credibility's sake, I cannot go out there with numbers I have to pull back.

Nicholas Kristof, New York Times

Sheryl had been calling around to hospitals and getting accounts of the death and injured toll, so we had figures and some of these were official numbers. Some of them were from friends who happened to be at that hospital. Then there was an order not to give out numbers. But this number of twenty-six hundred or twenty-seven hundred that supposedly originally came from the Chinese Red Cross, we heard that very, very early. It seemed to us too early to be an authentic number. I was very suspicious. It didn't jibe with the figures that I did have. In addition, there's a well-known correlation between the number of dead and the number injured. If you have twenty-seven hundred dead, you're going to have somewhere between five and ten times as many injured. It was clear that there weren't that many people who were seriously injured. It was also clear that people were exaggerating. That is something that in journalism we see—when terrible things happen, victims lie as well as perpetrators. I was very suspicious of some of these huge numbers going around and pushed back and wrote an article suggesting that it was a lot lower. In retrospect I think that was right.

Jim Laurie, ABC News

We were never able to determine the extent of the deaths and injuries that night. All we knew was that there were tremendous numbers and that the hospitals

were in a panic mode. My view is that whether it was a hundred or a thou-
sand, it was incredibly devastating, not only for the people who were killed,
but for the reputation of China.

Shortly after returning to the CNN office at the Great Wall Sheraton Hotel
that Sunday morning, I received a tip from a Chinese friend that there were
rumors the army might raid the hotel and seize our tapes. Concerned about
preserving the record, I brought the tapes to the U.S. embassy. Press counselor
McKinney Russell, who was a good friend, let me in. But Russell wouldn't
speak because he feared the embassy was bugged. Instead, we exchanged
notes. I explained my concerns, and he agreed to keep the tapes for us until
things calmed down. In the end, the raid never took place, but the tapes
remained at the embassy for several days.

Later on June 4, Richard Roth and Derek Williams of CBS were released.

Richard Roth, CBS News

I had been injured but not seriously. I was hungry and dirty and tired but oth-
erwise OK. We walked as a group to a nearby hotel. The first person that
greeted me was Keith Miller, an NBC correspondent and old friend of mine.
And he greeted me as if he had been led to believe I was dead.

THE MAN IN FRONT OF THE TANK

The next morning, Monday, June 5, Liu Heung-shing, who'd temporarily
taken over as the AP's photo editor, asked Jeff Widener to get some shots of
Tiananmen Square from the Beijing Hotel.

Liu Heung-shing, Associated Press

We get this message from headquarters that said, "Can you get us a picture of
the empty square? We want to see what the square looks like."

Jeff Widener, Associated Press

I had a jacket, and I hid my camera equipment inside it. I had a very long
400mm lens, but it was slender, so that went into my left pocket. I had a

doubler for the lens, and it went into another pocket, film in my underwear, and I had a camera body stuck in my back pocket. I'm biking towards the Beijing Hotel about two miles away, and there's just debris, charred buses, and rocks on the ground. I thought, well this is not too bad. I can hear some sporadic gunfire in the distance, it doesn't seem too close. All of a sudden, I'm getting to this large bridge, and there's four tank barrels coming up as I go. It's manned by soldiers with heavy machine guns. I'm wheeling my bicycle past this thinking I can't believe I'm doing this.

I finally get to the hotel. I hear rumors that other journalists had had their film and cameras confiscated. I had to figure out a way to get into the hotel. I had no idea how. When I get there, I look inside the darkened lobby, and there's this college kid that had a dirty T-shirt, shorts, sandals. I walked up to him and said, "Hi, Joe, how you doing? I've been looking for you." Then I whispered, "I'm from Associated Press, can you let me up to your room?" He picked up on it right away. He said, "Sure, come on." We go up to his room, which is on the sixth floor. I start taking pictures of some of the tanks as they came by— they'd push some of the burned-out buses. Sometimes you'd hear a little ring of a bell and they've got a cart with a body or injured being taken somewhere to a hospital. I photographed that for a while.

Jonathan Schaer had set up a camera on the balcony of CNN's hotel room.

Jonathan Schaer, CNN

We had a camera there. Trying to stay awake. We had been up for hours and hours and hours. The night before we were just getting the best video we could. You could see kids coming out on stretchers.

Terril Jones, Associated Press

I was standing in front of the Beijing Hotel on the street level and had a camera. I knew that soldiers had gone around in trucks broadcasting that anybody using a camera or binoculars could be dealt with on the spot. I asked somebody, "What does that mean?" And he said, "It means you could be shot on the spot." We heard gunshots coming from the direction of the square. We could hear these tanks.

Jeff Widener, Associated Press

I had a concussion and was really spaced out. I hear the noise of the tanks, and I go to the window. I remember very clearly that balcony, because right above my head there was a bullet hole, so I knew they could easily pop a shot off. I see this long column of tanks coming down the road, and I'm thinking, "Well, that's not a bad picture. I've got a long lens. It'll be a nice compression shot." And this guy with shopping bags walks out in front and starts waving the bags.

Jonathan Schaer, CNN

Another cameraman said, "Hey, look at the guy in front of the tanks!" I just zoomed in on it and started videotaping it. When the column stopped and the man blocked the tanks, they were trying to scare him off by shooting over his head. Well, shooting over his head was basically where our position was—it was the fifth floor or the fourth floor, whatever balcony we were on—but the bullets were so close you could hear them whizzing by. At that point, we just locked the camera down. I lay down and looked over the balcony. It was just too dangerous. There were bullets ricocheting around.

Jeff Widener, Associated Press

I'm just waiting for him to get shot, holding the focus on him, waiting and waiting. It's too far away. I look back at the bed, and I had that lens doubler, which would make my 400 an 800. I had to think, "Do I gamble. Do I go back to the bed? Maybe I lose the shot, or do I just shoot this wider?" So I took a chance. I ran to the bed, got it, put it on the camera, open the aperture up all the way. One, two, three shots.

Terril Jones, Associated Press

People were fleeing, scattering from where I was standing. They were running away from the direction of the tanks back to where they could duck down a side street. I lifted the camera. I took only one shot, and then I ducked away, because you don't know where the bullets are being aimed at.

Jeff Widener, Associated Press

Then it was over. Some people came, they grabbed this guy, and they ran off. I remember sitting down on this little sofa next to the window and the student said, "Did you get it? Did you get it?" I said, "I don't know, I really don't know." I was really bothered because I thought I must have blown it. But something in the back of my mind said maybe I got it, but I'm not sure.

Liu Heung-shing, Associated Press

He called me on the phone, he said, "Liu. I have this image. I think I got it. There's this man in front of the tanks." And I just instinctually fired off some advice, "OK, roll the film up and remove that roll from your camera. And separate them in two places." I said, "Leave your camera and leave your [camera] body in that hotel room and come downstairs to the lobby." Sometimes in those early days we have a lot of foreign students. I said, "Find one young man or woman, and see if they want to bring that roll of film."

Jeff Widener, Associated Press

I took the film and asked him [a foreign student] if he could take all my film and smuggle it in his underwear and ride the bicycle back to the AP office.

Liu Heung-shing, Associated Press

Another forty-five minutes passed. An American guy with a ponytail and a backpack showed up with an AP envelope and said, "Is there a Mr. Liu here?" Our Japanese photographer soaked the film. And I came out, and I looked at that frame—and that's the frame. It went out.

Jonathan Schaer, CNN

We didn't really know what we had on the tape until we went back and looked at it. We took it back to the workspace where we had this gizmo that could send video. It was a prototype that Sony had given us to try out. It would scan one frame of video. It would take like an hour to do one frame and send it over a phone line. I think we sent five frames of it, made copies of the tape, and sent it to the airport, where we found a tourist to take it to Hong Kong.

Jeff Widener, Associated Press

The next morning, I pedaled back to the AP office. I look at the clipboard, and there are messages from all over the world. It was amazing. There were congratulations from the president of AP, congratulatory messages from all over the world.

John Sheahan, CBS News

No one who has ever seen that is going to forget that picture.

Jeff Widener, Associated Press

When I took the photo, it didn't seem unusual. It didn't sink in till later that I had something really big. It's taken on a life of its own. I suppose for a lot of people, it's something personal, because this guy represents everything in our lives that we're battling, because we're all battling something. We're either battling to pay the rent, or we're battling a boss, or we're fighting for something in some small or big way. We still don't know who this guy is. It's almost appropriate because it's almost like the Unknown Soldier. He's really become a symbol for a lot of people. Folks get really passionate about this image. For me, it was just another assignment. I never dreamed that this thing would take on the stature that it's taken on through the years, and it seems to get bigger and bigger. It's amazing, really.

For me, the man in front of the tank is unquestionably one of the great iconic images of the twentieth century. Decades later, the identity of the young man remains unknown, but the photo endures as a symbol of the individual standing up to the power of the state.

In the rush of events, Terril Jones didn't look at his film closely and promptly forgot about it. It would be twenty years before his photo, the only one of the man in front of the tank taken at street level, was published.

THE FALLOUT

That same day, the dissident physicist Fang Lizhi sought refuge at the American embassy, after hiding out in a hotel room being used by Jay Mathews of the *Washington Post*, who'd flown in to help Dan Southerland. U.S. diplomat Raymond Burghardt handled the cloak-and-dagger operation.

Raymond Burghardt, State Department

People were shooting on the streets. It was a nightmarish atmosphere. We went and picked them up in a hotel and brought them lying on the floor of the van to the embassy, where he stayed for a year until he got out.

Meanwhile, rumors swirled around Beijing that the military had split over the crackdown—spurred by the PLA opening fire at an apartment block housing U.S. journalists and diplomats. Dan Southerland had just sent his wife and son to the airport.

Dan Southerland, *Washington Post*

I had to pay two hundred dollars for her to get to the airport, because they had to dodge columns of tanks and burned-out buses. She stayed at the airport hotel until she was able to get a flight. Back at the compound, I was trying to sleep, and all I hear is automatic weapons fire hitting something near my apartment. It was very loud. I rolled out of bed and barely get to the phone and called Washington and said, "I don't know what's going on here and I don't know what time it is but listen to this." And I held up the phone. We couldn't figure out what they were aiming at, but everyone was lying low.

Larry Wortzel, U.S. Embassy Defense Attaché

Part of what precipitated the embassy building being shot up was that a CNN crew had been up there the day before observing events and taking footage, and some of them used my balcony. And the next day, I was actually warned, "Don't be in your apartment after 10 AM," and my apartment took around forty rounds. They just shot the place up, and I think that was to shut down CNN and other reporters.

Dan Southerland, *Washington Post*

I think I was the first to report that the thirty-eighth army, its commander would go into a hospital and claimed he could not function. These were Beijing-based troops, and they didn't want to fight their own people. I was able to pick that up, so I think there was tension in the army.

In the fevered atmosphere of the moment, such reports sparked rumors of possible civil war.

John Sheahan, CBS News

There were crazy rumors about, oh well, these troops from this province and these troops from this province, they are really sympathetic, and they are turning antigovernment.

Terril Jones, Associated Press

It's a kind of rumor people liked to believe, especially journalists. It is a good story. People wanted to believe there was a conflict within the Chinese leadership because they didn't want to believe that all the sides were arrayed against the people.

The rumors led some journalists to speculate about civil war, their reporting buttressed by insights from one Western defense attaché.

Larry Wortzel, U.S. Embassy Defense Attaché

It was bullshit. And it was spread by a single defense attaché from a large ally way south in the Pacific where they speak with funny accents and there are kangaroos. He apparently heard the rumors, saw tanks opposite one of the intersections facing in all four cardinal directions, and decided that was a defensive position. He had no idea what he was talking about.

Adi Ignatius, *Wall Street Journal*

I think my biggest regret as a correspondent was in cowriting a piece that gave credence to the civil war scare. We were hearing this from fairly senior diplomatic sources. We were hearing it from normally reliable Chinese sources. I don't think the reporting was correct, and I regret that we ran a piece that seemed to give credence to it.

Nicholas Kristof, *New York Times*

I don't think it was the finest moment of journalism.

As an uneasy calm slowly returned to Beijing, the government issued a most-wanted list. Fang Lizhi and several student leaders, including Wuer Kaixi, featured prominently.

Right after the crackdown, Jim Laurie of ABC had videotaped a man, Xiao Bin, who was bitterly denouncing the crackdown to a group of bystanders.

Jim Laurie, ABC News

We brought the camera in, and he kept talking, He was exceedingly animated. At that point there were no satellite feeds out of Beijing, so we sent the tape off to Hong Kong. And the tape was transmitted on the Pacific Ocean satellite to California and on to New York in a raw form.

Two days later, Laurie turned on Chinese TV. The Chinese had intercepted the ABC satellite feed and taken the raw footage of Xiao Bin.

Jim Laurie, ABC News

We see the video of him that we had shot declaring, "The bastards have killed thousands, I saw the tanks roll over them." Then was the super, "Please report this man if you know him to local public security. He is wanted for rumor-mongering." We realized that we had just gotten this fellow into some pretty serious trouble.

Xiao Bin was sentenced to ten years in a labor camp.

Jim Laurie, ABC News

I had covered wars, been through Vietnam, been through a lot of experiences, but to put somebody in jail, which is what we in essence did, is pretty devastating.

Meanwhile, the government went after the American press.

Al Pessin, Voice of America

In the days after the massacre, some strange things started to happen at the VOA office. We got a lot of phony phone calls. We would pick up the phone, and the other end would say, "Is this VOA?" in English. And I'd say yes. And they'd say, "Fuck your mother." This was eerie, and a little bit scary.

On June 14, Pessin was summoned by the police.

Al Pessin, Voice of America

An official read me an order, including a long diatribe against VOA's coverage of the lead-up to and the massacre itself, and then ended with the phrase saying that I was being expelled from China, starting seventy-two hours from now.

The same thing happened to John Pomfret.

John Pomfret, Associated Press

I was pretty nervous. I'm interrogated about my activities around Tiananmen Square and my relationship with the PLA officer [whom Pomfret had met and befriended in the square before the crackdown]. I'm like, "yeah, I know him." He had a perspective that was really helpful, but in terms of state secrets it didn't even pass the sniff test. But they were pushing on that door, and I pushed back and denied and denied. Then they left. About three minutes later they came back with a blue document that said you're both unfriendly and uncooperative, and we're giving you three days to leave China. About an hour later, I was on the nightly news along with Al Pessin as the two resident correspondents being expelled. I spent my whole life trying to get to know China. I planned to spend many years there, and suddenly that little dream just sort of popped. I had a sense of being lost because I had adopted China as this second home.

And the state propaganda machine went into overdrive, attacking foreign reporters for using the press shorthand of the "Tiananmen Square massacre," even though it alleged there was scant evidence anyone died in the square itself.

Cynde Strand, CNN

You could say there was a massacre around Tiananmen Square, but you couldn't say there was a massacre in Tiananmen Square, because they were going to just shove the students out. And that's what they did.

Terril Jones, Associated Press

The government did try to use the media's blanket description of the "Tiananmen Square massacre" against the media.

Melinda Liu, *Newsweek*

It also allowed for the sort of linguistic loophole where the Chinese authorities could say nobody died in the square. It became clear afterwards that the vast majority of casualties actually occurred west of the square.

Richard Roth, CBS News

People have said to me—they say to me even now—what's the difference? There were a lot of people killed that night. Well, the difference is place and circumstances. And the difference is truth. And the difference is, getting the facts right matters.

As Al Pessin was packing to leave Beijing, he got a phone call at the VOA bureau.

Al Pessin, Voice of America

I was sitting at my desk and the phone rang. And again, a Chinese man speaking English, saying, "Is this VOA?" And I thought, "Oh no, not again. Am I getting even more of these phone calls?" And I said, "Yes, this is VOA." And he said, "OK," he said, "Don't be discouraged." And I said, "What? Excuse me?" And he said, "Don't be discouraged." And I said, "OK, don't you be discouraged." He said, "OK." And we hung up.

Two weeks after the crackdown, the Chinese Foreign Ministry invited foreign journalists to visit the square. All was quiet. A military spokesman insisted no massacre had occurred anywhere in Beijing.

Cynde Strand was on the tour. In her pocket, she had a lucky charm she always carried.

Cynde Strand, CNN

I used to have this rock, and I'd carry it with me. They finally opened the square and they took us on a tour. It was funny because I used to reach in to that rock all the time. You know, you do it without thinking about it. And then it was broken in my pocket. I remember thinking then, "Oh, the lies are too strong."

11

AFTERMATH

China entered the 1990s in a state of political deep freeze. With the fall of the Berlin Wall in November 1989, and the collapse of communism in Eastern Europe in 1990, followed by the fall of the Soviet Union in 1991, Party hard-liners in Beijing were determined to avoid a similar fate. After the army crackdown, they tightened control, imposing a stifling ideological orthodoxy, purging liberal figures associated with the protests, and tracking down and jailing activists who did not manage to escape. For American and other foreign correspondents in Beijing, the heady days of the late 1980s were replaced by an atmosphere of fear.

Dorinda Elliott, *Newsweek*

It felt like the Invasion of the Body Snatchers *had happened. It was like this was a different country. Nobody would talk to you. Everybody was terrified. It was just the most shocking and depressing thing I'd ever seen. We stayed for one more year, which was certainly the toughest year of journalism I'd ever done, because we couldn't talk to anybody. How you cover a story when no one will talk to you is a tricky dilemma. We lived in this compound. Every time I drove out of the compound, there would be two motorcycles a short distance behind me. They weren't hiding. They wanted me to know that they were there. And it was extremely effective. I assumed they wanted to see where I was going. They wanted to see who I was talking to. But the effect was that I then did not go see anybody for a year. I literally didn't see any friends for a year.*

Nicholas Kristof, *New York Times*

I'm usually a fairly mellow guy. We'd be driving along, and these state security goons would be tailing me, and I would go around a corner, and I would catch myself wishing those guys would slide out of control and go under a bus.

Adi Ignatius, *Wall Street Journal*

It really was a dark period. I remember from our compound you would occasionally hear, in the months after Tiananmen, gunshots at night and cars screeching. You'd just wonder what had happened. It was creepy and scary and very depressing.

Kristof's wife, Sheryl WuDunn, also a *Times* reporter, had just had a baby. The Chinese refused to give the child a visa.

Sheryl WuDunn, *New York Times*

I went to Hong Kong to give birth. Then I was ready to go back, and they wouldn't issue my son a visa. We were supposed to get the proper visa because he's going to be part of our family. We need to have a residence permit, and they just wouldn't give it. We got him a tourist visa. I went to the Foreign Ministry with my little baby to explain he's living with us and we'd like to get a visa. It was, "Sorry, we can't give you one." The only thing we could surmise was that they didn't like what Nick was reporting. I kept pleading, and finally, near the expiration date of his tourist visa, they did grant it. I think it was them trying to teach us a lesson.

Kristof's reporting had apparently angered hardline Premier Li Peng.

Nicholas Kristof, *New York Times*

I wrote some articles about Li Peng that got his office very upset. I thought State Security was trying to set me up. There were some phone calls. There was some Chinese woman who called me up and she wanted to sleep with me. There were a few other things to me that seemed to be setups. We heard from Chinese friends that the government was maybe looking to kick us out. Then I met the vice minister of State Security. He said there is this debate about what to do with you. He counseled me to write a letter. He said, don't apologize, but he had a couple of points—that you regret there had been misunderstandings and you look forward to improved Chinese-American relations, something along those lines. I wrote such a letter and things ultimately improved, but there was a long period there where every time we left our apartment, we were followed.

THE FATE OF FANG LIZHI

Meanwhile, Fang Lizhi and his wife remained in the U.S. embassy, safe from the Chinese security agents stationed outside, but with no clear path to freedom. In late November 1989, Fang was awarded the Robert F. Kennedy Human Rights Prize. Orville Schell was asked by Senator Edward Kennedy to travel to Beijing to find out if Fang would accept the reward, given concerns it might complicate his situation, and also to see if he could learn more about the physicist's condition.

Orville Schell, *New Yorker*

I didn't know if the embassy would allow it. I got picked up at my hotel by the local CIA operative, who wouldn't let me talk in the car. Ambassador Jim Lilley summoned me to have dinner. I went to the residency. We were having dinner. He put his finger to his lips and beckoned me. I followed him through the kitchen and down the stairs into the courtyard, very dark, across to some low-lying place. He knocked on the door. It opened. We went inside. There were a couple of guards. We went to another door and knocked. It opened up, and there was Fang Lizhi. We had a long conversation, and it turned out he wanted the award.

After secret negotiations lasting for months, in June 1990, China's leaders finally allowed Fang and his wife to leave for the United States, ostensibly for medical treatment. But for some reporters, the constant surveillance, pressure, and depressing overall situation became too much.

CHANGING OF THE GUARD

Adi Ignatius, *Wall Street Journal*

The year after Tiananmen was so awful that we burned out pretty quickly. 1988 was the most exciting year of our professional life, our happiest professional year. It was so incredible, so exciting. We made more long-lasting friends in Beijing than we ever have made anywhere else. Then after Tiananmen, it was just such a dark, restricted environment that we just really didn't want to stay longer than we had to.

By 1990, Ignatius and his wife, Elliott, were among a growing number of bitter and disillusioned Tiananmen veterans leaving China for other assignments.

Lena Sun, a Chinese American who had been one of a very few Americans permitted to study at Peking University in the late 1970s, before normalization, replaced Daniel Southerland at the *Washington Post.*

Lena Sun, *Washington Post*

Arriving after Tiananmen I think was one of the most difficult periods for American journalists. People didn't want to talk to you—understandably. American journalists were singled out for more scrutiny. It was hard to convince people to want to talk to you.

James McGregor, who'd been based in Taiwan for the *Wall Street Journal* since 1987, took over the *Journal*'s Beijing bureau from Adi Ignatius in mid-1990.

James McGregor, *Wall Street Journal*

I arrive in China post-Tiananmen, and it's very depressing. All the correspondents talked about was Tiananmen. Every dinner, that's all they would talk about, "Where were you? What did you see?" People were very bitter. I think that most of the journalists there at Tiananmen really had to get out. Most of them had left in a year or two, because they had gone through the whole thing, and felt angry and disappointed. The eighties were a time of expectations and hope in China. And then Tiananmen, boom, just kind of changed all of that.

THE SHADOW OF TIANANMEN

Meanwhile, the Communist Party remained consumed by the fear it would meet the same fate as the Communist regimes of Eastern Europe and the Soviet Union.

Lena Sun, *Washington Post*

I think there was a real fear among the Chinese elite that if they did not maintain the lid on stability that they would go the way of the Soviet Union and Eastern Europe. There was always that tension, and there was always that, for the reporter, to try to compare China to the Soviet Union.

The shadow of Tiananmen Square and the ongoing repression unquestionably affected the coverage of the country.

Jaime FlorCruz, *Time*

It did dominate our reporting on China-U.S. relations, and on China's relations with the outside world.

Sheryl WuDunn, *New York Times*

I think it totally shaped the way coverage was run. We didn't have something to put in its place. We didn't have anything as dramatic.

State Department official J. Stapleton Roy was appointed U.S. ambassador in 1991, succeeding James Lilley.

J. Stapleton Roy, U.S. Ambassador

Tiananmen had an emotional impact in the American people. You couldn't have a story on China on U.S. television without a picture of the student standing in front of the tank. That means that every time you touched on China, you had a pejorative image of China as part of the story.

Ted Koppel, who had been the host of the enormously successful ABC News broadcast *Nightline* for more than a decade, had returned to Beijing just after the crackdown, and produced a documentary called *Tragedy at Tiananmen.*

Ted Koppel, ABC News

TV reporting is very basic, not very nuanced, not very sophisticated. The pictures always have more of an impact. Pictures mean more than the narration.

The words are kind of incidental. And until the age of the Internet, television was still the great means of communication.

J. Stapleton Roy, U.S. Ambassador

Unfortunately, the powerful images were the negative ones. To the extent the media only wants to show powerful images, there's going to be a certain self-selection process of what they show. This is a frequent complaint of government officials in dealing with the media, which is the media prefers to run with a story even when it's not completely accurate because it is more dramatic.

Hoping to blunt some of the negative publicity, in May 1990, Jiang Zemin, the Party secretary in Shanghai who had been appointed Communist Party general secretary after the ouster of Zhao Ziyang, agreed to speak with Barbara Walters of ABC News. It was the first interview with foreign media that any senior Chinese leader had given since the crackdown.

Barbara Walters, ABC News

Henry Kissinger vouched for me. So Jiang Zemin sat down very pleasantly, smiled a lot, cold eyes, big smile. About Tiananmen Square, he knew a little English, and he said, quoting Shakespeare, "Much ado about nothing." Perhaps the scariest moment for me was, in the middle of the interview, I produced a photograph, which I was sitting on, of the young man who stopped the tanks. We did not know what had happened to him. I asked this of Jiang Zemin and did not have him get up and walk off, or not have them say to me, "Ms. Walters, you are a spy. We are getting rid of you or putting you back on your plane and go home." It took a lot of courage, but it was such a famous photograph that I had to show it. I don't think they were thrilled with the interview.

ABC News, Jiang Zemin Interview

WALTERS: Do you have any idea what happened to the young man?
JIANG: I think this young man will be not killed by the tank.
WALTERS: But did you arrest him? We heard he was arrested and executed.
JIANG: I can't confirm whether this young man you mentioned was arrested or not.
WALTERS: You do not know what happened to him.
JIANG: But I think—never killed.

As the first anniversary of the crackdown approached in June 1990, tension in Beijing increased. The authorities, determined to prevent any commemoration, flooded the city with soldiers and police and sealed off Tiananmen Square. Reporters and camera crews who ventured into the square were roughed up or detained. That night, many journalists gathered outside Peking University. We could hear students chanting, but couldn't get into the campus, and were eventually chased away by police. CNN soundman Mitch Farkas and others were held at gunpoint with their hands and legs apart against a wall, while a reporter for the *Los Angeles Times*, his photographer wife, and a German TV reporter were beaten. Formal diplomatic protests over the treatment of the press were made by the American, German, and other embassies, but fell on deaf ears. Relations between the Western media and the Chinese government fell to their lowest level in years.

FRIENDS AND SOURCES

During the Tiananmen protests, Nicholas Kristof and Sheryl WuDunn had become friendly with a Tsinghua University student named Liu Xiang. Arrested after the crackdown, he had managed to escape the city, but in June 1990, returned to Beijing to ask the couple for help in fleeing the country.

Sheryl WuDunn, *New York Times*

He worked for us for a while. He was amazing, just wonderful. We just relied on him so much. We got to know him quite well.

Nichols Kristof, *New York Times*

He had once signed us into Tsinghua. After the crackdown, he tried to deny everything, but they had on paper him signing us in. He claimed he had just met us on the street, but they were suspicious. He fled and tried to get to Hong Kong. But he was arrested, put in prison. He eventually escaped. He came back to Beijing and met secretly with Sheryl and me and asked for our help fleeing China. We didn't know what to do. We trusted Liu Xiang, but he also acknowledged that he had been in prison. You could easily imagine a deal whereby he would be released from prison if he would entrap us. We were very torn about our ethical obligations. On the one hand, here's a nineteen-year-old kid who, if we didn't help him, probably would be arrested. On the other hand, if we did help him, it wasn't clear that he would necessarily get abroad, and not only would we get kicked out of China, but the New York Times *bureau would probably be closed, and that would be a betrayal of our obligation to the* Times. *There's also a sense that if you're in a country, you obey the laws and don't go around helping felons leave the country. Sheryl and I debated this on long walks. Finally, Sheryl said, "Look, he helped us. He helped our readers. We've got to do something." So we very carefully helped him in ways that were deniable, in places where we were sure we weren't being filmed, and he was able to escape to Hong Kong. I flew down to Hong Kong and helped him secretly get to the United States. It was utterly unprofessional, but we were very glad we did.*

Kristof and WuDunn became obsessed with countering the Chinese security apparatus.

Nicholas Kristof, *New York Times*

We were so careful. On our vacations, we would read spy novels, just to figure out how they did this. They would put a hair across their safe to see whether someone had actually opened the safe and would know if the hair was gone. We really did use that method because we were just so worried we would get someone in trouble.

Stifled in so much of her reporting, the *Washington Post*'s Lena Sun was able to resume a friendship she'd made as a student in China in the late seventies with a young man named Bai Weiji, who'd become a Foreign Ministry official.

Lena Sun, *Washington Post*

When I knew him as a student, his whole desire was to be a U.S.-China specialist. He read every book about China in English. He was always explaining Party politics, what was going on. We became good friends. I found him useful in helping to explain what was going on, which was very opaque. I was friends with his wife too. Her English was really good. He would give me internal analyses of what was going on. She would translate them, and it was very useful.

In May 1992, police raided Sun's office in the so-called diplomatic compounds where foreign reporters were required to live.

James McGregor, *Wall Street Journal*

We and Lena lived in the same building, and her son, Benjamin, was really good friends with my daughter Sally. They were really little then. We pull up and Benjamin was on the balcony, the second floor of building seven, and he said, "Bad guys! Bad guys!" Then we went to our apartment and figured out what was going on.

Lena Sun, *Washington Post*

When I opened the door, there were people in uniforms saying they needed to go to my office. We had our little standoff, in which they demanded that I open all my drawers. I'd called the U.S. embassy, and people came over and they stood outside. The bottom line was they found some translated documents and insisted that I sign some confession. In the end, my friend Bai Weiji was charged with treason and sentenced to ten years in jail. His wife was sentenced to six years in jail. They had a little kid who was, I think, younger than my son at the time. Bai was taken away a couple of days before she was, and she called up, she wanted to know whether I would adopt her little girl. That was a heartbreaking conversation. I told her I'm not going to take your child away from you. They had relatives, and eventually the child was raised by the relatives. They both served some jail time, but not the full sentence. I felt guilty. He knew a lot of journalists, but maybe because I was the Washington Post, I was a bigger fish, so they chose to use that as an example.

Sheryl WuDunn, *New York Times*

The night we heard about what happened to Lena's friend, Nick and I just couldn't sleep. I thought—my goodness is there a chance this could happen to one of our own sources? It shook me to the core. It was just chilling.

Nicholas Kristof, *New York Times*

It was really nerve-racking. We had these Chinese friends. We cared very deeply about their safety, and I was terrified we were going to get them in trouble. We stayed up tossing and turning all night, thinking that could have been our friends, and feeling that we wanted out, because at some point our luck was going to run out, and our friends would go to prison.

THE THIRD ANNIVERSARY

That June was the third anniversary of the Tiananmen crackdown. Chito Sta Romana, the onetime Filipino dissident who had come to China with Jaime FlorCruz in 1971 and, like FlorCruz, had stayed, was now the producer at the ABC News Beijing bureau. The ABC correspondent was Todd Carrel, a Chinese speaker who had been based in Beijing since 1985. On June 4, Carrel went to the square to check out a tip that a lone protestor was planning to unfurl a banner.

Chito Sta Romana, ABC News

Our cameraman was on vacation, so he took the camera himself. The guy unfurled a banner, and Todd tried to film it. But there were all these plain- clothesmen who saw him and tried to get the camera away from him. Todd resisted. And these guys had something in a white cloth that they were swing- ing at Todd and hitting. They broke the camera, broke the lens. They got Todd and then dropped him off at the police station. And they worked on him. When Todd came back to the office, he looked fine—a little bruised but fine. And we were able to offer a spot that night for ABC's evening news.

ABC News Broadcast

TODD CARREL: Plainclothes policemen from all over the square descended on us and the man and began beating us and grabbing him.
PETER JENNINGS: And did the authorities have any hesitation in beating up on you and the lone demonstrator?
TODD CARREL: Absolutely not. But these authorities were plainclothesmen. We were later beaten by uniformed police. But they were all the same, part of the big security apparatus of a police state.

But something was clearly wrong with Carrel.

Chito Sta Romana, ABC News

The next day, he didn't come to the office. I said, "What's wrong?" He said he was staying in bed. It went on for a second day, and we started to wonder what's happening. Todd said something's wrong. He talked to New York, and they said we want you to go to Hong Kong for a checkup. He was gone for a couple of days, and then he came back. He said the doctor said I'm clear. But there was something wrong. He still couldn't walk. He couldn't work long hours or regular hours. And he would go back and rest again. Finally, he talked to New York, and they said go back to the States. We'll have it examined. It turned out there was something in his spinal system and he had to go through a series of tests, CAT scans and MRIs. In the end, he never came back. He was a broken man. And up to now, he can't really stay out. If you go out to dinner, he has to lie down. He could never sit for a long time. That's a permanent disability. Of all the foreign journalists, he is certainly one of the worst victims.

With permanent damage, Carrel was forced to leave China and give up his career as a reporter, eventually taking a job as a university journalism professor.

"CODDLING DICTATORS"

The ongoing repression, and the still powerful images from 1989, continued to make the human rights story the dominant narrative in U.S. media coverage of China. With a presidential election in 1992, Democratic candidate Bill Clinton attacked President Bush for being "soft" on China.

James Baker, Secretary of State

I remember when we were running for reelection in 1992 against Clinton, he accused us of "coddling dictators," which I guess was a good political stratagem in the United States.

Almost from the moment the shooting stopped in June 1989, Bush had sought to prevent U.S.-China relations from collapsing.

James Baker, Secretary of State

President Bush called Deng Xiaoping. Deng had been a very close colleague of President Bush when he was there as head of the U.S. Liaison Office. They knew each other. Deng Xiaoping wouldn't take the call, and that angered Bush.

The president then ordered his national security advisor, Brent Scowcroft, and deputy secretary of state, Lawrence Eagleburger, to make a secret trip to Beijing in July 1989.

James Baker, Secretary of State

The rationale for that trip was to let the Chinese know, with presidential envoys, that President Bush wanted to keep this relationship going, even though he was extremely disappointed with the behavior of the Chinese government. He didn't want to break off the relationship. He felt that in the end, it was extraordinarily important to try to keep things moving in a positive direction. We sent them over to make that point.

Five months later, Bush sent the two men on a second trip, which was made public. The day their arrival in Beijing was announced, I happened to be at a reception hosted by the All-China Journalists Federation. It was one of the few occasions where we could interact with Chinese officials in the months following the crackdown. In a casual aside, a Chinese journalist said to me, "You know Scowcroft and Eagleburger were here in July." I expressed surprise, and he told me a few more details, probably based on an internal document he had seen. To learn that Bush had secretly sent two envoys to Beijing within weeks of the crackdown was a big story, but I had no way to confirm it, and didn't want to get this man in trouble. I called the CNN Foreign Desk, told them what I had heard, and the CNN White House correspondent was able to confirm it with Bush's press secretary. The news created a firestorm of criticism in Washington. At no point did I mention where I heard the story, but I later learned that the Chinese journalist had been identified as my source and disciplined.

When Clinton took office in January 1993, he appointed Winston Lord to be assistant secretary of state for East Asia.

Winston Lord, Assistant Secretary of State

Clinton during his campaign, like most presidents in campaigns, was quite tough on China, particularly the human rights dimension. By the time he got in, there was great pressure to either cut off what was called Most Favored Nation [MFN] trade status or load it up with conditions. We confined it to human rights alone. There is no question it did dominate the relationship.

China scholar Kenneth Lieberthal served as Clinton's top Asia expert in the president's second term.

Kenneth Lieberthal, National Security Council

The Clinton administration came into office in the context of very, very nega-
tive views about China, especially on human rights issues. He did try to con-
nect specific progress in human rights issues in China to the annual renewal
of Most Favored Nation trade status.

A traditional term for simply normal trade relations, MFN was something
of a misnomer. But for China, as a nonmarket economy, the status had to be
renewed by the U.S. Congress every year. If not, Chinese exports would be
effectively frozen out of the American market. In the heated atmosphere following the Tiananmen crackdown, it came to be seen as a tool the new administration could use.

Kenneth Lieberthal, National Security Council

The Chinese were determined to convey to the Clinton administration that if
you seek to leverage how we govern our people for favors in terms of American
policy, forget about it. The Chinese made very clear that they would rather lose
MFN trade status than to succumb to blandishments from this new American
administration. At the end of the day the Clinton administration backed down.

The battle over MFN became a staple for the Beijing press corps.

Sheryl WuDunn, *New York Times*

The big story was MFN. We didn't know what was going to happen on human
rights. We didn't know if there was going to be a big clash between the U.S. and
China at some point.

James McGregor, *Wall Street Journal*

Every year when they had the vote to renew it, it set the image agenda for China
in the U.S. That was the story that people chased. But we're in China, and we're
seeing a whole other world. We're seeing China rising, we're seeing a lot of prob-
lems, and, of course, we're seeing a lot of human rights problems etcetera, but
there's this whole other aspect—that China is on the move.

FIGURE 1. John Roderick of the AP with Chairman Mao at the Communist Party's headquarters in the remote northwestern town of Yan'an, 1946. Between 1945 and 1947, Roderick spent seven months there, developing unusually cordial relations with Mao and other top Communist leaders. Associated Press Photo.

FIGURE 2. Stanley Karnow arrived in Hong Kong in 1959 for *Time* magazine, but soon moved to the *Washington Post*. He covered the Cultural Revolution and the Nixon China trip in 1972, although the president so hated the *Washington Post* that he tried unsuccessfully to have Karnow banned from the traveling press corps. Courtesy Catherine Karnow.

FIGURE 3. Seymour Topping of the *New York Times* meeting Premier Zhou Enlai in 1971 in Beijing. Topping had covered the Chinese civil war for the Associated Press. His father-in-law, Canadian diplomat Chester Ronning, had known Zhou in the 1940s and helped arrange Toppings's visit in 1971. Courtesy Audrey Topping.

FIGURE 4. President Richard Nixon poses with the journalists who accompanied him to China. Barbara Walters of NBC is to Nixon's right. Just behind her is CBS News anchorman Walter Cronkite. Kneeling to Nixon's left is CBS News White House correspondent Dan Rather. Richard Nixon Presidential Library and Museum.

FIGURE 5. U.S. network TV crews on the Great Wall of China waiting to cover Nixon's visit. The White House designed the trip as a "television extravaganza," convincing the Chinese to allow unprecedented live coverage of the president's activities. The images helped consolidate public support in the U.S. for Nixon's dramatic diplomatic breakthrough. Courtesy Ed Fouhy.

FIGURE 6. Richard Bernstein of *Time* on a Chinese train, late 1970s. To travel outside Beijing, resident foreign correspondents were required to apply for permission ten days in advance, and were usually accompanied by government minders who monitored their reporting activities. Courtesy Liu Heung-shing.

FIGURE 7. Jim Laurie of ABC shooting video in Beijing in 1981. The American networks were not initially allowed to station camera crews in Beijing, so when ABC, NBC, and CBS opened their bureaus, the correspondent had to do all the shooting as well. Courtesy Jim Laurie.

FIGURE 8. CBS Beijing bureau chief John Sheahan with Deng Xiaoping as *60 Minutes* host Mike Wallace looks on. Wallace's interview with Deng in 1986 was the first time a top Chinese leader had done a one-on-one interview for American television. Courtesy John Liu.

FIGURE 9. Edward Gargan of the *New York Times*, Jaime FlorCruz of *Time*, Stefan Simons of *Der Spiegel*, Joseph Reaves of the *Chicago Tribune*, and Richard Hornik of *Time* covering the Communist Party's thirteenth Congress at the Great Hall of the People in Beijing, October 1987. In a sign of greater openness, this was the first time foreign journalists were allowed to cover a Party Congress. Courtesy Robin Moyer.

FIGURE 10. *Newsweek*'s Dorinda Elliott with dissident astrophysicist Fang Lizhi at a Christmas Party in Beijing, December 1988. The outspoken Fang was a favorite among Western journalists. Six months later, following the crackdown in Tiananmen Square, Fang became one of the most wanted men in China, and sought refuge in the U.S. embassy for a year before being allowed to leave for the United States. Courtesy Dorinda Elliott.

FIGURE 11. The CNN Beijing bureau—correspondent Mike Chinoy, camerawoman Cynde Strand, and soundman Mitch Farkas—in Lhasa, Tibet, 1988. The network's live coverage of the Tiananmen Square crisis in 1989 was the earliest example of what became known as "the CNN effect"—the power of real-time television reporting to shape public opinion and drive policy responses in Washington and other capitals to crises around the world. Courtesy Mike Chinoy.

FIGURE 12. Nicholas Kristof and Sheryl WuDunn of the *New York Times* outside the Times Beijing office, 1988. After covering Tiananmen Square, the husband-and-wife team struggled in their reporting to reconcile the Communist Party's heavy-handed repression with the remarkable economic dynamism that emerged in the 1990s. Courtesy Sheryl Wudunn.

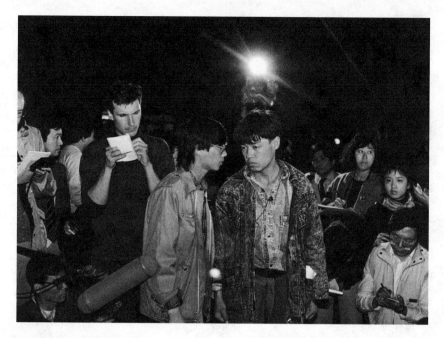

FIGURE 13. John Pomfret of the AP in Tiananmen Square with student movement leaders Wang Dan (l) and Wu'er Kaixi, May 1989. Pomfret was among those who witnessed the army crackdown on the night of June 3–4. Two weeks later, he was expelled from China, but was allowed to return for the *Washington Post* in the late 1990s. Courtesy John Pomfret.

FIGURE 14. Kathy Chen of the *Wall Street Journal* with the Public Security Bureau officials, mid-1990s. Chen befriended children of senior Chinese officials and other "princelings," whose wealth and influence grew as the China boom took off. Courtesy Kathy Chen.

FIGURE 15. The *Wall Street Journal*'s Joseph Kahn interviewing one of China's early stock market traders in Shanghai. The *Journal* opened one of the first American news bureaus in the city in the mid-1990s to cover China's dramatic economic growth, including the first Chinese stock markets. Courtesy Joseph Kahn.

FIGURE 16. Ching-Ching Ni of the *Los Angeles Times* on a reporting trip in impoverished Guizhou province, early 2000s. A naturalized American, Ni was the first person born in the People's Republic to work as a foreign correspondent in China for a U.S. news organization, and devoted particular attention to reporting on what she called "the underbelly" of the Chinese economic miracle. Courtesy Ching-Ching Ni.

FIGURE 17. Melissa Chan of Al Jazeera English interviewing a child living alone in the countryside while her parents worked in the city. Suspicious local authorities complained, and an irate Foreign Ministry official warned the newly arrived Chan that "if Al Jazeera is going to act like BBC and CNN, we're going to start treating Al Jazeera like BBC and CNN." Courtesy Melissa Chan.

FIGURE 18. Austin Ramzy of *Time* with survivors of the Sichuan earthquake, 2008. The Chinese government initially allowed surprisingly unrestricted foreign news coverage of the quake's aftermath, but imposed sharp curbs when journalists began reporting on how corruption in construction projects had caused many poorly built structures to collapse. Later, when the *New York Times* hired Ramzy, Beijing rejected his visa application, and he was forced to leave China for Hong Kong. Courtesy Austin Ramzy.

FIGURE 19. Paul Mozur of the *New York Times* tries on facial recognition glasses used by police at the Zhengzhou train station, 2018. China's use of advanced technology to create a high-tech authoritarian state in the years after Xi Jingping came to power became a central feature of journalistic coverage. Courtesy Paul Mozur.

FIGURE 20. Chao Deng of the *Wall Street Journal* and Chris Buckley of the *New York Times* leave Wuhan as the two-month COVID lockdown there is lifted. During the lockdown, the government ordered both to leave the country, part of a wave of expulsions that dramatically reduced the number of American journalists working in China. Courtesy Chao Deng.

12

A TALE OF TWO CHINAS

In February 1992, Deng Xiaoping, by now officially retired from public life, visited Shanghai and the Shenzhen and Zhuhai Special Economic Zones in southern China, which he had been instrumental in setting up in the early 1980s. The visit took place amid a continuing political struggle within the leadership. Following the crackdown in 1989, Party hardliners had advocated not only crushing any moves toward political liberalization, but also rolling back the market-style economic reforms Deng had pioneered and reasserting state control over the economy. This, they argued, was the only way to ensure the Party's continued survival. Deng, however, especially in the wake of the collapse of the Soviet Union in 1991, reached the opposite conclusion— that only accelerated economic reform, and the attendant economic growth, could help the Party stay in power.

In a sign of the resistance he faced, Deng, despite his immense prestige, organized his trip in secret. Initially, his talks and meetings with reform-minded officials in the two zones were ignored by the Party-controlled media. Journalists in nearby Hong Kong got wind of Deng's presence, however, and after a flurry of reports appeared in the Hong Kong and international press, Deng's calls for faster reform and greater openness to foreign investment and enterprise finally received coverage from the central media in Beijing. The journey became known as the Nanxun, or "Southern Tour," language previously used to describe travel by the emperor and his entourage in long-ago dynasties. For the eighty-eight-year-old Deng, it was a final political initiative, but it was enough to break the deadlock within the leadership and spark a new wave of entrepreneurial energy that would usher in decades of astonishing economic growth.

Orville Schell, *New Yorker*

Deng Xiaoping was on the march again. When he went to Shenzhen in 1992, it was clear that he had thrown half the reform program out of the window, but it was the half that he never really subscribed to anyhow, the political reform. He was back, going to ram home a new program of economic reform. That was a monumental moment, as monumental in a way as when Deng Xiaoping came to America in 1979.

Sheryl WuDunn, *New York Times*

I think the foreign press focused too much on human rights, and they missed the economic story. What was going on was this economic dynamism. It was a dynamo. This was the beginning of the economic revolution.

J. Stapleton Roy, U.S. Ambassador

It wasn't until Deng visited southern China and declared that the new economic zones there were the right way to go that the tide turned, and the hardline elements were essentially purged during the fourteenth Party Congress in the fall of 1992. Beginning in 1993, China's economy started taking off. The American business community noticed this immediately, and they began to flock into China. Every American during 1993 who visited China was shocked to discover that the circumstances in China were so much better than was being reported in the American media. I raised this with the American journalistic community and said, "Why is it that your reporting is giving a totally distorted view of China?" I remember some of the responses—that the incentive structures were set up so that if you reported negative things about China, you got front-page coverage, and if you reported positive developments in China, either it wasn't reported or it got buried in rear pages. Journalists are human beings like everyone else, and they like front-page stories. There was a built-in incentive bias in a free press that resulted in a very distorted view of what was being reported out of China.

"YOU COULD FEEL IT COMING"

Slowly, however, American journalists did begin to shift their focus away from human rights and toward a country consumed by a gold rush.

Lena Sun, *Washington Post*

You could see it bubble up, this desire, this rush to embrace materialism.

James McGregor, *Wall Street Journal*

They were so eager for foreign investment. Because I was from the Wall Street Journal, *they wanted to know how I could bring in foreign investment. Every time you'd go to an economic zone, or meet a mayor, or even a governor, Party secretary, who were all pretty accessible those days, they'd all tell you the same things. They'd say, "OK, you're from the* Wall Street Journal. *How can we get more foreign investment? How can you help us?" I remember being in Wenzhou, a place of pretty deep capitalism, and I was sitting with this guy. Deng had just gone on his trip to the south. This guy pulled out plans for a bank and said, "I've been waiting for this, and now I can finally go through with this," even though private banking was still illegal. That meeting in Wenzhou was an "aha" moment for me. In business, you could smell it and feel it coming.*

Andrew Browne had started out as a reporter for the *South China Morning Post* in Hong Kong in the 1980s. Now with Reuters, he set up the first Western news bureau in Shanghai, which soon became the epicenter of the emerging boom.

Andrew Browne, Reuters

After 1989, the conventional wisdom was that this was a big setback for economic reform. I think a lot of the businesses felt exactly same way. They had all left after 1989. The banks, big multinationals, pulled people out. Then you had this amazing episode, the southern tour, and it flipped the atmosphere. Shanghai had really been electrified by Deng Xiaoping's trip. After the southern tour, Reuters decided they needed to open a bureau in Shanghai. The city itself was changing visibly. The topography of the city was being transformed.

The economy was taking off. This was now China's market economy. From a news perspective, it meant we had to suddenly take teams of reporters who had been pretty much geared to the political/social story and repurpose them for covering markets. And such a creature didn't exist. There weren't reporters at the time who understood, and I didn't myself, how do you cover a futures market? And there were a dozen, two-dozen futures markets suddenly set up all over China. Plywood futures in Suzhou. Mung bean futures in Dalian. Grains futures in Zhengzhou. And these were big markets.

Marcus Brauchli had worked for AP-Dow Jones in the mid-1980s covering the Chinese economy from Hong Kong. In 1987, he joined the *Wall Street Journal*, based first in Europe and Japan, before returning to Hong Kong in 1992, and then moving to China.

Marcus Brauchli, *Wall Street Journal*

The Journal *covered China a lot more aggressively than our big newspaper rivals did through most of the 1990s, because we saw it as a central story for our core readership, which is business. It's not that we only covered business stories. You can't cover China meaningfully without understanding the politics, because they have such profound impact on business. But it was a story that really was about economic advance. We had opened the first American news bureau in Shanghai in '93 or '94 with Joe Kahn. We hired Joe from the Dallas News. I decided to move the bureau chief's job to Shanghai instead of Beijing to signal that we were about covering the socioeconomic changes in China, not the pronouncements of various government agencies.*

Joseph Kahn had earned an MA in East Asian studies from Harvard and arrived in Beijing for the *Dallas Morning News* in 1992. In 1993, he joined the *Journal*'s new Shanghai bureau.

Joseph Kahn, *Wall Street Journal*

Shanghai had only recently been opened up to foreign journalists. The foreign press was very small. The Wall Street Journal *set up an office. Then the Associated Press. A short time after, so did the* New York Times. *Then there were a couple of Japanese organizations. But when we formed the first Foreign Correspondents Club in Shanghai sometime in late '93 or early '94, we could all sit around one dinner table in a restaurant, including the Japanese. It was pretty tiny. But Shanghai was viewed by the leadership as a bigger experiment than the southern China, Shenzhen, Guangzhou openness to foreign investment had been. They were now willing to experiment with economic reform in a much larger and, for the Party, a much more vital center of industry and commerce. My initial foray there was about the revival of the spirit of economic reform. People were looking to get ahead. You could sense the energy. The big excitement was about the creation of domestic stock markets. The financial industry was getting a fair amount of buzz and attention as being a real sign of forward progress. There was a culture of investment, not all of it very healthy, much of it pure speculation. But that gave a little inkling that we were in a new era, where capital was being freed up and people were being allowed to invest their money in new ways.*

James McGregor, *Wall Street Journal*

The first business story I wrote in China was about a guy nicknamed "Millions Yang" in Shanghai, who had cornered four or six stocks on this illegal market. And then one thing led to another, and the markets just exploded.

Lena Sun, *Washington Post*

At the time there were all these millionaires in the making. Some of them were local in Beijing and I was writing about them. That was really new. You just couldn't believe that they were doing that. It was a sign of people really deciding, "OK, we're going to go for it, we've got the green light."

Kathy Chen, a Chinese American who had started her journalism career writing for an English-language newspaper in Taiwan in the mid-1980s, was assigned to the *Journal*'s Beijing bureau. She soon started hanging out at a riding stable just outside the capital run by a former senior military officer and catering to China's new rich.

Kathy Chen, *Wall Street Journal*

A lot of the kids of the military leaders used to go there and they brought their own horses. It was just the beginning of the Chinese who were getting very wealthy off these business opportunities opened up by Deng's southern tour.

They were feeling that they wanted to really live, so they bought horses. They bought dogs. Those were sources that turned out to be really helpful, because there were people you met outside of the official channels, who heard rumors, who knew things. For example, I did a story about princelings and how they were involved in business. I was trying to capture the go-go Wild West atmosphere of Chinese scrambling to make money after '92. Everybody was trying to set up their own business and enjoying the fruits of their wealth. Trying to cover all that was really fascinating.

MACHO SINO GIRLS

Chen found that being Chinese American was a huge advantage.

Kathy Chen, *Wall Street Journal*

Part of the thing was that people kind of accepted you as Chinese. They would tell you things like, "Oh, you understand. You're a Chinese person." But they kind of automatically expected you to take their position. "You're patriotic. You understand what China's going through." But it also allowed me to melt into the crowd at times, which was very helpful, because back in the early 1990s, the State Security police were all over the place.

The *New York Times*'s Sheryl WuDunn had the same experience.

Sheryl WuDunn, *New York Times*

It was much easier for me to operate in China because Nick just stood out so plainly, whereas I could really blend in. People would often prefer to meet with me than with him. People did not feel threatened by me. I think that ultimately helped me and other Chinese American reporters.

But looking local had its drawbacks, as WuDunn discovered at a party attended by the minister of construction.

Sheryl WuDunn, *New York Times*

Some of his representatives came over to me and said, "The minister would like to have a dance." I said, "Oh, sure." I had a dance, and then he really started doing a lot more than just dancing. I kept pushing back. I said,

"Wow, he's really being aggressive. I know what I'll do. I'll tell him I'm from the New York Times." *And that really did startle him. He thought that I was one of the secretaries there. I guess, on the one hand, that's the good side, because you blend in like you're a Chinese. On the other hand, you also get treated like a Chinese who sometimes are not treated very well if you're a young woman.*

WuDunn, the *Washington Post*'s Lena Sun, and some other women foreign correspondents formed an informal club.

Lena Sun, *Washington Post*

It turned out there were all these women who were ethnic Chinese working as journalists in China. And we decided that we would have this group, and it was called MSG, Macho Sino Girls—we give you a headache.

Sheryl WuDunn, *New York Times*

It was just a matter of getting together every once in a while and commiserat[ing], shar[ing] war stories, because there were just a few Chinese American girls together, so we would just meet everyone, I think it was once a month, or every two months. It was just a lot of fun.

TRANSITIONS

Also joining a rapidly changing U.S. press corps was Wen-Chun Fan, a Chinese American who had studied at Peking University. He was hired as a cameraman by CNN.

Wen-Chun Fan, CNN

I think it was really helpful in terms of being able to blend in. And people wouldn't automatically associate you with being a journalist. And I spoke Chinese without an accent, so it would be fine. People would think I was a local, so it was an advantage.

Another new addition was Ian Johnson, who had studied Chinese in Beijing from 1984 to 1985, became the *Baltimore Sun* China correspondent in 1994, and then joined the *Wall Street Journal* in 1997.

Ian Johnson, *Wall Street Journal*

My university had an academic exchange program with Peking University and in 1984 I went for a year. I realized how much I liked the place. I decided I wanted to be a foreign correspondent. In 1994, I felt that there was a generational change going on. Correspondents who had covered Tiananmen Square were slowly leaving or had already left, and there were people coming who hadn't covered Tiananmen.

In the years after the Tiananmen crackdown, United Press International's bureau chief David Schweisberg had continued to win respect for his insightful reporting, and his willingness to challenge Chinese officials. On one occasion, in response to a question about Tibet, a Foreign Ministry official launched into the standard recitation of how criticism of China's Tibet policy "hurt the feelings of the Chinese people." Schweisberg retorted, "Oh come on. You know as well as I do that the Tibet question doesn't hurt the feelings of the Chinese people. What hurts the feelings of the Chinese people is inflation and corruption."

But, especially as the social climate became more relaxed, Schweisberg also became, as one colleague put it, "the original blues brother of Beijing." Wearing his trademark Stetson hat and sunglasses, a cigarette between his lips, he was an enthusiastic proponent of China's burgeoning youth culture, holding unofficial art exhibitions in his apartment and arranging venues for local rock 'n' roll bands that were beginning to emerge. He was also a member of Beijing's first expat rock group, the Back Door Band (a sardonic reference to China's ubiquitous official corruption), jamming with the likes of famed Chinese rocker Cui Jian and the controversial all-girl band Cobra.

In November 1993, Schweisberg, who'd been warned by his doctor that the pressures of his job and his hard living were jeopardizing his health, collapsed and died of a heart attack. He was just thirty-nine. He had been my best friend in Beijing, and it was a bitter blow. A number of us organized a memorial. Dozens of Chinese musicians, artists, and dissidents attended. I remember thinking to myself, "Even now, Schweisberg has better Chinese contacts than almost any other journalist!"

BREAKING THE IRON RICE BOWL

To the surprise of many correspondents, Jiang Zemin, who'd replaced the liberal Zhao Ziyang during the crisis of 1989, emerged as a strong supporter of Deng's reforms. Jiang was assisted by Zhu Rongji, the charismatic, blunt-talking former mayor of Shanghai.

Joseph Kahn, *Wall Street Journal*

Zhu Rongji had a very positive reputation as a pragmatist, a problem-solver. Zhu was respected in the Shanghai context as someone who got things done, who understood economics, of being very hands-on. There was a strike—he figured out a way to defuse it. There was a crisis between foreign investor and Chinese joint-venture partner—he sat them down and talked them through it and came up with a solution. That was Zhu Rongji's reputation. As he started to rise in the central government, I think that was somewhat coincident with the rising expectations that maybe reform was real this time around.

Ian Johnson, *Wall Street Journal*

We did quite a long interview with Zhu. As usual, we had to submit five or six questions in advance. He basically said, "I've seen your questions. Do you want me to answer any of them? If not, why don't you start asking questions?" We were like, "Whoa, this is good," and we started asking questions. This guy was more like a British prime minister, used to the question-and-answer session. He could sit there and talk about anything. Our CEO, Peter Kann, who had also been a foreign correspondent in Asia twenty years or so earlier, asked a question. "One of the most enduring images for Americans," he said, "is of the man standing in front of the tank in Tiananmen Square." And Zhu Rongji said, "One of the enduring images that we have of the United States is a little girl being napalmed on the streets of Vietnam." He said, "In China, we didn't kill the man, but you guys napalmed the little girl. Who's worse?" And were like, "touché." And this was unprepared. He was the kind of person that can think up such answers.

One of the key reforms Zhu spearheaded was the restructuring of China's inefficient, money-losing state-owned enterprises—shattering the cradle-to-grave provision of jobs and welfare benefits that had been a hallmark of the Chinese system.

Ian Johnson, *Wall Street Journal*

Zhu was the most arrogant SOB you've ever met. He was also one of the most brilliant SOBs you've ever met. The problem was he knew it, and he was so arrogant and insufferable. And you can only imagine what it'll be like if you were some SOE [state-owned enterprise] flunky who was losing money or doing something terrible. Zhu would give you a tongue-lashing. The story of how he pushed through reforms was legendary.

Charles Hutzler, who received a degree in East Asian studies from Yale and studied Chinese in Taiwan, joined the AP's Beijing bureau in 1995.

Charles Hutzler, Associated Press

It was a period of shock and pain, especially in urban China, where you had state-run factories in many cases laying off almost all their workforce. If you went to towns in the northeast, real centers of the state-run economy, of heavy industry, these were communities in great pain.

Joseph Kahn, *Wall Street Journal*

When you went up to northeast China, for example, to cover one of these mass layoffs at a steel mill, once you were seen in the crowd, you were often singled out by thugs, plainclothes police officers or people employed by the factory, who would unceremoniously spirit you away and hold you for interrogation. You knew they were not going to do anything to you because they had no real legal power, but you would end up wasting six or eight hours. There was no physical threat, but there was a real threat that you were going to spend a couple of days and lose your story. If you were traveling with a photographer, the film would be taken. If you were traveling with notes, you were going to lose your notes. You would never travel with a laptop because they were going to want to look at your computer. So you had to prepare yourself for those kind of low-level confrontations, which were more annoying than scary, but annoying enough that you really had to think about swooping in and getting enough and getting out within twenty-four hours. That was the way you covered an ongoing protest.

IN SEARCH OF FORTUNE

As the restructuring helped to reinvigorate a long-moribund economy, one of the big stories was the movement of people from the countryside to the coastal areas, where a rapidly growing number of foreign-funded factories were located.

Kathy Chen, *Wall Street Journal*

At that time, there were about one hundred million migrant workers—farmers, peasants, mostly young people who would flock from the countryside to the cities in southern China along the coast and find factory work. We wanted to do a story. A lot of the people came from the poorer inland provinces like Sichuan. Back then we had to get permission to go anywhere outside Beijing to do any reporting. We reached out to the local Foreign Ministry people. I told them I wanted to follow some migrant workers as they made their trip to the coast. They actually found me a bunch of girls in their late teens who were making this trip. I went out to Sichuan to this little village and met them.

They were taking a five-day bus ride. We were going to somewhere on the coast. I didn't know where or what factory they were going to. I just got on this rickety bus with them. We went through Guilin and Guizhou, some of the poorer parts of the country. For these girls though, it was both exciting and a little scary and extremely uncomfortable at the beginning, because so many of them were carsick and so they would all be throwing up outside of the windows. There was no shower. Everybody went to the bathroom whenever they stopped, and brushed your teeth, if you were lucky. It was five days of this. By the end of it the whole place smelled like vomit and sweat. It was really disgusting.

We ended up in Guangdong, at a Mattel Barbie doll factory. Mattel had dorms. The girls all had IDs. I didn't follow them in on the first day, but I was able to sneak in later because I looked Chinese. I was able to see the conditions of the dorms and talk to them and follow up on what they were doing, which was stitching hair onto the scalps of Barbie doll heads for a couple hundred dollars a month.

But it wasn't just a story of exploitation, which was the easy line to take. They were living fifteen to a room, a couple of bathrooms that were holes in the walls, running water sometimes, very few days off, working ten-hour days or longer. But for the girls it wasn't all awful. They saw it as a real adventure. It gave them a way to get out of the boredom of the villages, where they really had nothing to do and there were no job opportunities.

Marcus Brauchli, *Wall Street Journal*

She had the advantage of looking like many of the people she was traveling with, so she slipped right in. And she wrote an incredibly poignant and powerful story about what this internal migration is like, the human side of this emerging economic powerhouse. That's a story that I think really began to shape the world's understanding of how China really worked.

SIGNS OF RELAXATION

Kathy Chen's ability to make that trip was one sign of how the economic liberalization was beginning to lead to better working conditions for foreign reporters.

Charles Hutzler, Associated Press

I think by the mid-1990s, it had become easy to travel around, and especially to go to other cities, and not stand out. You could actually do reporting for a few days in different cities without having the police track you down. The smart Chinese companies were more than willing to have foreign reporters come and talk to them, and this was happening throughout society.

For foreign journalists to travel outside Beijing, though, it was still necessary to get permission from the local Foreign Affairs Office. But the hunger for money made that easier too.

Ian Johnson, *Wall Street Journal*

If you can come up with a halfway plausible idea to go somewhere, you could get approval. You still had to contact the local waiban *[Foreign Affairs Office] and fax them the themes, where you wanted to go, what kind of people you wanted to interview, and it would take them a week or two to get back to you. But they would often arrange it for you. Partly because they were motivated by money, the Foreign Affairs Office would start charging a day rate for their people, which is kind of fresh if you think about it. You are paying for someone to mind you. But they said they were a guide, and you had to pay for a car and a driver. And they would also put you in a local hotel, and they probably had some relationship with the hotel, and were probably making a kickback off this. So they were kind of eager, depending on their entrepreneurial spirit.*

From his base in Hong Kong, Keith Richburg, who had previously been based in the Philippines and then in Africa, was traveling regularly to Beijing for the *Washington Post*.

Keith Richburg, *Washington Post*

That was an amazing time to cover China. Where the tanks once rolled, I was seeing signs for Hennessy cognac. I was seeing signs for luxury goods. I was thinking to myself—this is some amazing transformation going on. Beijing was really exploding. It went from being this difficult place for correspondents to live to actually being kind of fun. This was only five or six years after Tiananmen. They really wanted to be as helpful as they could to journalists. I used to go out to dinner with Foreign Ministry spokesman Shen Guofang and his wife. Kathy Chen of the Wall Street Journal*—we used to take Shen out bowling. You actually could develop personal relationships with people.*

The reporters began to cover a new, post-Tiananmen youth culture.

Keith Richburg, *Washington Post*

There were a lot of journalists who were pretty scarred by Tiananmen Square. They were there. They saw what happened. They had friends who had to leave the country, or who were unaccounted for or missing. And then there were other journalists who came in and saw that China was a booming, bustling place and it was changing before our eyes. And we just wanted to cover that part of China that was changing, and not be trapped into writing about the ghost of Tiananmen. I was able to bring this fresh eye. There were a lot more clubs and places to go eat, and places to party. I covered the story of the first big American-style megadisco that opened in Beijing, called Nightman. I did stories about the first computer matchmaking service for Chinese. I wrote a story about the first sex shop for women opening outside of Beijing. I was able to write a story about the rising divorce rate. There were all these things going on in society that were absolutely fascinating.

THE SHANGHAI BOOM

Marcus Brauchli, *Wall Street Journal*

Shanghai was a fun place to live—a place where there weren't the controls you had in Beijing. The energy was just pounding. You had thirty million people on the make. I used to say China's not a free-market economy, China's a free-for-all economy. Everybody was trying to do something in Shanghai in those days.

I had first visited Shanghai in 1973. Everything was drab and rundown. Everyone seemed to be wearing blue-grey Mao jackets. By early evening, everything had closed. The streets were virtually deserted. I returned to Shanghai frequently over the years, and by the mid-1990s, as I was winding up my time as CNN's China correspondent, you could really start to see the changes. People—especially young people—were wearing much more stylish clothing. The billboards were full of advertisements for Western consumer goods, and department stores were full of color TVs, refrigerators, and air conditioners. The streets were packed and illuminated by neon signs at night. It really felt like a boomtown, like Shanghai was on its way to recapturing its pre-1949 glory.

Marcus Brauchli was so caught up in the go-go atmosphere that he opened a bar with a friend.

Marcus Brauchli, *Wall Street Journal*

We had very strict rules at the Wall Street Journal *about what you could do, so I got in touch with a lawyer, and said, "Would it be alright if I invested in this restaurant/bar that some friends and I are thinking of opening?" They said, "As long as you don't write about restaurants and bars in Shanghai," which I thought would be no problem at all. So in 1997, I and a friend opened a bar and restaurant called Park 97. It was just a lounge and nightclub scene, something fun to do. It was several thousand square feet. We actually had too much space. We had to rent out part of it to an art gallery, Shang Art, which became the biggest contemporary art gallery in Shanghai. It had a restaurant because we thought you needed a place to go outside of hotels, and it had this lounge with these booths, and behind the booths on the wall was a sort of exaggerated stylistic painting of a rotund obese naked woman.*

Brauchli and his wife, *Los Angeles Times* Hong Kong correspondent Maggie Farley, also organized an annual ball at Shanghai's legendary Peace Hotel, which had been the center of expat life before the Communist revolution.

Marcus Brauchli, *Wall Street Journal*

My wife was in Hong Kong. I was in Shanghai, so we had what we called the commuter's ball I organized every October. In Chinese we called it the waidiren wanhui, *the migrant worker's evening party. And we'd invite several hundred people to come and usually in an old colonial-style building. We'd have a jazz band. It would be a good party.*

Andrew Browne, Reuters

It was a party time in Shanghai. The commuters' ball in the Peace Hotel. It wasn't just a party for China. This was a regional party. People flew in from everywhere. Shanghai was the aspirational place. You wanted to be there. It's where things were happening. It's where China was reinventing itself.

Keith Richburg, *Washington Post*

I call that the golden age of covering China. It really was.

THE DENG XIAOPING DEATHWATCH

As China continued to open up, however, a cloud was hovering over the country. Deng Xiaoping was in his nineties and visibly failing. The People's Republic had a history of tumultuous leadership transitions. When Chairman Mao died, his widow, Jiang Qing, who had sought to seize power, was purged and put on trial. During the Tiananmen Square crisis, Deng Xiaoping's designated heir, Zhao Ziyang, was ousted and spent the rest of his life under house arrest. For the foreign press, the Deng Xiaoping deathwatch became an all-consuming obsession.

Keith Richburg, *Washington Post*

The Deng deathwatch was pretty amazing. He loomed over China. There could be turmoil. There could be factions fighting within the military. So, the rule was we could not leave China uncovered for a single minute while Deng Xiaoping was still clinging to life. China being China, we never had any real information. Any time there was an official event and Deng didn't appear, we would automatically think, "Oh my God, he's probably dead or dying."

Charles Hutzler, Associated Press

We never could leave the office unstaffed. This was before the days of supremely portable communications. So we were constantly on deathwatch.

Lena Sun, *Washington Post*

It was a constant preoccupation for reporters. After Deng, what will happen? Will there be chaos? I remember that every time there was a murmur or a whisper that Deng had died, and this happened hundreds of times, I'd get an email or a telex from my editor saying, "Hearing from good sources that Deng has died." I remember one time I got these telexes I was in Yunnan. I was in a hotel. The pillows were made of like barleycorn inside. I said, "I don't even have access to telex. What do you expect me to do?" That was part of this constant obsession people had about Deng's health. You constantly had that worry: What will I do if Deng dies?

Ian Johnson, *Wall Street Journal*

There were all these scenarios. There might be war, there might be this, there might be that. That Jiang Zemin only was there for the graces of Deng Xiaoping. When he left, there are going to be other people that would take over or push Jiang Zemin out of the way.

On the evening of February 19, 1997, Deng Xiaoping died. Rebecca MacKinnon, a fluent Chinese speaker who'd lived in Beijing as a child with her parents, who were China scholars, returned to the country as a producer in the CNN bureau.

Rebecca MacKinnon, CNN

I got a call from a Chinese friend saying, "It looks like he might have really died." I said, "Is this a rumor or is this real?" He said, "This is real." It had to do with a communication that had gone to somebody very senior at China Central Television [CCTV] being told to get ready. They wouldn't have gotten that communication unless it was real. I rushed back to the bureau, and started putting together notes, watching the wires and Xinhua. We needed more confirmation. False rumors of Deng's death had caught many a journalist in past. Mei Yan, who was working as an assignment editor on the CNN International Desk at network headquarters in Atlanta, is from China and had high-ranking connections both through her family and professionally. She managed to confirm it through a relative of somebody high-ranking in the Chinese elite. We decided to go with it. It wasn't very long after that that

Xinhua started coming out with the news. The significance was this was very much the end of an era. It also marked a great deal of uncertainty, because of course Deng had been the architect of reform, and there was uncertainty kind of as to what direction Jiang Zemin and Zhu Rongji would take after Deng had passed on.

The formal transition to Jiang Zemin, however, proved surprisingly anticlimactic.

Jaime FlorCruz, *Time*

The expected political crisis or protest out in the streets or factional divide spilling over into the streets of China didn't happen.

Rebecca MacKinnon, CNN

For ordinary people it was completely uneventful. It was so different from Mao's passing. That was kind of like a mountain fell down and the Earth moved, and nobody was sure what the world would be like the next day, because he was so central to everything. But with Deng's passing, people had mixed feelings. People on the street, when you asked them what they thought, were like, "Well, I have to go to work and I have to get on with life," and so on.

Charles Hutzler, Associated Press

This was a great sign of the degree to which China had become a more normal society. For most people, there might have been a twinge of sadness, but most were interested in getting on with their lives.

As they covered the reaction to Deng's death, the reporters also found that for many Chinese, his role in changing China far outweighed his responsibility for Tiananmen Square.

Keith Richburg, *Washington Post*

I went to Shenzhen and started talking to anybody I could about what Deng had meant to Shenzhen. The first thing I saw when I got in a taxi at the train station was a huge portrait of Deng smiling over the city. Even the ubiquitous taxi driver who we all quote started telling me what a good man Deng was.

I found there was real affection for Deng. Not that many people mentioned Tiananmen Square. They mentioned the fact that this place was booming. His death ended up being kind of a nonevent. We all thought it would be a huge event, but the Chinese were actually far more ready for it, and far more accepting of it than the foreign press was at the time.

NEW FACES

In the wake of Deng's passing, there were some significant changes in the American press corps, including the return of John Pomfret, who, as an Associated Press correspondent, had been expelled from China in the wake of the Tiananmen crackdown, and had spent the years since covering the war in Bosnia for the *Washington Post*. But to get a visa, Pomfret had to write something Beijing could interpret as an "apology."

John Pomfret, *Washington Post*

I wrote a self-criticism but writing it so that if one day it was published in the People's Daily, I would be not embarrassed. But I knew I had to express a personal sense of maturation, if you will, or understanding, which I did. And it was relatively easy, because I said I was in Bosnia for four years, and I understand what chaos is, and I wouldn't want chaos visited upon by any country, China being one of them. That is from the heart.

The government approved his journalist's visa. After several years away, mostly covering the war in the Balkans, Pomfret was amazed by what he found in China.

John Pomfret, *Washington Post*

I appreciated very deeply the fact the Chinese wanted to build roads and [unlike in war zones] didn't want to mine them. That helped add a certain level of understanding when writing about this place. When I came back, that energy from the south had moved to the north, and the whole country had been caffeinated, and the whole China is go-go China.

Melinda Liu, who'd opened the *Newsweek* bureau in 1980, also returned for a second assignment, and had a similar reaction.

Melinda Liu, *Newsweek*

This is like a whole new world. There are physical things that might seem familiar, but then if you dig underneath them, it's totally not what you thought it would be. China was moving out of not only its own past, feudal past, Tiananmen past, Maoist past—that was all going away. And it had begun to embrace the future—the new stuff, the Internet, market economy, and all these things.

Elisabeth Rosenthal, who had been trained as a doctor and was covering health issues in the United States, arrived for the *New York Times.*

Elisabeth Rosenthal, *New York Times*

I was not a China person. The Times *was looking to expand the bureau to two people. We were looking for a foreign assignment, my ex-husband and I, and we were looking at the bureaus that were open. We wanted to go someplace where we thought there was a compelling political story, so Beijing became our target. Luckily for me, it was a time when social issues like education, health, family were really exploding in China, so it seemed like a good fit.*

Like Melinda Liu, Rosenthal was impressed by what she saw.

Elisabeth Rosenthal, *New York Times*

We met Chinese who were buying their first cars or flats. They were going on their first vacations. They were taking these road trips. I knew a kid who was a student at Peking University, and when the NBA playoffs were happening, I said, "Can I come up and watch them with you and your friends?" I remember being crammed into a dorm room with these six kids in basketball attire going berserk over the NBA playoffs. It was telling that they would let me be in their room as a foreign journalist. If they had been having a political conversation in that room, that would have been a no-go. But basketball was OK. Still, it was a real time of transformation. From a social perspective it was a pretty extraordinary time to watch this society open up.

The Chinese media, long tightly controlled, reflected this greater openness.

Jaime FlorCruz, *Time*

They started to be more robust and to a certain extent freer to write—not about sensitive topics—but beyond those topics, to write various stories in a more interesting and real way.

Elisabeth Rosenthal, *New York Times*

You began to see the media open up on social issues. We had read a story about Gao Yaojie, a physician—an elderly gynecologist in Hunan province—who was working with sex workers, teaching them about STDs. And I thought that's an interesting little feature story.

Despite the relaxation the Chinese press still faced significant restrictions. The correspondents found that frustrated Chinese journalists themselves often became important sources.

Rebecca MacKinnon, CNN

I had friends who worked in the Chinese media in the nineties. There was certainly kind of a relationship by which there were some things your Chinese friends knew they would never get published or aired in the Chinese media but wanted it to get out.

THE HONG KONG HANDOVER

On July 1, 1997, Britain handed Hong Kong back to China. For the Chinese leadership, regaining sovereignty was a moment of supreme importance, rectifying what Beijing saw as a national humiliation. Beijing promised that Hong Kong could retain its freewheeling way of life under a formula called "One Country, Two Systems." For the American and international press corps, charting how a Westernized, capitalist colony would be absorbed by a state led by a Communist Party was a major story.

Keith Richburg, *Washington Post*

I was there for the handover. That was why the Washington Post *decided to open a bureau in Hong Kong, just to be there for the handover. That was going to be a dramatic time to be there.*

I had finally left Beijing and moved to Hong Kong to head a newly established CNN bureau. The idea was that the handover was going to be a huge story, and CNN sent anchors, correspondents, and camera crews from the United States and Europe to cover it. But after the drama of the handover ceremony, life largely went on as normal and the situation in Hong Kong was quickly overshadowed by other news.

Indeed, it would be more than twenty years before the fears so widespread in 1997 that China would not honor its pledges to preserve the territory's freedoms proved true. Only in 2020, following months of sometimes violent predemocracy, antigovernment protests, did Beijing impose a draconian national security law that led to the arrests of virtually all opposition voices and the stifling of Hong Kong's once-lively press.

On July 1, 1997, however, the images of Communist Party chief Jiang Zemin and Premier Li Peng, widely reviled in the West as the "butcher of Beijing" for his role in 1989, standing next to Britain's Prince Charles and Prime Minister Tony Blair, became a symbol of how China's leadership was emerging from the shadows of Tiananmen Square. A further step in that direction came in October 1997, when Jiang Zemin paid a state visit to the United States, which Bill Clinton reciprocated by visiting Beijing in June 1998. Clinton had dropped his efforts to link the renewal of Most Favored Nation status to China's human rights record, and both summits were designed to stabilize Sino-American relations. But the legacy of Tiananmen continued to shape the relationship, leading to a remarkable televised exchange between the two leaders in Beijing.

CLINTON: We still disagree about the meaning of what happened then. I believe, and the American people believe, that the use of force and the tragic loss of life was wrong.
JIANG: With regard to the political disturbances in 1989, had the Chinese government not taken the resolute measures, then we could not have enjoyed the stability we are enjoying today.

THE TENTH ANNIVERSARY

With the arrival of 1999, the tenth anniversary of the Tiananmen crackdown was approaching. It would turn out to be a tumultuous end to the decade. At CNN, Rebecca MacKinnon, now the bureau chief, began assembling a tenth-anniversary documentary, working with Chinese American camera-man Wen-chun Fan.

Rebecca MacKinnon, CNN

We had a conversation about an hour-long special and dividing it up in such-and-such a way, and here are some of the elements that we might want to include. I knew that if we waited until close to June it would be hopeless. There would be no way we'd be able to interview anybody. We had to think far in advance and start collecting interviews right away.

They decided to try to interview Ding Zilin, the mother of a student killed on June 4, 1989.

Rebecca MacKinnon, CNN

Ding had become a leader of the movement of bereaved families trying to get recognition for their loved ones' deaths. Of course, her house was always watched. So Wen-chun and I decided that Chinese New Year was a great oppor-tunity to pay visits to elderly people. Wen-chun had a lot of experience in outsmarting the authorities and was very creative. He dismantled the camera, put it in a gym bag, put on not very nice clothing. It was winter so I covered myself up and we just showed up at her house unannounced. We had parked the car far away, masquerading as people going to see grandma, got into the apartment, and managed to interview her. Because that was successful, we thought maybe we should try doing this with a few other people.

They decided to contact an even more controversial figure, Bao Tong, who had been secretary to Zhao Ziyang in 1989, had been jailed for eight years, and was now under house arrest.

Rebecca MacKinnon, CNN

Wen-chun dismantled the camera. I wore a Chinese coat with a hood. We got a plastic bag of Chinese medicine and a fruit basket and parked the car quite far away, and walked over, managed to walk right up to his apartment, knocked on the door. He opens it. "Hi, we're CNN." And he's like, "Oh great. Wait in there. I'll be right there." Wen-chun reassembled the camera, took a tape out of his back vest in his pocket, and we proceeded to do the interview, in which

Bao was scathing about the current generation of leaders, who he called the successors of Deng Xiaoping's mistakes, and placed the blame squarely on Deng. It was quite an interview.

Wen-Chun Fan, CNN

We pretty much knew that we would be intercepted by the security guards when we left the apartment, so we gave the tape that had the interview on it to Bao, and we would arrange to pick it up some other time in some other place. But we figured the security people knew what they were doing, and they'd ask to see that tape, and it would look dumb if we showed up with a camera with a blank tape inside.

Rebecca MacKinnon, CNN

And we proceeded to record an exchange in which I pleaded with him to grant an interview, and he continued to politely and steadfastly refuse. He said, "Oh I'm very, very sorry. It's really inconvenient for me to accept this interview at this time. I really don't think it's a good time."

Wen-Chun Fan, CNN

We walked out of the apartment with that tape in the camera, and, sure enough, the security guards stopped us. We were taken to a room. They asked us a lot of questions.

Rebecca MacKinnon, CNN

They mainly dealt with, "Why were you conducting this interview without permission?" I said, "He refused to grant the interview, and the tape is in the camera." They asked to see the video. We played it back to them. There was Bao saying, "I don't want to be interviewed." That was our story. We had to sit around for several hours while they found somebody from the Foreign Affairs police to sign off on all the paperwork for our detention. They gave me tea. I tended in these circumstances to play slightly dumb, like, "Oh, I didn't realize I had broken any rules here." But to be very friendly and generally not try and argue or be confrontational, since that never really gets you too far. I remember shaking hands with them as I left and saying, "We have a job to do and *you have a job to do and sometimes that requires that we have situations like this, but it's not personal." That kind of conversation, shaking hands, "Bye-bye, have a nice Chinese New Year," and we go off. Then, of course, the interview aired on June 4. I had an opportunity to meet Bao Tong's son a couple of months later, and he told me that several of the officers we met that night were fired because of this. The Foreign Ministry was very upset. They were making noises that my visa was coming up soon, and they may or may not feel like renewing it. And that we had lied to the police. It caused great consternation.*

WTO AND THE BELGRADE BOMBING

In the meantime, Zhu Rongji, who'd become premier, was struggling to conclude negotiations with the United States on China's entry to the World Trade Organization, a key move to accelerate the process of economic reform. In early April 1999, Zhu flew to Washington.

Kenneth Lieberthal, National Security Council

A major objective of that visit was to reach final agreement, nail down the final few terms. That would have been a huge step in U.S.-China relations, and a huge step in China joining the WTO.

Marcus Brauchli, *Wall Street Journal*

Joe Kahn and I went with Zhu Rongji. They didn't let us travel on the plane with him, but we could travel in parallel with the Chinese delegation and then they arranged for us to be on their motorcade, sort of like American journalists are with the American president, which was fascinating because that suggested a degree of sophistication hitherto unseen in Beijing. He went to Washington, saw President Clinton, and for whatever reason the White House wasn't ready to deal on WTO. And Zhu Rongji was put out, because I think he thought that he had come all this way in part to sign the deals so that China could become part of WTO.

Kenneth Lieberthal, National Security Council

Clinton didn't want to sign a deal that Congress would not support, and there was still a little work to do on that. Zhu felt humiliated. In China, Zhu came under enormous criticism for having given away the store. The White House came under enormous criticism on this end, "Why didn't you sign the deal? It was such a good deal!" Both of the people who were in the room trying to make something happen ended up being losers.

The tension created by Zhu's unsuccessful visit was fueled by U.S.-led NATO air strikes that spring on Yugoslavia in response to the Yugoslav ethnic cleansing of Albanians in Kosovo. China opposed the U.S. military campaign. Shortly after Zhu returned to China, with the differences over Beijing's WTO membership still unresolved, Sino-American relations took a dramatic turn for the worse.

Kenneth Lieberthal, National Security Council

The phone rang. It was the Situation Room at the White House saying, "Mr. Lieberthal, we are watching CNN report that U.S. planes have just bombed the Chinese embassy in Belgrade." The Chinese had been extremely critical of our campaign in Yugoslavia. They immediately felt the bombing of their embassy in Belgrade was a specific targeted move by the U.S., both to reduce their capabilities and punish them and humiliate them by bombing their sovereign territory, which an embassy is, without warning, and as it turns out, killing some embassy staff.

Washington portrayed the bombing as a targeting error, but the reaction in Beijing was immediate and furious.

Elisabeth Rosenthal, *New York Times*

Suddenly, the U.S. became public enemy number one. To do reporting, you had to go into the crowds outside the U.S. embassy. There were a lot of hotheads. Things were being thrown. You didn't want to go out there and say, "Hey, I'm an American reporter," but you had to get your quotes. It was tense and a little frightening.

Rebecca MacKinnon, CNN

People started throwing bricks and bottles. I was doing a live phone report. I'm describing the protesters trying to light the flag on fire, throwing bottles, and shouting epithets. Some people near me start shouting. I said, "Yeah, and they're shouting at me, too, because they think I'm American." The anchor says, "What are they shouting?" I'm like, "Well, I can't repeat it on air." And he said, "Well, what else are they doing?" I'm just like, "Well, this gentleman here is saying something quite obscene. Whoops, he hit me. I have to go." At which point the man who had hit me and a few other people near him were yelling, "Da ta! Sha ta! Hit her. Kill her." Fortunately, there were some people who pulled me away. I ran off. People who were watching CNN who knew my parents immediately called my parents, who were rather freaked out. I was fine, but the fact that that was on air, the fact that we continued to report, the fact that I'd been attacked by somebody in the mob had greatly upset the Chinese Foreign Ministry. Usually, the argument they made was that "The things you are reporting are not constructive for U.S.-China relations." My response was a little more polite version of, "Well, if you weren't doing it, we wouldn't have to report it."

THE "EVIL CULT"

The embassy protests added to tension in Beijing that had been heightened just a few days earlier, when ten thousand members of the Falun Gong spiritual group had suddenly materialized outside Zhongnanhai, the compound where the Chinese leadership lives and works, demanding official government recognition. Founded in 1992 by Li Hongzhi, a former trumpet player, Falun Gong drew on China's long tradition of *qigong*, a series of breathing and meditation exercises. But Li added a series of moral teachings, as well as some highly unorthodox theories, such as a belief that aliens were taking over the world. Whatever its idiosyncrasies, the group became increasingly popular.

Jaime FlorCruz, *Time*

I remember walking up to them. I introduced myself as someone working for Time *in Chinese, and asked, "Can you tell me what's going on? Why are you here?" None of them would talk. Zip. Zero. Nothing.*

Rebecca MacKinnon, CNN

We went down to the area around Zhongnanhai. It was so bizarre. There were all these middle-aged, ordinary-looking people, who were clearly not sophisticated Beijingers but from elsewhere, just sitting there meditating. Many of them didn't want to be interviewed. Whoever they were, whatever their purpose was, protesting near the leadership compound was obvious political dynamite.

Craig Smith, who had become interested in China as a college student after reading the reports of Fox Butterfield, had worked in Beijing as a businessman in the 1980s. After four years with the *Wall Street Journal* in Hong Kong, he moved to the *Journal's* Shanghai bureau in 1997. Even before the protest, Smith had already been looking into the Falun Gong.

Craig Smith, *Wall Street Journal*

I began seeing in the parks at dawn all these crazy exercise routines. I went early one morning to catalogue all these different regimes. There were people banging themselves against trees, people walking backwards, a group that would shout a magic number at the top of their lungs. It was clear from talking to the people involved that these were cults more than exercise routines. So, I set out to do a story on the rise of cults in China.

Smith managed to secure an interview with Falun Gong spiritual leader Li Hongzhi, who had left China in 1996 and now lived in New Jersey.

Craig Smith, *Wall Street Journal*

I thought we established a rapport. I said to him, "Where you lose me is when you start saying things like you can fly. Why do you have to do that? You have a very credible and valuable moral system that you are teaching. Why do you have to talk about things like flying?" He got really agitated and said, "I can fly. There are a lot of people that can fly, there are people in America that can fly." The rest of the interview was downhill from there. Then came the April event which challenged the government. And I had an interview with Li Hongzhi in my notebook. I pounded out a leader, and that morning, on the cover of the Wall Street Journal, *we have an interview with the leader of this group, where everyone else couldn't even get the name right, and everyone else was scrabbling to figure out what this group was.*

Nonetheless, the Falun Gong's popular appeal was one sign of a search for moral values at a time of bewildering change. But for China's leaders, the fact that an unauthorized demonstration by ten thousand people had been planned right under the noses of the security apparatus was terrifying.

John Pomfret, *Washington Post*

I was there when they surrounded Zhongnanhai. I always thought it was a difficult story to write for the Western audience, because Li Hongzhi, the leader of the sect, encouraged his people to put themselves into harm's way. He put on his website, "If you don't confront, you are not a Falun Gong practitioner." In the early part of the crackdown, they protest in front of Zhongnanhai. Jiang Zemin gets a bug up his ass about the whole thing and decides they have to crush it.

Covering the crackdown on what the Chinese government called the evil Falun Gong cult became a staple of the China beat, to the discomfort of many correspondents.

John Pomfret, *Washington Post*

Li [Hongzhi] did odious things, and of course the Communist reaction to that was odious as well. But when you have two grey characters, it's difficult for a Western audience. The ones that wrote the stories in black or white got more traction in the West, but I felt the story was true. And the discussion about the Falun Gong and their lives, twenty minutes into the conversation, you begin to realize that some people's beliefs systems are just nutty. It has a wackiness that needs to be written about. But as you do that, the victims become less sympathetic.

Rebecca MacKinnon, CNN

I think the Chinese Communist Party versus the Falun Gong—in the international media the storyline was the innocent religious activists versus the thugs. Unfortunately, what it felt like covering the story, it was the fruit loops versus the thugs. I mean, you just felt icky about the whole story. But you shouldn't get thrown in vans and beaten and tortured if you want to believe in some weird cult leader, as long as you're not going around murdering people.

THE FIFTIETH ANNIVERSARY

But the push for economic reform continued, with Zhu Rongji finally reaching a deal with the United States for China to enter the World Trade Organization.

Andrew Browne, Reuters

It was a massive game-changer. Suddenly they had real competition inside China. And this was Zhu's game plan all along—bring in foreign players, intro-duce competition, strengthen our domestic champions.

John Pomfret, *Washington Post*

It was a transformative deal for China. If you look at China's trade statistics after 2001 it's just insane explosion. It's amazing how they were able to profit from it. That was an extraordinary turning point for China. That was a huge accelerator.

In the fall of 1999, China marked the fiftieth anniversary of the founding of the People's Republic with the biggest parade in Tiananmen Square in years, presided over by Jiang Zemin, who reviewed a long parade of military hardware. After a turbulent decade, it was a chance for China's leaders to trumpet their successes. Even normally cynical reporters acknowledged how dramatically things had changed.

Craig Smith, *Wall Street Journal*

I think people frankly underestimated the nimbleness and flexibility of the Communist Party. You look back at the late nineties and you see tremendous strides. No one ever thought it would develop to that degree.

Marcus Brauchli, *Wall Street Journal*

There is with China a huge amount of very positive change that gets overlooked in the kind of snapshot analysis that gets done. If you take a dynamic picture of China, and you look where China came from—and this is important to do on any story, but particularly important in China—you'll see that China has actually continued to advance.

But for the American press corps, the dizzying changes meant only a mod-ification, not an end, to the intimidation, surveillance, and pressure they faced. As the year—and the decade—drew to an end, the Beijing Foreign Correspondents Club produced a gag video for its annual Christmas party, to take some of the sting out of living and working in China. It featured

Norman Bottorff of the AP playing a journalist driven mad by the city's pervasive cockroaches. To root out the insects, he ventures into the filthy basement of the so-called "diplomatic compounds," where foreign reporters were required to live. There, he discovers a Chinese police team, led by CNN's Wen-Chun Fan, who played the part dressed in full police uniform, spying on a female Western reporter in her bathrobe. Then Bottorf encounters an "evil cult"—not the Falun Gong, but one devoted to the worship of *Time* magazine's Jaime FlorCruz. A dozen journalists sit on the floor, hands clasped, chanting in unison, "See Jimi. Be Jimi." The scene drives Bottorf over the edge. He goes crazy, battering FlorCruz and his devotees with a giant club while shouting, "This evil cult must die!" The absurd drama generated many laughs at the FCC Christmas gathering—but they were knowing laughs, because for all the zaniness, the film accurately captured at least part of how many American and other foreign correspondents felt about their fascinating, and maddening, beat.

13

THE NEW MILLENNIUM

In 1967, at the height of the Cultural Revolution, Ching-Ching Ni was born in Beijing. At the age of twelve, she moved with her mother to the United States.

Ching-Ching Ni, *Los Angeles Times*

After Nixon came to China, I learned that my grandmother had another daughter that she sent to America in the 1940s. They didn't see each other for a quarter of a century. She came back after Nixon's visit to see her mother. She was our connection to the U.S., and that's how we were able to come to America.

In 2000, now an American citizen, she became the *Los Angeles Times* Shanghai correspondent—the first person born in the People's Republic to work as a foreign correspondent in China for a U.S. news organization.

Ching-Ching Ni, *Los Angeles Times*

What makes me unique is that I was born Chinese but grew up as an American and came back as an American foreign correspondent. This was not only a professional dream come true. It was a journey of personal discovery. I left just as China was starting to change in such dramatic ways that, by the time I came back, it was beyond recognition. I wanted to know that China. And I wanted to share what I learned with my American readers.

A lot of people were confused by me, because I looked Chinese, but spoke English and also spoke Chinese like a local. They didn't know what to make of me. They didn't understand what the LA Times was. They used to ask me, "Do you write in English or Chinese?" They had no idea. And the worst of it is that, sometimes, they think you're a spy.

By the time I arrived, China was changing so much that the challenge was which China story to cover. China had so many different faces. Most of us had a hard time figuring out which story really captured what China was. I think Chinese people themselves were struggling with who they were, where they'd been, or who they want to be. What helped was to look for stories that said a lot about the dramatic changes that were going on. But it was very hard. It was sort of like the blind man and the elephant. You know there's so much, whatever part you covered, but it was hard to know whether it gave you a full picture of what China really was.

Ni began her assignment by searching for traces of the China she remembered. She had grown up watching the revolutionary operas of Chairman Mao's wife, Jiang Qing, like *Taking Tiger Mountain by Strategy*. The opera's star, Tong Xiangling, had become a national icon. Ching-Ching set out to find him.

Ching-Ching Ni, *Los Angeles Times*

He was like the Arnold Schwarzenegger of the Cultural Revolution, Madame Mao's favorite opera singer. I remember singing his songs as a child. Where is he twenty years later? Selling noodles in Shanghai! He opened his own noodle shop. Is he a very good businessman? No. But he was surviving and trying to reinvent himself.

There was the Red Detachment of Women ballet that Nixon saw. Because my mother worked at the Central Ballet in Beijing, I grew up backstage watching rehearsals of the Red Detachment. I wanted to know what happened to these people. When I went to Hainan, the location of the real Red Detachment of Women, I learned that there was a theme park built around them. You know what they did? They brought back the women who were girl soldiers, the real women portrayed in the ballet. Now they're like ninety years old. They're like little monkeys in a circus! They parade them out and dress them up as soldiers with the red star over their heads, and people come and look at them. That story only I know because I grew up watching the Red Detachment of Women. And I was able to go in there and interview these real women that the ballet dancers tried to imitate. To me that was more interesting because it's so odd and jarring.

A HUGE NATIONAL TRIUMPH

From Maoist hero to private businessman in Shanghai, from revolutionary heroines to tourist attractions—the icons of Ching-Ching Ni's youth had become symbols of how much China was changing. The scale of the change was brought home to the rest of the world when, in the summer of 2001, Beijing was awarded the right to host the 2008 Olympics. It was just a dozen years after Tiananmen Square. The decision set off huge celebrations.

Hannah Beech, who had been based in Hong Kong for *Time* magazine since 1997, had moved to Beijing in 2000.

Hannah Beech, *Time*

It was a moment of huge national triumph. I happened to be near the Mao portrait on Tiananmen Square and the crowd was moving forward, and it was this moment of release. There was almost anarchy on the streets, in a way that we all compared to the other moment where there had been anarchy on the streets. But it was this incredibly joyous moment. I had people come up to me and say, "China is number one. China is number one." I thought "Fair enough." You could see the patriotism, the nationalism, that of course is such a part of the narrative now, manifest itself.

Beech was the daughter of legendary American war correspondent Keyes Beech, who had covered World War II, the Korean War, and Vietnam, and a Japanese mother, who was also a journalist.

Hannah Beech, *Time*

I was born in Hong Kong. I grew up overseas. I'm half-American, half-Japanese. I went to British school. I'm sort of the quintessential expat brat. My father was a journalist, my mother was a journalist, so I wanted to be anything but a journalist. But I think at a certain point, having grown up living overseas, watching what my parents did, you either follow in their footsteps or you move to Iowa and never move, and I chose the first option.

For Beech, as for the rest of a rapidly growing U.S. press corps, making sense of China's transformation became the central theme of their reporting.

Louisa Lim, who did a degree in Chinese studies at Leeds University in England and had been an editor and translator at a state-run publishing firm in Beijing, had begun her journalistic career in Hong Kong in the mid-1990s, working for a local newspaper and TV station. She then spent three years as a BBC correspondent in Beijing before joining U.S. National Public Radio as a correspondent in Shanghai.

Louisa Lim, NPR

The theme everybody was interested in was the exploding Chinese economy. That was the rationale for setting up the NPR Shanghai bureau. They wanted more reporting about the economy, more reporting from outside Beijing about how China was changing. I tried to cover stories I felt were really important that were not being covered—those more unspoken shifts that were happening outside the major urban centers.

Michael Forsythe, who had spent seven years in the U.S. Navy and then taken an intensive Chinese-language program at Tsinghua University, joined a still small Bloomberg News bureau in Beijing.

Michael Forsythe, Bloomberg News

The big story was opening up, the WTO accession, the rapidly expanding economy. I was a jack of all trades. One day I'd be covering automobiles, the next day banking. I certainly was one of the reporters writing the generally positive story about China at the time. I was in a business news organization and focused on that.

Joseph Kahn had by now left the *Wall Street Journal* for the *New York Times*.

Joseph Kahn, *New York Times*

China's place in the world had become significantly more important. The growth rate was very high. People were wide-eyed about China's potential. By 2002, everybody was enamored of China's rising place in the world. I was a little bit dubious. Some of the underlying problems I had seen before were still present. They obviously had a track record of success and growth, but the underlying human rights problems were still a big issue. Unanswered questions about political stability. As I got into my tour, I also found that there were big problems with the legal system. There were enormous problems with the environment.

You started to see kind of routine cases of mass unrest and protest in the streets that became a big part of the coverage.

A DIFFERENT WAY TO COVER CHINA

Missouri native Peter Hessler, who'd studied creative writing at Princeton, had spent two years as a teacher for the Peace Corps in Sichuan province in the 1990s. He was now back in China, struggling to make it as a freelance reporter.

Peter Hessler, *New Yorker*

I wanted to be a novelist and short story writer and then burned out on that and took a trip around the world. That took me through China when I was twenty-five. It was 1994. I showed up in Beijing and something about Beijing just grabbed me. There was an energy. There were all sorts of things going on. I decided to come back, and joined the Peace Corps. I thought that would be a good way to learn the language and get a background of the country. But I didn't start thinking of myself of a journalist until I finished my time in the Peace Corps and wrote my first book, River Town. *[The book, a description of Hessler's time in the small town along the Yangtze River where he served in the Peace Corps as a teacher, was a critical success.] After that experience, I decided to go into journalism. I got a part-time job as an assistant in the* Wall Street Journal *Beijing bureau. I would go to Hong Kong every six months and over to Shenzhen, across the border, and get a business visa, basically freelancing illegally.*

Hessler discovered that some of his former students had joined the millions leaving the countryside for factory jobs in coastal boomtowns like Shenzhen.

Peter Hessler, *New Yorker*

The sense of movement, people leaving home, is such a fundamental characteristic of this generation. I was very fortunate because my students and the people I became friends with in the town where I was a Peace Corps volunteer were of this generation that was moving from the countryside. Most of them were from farm families. Their parents had been quite poor. Now they're basically becoming urban people. I had a former student who was living in Shenzhen. She was working at a factory, and I started tracking her story and meeting her friends. One of the things that was interesting to me about

Shenzhen was that it had been written about as an economic story. There wasn't a lot of emphasis on their personal lives and interests. It was a place where people were becoming individuals. It was a story about individualism in China.

On one visit to Shenzhen, Hessler found a restaurant whose most famous dish was rat.

Peter Hessler, *New Yorker*

I figured, this is great, I'll do a taste test. I hung out with the rat restaurant guys. The guy showed me the rat and asked me if it was OK, just like they do with a fish. I said, "That's great," and he took the thing by the tail and swung it and, whack, hit its head on the cement, and that was it, and it was on my plate in ten minutes. I wrote this story and sent it to my former teacher at Princeton, John McPhee, who said, "This is great." He sent it to David Remnick and Remnick bought it and said, "Do you have any more things like this?"

Remnick was the editor of the *New Yorker*. Soon, Hessler became the magazine's first full-time correspondent in China.

Peter Hessler, *New Yorker*

It's very unusual for them to have people based overseas. The fact that they were willing to have a guy in China, especially a young guy, shows that they did understand that it mattered. I ended up having quite a bit of freedom. It wasn't always easy, because I was dealing with China, and on the other side, trying to figure out the New Yorker, *and the* New Yorker *can be just as complicated as the Communist Party.*

But writing for the *New Yorker* meant Hessler didn't have to cover breaking news. Instead, he wrote long-form pieces that chronicled the deeper ways that people were changing.

Peter Hessler, *New Yorker*

I decided it was a different way to cover China. My feeling probably comes from having a sociologist father. I felt like the way to cover China was basically following people or communities over periods of time, because of the way things were changing, describing that change, but also watching and observing how people respond to change.

"IT'S NOT EASY TO DO COMPLICATED"

Meanwhile, as the economy grew, conditions for Western reporters gradually began to improve. Barry Petersen, a veteran CBS News correspondent who had been with the network since 1978, had been traveling to China from his base in Japan since the mid-1990s.

Barry Petersen, CBS News

What escaped our attention until we were able to travel was that a lot of this change and progress was happening all over China. You could go to cities of ten million people whose names nobody would ever know. Ten million's bigger than almost any city in the United States. They had five-star hotels. They had a Mercedes dealership. You could really see that the effort to get prosperity across the country was working.

For Peterson, as for correspondents from the other U.S. networks, the challenge was getting on the air with a story that was more a process than a dramatic event.

Barry Petersen, CBS News

In TV news, it's not easy to do complicated. There's not a lot of interest in foreign news in the U.S. People just don't care that much unless it's a war that Americans are fighting in. There's kind of a bias. The leadership of the Communist Party in China changes or massive flooding in St. Louis—which one do we go with? Well, you're going to go with flooding in St. Louis.

Rebecca MacKinnon, CNN

This was always a challenge because China was a feature story a lot of the time. Breaking news was important, too, but the story about the rise of the middle class, or the rise of certain industries, or the rise of local tycoons. It was all stories about individuals. You'd have to find characters who embodied what was going on. We tried to travel as much as we could to tell these stories about individuals

*who were either creating change, or beneficiaries of change, or sometimes victims
of change, but to really try and personalize what was happening and then connect it with kind of the broader trends. But it's a hard sell for television.*

And it wasn't that much easier for print reporters.

Charles Hutzler, Associated Press

*You cannot re-create the complexity of this place in six hundred words, in a
thousand words, even two thousand words. You hope that you get a piece of it,
and that, over time, you build a body of work that lets people know what's really
going on.*

Many print journalists found that covering the dramatically growing Chinese economy offered an effective way to explain China. As a student at
Boston University, David Barboza had interned for Fox Butterfield, who'd
opened the *New York Times* bureau in 1980 and then became the paper's correspondent in Boston.

David Barboza, *New York Times*

*I already had somewhat of an interest in China and had Fox Butterfield's book.
It was soon after that I ended up as Fox's intern, so I also got to go through a
lot of his files. His papers are in his office, so I started to read a lot. My interest
was looking at the stuff, reading about what Fox did. I kind of worshipped Fox
for a while there, and I read all of his works, and studied what he wrote.*

Now a *New York Times* correspondent in China himself, Barboza was following in Butterfield's footsteps. He was assigned to Shanghai to cover the
economy.

David Barboza, *New York Times*

*My first major story from China was a look at textile cities to see how China
works. How businesses work, how its industries do sourcing, and how they have
cities that specialize in one thing. They have underwear city, they have bra city,
they have suit city. I think I started my story in sock city, which makes like eight
billion socks a year, which is just incredible.*

By now, Andrew Browne had left Reuters for the *Wall Street Journal*.

Andrew Browne, *Wall Street Journal*

Localities all over China were setting up industrial parks looking for foreign investors. They figured if they could get some positive publicity, if the mayor could be interviewed, if local businesses were featured, maybe the foreign investors would come, so we were very welcome. We were the vanguard of the investment wave.

PERSONAL CONNECTIONS

Rebecca MacKinnon, CNN

It was quite easy to make Chinese friends. There was this trend of people starting to leave their government jobs and go into business. A lot of the people I got to know were working in the arts, or in entrepreneurial-type professions where having a foreign friend wouldn't lead to a slap on the wrist from your work unit, who enjoyed being friends with foreigners. By that point, enough people were no longer afraid of associations with foreigners and actually felt that they benefited from a personal standpoint. And there were a lot of foreigners who were dating Chinese. I dated a Chinese man quite a number of years. And there was a whole community of couples, Chinese and Western couples, quite a lot of marriages and babies. It was definitely very different from earlier eras.

John Pomfret of the *Washington Post* met his future wife, a Western-educated Chinese, while showing his boss around China.

John Pomfret, *Washington Post*

There was this great woman who just got her MBA from Harvard and was working at McKinsey and wanted to do a travel company. She was arranging a three-day hike. I love backpacking and hiking. We went off and basically did a three-day hike with my boss from the Post. *We got to know each other and became boyfriend and girlfriend and we got married. I've always said that it was because of him I have three kids and a marriage. The* Washington Post *is a full-service organization. It was my work unit that introduced me to my bride as well as gave me a steady job.*

Ching-Ching Ni fell in love with a Chinese man whom she eventually married, but not before the police let him know they were watching.

Ching-Ching Ni, *Los Angeles Times*

The long arm of the state has ways to intimidate. My husband is Chinese. When we first met, he was taken out to tea [a euphemism for being called in by the police]. They knew everything about him, probably knew more about him than I did at the time. It was really hard. He was a Chinese national. I'm an American journalist. They want to signal to me there are lots of ways they can intimidate you. Basically all of us knew that even though China was freer than ever, and we as journalists had more access than ever, we were watched constantly.

THE DARK SIDE

Evading scrutiny was an ongoing challenge, especially when covering the darker side of China, which many correspondents felt was crucially important.

Hannah Beech, *Time*

We have to be the voice for the voiceless. I know that sounds ridiculously idealistic, and it's one of the reasons that we're criticized often in China. "You only focus on the bad stories," but we see our role as the checks and balance against the government that happens to be in power. That is for me, and for a lot of foreign journalists in China, a really important mission.

Ching-Ching Ni, *Los Angeles Times*

I was interested in the forgotten stories, the underbelly of the China miracle, the dark side, the people that no one gets to. If nobody is talking to them, history would not know about them. The more of those stories that we can get out, the more complete a picture we can paint. I was in Tibet on one of these government-organized tours. This is when it really came in handy to know the language and blend in. There are ways you can leave the tour and try to capture a bit of real life as opposed to the stage-managed thing. I was able to get a story about Tibetan women by observing that on the road, during the day, there are so many women working on construction sites. I was able to write a story by sneaking off to talk to these construction workers, young Tibetan girls mostly, about how they contribute to the economy during the day and by night. It's sort of like a twenty-four-hour cycle. By day they work on construction sites, and by night they work as prostitutes, serving the underground economy of men who work on the frontiers. It was a story I was able to get while on this officially sponsored trip.

One of the darkest stories was a virtually unknown AIDS epidemic raging in Henan province in central China. *Time*'s Hannah Beech and Elisabeth Rosenthal of the *New York Times*, who, with her medical background, had covered AIDS/HIV in the United States, both stumbled onto the story.

Elisabeth Rosenthal, *New York Times*

I had trained in New York during the height of the HIV epidemic, so I knew a lot about it and thought, "That's weird. Rural China? HIV/AIDS? Why would that be there?" I managed to speak to Gao Yaojie, the gynecologist who I had worked with very early on in my time there [on a story about STDs in China]. My Chinese wasn't very good. I thought I must be misunderstanding what she is saying. It sounded like she was saying there was this huge epidemic of HIV/ AIDs in rural villages. I was like, "That's really strange." But I had someone listen to the tape, and that was indeed what she was saying.

Hannah Beech, *Time*

People had gotten HIV/AIDS not from sexual activity, but from selling their blood. They were poor peasants who decided, "We need to make some money." They went to sell their blood, the needles weren't clean, and that's how the AIDS epidemic ended up spreading in Henan.

Elisabeth Rosenthal, *New York Times*

Through one person who knew someone who knew someone else, I organized a quick trip to the village. We did it at night, because you couldn't really go there during the day because you'd be kicked out. Someone brought us in in a bicycle cart with a tarp on the back. We were under the tarp, me and a translator. We had to do it in somebody's home who was willing to have a foreign journalist there. I remember seeing all the things I had seen in a hospital when I was in New York City in 1986. All the same infections, the coughs, the mouth sores. I knew they had HIV/AIDS. I started, as I usually did, assuming they wouldn't want their names used. They said, "No, we want our names used. We want the village named. Because we have this terrible disease." They weren't getting any help. They were just dying. They were like, "No, we want to be on the map. We want to be on the front page of the New York Times *because we've tried everything else and we're not getting help." So that started the reporting going.*

Hannah Beech, *Time*

I met with Dr. Gao. She gave me all her contacts. We went late at night. The photographer I was traveling with was Chinese American, and I look Chinese-ish, especially if it is night. If I was blonde, it would be harder. We snuck in and started walking around villages knocking on people's doors. We saw these freshly dug graves. And you start talking to people, and they understand that you're there to try to help or at least give them a voice, but at the same time they were very scared because they didn't want the stigma of being connected to this.

The Chinese authorities were not happy.

Elisabeth Rosenthal, *New York Times*

The initial reaction was being called into the Foreign Ministry, who said, "You didn't have permission to go there." But I think it started a process. As is always the case in China, there were people within the official structure who knew what was going on and really tried hard to do the right thing. It wasn't like everyone in the Ministry of Health was denying that HIV/Aids exists. There were people in the government who were quietly encouraging and helping me. It was really an extraordinary experience, and incredibly gratifying to me as a journalist, because having that publicity in the Western press did bring a lot of help. A lot more Western foundations got involved in HIV/AIDS in rural China. And the Chinese government admitted we have this HIV/AIDS problem. People in these villages started getting medicines. One extraordinary thing for me is, I went back some years later as a tourist with one of my kids, and people who I had assumed would be dead were alive and on medicine and doing OK. Once in a while in journalism, you feel like you made a difference.

THE SARS EPIDEMIC

Against a backdrop of continuing repression but remarkable economic growth, the Chinese Communist Party held its sixteenth Party Congress in late 2002. Fifty-nine-year-old Hu Jintao, a colorless, longtime Party apparatchik, replaced Jiang Zemin as China's leader. Still, the Congress was a watershed, marking the first orderly transfer of power, with no purges, upheaval, or drama since the founding of the People's Republic. It also approved allowing private entrepreneurs to become Party members. This step both acknowledged China's changing economic climate and was designed to co-opt the country's emerging business elite.

Barry Petersen, CBS News

It was evidence of a normal, orderly process that really started with Deng Xiaoping. You had these people who were groomed into these positions. It reflected the desperate hunger for stability. They didn't want upheaval. That's a running undercurrent in the Chinese Communist Party. They're always afraid that the place is going to come apart at the seams.

As Joseph Kahn noted in his report on the congress for the *New York Times*:

The Party is rewriting its constitution to declare that it represents "advanced forces"—capitalists—as much as workers and peasants. Rich people have begun joining the Party. Jiang Zemin has buried the last pretenses of socialism.[1]

Yet Hu Jintao had barely taken over before he faced a frightening new challenge. In early 2003, reporters heard rumors of a strange new respiratory disease. It became known as SARS—Severe Acute Respiratory Syndrome. It swiftly spread across China and beyond. But as the anxiety and the death toll mounted, the Chinese authorities said almost nothing.

Elisabeth Rosenthal, *New York Times*

Since I had a medical background, it was my story. It was a strange and scary time because the Chinese were not very good about providing information, so nobody really knew how dangerous this is, how many cases there were. There is a culture of hiding things that has often been state-sanctioned. It turned out that that lack of transparency about SARS in the early days in China helped the disease spread to many other countries. Everyone was scared, even me, and justifiably so. It could have been much better controlled if there had been transparency in the beginning.

Barry Petersen, CBS News

SARS marked something different for the Chinese. There was this effort to say it's not that big a deal, not telling people what was going on. Especially in China there was a real effort to quash this. We've got it under control.

Hannah Beech, *Time*

There were SARS cases all over China, and Hong Kong and Singapore. Mysteriously, there were supposedly no SARS cases in Shanghai. I started going with my assistant to a bunch of hospitals in Shanghai. At one of the hospitals there was a WHO group, including foreign doctors, who were looking at X-rays and medical files of some of the people who supposedly didn't have SARS. I attached myself to the group. As we were walking through, security officials said, "Are you with the WHO group?" I said, "Oh yeah. Sure." I stuck with them, and the WHO group, for whatever reason, allowed me to tag along. We looked at X-rays and medical data, which I took pictures of, that confirmed that some people actually did have SARS in Shanghai. I ended up writing a story about that. I got called to the Shanghai Foreign Ministry for lectures. At one point, they had gone through my resume and discovered that I had not gone to journalism school, so they brought in the dean of the journalism program at one of the local universities to lecture me on journalism ethics. They read me a three-hour lecture. I just sat there and took it, and smiled, and learned about Chinese journalism.

The unhappy Shanghai authorities also called Beech to a meeting with an official from the Ministry of State Security—where she had a surprise.

Hannah Beech, *Time*

The State Security is a scarier apparatus. I got a call from a guy saying, "I want to meet with you. I'm from the State Security. We need to discuss what you've been doing." I thought this was a bit concerning. Interestingly, he didn't want me to go to his office, but said, "Let's meet at the Starbucks in Xintiandi." Xintiandi is this very ritzy part of Shanghai. I said, "Okay." We sit down and he gives me a very half-hearted lecture about what I've been doing. Then he leaned in and said, "Can we talk off the record for a moment?" I said, "Sure." He said, "I have a daughter. Should I be sending her to school? Is it safe? Should I evacuate her and my wife to Hong Kong or to overseas? What's going on with SARS? Can you please tell me?" Here is this State Security official who is depending on a foreign journalist who he's been tasked to criticize to find out what's going on. It was such a revelatory moment for me.

Elisabeth Rosenthal, *New York Times*

I had gone down to one of the hospitals in Guangzhou that had a lot of patients, and we found families. You could walk into the ward where they were treating SARS patients. You could find people who had been discharged, people whose families had died. We went to the animal markets where people had gotten sick. I think we had done that before there was kind of an official whistleblower.

The whistleblower was an elderly army doctor, Jiang Yanyong. Only after he spoke out—to the Chinese press and to *Time*—did the government have to admit what was happening.

Hannah Beech, *Time*

It's incredibly powerful. I think one of the things you find with this job is you meet, particularly, older, brave Chinese who've just gone through everything. And they think, "You know what? Screw you, government. Screw you, regime. I'm going to do what I want." And they're the ones from the AIDS doctor in Henan to the retired military doctor in Beijing who are making a difference.

Barry Peterson, *CBS News*

Afterwards, they admitted that it was a big deal, and they didn't really have it under control. That was a time when the Chinese government had a chance to build trust with its people, and they didn't. It was a time to show the world they could be transparent, but they were afraid to.

An authoritarian system like China, however, had tools to control the outbreak that other societies did not. Philip Pan, who'd been born in the United States to immigrant parents from Taiwan and studied Chinese in Beijing in the 1990s, was now working for the *Washington Post*.

Philip Pan, *Washington Post*

I spent a week driving across northern China to get a sense of what the situation was. There were roadblocks placed at all these villages. The strategy was mass mobilization [of the Communist Party's enormous resources] and making sure the people could not transmit the disease. There was roadblock after roadblock where they were trying to prevent people going places.

THE CASE OF ZHAO YAN

In early September 2004, Joseph Kahn, citing two Chinese sources, published a story in the *New York Times* about former president Jiang Zemin being pushed out of his last post, as head of the Chinese military. Ten days later, Zhao Yan, the Chinese news assistant at the *Times* bureau, was arrested.

Joseph Kahn, *New York Times*

I heard from a couple of good sources that Jiang was being pressured to give up that final post, and I reported that. It was initially denied as rumor, but a short time later, Zhao Yan was arrested. He had had nothing to do with the reporting of that story. But it became clear they were asking him how that story got into the hands of the New York Times. *They did eventually arrest him and charge him with revealing state secrets.*

Philip Pan, *Washington Post*

Obviously, they wanted to know the source, and they were looking for a way to put pressure on the Times. *Zhao Yan was an easy target. I don't think Zhao knew the source, but because he was already known to the security services, it was convenient to bring him in. It might have happened to any of us. They could have done that to our assistant as well. Pressure the assistant to try to disclose the source. It was a very difficult time for the* Times.

Joseph Kahn, *New York Times*

I felt terrible. You get no information from Chinese judicial authorities. We didn't know if there would be charges or what they would be. It became a very drawn-out process of mobilizing our resources to figure out what was going on and try to get him released, first from custody, and then, months later, when there was some indication he was going to be charged, to hire lawyers and fight those charges. I felt pretty seized with the responsibility to do anything we could to get him out.

It took three years, but eventually, Zhao Yan was released.

His case highlighted one of the central questions that American and other foreign reporters struggled with—the status of the Chinese assistants who worked for them.

Andrew Browne, *Wall Street Journal*

You end up with this sort of two-tier bureau, where you've got the Chinese news assistants—not allowed to call them reporters, they can't go to certain events, press conferences, they don't get treated like Chinese sources in the same way— and then you've got the small group of reporters with foreign passports.

But the reality was that the Chinese assistants were indispensable windows into Chinese society, and, at many news organizations, were acting as reporters in all but name. Critical in developing story ideas, finding interviewees, translation, and research, the assistants were heavily involved in almost every aspect of coverage. However, since Chinese nationals were prohibited from having bylines in the international media, their names never appeared on the stories they helped to create. As Zhao Yan's plight demonstrated, news assistants were also often at greater risk than their employers.

THE RIGHTS LAWYERS

Joseph Kahn, *New York Times*

Partly because of Zhao Yan, I started spending a lot of time with a community of lawyers who were willing to take on some of the toughest cases. I ended up doing a series of stories about rule of law and the disappointment that there was still Party control of the judicial system and trying to reveal how that worked in practice, and how pressure was brought on lawyers. It was interesting to watch it unfold in real time, because foreigners had high expectations that China was actually building a legal system. A lot of Chinese lawyers did too. There was a real movement for constitutional rule. There were a lot of people who were getting legal training. There were lawyers looking to test the ability to enforce the letter of the law as it was written, when the letter of the law was not perfectly in sync with the Party's will. You saw a lot of experimentation going on, both at the local level and at the central level in Beijing. It was a pretty exciting time.

Indeed, by the middle of the decade, amid growing social tension over issues like forced abortions or farmers being forced off their land by developers, which often led to violent confrontations, a new generation of legal activists known as *weiquan*, or "rights protection lawyers," had emerged. Their goal was to use China's own laws to defend human rights.

Peter Ford, who had spent the previous fifteen years based in Europe, Moscow, and the Middle East, became the *Christian Science Monitor*'s China correspondent in 2006.

Peter Ford, *Christian Science Monitor*

I was surprised by how difficult it was to find out what was really happening, not just because the authorities generally try to stop foreign correspondents finding out if there's something remotely embarrassing to the authorities, but also because people themselves were not necessarily going to tell you the truth. But the lawyers were a very good source of stories, and a very good story in themselves, as to how they were expanding the field available to civil society through the law courts. They were having tremendous difficulties, but they were saying things that hadn't been said before. They were treating the courts in different ways. They were doing all sorts of theatrical actions to attract attention. It wasn't just dry briefs in court. They were really using law in a whole different way.

Among these rights activists was a young, self-taught, blind lawyer named Chen Guangcheng. At first defending ordinary people from the depredations of local functionaries, in 2005, Chen had brought a groundbreaking lawsuit against the local government in his native Shandong province for their brutal enforcement of the one-child policy.

Philip Pan, *Washington Post*

This blind rural activist found me in Beijing. He wanted to talk about abuses of the one-child policy. He was very charismatic. He wore sunglasses because he was blind, but it made him look quite fashionable. He was very well spoken. He was obviously well educated beyond the village. He showed me his law books, these braille books dated from the 1970s. He educated himself, and became this celebrity in his village, because he had challenged the government, sued them to get back taxes, and won. I think I was the first Western reporter to go down there and spend time with him. It was pretty amazing. Every time someone had problems with the government, they went to him. I spent two or three days following him around. We'd walk in, the crowds would surround him like a rock star. We published this story and other media picked up on this and it became a big international story.

Hannah Beech, *Time*

We got to know each other pretty well. He gave me contacts for some women who had recently undergone forced abortions. The last time we met in Beijing, I waved and said, "See you in a few days." I was going off to Shandong, his home province, to meet the women. A few hours later, he was detained. That began his long stints of jail and house arrest. I was the last foreign journalist to meet with him before he was picked up. So my photographer and I had a quick confab and we said, "We're still going to go." We drove out there late at night. In the middle of a field, we met with three women who had had forced abortions. Just incredibly personal, wrenching details. A woman who had been forced to—I guess it's called an "abortion" technically—but she was only a couple days to her due date. They strapped her down on the bed and injected poison into her belly, and then a few hours later she gave birth to a dead baby, which they then plopped into a bucket next to her. She had a name for the baby. Her husband was crying, and she was still strapped down. I'm talking with these women who've gone through incredibly traumatic experiences in the middle of a field, knowing that Chen Guangcheng has just been detained but not knowing what the ramifications of it were. The photographer (Taiwanese American Chien-min Chung) had a tough time because we were in the middle of a field at 1 AM. How do you take photos? He was very creative and ended up turning on the headlights of the car and shining it on these women and you got that sort of "deer in the headlights" look. It was a very powerful photo.

TWO COMPETING THEMES

The fate of the rights lawyers and other dissidents highlighted what was for many reporters the central contradiction in trying to make sense of China.

Longtime Australian TV news anchor Stan Grant had joined CNN in Hong Kong in 2000 and became the network's CNN China correspondent in 2005.

Stan Grant, CNN

The inconsistencies, on the one hand, of a country opening up economically and creating a lot more personal freedom for their own people, but politically still trying to control from the center at Beijing. That would obviously play itself out with human rights issues, issues of rule of law, various crackdowns the Party would impose on civil liberties and human rights organizations and activists. The heavy hand of the Communist state versus the opening up of the economy and increasing personal freedom was really fascinating.

The same year, Evan Osnos, who had studied Chinese in Beijing in the 1990s, arrived in China for the *Chicago Tribune* after a long stint in the Middle East.

Evan Osnos, *Chicago Tribune*

There were two dominant themes competing for attention. One was the classic story about China the last twenty-five [to] thirty years, the struggle between human rights and the Chinese political ethic, and how were these two going to fit together, and how was this China going fit into the world? Then there was this emerging story—the sudden onset of prosperity, and what that meant for people, both on a macro basis, but also on an individual basis, how it's changing people's lives. You have this schizophrenic story. You could write on Monday about a dissident and on Tuesday about the ribbon cutting at the world's largest airport. Trying to put these two side by side in your own head was hard enough. Trying to put them into the same story was difficult. To me, that sense that you had to allow these two narratives to coexist became a very important part of how I looked at the story, because I felt the longer I was there, telling one of those stories without the other in the same frame felt inadequate. I felt like I was doing a disservice to the reader to tell just one of them, and so I started looking for opportunities where I could put these two narratives into a kind of harsh juxtaposition with each other.

John Pomfret, *Washington Post*

The most interesting thing is the economic development and the changes in terms of the fact that people were leaving home, going away for long periods of time, alienated relations with parents, how that created this incredible social change here, sped up by China being sucked into the global community. That story for me was the most fascinating one.

Evan Osnos, *Chicago Tribune*

What was going on was also an interior transformation, where people's conception of themselves as individuals and their relationship to the state was all in flux. It was changing just as rapidly and just as dramatically as the physical landscape. The challenge became how to capture that? How do you get inside people's lives and inside their stories?

China was opening up, changing almost beyond recognition, although for the American press corps, much of it remained frustratingly inaccessible.

14

TREMORS

By the mid-2000s, the skyline of Beijing was changing. With the 2008 Olympic games approaching, the government was devoting massive resources to making the capital an international showcase. When China sought unsuccessfully to host the 2000 games, the official slogan was "a more open Beijing awaits the Olympics." At the end of 2006, with the games less than two years away, the government announced a dramatic liberalization in the rules governing foreign journalists.

Peter Ford, *Christian Science Monitor*

The rules were changed to satisfy the International Olympic Committee about press freedom. This was the first time that foreign correspondents were allowed to go out of Beijing without asking permission first. You were technically allowed to speak with anybody who was willing to speak to you.

Joseph Kahn, *New York Times*

There was a pretty sincere commitment by the media authorities in China to fulfill their obligations in hosting the Olympics to allow more unfettered coverage of national events by the foreign press corps. In the run-up to the Olympics, they liberalized reporting rules for travel outside of areas like Beijing and

Shanghai, dropped the requirement for prior approval, and restricted how much officials could interfere with you when you were there.

Andrew Browne, *Wall Street Journal*

The period ahead of the Olympics had a real sense of opening and possibility. Everything appeared to be heading in the right direction. From a reporting point of view, we were told the Olympics was going to be the turning event for us, that we would have freedom to travel around the country. China was opening and it would open to us as foreign reporters.

Barry Petersen, CBS News

We could go anywhere. We can just get on a plane and rent a car and arrange a hotel, that kind of thing. It gave us extraordinarily more freedom to do the kind of stories we wanted to do, which were two parts—talking about China as a growing economy, what that's going to mean to the U.S., but also taking people into the heart of China, which we had not really been able to do.

Away from Beijing, though, whatever the new rules, the correspondents frequently found that it was the same old story.

Peter Ford, *Christian Science Monitor*

The problem was local authorities, who didn't want Beijing to know that something embarrassing was happening on their patch. It wasn't that those authorities were worried about what people were going to read in Berlin, Boston, or Timbuktu. They were worried that via Berlin or Boston or Timbuktu, Beijing would find out about it.

Louisa Lim, NPR

We all wanted to test the rules, so we trotted out to the countryside carrying our copies of the regulations, to discover that, although the regulations were there on paper, on the ground, there was still this sort of extreme reluctance by local officials to allow you to interview people and to talk to people.

Joseph Kahn, *New York Times*

You pretty routinely would confront local officials who would forbid you from doing any serious reporting or took your notes or otherwise intimidate you, but legally, they had no grounds to do that.

THE POISONING OF LAKE TAI

In early 2007, Kahn had established contact with a former factory salesman named Wu Lihong, who had become an environmental activist. For years, Wu had waged a one-man campaign to name and shame the hundreds of chemical plants, textile mills, and other factories that had been discharging industrial waste in to the once-pristine waters of China's third-largest fresh-water lake, Lake Tai.

Joseph Kahn, *New York Times*

Wu Lihong persistently called attention to the effluent that flowed into the lake that led to choking infestations of algae that came close to killing the lake. He took the battle repeatedly to local officials. He was intimidated and warned, and there were also a number of inducements to him, including opportunities to become "consultants" to local companies and that sort of thing, which were pretty thinly disguised bribes. But he rejected them, and continued to call attention to the pollution there, and he was brave enough to have open lines of communication to journalists like me.

That spring, as Lake Tai became so polluted by algae that it turned green, and millions of people were forced to find alternative sources of water for drinking and cooking, Wu Lihong was arrested.

Joseph Kahn, *New York Times*

I spent a lot more time there after he was jailed, re-creating his story of activism. I knew when I went that I had a very short window to do reporting. To do one big piece on him, I went three separate times, each for very short stints, to see people I had arranged in advance. I knew that when I went to see them, that was immediately going to call my presence to the attention of local officials, and I would have a very short time before I was either kicked out or those

people were told not to talk to me. I never sensed the top environmental offi-
cials, much less the top Party officials in Beijing, were trying to suppress the
story. Your big adversaries were the local, provincial-level interests that didn't
want to create any kind of disturbance, didn't want a thorough investigation
into why a big lake like [that] had become so heavily polluted. Once you got to
the top level, there was actually a certain amount of encouragement for in-
depth reporting about environmental abuses at the provincial level. So I never
was punished for environmental reporting on big local problems like that.

"THE AUTHORITIES WERE ABSOLUTELY TERRIFIED"

Also in 2007, Melissa Chan, a Hong Kong–born Chinese American who had
studied at Yale, became the Beijing correspondent for the English-language
network of the Qatar-based Al Jazeera.

Melissa Chan, Al Jazeera

As a Chinese American, I went in wanting to be very fair to China and feeling
that it was being unfairly covered to a certain extent by Western media. I was
working for this channel that really wanted to turn things on its head, Al Jazeera
English, with this mandate to question and do things no one else did. But at
the end of the day, as you start traveling, and we traveled a lot, you start seeing
things. The bottom line is that shitty things are happening to people in China,
and the reason is the government.

One of her first stories was a feature about a child living on a farm while
her parents worked in the city.

Melissa Chan, Al Jazeera

I was so naïve. I was thinking, "What's the harm of that?" We spent the morn-
ing with this little girl. She mainly took care of herself. She cooked her break-
fast, went to school, and then came back. It was rural, pastoral. There were
chickens running around, a Chinese village, and a little home. I thought it was
just a nice color piece. The local authorities were absolutely terrified. They found
out when we filmed the little girl going to school. Suddenly we were surrounded.
They even locked the courtyard, and refused to let us out, and started asking
a lot of questions. Eventually things got sorted out, and we were let go. But back

in Beijing, I got a call. I guess the local authorities in Anhui reported it. And the Foreign Ministry very angrily said, "If Al Jazeera is going to start acting like BBC and CNN, we're going to start treating Al Jazeera like BBC and CNN." And then they slammed the phone down.

Ian Johnson of the *Wall Street Journal* had left China in 2001 for Berlin and had written a book about the Falun Gong. He was now trying to get back, only to discover the Chinese wouldn't give him a visa.

Ian Johnson, *Wall Street Journal*

I published a book that was partly on the Falun Gong and partly on other civil society protests. In January 2007 we applied for me to come back again with the Wall Street Journal. *In June, they called the bureau chief and the foreign editor, basically banged their shoe on the table and said that "this guy is never coming back into China. He has violated all kinds of rules and regulations." They were adamant that I could not get back in.*

Rupert Murdoch's News Corporation had just acquired the *Wall Street Journal.* Johnson enlisted the help of former CNN international desk editor Mei Yan. Her father had been a high-ranking Communist official, and she now headed News Corporation's government relations office in China.

Ian Johnson, *Wall Street Journal*

The way these things work is you have to soften up the bureaucracy. I got good advice from John Pomfret, who said you probably have to write something like a self-criticism but just imagine it's going to be published on the front page of the People's Daily *tomorrow. In other words, don't write anything that you'll regret if it becomes public. Don't say you wish you hadn't covered Falun Gong or whatever. So I wrote a carefully worded letter about how I'd gotten involved in China, and what I hoped to accomplish next time around, and how I was older and more mature.*

At the end of it all, you have to get a very high-level person, an old "friend of China" or somebody with some pull, who can see a minister and kick down the final door and get you in. This is sort of the pattern for other people who have been banned from China. The Journal was just being sold to News Corporation, which was headed by an old "friend of China," Rupert Murdoch, but nobody was going to go up the ladder to ask him for help, because everybody was worried about their job. The problem was to get Murdoch on board. Mei Yan's father had been minister of broadcasting back in the old Communist system, so she was pretty plugged in. She was like, "We've got to get you back in here. We can't have you banned." I was in Berlin, and she told me that Murdoch is coming to Beijing tomorrow. She said, "We need to get something in his hands and get him involved. Send me a one-paragraph synopsis of your case." And she went with Murdoch, who was going to see the state council information office minister. She put it in front of Murdoch. He didn't know from Adam, obviously. He's like, "Oh, it's a bit of a complicated situation, but if you say so, Mei, why not?" He went in, and by all accounts gave a great little talk. And said, "I've got this little favor. This fellow, he wrote some articles, who knows if they were right or wrong, but it was ten years ago. Forget about this. Give him another chance, just for my sake." And the minister said, "I'll see what I can do."

Soon after, the Chinese promised Johnson a visa for the Olympics. He got a full accreditation in 2009.

DISSIDENTS

The approach of the Games, and the hope it would bring greater liberalization, also inspired China's dissidents. Among them was the prominent intellectual Liu Xiaobo, a literary critic and university professor who participated in the Tiananmen Square protests and was subsequently jailed for twenty-one months. He was imprisoned again in the mid-1990s for three years, but after his release continued to speak out about democracy and human rights.

Evan Osnos, *Chicago Tribune*

I met Liu Xiaobo in 2007. He'd been writing criticisms of the state for a number of years. I went to see him to talk about what the Olympics was going to mean for China. Liu was optimistic. He felt that this moment in the spotlight, in which China was pulled into the international system in a new way, would pressure the leadership to honor some of the constitutional commitments that it had made, or commitments to international organizations. And he showed me a letter that he was writing that was going to be distributed and signed by a bunch of other dissidents.

Joseph Kahn, *New York Times*

I always felt he was a quiet, unrepentant dissident of the kind that I thought China had made a decision to allow to exist as long as they stayed somewhat subterranean. That was my impression.

Evan Osnos, *Chicago Tribune*

Liu was also a devotee of the Internet. He called it "God's gift to China." As a dissident, as an activist, it was transformative. "Before the Internet," he said, to sign a petition, "you had to spend weeks crisscrossing the city on buses and trains, trying to get people's signatures—all of this done, of course, in secrecy because you were afraid you were going to get caught. Once the Internet made it possible for you to be in contact with people all over the country, you could assemble signatures and support and debate ideas and documents in real time."

To host the Olympics, the authorities embarked on an extraordinary construction boom to create venues like the much-heralded Bird's Nest stadium, which was codesigned by the artist Ai Weiwei. But Ai soon became a critic of the entire Olympic extravaganza.

Evan Osnos had by now replaced Peter Hessler as the *New Yorker* China correspondent.

Evan Osnos, *New Yorker*

I got interested in Ai Weiwei around the time of the Olympics. He was an emerging international artist. He had been hired as one of the architects on the Bird's Nest stadium. That was a familiar trajectory—a guy who's gotten some international attention and the embrace of the Party to the degree that they have elevated him and allowed him to have this important, high-profile job. But instead of moving smoothly along that trajectory into being an "official intellectual," he upturned the apple cart. The more he learned about it, the more he came to believe it was, as he put it, "a fake smile." He didn't believe it was a sincere gesture of openness to the world. He thought it was in the end a nationalist project, and that put him on a collision course with the state.

This is a guy who could've been one of the art stars of this period. He could've sold his work internationally for a huge fortune. He could've had a companionable relationship with the Party. But instead, he pushed back. He kicked them in the face. And while he was doing it, instead of alienating the public, there were people all over China who were beginning to see something that resonated with them in his very idiosyncratic struggle. In some ways, Ai Weiwei's turn towards dissent was also a reflection of the role of the Internet. He played the Internet like an instrument. He mastered it, more than anybody else had, and faster than anybody else had. He was putting out hundreds of photos a week. Even before there was a thing like Instagram, he was using the Internet for that purpose. He was blogging, and he was taking it on in a political way. He made the Internet accessible to people who had previously imagined that it wasn't something for them.

THE CHINESE INTERNET: "A NATIONWIDE TIP LINE"

For the correspondents, the Internet, in particular Weibo, the Chinese version of Twitter, was providing a remarkable window into Chinese society.

Melindia Liu, *Newsweek*

The Internet was not nearly as constrained as it is now. There were people seeking freedom and their identity online.

Louisa Lim, NPR

Suddenly the Internet, and especially Weibo, was this ginormous nationwide tip line where you could find extraordinary stories and contacts and pictures and proof videos. It was extremely important in reporting.

Joseph Kahn, *New York Times*

The microblogs became an extremely easily accessible and popular way for ordinary people to express their views and communicate. There were dozens of examples of cases of abuse and corruption that were being exposed. I felt, and think many others in the media did, that this really was a genie that was going to be hard to put back in the bottle in terms of open expression by people who had long distrusted their own state media and were now creating and consuming information that was outside the traditional channels of control. As a tool for foreign correspondents, it was an absolute bonanza.

Philip Pan, *Washington Post*

It was a window into society that you could really monitor. It had an impact on journalists but also on how fast things moved in China. It was a catalyst. A story could blow up very quickly because of the Internet.

RAZING THE *HUTONGS*

As the government's grand Olympic project moved ruthlessly ahead, one key feature was to rid Beijing of many of its historic *hutongs*—neighborhoods of narrow alleys lined with quaint but often dilapidated courtyard homes, dating back decades, often inherited by the new middle class.

Peter Ford, *Christian Science Monitor*

You couldn't live in Beijing and not see what was being knocked down or hear from people who were living [in] the places that were being knocked down. There was a great deal of activity amongst people who were losing their homes, getting in touch with foreign journalists. They were very moving stories, and often cases of tremendous injustice. There was a great deal of the negative aspects of Beijing's development to report on, which of course the Chinese government objected to enormously.

Stan Grant, CNN

There were stories that we did about moving people forcefully from their homes, people trying to cling to their homes while they were being torn down around them. A couple of instances of people that we'd interviewed taken away, held under house arrest, beaten up. We were detained and slapped around on a couple of occasions.

Barry Petersen, CBS News

If they needed to cut a swathe of five blocks to do something, there were no meetings, no lawsuits, no input, no nothing. They just went in and told people, "OK, you're out of here." To their credit, they didn't throw people onto the streets. They took people out of these areas and put them into high rises. They did give them a better standard of life. The complaints from most people were about losing their neighborhoods because they'd lived there for decades or even generations. When you take people like that and put them in a high rise, you lose all sense of neighborhood. They got a better standard of life but they felt like they lost part of themselves.

Ching-Ching Ni, *Los Angeles Times*

There was no more of the Beijing I recognized as a child. There were communities where they knocked them down, rebuilt them, or just simply painted them on one side so the traffic passing by would look at a more sanitized neighborhood. Only Tiananmen Square was still there.

For the authorities, though, and, indeed, for many Chinese, the transformation was essential as China prepared for its grand entry onto the international stage.

Charles Hutzler, Associated Press

The government had hyped the Olympics and there was a lot of genuine public emotion that the Olympics was going to be this high for China, it would be a game-changing event for international perceptions of China.

Evan Osnos, *New Yorker*

The Olympics were important to China on a much deeper level. This is about China's reentry into the world in a variety of ways. What was going on was also an interior transformation, where people's conception of themselves as individuals and their relationship to the state was changing just as rapidly and just as dramatically as the physical landscape.

ANTI-CNN.COM

To Beijing's consternation, in March 2008, on the anniversary of the uprising against Chinese rule in March 1959, riots broke out in the Tibetan capital, Lhasa. Ethnic Tibetans went on a rampage, attacking Han Chinese and their shops, hotels, and businesses. Dozens of people were reported killed. The Chinese authorities did not allow American or other foreign journalists to witness the unrest. The prevailing Western narrative, widely reflected in the press coverage—of Tibetans resisting oppressive Chinese rule—ran directly counter to the Chinese narrative. This blamed the violence on Tibet's exiled spiritual leader, the Dalai Lama, and advocates of Tibetan independence, supported by an allegedly biased Western press. Soon, the Western media came under fierce attack, both from the Chinese government and from the Chinese public, especially on the Internet.

Joseph Kahn, *New York Times*

There was very strong moment of Chinese nationalism—a feeling among a number of Chinese I knew that both the riots in Tibet and the various controversies over the Olympics were somehow manipulated by the foreign media to undermine the message China was trying to send to the outside world. I don't think the coverage was manipulation by the foreign media, but I can understand why Chinese, in their moment of national glory, felt that way. I also understand why people in Tibet might have wanted to take the opportunity of intensive international attention to get their message out there as well. The media was caught between those two forces.

CNN became a particular target, especially after an editor at CNN headquarters in Atlanta cropped a photo of the Lhasa violence for stylistic reasons and put it on the CNN website. Tomas Etzler worked as a correspondent for Czech TV and freelanced as a producer and reporter for the CNN Beijing bureau.

Tomas Etzler, CNN

It was a wide photograph of Chinese military trucks on the left side of the picture, and on the right side of the picture were Tibetans throwing stones at them. Somebody cropped the Tibetans out and put this photograph on the CNN website. And it created another huge wave of anti-CNN feelings. And it was at this point that the Anti-CNN.com website was launched.

Even though the photo was captioned, "Tibetans throw stones at army vehicles on a street in the capital Lhasa," the "Anti-CNN.com" website got millions of Chinese supporters.

Tomas Etzler, CNN

There were a lot of threats. The CNN bureau was receiving daily hundreds of death threats. The bureau had to evacuate to a nearby hotel because there were so many threats. And when they moved back, there was a police presence in front of the bureau. It was quite intimidating.

Wen-Chun Fan, CNN

It did get very scary. At one point, we could not answer the phones. We could not even really turn on the fax machine. We couldn't operate. We couldn't really go cover anything, because the minute we told people we were from CNN, they'd be very hostile or they'd be like, "Yeah, I don't think it's a good time."

CNN was not the only foreign news organization to become a target.

Charles Hutzler, Associated Press

It was dicey. I stopped using my mobile for a while. What I became really worried about—because a lot of the threats became "We're going run you over" or "We're watching you. We know where you live"—was collateral damage, especially of my family or my colleagues.

David Barboza, *New York Times*

I wrote two or three stories about Tibet. That's the first time I had gotten hate mail in China. Some were threatening we're going to kill you and your wife, and I wasn't even doing anything. It's not just CNN, it's the foreign media.

Louisa Lim, NPR

I was sharing an office with Quentin Sommerville of the BBC, their Shanghai correspondent. He had asked a question in a press conference that had been televised live about what steps the government would take to protect the Olympic torch on its tour of Tibet. After that, he got death threats, and someone put our office address on the Internet. All our assistants were harassed and told they were traitors. There was this real atmosphere of absolute fear. Looking back now, this was the beginning of a move towards a much more nationalistic China.

After the unrest was suppressed, the government took a small group of reporters to Lhasa to show that everything was fine.

Charles Hutzler, Associated Press

They tried to script everything. But this backfired. When we were taken to the Jokhang Temple, the holy shrine of Tibetan Buddhism, twenty to thirty young monks came out. They started saying how we were being led on this sham trip, that the shrine had been closed since the riot, that the believers were all Communists brought in by the government. They also talked about their own grievances and how they wanted the Dalai Lama to come back. Because I was there with a colleague from AP TV, the story was instantly everywhere. The government was really unhappy. When we got back, somebody put my contact on the Internet, and we started to get death threats from angry patriotic Chinese. Our contacts were put under the title "American journalists that fabricated information in Tibet."

Following the Lhasa riots, anti-Chinese protests dogged the progress of the Olympic flame through Europe and the United States, further inflaming Chinese public opinion. In Beijing, the government had months earlier decided that the flame should be carried to the summit of the Chinese side of Mount Everest in Tibet. Now, the political significance for Beijing of producing such a triumphant image—China Central Television was planning to broadcast the ascent live—became even more important as a dramatic counterpoint to the riots in Lhasa. A small group of foreign reporters had been invited to cover the event from Everest base camp, among them CNN producer Tomas Etzler.

Tomas Etzler, CNN

The planning started extremely friendly. We were told we would go to Lhasa and have at least a week before we get to base camp, which is over seventeen thousand feet above sea level so we can get acclimatized. Then came the Tibetan riots. They renewed the conversations, but it was not friendly anymore. They said we will have two days to get there. There were supposed to be twenty foreign journalists going. In the end, only eleven went. We arrived and the Chinese media were filming our arrival. The moment they figured out I was from CNN they were asking if CNN should apologize. I said, "This is a question way above my level. I am here not to talk politics. I'm here to cover an incredible sports achievement." I refused to talk about it.

The Chinese had originally said that the foreign reporters would be allowed to stay at the Everest base camp.

Tomas Etzler, CNN

They promised us we'll have unlimited access to all the climbers. But a lot of these climbers were Tibetan climbers. They were really paranoid, afraid some activists might make it up there with Free Tibet banners and this would be broadcast live. So they didn't want us in the base camp. We were maybe two kilometers away in some small facility, just wooden shacks. I remember one guy from the Kyodo Japanese news agency was a climber. He said, "I am going to the base camp. They promised us this. I am a climber. I can go around." He left. One hour later, he was brought back, escorted by two soldiers with Kalashnikovs. They were very uptight. There were about seven hundred Chinese soldiers stationed there. We were told not to film, and when I tried to film a standup with them, I was stopped. When the climbers reached the summit, they took us to the base camp to see the celebrations. Everyone was really happy, especially CCTV, because they managed to actually bring live pictures from the top of Mount Everest.

THE SICHUAN EARTHQUAKE

On May 12, 2008, Sichuan province was hit by a massive earthquake. Over seventy thousand people died. Edward Wong, who had a graduate degree in journalism from the University of California, Berkeley, had just arrived in Beijing for the *New York Times* after spending four years covering the war in Iraq.

Edward Wong, *New York Times*

The Sichuan earthquake was the first story I covered in China. We felt the tremors in Beijing, and I got on a plane to Chongqing. They had already shut down the airport in Chengdu. We landed in Chongqing and scrambled to get a car to drive hours west out to the earthquake zone. Of all the stories I covered in China, the Sichuan quake was the closest story in terms of a parallel to Iraq. When I got into Dujiangyan, which was one of the hardest-hit towns, I saw buildings that had been turned into rubble, and bodies protruding from buildings. It was a tough scene to take in.

Like Wong, Al Jazeera's Melissa Chan was among the first Beijing-based reporters to reach the scene.

Melissa Chan, Al Jazeera

The earthquake took place at around 2 PM local time in Sichuan and we got there about 2 AM that night. We tried to get into Beichuan [a town of 160,000 close to the epicenter of the quake]. We were the first group there, and local officials tried to stop us. We argued for hours. Finally, were allowed to go.

Tomas Etzler made his way to the quake zone as a cameraman for CNN.

Tomas Etzler, CNN

It took us twenty-four hours to get there because the roads were broken. There were huge landslides. We hitched a ride, then we had to hike a little bit, and hitch another ride with medical teams. And the Chinese military invited us to come with them. I could not believe the Chinese military would be so inviting. Some of the soldiers even offered to carry my gear. So, animosities between the foreign press and Chinese authorities were kind of erased at the beginning. I had Chinese military helping me on several occasions to carry stuff across landslides and everything because it was really dangerous. I was really, really impressed. Still, there were people there who told us, because we needed to get across the river for example, they said, "We will only help you if you can prove to us you are not CNN." Even in those small villages, they knew about this CNN issue, that CNN had become so unpopular in China in that year. So, I always told them I am with Czech television. So, we managed to get across.

Edward Wong, New York Times

I went to a hospital and interviewed a family that had survived. The husband and wife had been trapped in a house when it collapsed. When I walked into the hospital room, I looked at the wife lying there in the bed. The husband was sitting next [to] her. I saw that her legs had just been amputated. She had both legs cut off. They sat there and told me the story of how they had been buried alive in their house, and they thought that they would die at that moment. And they told each other they would survive for their daughter, and they held to each other and stuck it through and then rescuers eventually got to them, but not in time to save the woman's legs, which had been trapped in the rubble. That story still haunts me today.

As the scale of the disaster became apparent, many Chinese journalists and bloggers traveled to Sichuan, and, along with the foreign press, were given surprising freedom to report.

Louisa Lim, NPR

Early on, the rescue and relief operation were so intense that the Chinese had an interest in getting the rest of the world to see what they were up against, so they had an interest in allowing open reporting. It was the most exciting time that I was in China as a journalist, the only time where I felt I was working alongside Chinese colleagues, working together. It seemed suddenly as if the local officials were so helpful to the foreign media, and everybody was so nice. It was a little window as to what reporting might be like without all that harassment.

Ching-Ching Ni, *Los Angeles Times*

The Chinese journalists can do one heck of a job if they weren't shackled, and during the earthquake, they were able to do some amazing work. They were free to cover the story. And I have to say—I was there as a reporter, but I was also a consumer of the news that they were producing, especially of TV. I remember they were covering the death of this young man who was buried under a building. Only his head was halfway out, and this reporter was talking to this man as he was dying, you know feeding him a sip of Coke, as he was talking about his hopes and dreams of what he would do when he gets out. And we watched this throughout the day on Chinese national television, and I was crying, the whole country was crying. It was incredible what the Chinese journalists are able to do once they're free.

Louisa Lim, NPR

I remember going to these tents and asking for figures of how many people had been displaced, and being given these lists of numbers and figures and thinking, "That was unbelievably easy—what happened?" Suddenly, everything was open, and we were working with our Chinese colleagues and exchanging tips on the same stories, and it was fantastic.

One by-product was an abrupt change in Chinese public opinion about foreign reporters.

Edward Wong, *New York Times*

During the earthquake, the controls operating on the foreign journalists in a news environment had loosened. We could travel anywhere we wanted, although there was the danger of the aftershocks, but we could go and talk to people, and people were eager to speak to us. It was an interesting moment following the Tibet uprising because it earned China more goodwill in the international sphere, and within China it earned foreign journalists more goodwill after the huge backlash during the Tibet uprising.

Then, the story began to change. It became clear that a disproportionate number of collapsed buildings were schools, apparently because, due to the corruption of local officials, they had not been built to adequate standards. In contrast, many government buildings in similar locations suffered only minor damage.

Melissa Chan, Al Jazeera

Suddenly there were a lot of questions about these elementary and middle schools and why all these students died, and the comparison of the government buildings that didn't crumble, and the schools that crumbled immediately. Foreign reporters started picking up on it and covering it. Suddenly the attitude in Sichuan changed. No one was allowed to cover anything. The same old stuff happened again. You tried to talk to parents. Some of them would defy authorities. They were angry. They had lost children, in most cases their only child, so they wanted to talk to journalists. But it suddenly became a lot harder. Authorities would follow us and essentially prevent any journalism into what had actually happened at these schools.

Ching-Ching Ni, *Los Angeles Times*

It really just hit you about the people left out of this economic miracle. The schools that collapsed, the families that lost their only child. I think for me that was when China became more than just a story. It was too personal for me. It was one of the hardest stories to cover because to see so many dead children who look just like my own, it was very hard to be just a reporter at the point.

"ONE WORLD, ONE DREAM"

As the Olympics approached, with the government trumpeting the slogan "One World, One Dream," the international outpouring of sympathy over the quake, coupled with China's dramatic economic progress, shifted the focus and tone of much American press coverage. NBC News anchor Tom Brokaw first visited China with President Gerald Ford in 1975. He'd returned in the 1980s, including immediately after the Tiananmen crackdown. He was astonished at what he saw now.

Tom Brokaw, NBC News

I wanted to grab my NBC colleagues and say you are not going to believe what this place was like twenty years ago. You cannot believe this. What they have done in a short amount of time is historic beyond my ability to describe it.

Barry Petersen, CBS News

They wanted the Beijing Olympics to be a spectacular moment of China coming out to the world. To the Chinese, this was legitimacy. They're one of the big guys now. They can put this event on. The point was to show the world they were a twenty-first-century country, that they were big and good and the architecture glistened and the skies were clear, and they did it.

How the Chinese cleared their normally polluted skies became a major Olympic story. Barbara Demick had recently moved from Seoul to become the *Los Angeles Times* bureau chief.

Barbara Demick, *Los Angeles Times*

We ended up writing a lot about air quality. That was really the beginning of the surge of stories about Beijing's air quality problems. I wrote a lot about the weather modification bureau. I loved weather modification. It was a very interesting story.

Barry Petersen, CBS News

They installed a very sophisticated system, going out a couple hundred miles, to deal with the issue that they were most afraid of, which was air pollution. And the days of the Olympics were some of the most spectacular, clean air days that I spent in Beijing, a city which is almost as famous for its pollution as it is for anything else. They shut down places like a hundred miles away if they thought the air currents were going to bring bad air or pollution into Beijing.

Hundreds of foreign reporters were granted visas for the Olympics.

Edward Wong, *New York Times*

But at the same time, there was a huge clampdown on protest, on dissenters. They shipped people out of Beijing. They wanted to make sure there were no troublemakers around, that the press wouldn't see anything that Chinese officials didn't want them to see. On the surface, there was this looser atmosphere, but behind the scenes, they were getting tighter, and they were making it harder for journalists to report on the real social issues going on in China.

Peter Ford, *Christian Science Monitor*

While they had this protest area set up, anybody who went near was in serious trouble. That didn't stop petitioners getting to foreign correspondents. But the overall Olympic atmospherics were great, the logistics were fantastic, and it worked brilliantly.

Louisa Lim, NPR

There was this huge upsurge of patriotism. I remember watching the opening ceremony with a family who'd been evicted from their house to make way for the Olympic stadium. They were so proud. They really didn't seem to mind that

*their entire lives had been uprooted to make way for this extraordinary dis-
play of national pride and strength. That was when I began to tell that the mood
had changed in a way that there was no turning back. This was the beginning
of a much more nationalistic China. I think those were the themes that we then
saw in the opening Olympic ceremony, themes that President Xi Jinping has
continued to develop.*

Edward Wong, *New York Times*

*I was roaming the streets of Beijing talking to people watching the opening cer-
emony on the big screen. People were very proud. They said it was a symbol of
China rightfully taking its place as one of the preeminent nations of the world.
There is this strong sense of nationalism. They were very proud of China getting the Olympics.*

But Ching-Ching Ni, who'd been born and raised in Beijing, watched the
spectacle with decidedly mixed emotions.

Ching-Ching Ni, *Los Angeles Times*

*The earthquake had really made me feel differently about the whole China
story. When you're growing up in Communist China as a Communist Chinese,
you believe everything you're told. But as an American journalist, you're trained
to look beneath the surface. And you're face to face with the real people of China.
And their stories are so far away from Beijing. The people I talked to that year
across China, they're suffering in ways where the Olympics had nothing to do
with their lives. It was really hard to feel too much.*

Four months after the Olympics ended, Liu Xiaobo and three hundred
other intellectuals and dissidents signed a document called Charter '08. It
was a sweeping call for political reform, including free elections and the end
of one-party rule, inspired in part by the government's promises of a more
open China because of the Olympics.

Evan Osnos, *New Yorker*

*Because Liu had become one of the authors of Charter '08, even before it was
made public, the police showed up at his front door. He was detained and eventually put on trial and sentenced to eleven and a half years.*

"I DON'T CARE IF PREMIER WEN JIABAO SIGNED THIS LAW"

Soon after Liu's arrest, Al Jazeera's Melissa Chan went to Liu's apartment block hoping to interview his wife. Chan brought the Foreign Ministry's booklet of more liberal rules about the press issued in the run-up to the Olympics.

Melissa Chan, Al Jazeera English

There were unidentified men guarding the access to her apartment complex. We had already called her. I went there and this guy refused to identify himself. I said, "I want to interview somebody in this apartment complex. Here is this booklet, in English and Chinese, of the Chinese law saying that foreign reporters can interview whoever we wish so long as they agree." I said, "Look!" and I turned the page. It said, "Premier Wen Jiabao signed off on this law." This unidentified man, probably twenty minutes from Tiananmen Square, looks at me and says, "I don't care if Premier Wen Jiabao signed this law or not." It really says something about the rule of law in China, but also about that specific set of rules for foreign correspondents, governing foreign correspondents, and how it really didn't work.

Chan never got the interview. In 2010, while serving his sentence, Liu Xiaobo was awarded the Nobel Peace Prize. Seven years later, still in custody, he died of cancer.

15

CONTRADICTIONS

In November 2009, newly elected U.S. president Barack Obama made his first state visit to China, looking to forge a new kind of partnership with Beijing. Obama was the first president in years to take office having not criticized his predecessor's China policy. George W. Bush, who had initially seen China as a strategic competitor, changed his tune after the terror attacks of September 11, 2001. Preoccupied with the wars in Afghanistan and Iraq, he sought to maintain good ties with Beijing, even attending the opening of the 2008 Olympic games. In his desire for better relations, just weeks after his inauguration, Obama sent Secretary of State Hillary Clinton to China, where she signaled the administration's intention to downplay human rights in the hope of enhancing cooperation on issues like the economy and climate change. To further avoid antagonizing Beijing, Obama himself declined to meet Tibet's spiritual leader, the Dalai Lama, before making his China trip.

However, in the wake of the global financial crisis of 2008–09, from which China emerged relatively unscathed while the United States suffered a deep recession, the Chinese Communist Party saw Obama's gestures as signs of American weakness. Although facing a host of complex challenges—a growing gap between rich and poor and between the booming coastal areas and the impoverished hinterland, rampant corruption, ethnic tension between Han Chinese and the country's Uighur and Tibetan minorities—a confident, indeed cocky, Chinese leadership subjected Obama to the shabbiest treatment ever given a visiting American president. Edward Wong was one of the reporters covering the three-day trip.

Edward Wong, *New York Times*

Obama wanted to have an open discussion with students, but the dialogue that eventually took place, sort of a town hall–style meeting, was very stilted. He wasn't allowed to hold a press conference where there was a Q & A afterwards. The very tight controls on the White House during that visit were in a continuum of growing Chinese confidence and exertion on other countries. That was right around the time China was getting much bolder in its foreign policy— making louder declarations about territories in the South China Sea, for example, and very vocally pushing back against the U.S. on a wide range of issues, whether it was cyber security or trade practices or human rights.

China's leaders were unquestionably emboldened by their ability to ride out the crisis as the Western financial system imploded. Austin Ramzy, who'd studied Chinese in college and then in northeast China, was now in Beijing for *Time.*

Austin Ramzy, *Time*

There was this real sense of increased confidence, less concern about what the rest of the world thinks, a sense that this was China's time, that the U.S. is in decline and no longer the sense that China needs to be beholden to the U.S. or appease the U.S., or to respond to U.S. interests."

Edward Wong, *New York Times*

The global financial crisis that started in late 2008 was a huge inflection point in China and within the Party leadership. We started hearing lots of things being said in China about how the American system was broken, how the capitalist system that was being promoted in the West couldn't work for other countries, that it would lead to dire consequences. China was saying that its Party-led version of the capitalist system was the appropriate model for China and for the rest of the world.

Hannah Beech, *Time*

Very educated young Chinese who were connected to the Internet did not say, "Oh, we want a democratic system." They said, "No. The Chinese system works. The Chinese model of growth works. And you guys in the West, your economy is going downhill, your politics are going downhill. We've got it figured out."

After six years based in Washington, where he covered campaign finance and elections, Michael Forsythe returned to Beijing earlier in 2009 for his second stint as a Bloomberg News correspondent. His focus now was entirely on the Chinese economy.

Michael Forsythe, Bloomberg News

The first year I was back, it was amazing to me to see the incredible wealth that had been built up. Many, many people in the middle class were far better off than they were even six years ago.

For his first reporting trip, Forsythe went to Shijiazhuang, a drab, nondescript city 160 miles southwest of Beijing. He was astonished by what he saw.

Michael Forsythe, Bloomberg News

My first really memorable story was going to Hebei province, to Shijiazhuang, and going to a Gucci store there, and the Starbucks in Shijiazhuang, which was still a pretty poor city.

"IT'S NOT A BANG-BANG STORY"

Figuring out how to explain to editors, readers, and viewers the scale of the change, and what it meant—for ordinary Chinese and for Americans— became a central challenge for the U.S. press corps.

Stan Grant, CNN

For CNN, being an American organization, the obvious point of interest to the story was China versus the U.S. What does China's rise mean for the United States? How was the U.S. dealing with a potential rival the size of China?

But for TV reporters like Grant and his colleague, Korean American Eunice Yoon, conveying China's internal complex internal dynamic was a challenge.

Eunice Yoon, CNN

China is not a bang-bang story. It's not like stories in the Middle East, where there are all these amazing events happening in front of you.

Stan Grant, CNN

In terms of the backstory, the nuance, the analysis of the change taking place—that was increasingly difficult to sell, because they're looking for the big bang. They're looking for the spectacular. The day-to-day machinations of Chinese society and politics outside those spectacular stories were particularly hard, because you're competing against other spectacular stories around the world.

Rob Schmitz, who had served in the Peace Corps in China in the 1990s with Peter Hessler, was now a correspondent in Shanghai for the radio business program *Marketplace*.

Rob Schmitz, *Marketplace*

In the Peace Corps, I got a good sense of how rural Chinese think and what their hopes and their dreams were. Those two years are very important to me. I learned a lot. It was very eye-opening and, in many ways, inspired me to later become a journalist.

Schmitz decided to use the street on which he lived in Shanghai to illustrate how China was changing.

Rob Schmitz, *Marketplace*

I did a yearlong series on the people who lived and worked on the street that I lived on. Every month, I reported about someone. It gave me time to focus on where they were in their lives, how did they fit in China's economy, and where did they see themselves in China. Where did they see their future? What were their dreams? What were their hopes, and hopes for their children? I had a lot of time to talk to these folks. I followed them around. I watched them work. In many ways, these are the stories that get to the heart of China—stories of real people who are trying to make it in the fastest-changing economy in the world.

At the *New Yorker*, Evan Osnos was not under pressure to cover breaking news. So he, too, did articles about the neighborhood where he lived—specifically, a stall outside his front gate in Beijing.

Evan Osnos, *New Yorker*

The China story was so vast that my solution, just mentally, was to shrink the field of view down to as narrow a target as I could. I lived in a courtyard house in a hutong *[a traditional lane], on the west side of the old city in Beijing. I started paying attention to a stall right next to my front door. They sold biscuits, and I got to know the person who ran the shop. Then overnight the place shut down. I asked the woman who was running it why. She explained some of the economic forces at play when you're a little shopkeeper in Beijing. It was replaced by a breakfast pancake shop, a jianbing shop, so I got to know a little about the economics of that business. Then that place closed. Finally, a brothel took over that same space. I thought, "OK, the brothel business is proven. That's probably going to have a future." And then the brothel shut down after a few days. I started to think—What is wrong with this area? Then, finally, a hardware store moved in that sold construction materials. That survived. I decided that maybe the definition of a housing bubble is when a hardware store lasts longer than a brothel in your neighborhood.*

THE WEALTH GAP

Indeed, the construction boom became a feature of the Chinese landscape, fueled by huge amounts of state money pumped into the economy to counteract the impact of the global financial crisis. The resulting growth continued the process of lifting hundreds of millions out of poverty. It also produced a new class of exceptionally wealthy Chinese, many with connections to the top leadership.

Almost a decade after his first China posting, Jeremy Page, who had worked in Beijing in the late 1990s for Reuters, and then had served as Moscow correspondent for the *Times of London*, returned for the *Wall Street Journal*.

Jeremy Page, *Wall Street Journal*

The thing that struck me was how much Chinese society had changed while I'd been away, and how little the Party had changed. It was obvious this tension was becoming more acute. The issue that really caught my eye was this question of princelings [a term used to describe the wealthy and powerful relatives of senior Communist Party officials] and their role in the Party elite, and the extent to which they dominated both political decision-making and economic decision-making and to a large extent [were] reaping the benefits.

Michael Forsythe, Bloomberg News

The bling you saw on Beijing streets exceeded any bling you would see even in Los Angeles, or London or New York. It was quite striking. It really struck a nerve with me. And that became a big theme of my reporting—the wealth gap and looking at the money behind the politicians.

David Barboza decided to do a series on the relationship between the government, big business, and private entrepreneurs.

David Barboza, *New York Times*

The idea was to do five or six stories on state capitalism and end it with how the children of the leaders are involved in business. I had thought we might do a map of where they went to school, and where they worked, and do this big chart. I collected a lot of files on princelings, and I had taken notes over the years about different princelings being involved in this and that. My hope was to find something new.

The explosion of corruption and the growing wealth gap fueled social tensions that became a central theme of American reporting on China.

Hannah Beech, *Time*

There's a huge difference between Beijing, Shanghai, and the rest of China. It is so impressive when you drive around Shanghai. You see the gleaming buildings and the striving, stylish people. It's as if you're saying New York, the Upper West Side, is what the U.S. is. You cannot make that kind of assumption. In

China, the differential between Beijing and Gansu [an impoverished province in western China] is huge.

Keith Richburg, who'd been in and out of China for years, became the *Washington Post's* Beijing correspondent in 2009.

Keith Richburg, *Washington Post*

This problem of land being confiscated with very little payment back to the original owners was a huge issue. I went down to Hainan Island, where villagers were complaining about their traditional farmland and forestland being taken, and golf courses and hotel resorts being built, because the Chinese government decided they wanted to turn Hainan into the Hawaii of China. It was absolutely fascinating. Everybody knows about these issues there. They all can tell you the names of the developers. They can always tell you who the corrupt officials are.

I also went to Shanghai right after the announcement that Shanghai Disney was opening and found there were more than one hundred residents of this area who were basically being told they had to move because Disney was somehow a public development project, approved, fast track, by the Shanghai government. There was one lone guy who refused to move because he felt that his parents had built that house, they'd sunk their pension money into it, and he was not going to leave. So they bulldozed all the houses around him. They cut off his water, cut off his electricity. They piled up the rubble from all the destroyed houses all around his lone house. And he stayed there with a Chinese flag planted on top of the house. He was in tears when I talked to him. Ultimately he had to move too.

THE URUMQI RIOTS

The gap between haves and have-nots was just one fault line in Chinese society. Another was between ethnic Han Chinese and the Muslim Uighur population in the western province of Xinjiang. China's largest region, bordering eight countries, Xinjiang was one of the most ethnically diverse parts of China. The majority population was Uighur. Mostly Muslim, they spoke their own language similar to Turkish, and saw themselves as culturally and ethnically close to the nations of Central Asia. Since the late 1950s, however, a mass migration of Han Chinese, encouraged by the central government, had been changing Xinjiang. With the Han now comprising over 40 percent of the population, the Uighurs felt increasingly marginalized in their homeland. In the summer of 2009, groups of Uighurs in the regional capital Urumqi engaged in demonstrations that turned violent. Nearly two hundred people died. Close to two thousand were injured.

Edward Wong, whose father had served in the People's Liberation Army in Xinjiang before emigrating to the United States, had just spent four years in Iraq.

Edward Wong, *New York Times*

The 2009 riots in Urumqi reminded me of my time in Iraq. As soon as we got the first news of civilian deaths in Urumqi, I flew out there. The situation there was as tense as anything I've reported on in China. Han civilians whose shops had been attacked and burned when the civilians themselves had done nothing wrong other than moving there.

Peter Ford, *Christian Science Monitor*

In Xinjiang, this was a massacre of Han people by Uighurs. It was not the Uighurs being the victims—and the Uighurs are traditionally the victims—so it was a story that China wanted to tell.

The result was that the authorities dealt with the press in a very different way than in previous cases of unrest in places like Tibet. Chris Buckley, an Australian who had received a PhD in Chinese studies from the Australian National University, covered the unrest for Reuters.

Chris Buckley, Reuters

The Chinese official position is that militants seeking violence in Xinjiang are largely the product of religious extremism imported from abroad. I think, at the time, the government was trying to show foreign viewership, in particular television, that this was what was happening in Xinjiang.

Edward Wong, *New York Times*

This was the Party trying out a new way of propaganda dissemination. Before 2009, when news broke in Xinjiang or in Tibet, as it did in 2008 during the uprising there, the Party would try and suppress coverage so the outside world only saw news coverage through the Party propaganda apparatus. It would keep foreign journalists from going. But when the Urumqi riots happened, there obviously had been discussion in the propaganda apparatus, and they said, "Let's allow foreign journalists out to Urumqi to see what's going on." Veteran China correspondents couldn't remember a moment like that. Everyone ended up working out of a hotel which had been set up as an official press center. There was a lot of wariness about filing stories from that hotel because we assumed that they were monitoring everything we were writing. But we were able to leave the hotel, wander through the streets, interview people.

Melissa Chan, Al Jazeera English

There was even a press room with people from the Foreign Ministry and the local waiban [Foreign Affairs Office] providing us Internet, providing us information, offering to take us around. We took them up on their offer. They took us to a heavily Uighur neighborhood where rioting had taken place. I think they miscalculated and thought they could take us there, we'd film, and we'd be on our way. What happened is everything went off script.

Austin Ramzy, *Time*

Suddenly the streets were filled with hundreds of protesting Uighur women.

Edward Wong, *New York Times*

And they were shouting, denouncing the Party, denouncing the controls that the Party had placed on Uighurs, and we were standing in the street interviewing these women who had their fists raised in the air.

Melissa Chan, Al Jazeera English

They were marching towards the Chinese military officers, chanting. Some of them started picking up objects like they wanted to throw rocks. The front lines were Uighur women, so it was a people power moment, and they knew that international media were there. The whole thing went off script. This is not turning out the way they wanted.

Chris Buckley, Reuters

It meant in practice this surreal experience of walking from one side of the city that was under guard of armed police into the Uighur neighborhoods and having these very candid, impassioned conversations with Uighur residents who felt they weren't being heard. I wanted to give their account of the events that led up to the bloodshed. It was one of the richest reporting experiences I can remember from this period of candor, when it was possible to talk to different sides.

It was also quite frightening, because what happened after the initial bloodshed, which was largely Uighur rioters attacking mostly Han Chinese, was this backlash from the ethnic Han residents. Thousands of people started heading towards the Uighur neighborhoods of Urumqi. Me and another reporter just got carried along by the crowd. It was this molten anger just looking for an outlet. After several hours of walking and filing reports, we ended up on the Uighur outskirts of Urumqi, watching these mobs of intensely angry Han residents looking to exact vengeance. There were some lynch mobs. Crowds banging on the doors and trying to break in with crowbars. What do I do if they break in, me as an individual? Am I about to watch a lynching? What should I do? Luckily, the crowd moved on and the police came in before I had to make that choice, but I'll never forget that painful half an hour watching that crowd trying to break in to a Uighur apartment block.

Melissa Chan, Al Jazeera English

Lesson learned. Never take foreign press around. I don't recall a time after where they would take us around in conditions like that.

Indeed, from that point on, the Chinese authorities severely tightened controls in Xinjiang, including on access by the foreign press, as Melissa Chan discovered when she returned six months later.

Melissa Chan, Al Jazeera English

We went to Urumqi, Kashgar, and Hotan. We're followed the entire time. When we were at the Beijing airport to fly to Urumqi, our Uighur translator and driver in Urumqi called to cancel. Police came to his house at midnight, took him to the police station, and forced him to hand over our emails. He called us as we were about to leave to say that he couldn't help anymore. We were driverless and without a translator. I said, "Let's just go. We're just going to have to wing it." For the entire time we were in Urumqi we were followed.

When we flew into Hotan, it was a small airport, and vehicles were already at the airport. By the time we loaded up and drove off, they were following us, two cars with about three or four men in each car.

We flew into Kashgar. I was very confused because no one was following us. I was very aware, keeping an eye out for cars and individuals. Our driver was Chinese and parked a little bit away from where we were filming. I did notice that somebody had gone up to him and asked him a few questions and walked away. I went to the driver and said, "What was that about?" The driver said, "That gentleman was looking for some journalists from the Middle East! And I said, 'No! No! No! Those are two Chinese girls and a European.' So this person just walked away." They knew Al Jazeera was in Kashgar and they were literally looking for three Arabs with turbans, so the Chinese authorities completely missed the fact that we were in the Old City. They saw us with a giant camera and just walked away. It's just wonderful because you think these guys are like Keystone Cops. Sometimes you can run circles around them. Other times you can't slip away from them.

16

THE TURNING POINT

The government's response to the Urumqi riots was a harbinger of things to come, both in Xinjiang and in the treatment of foreign journalists. But in much of the rest of China, the American press corps found a surprising openness, driven in large part by the dramatic growth of the Internet.

Keith Richburg, *Washington Post*

There were a lot more academics, think tanks, former Party officials, and newspaper editors who were willing to meet. I found that a uniquely open experience. You had this civil society community that we could talk to, we could quote in our stories. It became a whole other source of information. The newspapers, while not anything that in the West we'd consider aggressive, were suddenly actually behaving a little bit more like newspapers and writing stories about environmental problems and things like that. But the biggest change was that my return to China in 2009 almost coincided perfectly with the rise of the Internet, social networking, and Weibo [the Chinese version of Twitter].

Evan Osnos, *New Yorker*

It's almost impossible for me to imagine my experience as a reporter in China without having been there during this period of the Internet. When I was a student in China, there were a million people online. By the time I left as a correspondent in 2013, there were half a billion people online. During that period, it had two powerful effects. One was on the people who we were writing about who were suddenly finding themselves empowered with this new technological potential. It helped them find other people who were like them and gave them a new tool for registering their complaints and participating in a kind of public sphere that hadn't existed before.

Eunice Yoon, CNN

Social media is a great tool because people will post photos or talk about different issues. Obviously, there is a lot of censorship, but there is a certain window when something happens, and suddenly you will see a lot of people talking about that topic, or retweeting.

Edward Wong, *New York Times*

This completely changed China reporting for us. Now we had this window into things that were going on across the entire nation, and as soon as a big news event happened, people would jump on it.

Austin Ramzy, *Time*

It made a huge difference, particularly because China is such a large country, and it's basically just covered out of Beijing, Shanghai, and Hong Kong. In an ideal world, we'd have a bureau in every province, but the money is just not there for that. So you have to try and follow what's happening in these places. Before Weibo, there would be an incident somewhere. You might hear about it, but you'd be very limited in terms of getting witnesses, participants, anything like that. Sometimes you just had to find what the local telephone exchange was and start dialing random numbers until you got some poor person who picked up the phone and may have seen whatever protest or incident happened and could describe it for you. But with Weibo, you could find participants. It made it much easier to track down people. Even with the censorship, there was a lag—a period of hours, day after an incident, before the censors figured out what was going on and knew what words they should block—that you could find out things.

Evan Osnos, *New Yorker*

It made us as journalists much more powerful in our ability to find out what was going on much faster. The idea that you had to go out on the street to where you would interview five people walking in and out of a department store changed. All of a sudden it felt like—Why don't I just go online and look at the top five comments people are making on this website? The Internet became this incredibly powerful tip sheet.

Keith Richburg, *Washington Post*

I first discovered this when a driver in Shanghai was trapped in a sting operation. Shanghai police used to stop cars if they thought they were illegally picking up passengers and acting like taxicabs. This guy was driving his company's car. Someone flagged him down asked for a ride. A few meters later his car was stopped, and he was accused of being an illegal taxi. Of course, he protested, "I was just giving someone a lift who needed a lift. I didn't even know the person." But it was a sting operation. This guy could not get any redress. He ended up, in this act of protest, chopping off one of his fingers in front of the courthouse in Shanghai. This may have happened in the past, and we never would have known about it, but because of Weibo and social networking, this story went viral. I was in Beijing and heard this and immediately went to Shanghai to do a story. There were hundreds of people who heard of this story. Others who had been entrapped who were protesting outside of the Shanghai municipal building demanding their fines be returned. I thought, something is new in China now, that a story like this can go viral, and I can actually hear about it instantly in real time and get down to Shanghai and cover this.

In 2011, a high-speed train crashed near the coastal city of Wenzhou. Dozens of passengers were killed and many more injured.

Keith Richburg, *Washington Post*

My news assistant called me well before this ever appeared on any official news site because she was finding it on Weibo. The first reports about the crash and the first pictures from inside the damaged train came from people with cell phones who were posting it on Weibo.

Evan Osnos, *New Yorker*

This was the first national disaster that played out in real time on the Internet. The people who could afford to be on this high-speed train were people with cell phones and social media accounts. So when their friends and family and others began to complain about how this crash had happened and what were the underlying causes—Was there corruption? Were the construction standards poor? Was the train built too fast?—instead of people registering them quietly around the dinner table or going down to the town square and having a small demonstration, all of a sudden people were putting this stuff out on the Internet. The pressure was so intense, the Party couldn't ignore it. All of a sudden, those complaints were shaping the government's response. Premier Wen Jiabao took more than a week to visit the site of the crash. At the time, the state news service explained that he had been ill in bed. Immediately, people online found photos and news reports about him meeting with other leaders and visiting heads of state during that extended period, so that turned the propaganda upside down. The Wenzhou train crash for a lot of us correspondents crystalized the sense that the old rules that had applied not only to natural disasters but to big news events of political significance were changing fundamentally, because these issues were now going to be litigated in real time on the Internet.

ACROSS ALL PLATFORMS

The technological revolution was also having another dramatic effect on the way foreign journalists operated. Whether print, radio, TV, or a wire service, the demand from editors now was to service multiple platforms, all the time.

Stan Grant, CNN

It did increase the workload massively. Suddenly we were having to do wires for CNN, write feature stories for the CNN website, do CNN radio. It was a lot more onerous. The demands were greater. There wasn't a lot of downtime. What it came down to often was sacrificing sleep.

Keith Richburg, *Washington Post*

When you called up with a good story idea the first questions were, "When can you have it to us?" Number two is, "Is there any video to it? Are there any photos to it? What are the links we're going to have in it? What are the Internet elements? What are the audio-visual elements?" It became much more of a multimedia thing, as opposed to the old days, where you could just go with a notebook, and go off to a place and spend three or four or five days, or a week interviewing people and coming back and writing your story.

Many reporters felt the new technology and increased demands were, in some ways, impeding coverage of China, making it harder to get away from the wired cities and breaking news, or to work on stories in areas that required being out of touch with the head office.

Keith Richburg, *Washington Post*

It's a huge problem that you don't have time to think and analyze things anymore. It used to be when you were a correspondent for one of the major American newspapers, the New York Times, Washington Post, *or whatever, that we don't chase the wires. We don't write things everybody else is writing. The idea is the wires covered the spot news. We were supposed to be on the road, traveling, looking for trend stories, looking for the analysis pieces, the big takeouts. But we've become a wire service. They want us writing everything. We used to be able to go somewhere and spend a week talking to everybody and come back and give the definitive story on this topic. Because of the Internet and the competitive demands of the 24/7 news cycle, there's much more emphasis now on spot news and less interest in long-form front-page narrative that I think we did so well in the past.*

UNCOVERED STORIES

That trend had consequences.

Chris Buckley, Reuters

My feeling is that in telling the story of changing China, there's not enough attention on the lives and challenges of people who live in that massive swathe of China that's not on the eastern coast or the western periphery. It's the hundreds of millions of people who live in small towns and villages and cities from Hebei through to Qinghai. These tremendous changes that people are living through there have taken a life of their own and they deserve media coverage.

Barbara Demick was the only *Los Angeles Times* China correspondent, but she made a conscious decision to leave most of the big political stories to the wire services and spend most of her time outside Beijing.

Barbara Demick, *Los Angeles Times*

I liked to observe real life unfiltered by all the commentary in Beijing. What I was good at was picking a story far off the beaten path. My strength as a reporter has always been being sort of inconspicuous. Even though I'm not Asian, I have a way of putting on a big hat and flat shoes and dusty clothes, and just traipsing around. I was able to work in Xinjiang more or less unnoticed. I spent a couple of weeks traveling in Tibetan areas wearing a floppy hat and a facemask.

I got into very remote villages in Guizhou and Hunan doing child trafficking stories. There were a lot of stories about babies who had been confiscated by family planning for adoption in the U.S. and elsewhere. Contrary to everything that Americans have been told about Chinese throwing away their baby girls, a lot of them really love those baby girls. A few of these families had tried to get in touch with Chinese press or NGOs, but the Chinese press at that time was not able to report it. Some of them passed on the tips to me. In a very remote part of Guizhou, we had gotten a tip that family planning had confiscated large numbers of baby girls. They would look for a diaper or some of the clotheslines and listen for crying babies, and they would snatch the babies. I travel very, very low key. Since I'm print, I don't bring a big camera, just a tiny camera or smartphone. I look like a backpacker. I can usually get away with it. I don't look like what they think a journalist looks like. In this case we took a taxi and then walked the rest of the way. I've also been very lucky with taxi drivers. The right driver is sometimes more important than the right reporter. We found a driver who was helpful, and didn't like family planning, and got us to the right place, which involved putting stones in the river to drive over them.

At the end of that trip, I went to the orphanage where the babies had been taken. I knew that as soon as I walked into the orphanage, I would be picked up by the local authorities, which of course I was. They took myself and the assistant from my office to their offices, and then decided they would take us to dinner. This is one of the things that happen when you're reporting. Either you're kicked out, or you're treated to death by banquet. They decide to hold a banquet in your honor. That's a way of keeping you under control. These local officials really weren't evil. They felt that these peasants had too many children.

China had a one-child policy. These babies would be better off adopted abroad. They explained how they got about three thousand dollars cash for each baby and used the money for social services to take care of disabled children and the elderly. They did not feel like they were doing the wrong thing in confiscating the babies. It was the first time anybody had gotten any interviews at the local level about the dynamic of what was going on with these baby girls going into the adoption network.

Rob Schmitz, *Marketplace*

We get a lot of stories about urban China. We don't get enough stories about rural China, and I think the fate of China lies in their hands. When your first experience in China is in rural China, you learn that a lot of the issues the Western media talks about—like democracy, Internet censorship—are issues that most normal Chinese don't care about that much. Around the dinner table, they're talking about hukou [residence permit] issues, the internal passport system in China. That is a huge issue for rural Chinese because when they go to another city, they cannot have their children go to high school there. They cannot get health care benefits. They can't get their pension. They're talking about a sense of inequality in the system. That's what they care about. I think it's helped me as a reporter to try and get the most accurate story possible because my job is to cover the Chinese people and to cover what they think about the rest of the world. It's not to really cover the issues that I think reflect Western values.

THE "JASMINE REVOLUTION"

In the winter of 2011, popular uprisings fueled by grievances over inequality, corruption, and repression erupted across the Middle East, threatening autocratic regimes from Tunisia to Egypt to Syria. What became known as the Arab Spring soon had an impact in China.

Edward Wong, *New York Times*

Right after the Arab revolutions began, we started hearing talk on the Chinese Internet that maybe China should undertake similar types of protest. Messages started appearing that people who want political reform should gather on a Sunday afternoon at the shopping street of Wangfujing in central Beijing. When I and my colleague showed up there, we saw lots of plainclothes police officers and uniformed officers keeping a tight watch. We saw lots of Chinese shoppers. But we didn't see very many activists. Some of us didn't see any at all. Others saw maybe one or two people being dragged away by police. We weren't sure whether they were actual activists who'd shown up or innocent people passing by who looked like they might be activists. But it showed the paranoia within the security state.

Tomas Etzler, Czech TV, CNN

I took a small camera. The scene was very chaotic. People were asked on the Internet to bring a jasmine flower. When I arrived around 2 PM, there were already a lot of people, but most were media and police. I noticed there were a couple of people who actually put down flowers and they were dragged away by the police.

For several weekends after, the same scene was repeated. Despite the Internet chatter about a "Jasmine Revolution," there were virtually no demonstrators, just lots of journalists, and huge numbers of police, who became increasingly aggressive. One result was a sharp rise in threats and intimidation aimed at foreign correspondents.

Eunice Yoon, CNN

We saw more and more people getting harassed. I was physically lifted and grabbed along with my colleague. We were questioned about the footage and told it had to disappear. They weren't happy we had it.

Edward Wong, *New York Times*

One Sunday, there were very violent actions by the police against journalists. A photographer for the New York Times, *Shiho Fukada, and another photographer were set upon by police and dragged off into an alleyway, and then eventually bundled into vans. A Bloomberg videographer, Steve Engle, had been filming this, and plainclothes officers or thugs working for the police surrounded him, demanded that he stop filming, tried to take his video camera away, and then started beating him right there in the street. He eventually suffered a broken rib.*

The intimidation went to extremes Western reporters had never experienced in China.

Eunice Yoon, CNN

I was in my apartment. Somebody came to the door. I went to look in the door monitor who was there. It was a couple of guys who [were] wearing dark jackets and dark sunglasses. That was scary. I didn't know who these people were. They were buzzing at my doorbell very aggressively and it scared me.

Stan Grant, CNN

They would turn up at my house, asking my youngest son, who was ten or eleven at the time, where I was, starting to interrogate him. If my wife was at a coffee shop, then they were parked outside watching her all the time. There was a definite sense that they'd crossed the line here.

Tomas Etzler, Czech TV, CNN

You don't interrogate a child. That was harassment. That was an intimidation method. It was a message they were wanting to send to Stan Grant, and it made him very angry.

Hannah Beech, *Time*

My family and I went to Capital M, a restaurant right near Tiananmen Square, because there was an event for kids. A children's author had written a book about a rabbit who challenges the Chinese emperor, and he's mischievous, and does things that are not good for the emperor. We're all sitting there, and the adults are realizing this is an interesting metaphor for what's going on at the other side of Tiananmen Square. I look behind me and there are probably five or six Public Security Bureau guys sitting there, and they're trying to figure out, "What does this kid's story mean?" And we realize how ridiculous this is that they've dispatched this battalion of Public Security guys to come look at a kid's story.

Many reporters believed the government was wildly overreacting.

Edward Wong, *New York Times*

We didn't think anything like the Arab revolutions would happen in China. We knew that the economic conditions in China wouldn't push large numbers

of Chinese to push back against the Party, that the voices calling for this were
only a very small minority. We were very skeptical whether anything envisioned
by these mysterious dissenters on the Internet would materialize. But the Party
state thought otherwise.

"ALMOST IN THE SPY WAY"

American and other foreign reporters now found themselves tailed, harassed,
blocked, even beaten on an almost regular basis.

Peter Ford, *Christian Science Monitor*

The Arab Spring seems the time when the authorities thought they really do
have to worry about something—totally unrealistically. The foreign press was
seen as a vector for that sort of unrest. There was no Jasmine uprising in China
to match what was happening in the Arab world. There were more journalists
than demonstrators, and more police than journalists, and those police used
violence. The press corps felt constantly hemmed in and sometimes threatened,
either physically or professionally, by the authorities.

Keith Richburg, *Washington Post*

I think the Arab Spring uprisings marked something of a turning point for Chi-
na's relations with the journalists. They came to see the journalists as even
more of an enemy than they did before.

Louisa Lim, NPR

Increasingly, reporting in China felt like war zones, where you arrive some-
where, stay twenty minutes, and then move on because people will know that
you are there. The local officials would come, and you would get in trouble.
There started to be a real element of tradecraft, almost in the spy way. When
you wanted to go on one of these trips, you really had to plan—fly into another
province, hire a car, and drive, and then hire another car with local plates.
Where to stay so you weren't staying in hotels, how to get places without leav-
ing any kind of trace. That started to obsess us. I remember one trip where we
were going to sleep in one of these high-end prostitution establishments
because they don't take your details. It was Valentine's Day. It was full. So we

ended up sleeping in a café. Those were the things that you had to start thinking about.

But while doing a story in Hunan province about lead poisoning, Barbara Demick of the *Los Angeles Times* was one of many reporters who discovered that in the countryside, ordinary folks were often on their side.

Barbara Demick, *Los Angeles Times*

Outside of the big cities, I never heard "the foreign press has a plot against China and blah blah blah." People were very welcoming, especially to the American press. It was like, "You will tell our stories." They knew the limitation of their own press. In a small town near Zhengzhou, we were meeting a guy who had been trying to organize against lead poisoning from the factories in the area. We said, "Don't tell anyone we're coming. We're going to be very low key." When we arrived, we were followed immediately. We picked up a taxi driver. The driver was very obliging and really on our side. At one point, there was an unmarked van following us very closely. The taxi driver said, "I'm going to lose these people." He drove into a bus station where all the taxis were parked. The taxis there were green. He called a friend and told us, "Get out the back of the taxi, stay very low, and get into my friend's taxi." There were hundreds of identical green taxis, so we got out and into the backseat of the friend's taxi. As I was leaving, I said, "I want to pay you," and he said, "Oh no, you don't have to pay." I threw 100 RMB over the back seat for him and got into the other taxi. The guys just couldn't figure out where we'd gone.

THE TIBETAN SELF-IMMOLATIONS

Things became even worse in the spring and summer of 2011, when nearly a dozen Tibetan monks, nuns, and former monks burned themselves to death to protest China's continuing heavy-handed policies in Tibet.

Louisa Lim, NPR

The immolations were at their peak. It was so difficult to report from Tibetan areas. The way I operated was always to find the monastery kitchens, because they never put cameras in the kitchens, and you always had people in the kitchens. I remember we went to one kitchen and people said, "You must leave. If they see you here, they'll shoot us." I looked in the corner of the room, and the woman who was chopping was smiling, but her hands were shaking. We had had no idea, because people hadn't been to these areas, that it would be so dangerous for journalists to be there. There was this constant struggle. How do you report a story when you don't know how much trouble people are going to face by talking to you?

Stan Grant, CNN

We go to Sichuan and managed to speak to some monks who'd fled their village. Someone had obviously either informed on us or we'd been identified speaking to these monks. It became this cat-and-mouse game as we tried to get out of there with the material that we'd filmed. I remember getting back to the hotel and being tailed. We split up and got different taxis, and thought we'd throw them off our scent. We got in another vehicle to get to the airport. They were waiting for us at the airport and seized us. My cameraman and I were led away by a half a dozen men each. Our producer was Chinese American. She was dragged from the airport lounge, strip-searched, abused for being a traitor, a running dog, as they called her. They made threats against her family. They detained us for several hours and went through all our equipment. By the time they released us, they'd taken everything. We were put on the plane. It was very traumatic for our producer and ultimately contributed to her leaving journalism and pursuing another career. It was that traumatic.

BATMAN AND THE BLIND LAWYER

As 2011 drew to a close, tensions between the foreign press corps and the Chinese authorities remained high. Chen Guangcheng, the blind lawyer who'd challenged abusive practices by Chinese family planning officials, had been confined to his home in a village east of Beijing after being released from prison in 2010. In December 2011, actor Christian Bale, the star of *Batman* and other movies, set out with CNN's Stan Grant hoping to visit Chen and highlight his plight.

Stan Grant, CNN

He was making a film in China and wanted to meet Chen Guangcheng, being inspired by the stories that he'd seen us cover. We traveled there with him. A very heavy police presence around Chen's village was just impenetrable. We

were beaten by security and chased out of town. This time, they were beating up
a world-renowned actor, an Oscar winner, someone known to America, whose
celebrity really magnified this story and brought it to a much bigger audience.

Beijing increasingly began to threaten reporters that their journalist visas
would not be renewed. By now, the *Christian Science Monitor*'s Peter Ford
was president of the Foreign Correspondents Club of China.

Peter Ford, *Christian Science Monitor*

The Chinese authorities were trying to influence foreign coverage of China by
threatening to withhold visas. That was a violation of their undertakings and
a violation of international procedure. It's a violation of everything, and the
Chinese don't care.

Stan Grant, CNN

We got to the situation where my visa had to be renewed and we got down to
the last day. I was either going to get it approved or I'd have to leave the coun-
try. They'd been refusing and refusing to approve my visa until the very very
last minute to make this statement that they weren't happy about us. It was
directly linked to a couple of things—the Tibetan story and the Chen Guangcheng
story. There was a real sense there that the Ministry of Foreign Affairs had lost
the power battle with the Security Bureau, that this was now being run by the
thugs. It was a nasty atmosphere.

Melissa Chan, Al Jazeera English

I knew I was in trouble at the end of 2011 going into 2012. They didn't give me a
one-year visa. They gave me a two-month visa. I do not believe that had happened
for some time or had ever happened as a strategy. They were keeping me on a very,
very tight leash. After the two-month visa expired, I went in to get my visa
renewed, and they gave me a one-month visa. I knew I was really in trouble.

AIRPOCALYPSE

One story where the government couldn't prevent coverage was the environment. The country's atrocious pollution was something reporters lived
with every day.

Edward Wong, *New York Times*

I think "airpocalypse" was the day when almost everyone who had the option of getting out of China was asking themselves, "Why are we still living here?" And that episode inspired me to do a line of reporting on the concerns among Chinese over the poisoning of China. There's no other way to put it. China's being poisoned by its industrial growth. I think, besides corruption, the environment is a top issue on the minds of many Chinese.

Austin Ramzy, *Time*

You feel it in your lungs. It weighs on your consciousness. It's depressing. You go out and see grey skies and know it's not fog, but smog, taking minutes, hours, days off your life. It was oppressive, and became a big story, because most of the press corps is in Beijing. You don't have to go too far to find the story. It's right out your window. It's something that readers are very interested in. It's also the sort of thing that there's a growing consciousness within China about air quality.

The U.S. embassy in Beijing had started putting out hourly air quality measurements on its Twitter feed.

Barbara Demick, *Los Angeles Times*

I did the first story about the U.S. embassy's air quality monitor and how it had gotten a lot of people paying attention and looking at the numbers. That was one of the better things the U.S. embassy did in Beijing, because by publishing the air quality numbers, they really got people to pay attention, both foreigners and Chinese. That was for the good.

Edward Wong, *New York Times*

Middle-class and upper-class Chinese who were concerned about the air in Beijing started picking up on this. And this ties into the importance of social media in China. They started putting out the U.S. embassy ratings on their own microblog accounts. And some of these people have millions of followers. People said, "Why isn't the Chinese government putting out the same readings? Why do we have to go to the U.S. government to see these readings?" From

WikiLeaks we know Chinese officials approached the U.S. embassy and told them to shut down their air monitor because it would cause social instability in China. But because of a combination of that conversation and because of surges in pollution such as the "airpocalypse" in early 2013, the Chinese government decided they really had to bring down some of the barriers to transparent information. So it started letting state media report on pollution. We saw front-page stories about the air pollution. And then dozens around China now put out online their own air readings.

Eunice Yoon, CNN

You're seeing it all across the country, where people don't want to have chemical factories built close to them, or they don't want to deal anymore with [a] hazardous environment where they are literally cleaning, recycling with their bare hands. They don't want to have to live with the pollution, the polluted soil or polluted water.

Edward Wong, New York Times

I think the single story written from China that got the most reaction from readers is a first-person piece I did about living in China with a baby daughter, and some of the tough choices and the guilt that I felt about having her stay in China with me and putting out there the question of "Should I stay because of my own personal interest in China, or would it be better for her to leave?" This is a question a lot of Chinese who have that option of leaving are asking themselves now.

Eunice Yoon, CNN

It's affected my own life living here. For me personally it is difficult to deal with because you are constantly in situations where you or your colleagues feel you have to wear a mask all the time or you're checking to see what the air reading is.

FAKE NEWS

Pollution, repression, and corruption—the grimmest aspects of China— tended to dominate the coverage, overshadowing the country's amazing economic progress. But sometimes, things went too far. In January 2012, a report aired on Public Radio's hugely popular program *This American Life* about alleged abuses at a factory run by Foxconn that made Apple products in the southern city of Shenzhen. Foxconn was a controversial company. The world's largest electronics contract manufacturer, it had been dogged by claims of poor working conditions.

The report for *This American Life* was done not by a journalist but by American storyteller and entertainer Mike Daisey.

Rob Schmitz, *Marketplace*

I have This American Life *on my podcast list. It was Mike Daisey talking about his trip to a Foxconn factory that made Apple products in Shenzhen. I immediately thought it didn't sound right. The way he was talking about this factory that had guards who were carrying guns. I thought, maybe this is an exaggerated or fictionalized account of a trip to Shenzhen. But later in the broadcast, the host, Ira Glass, says they had fact-checked this. I rewound the podcast and listened again. Here was this man saying that he had seen guards with guns outside the Foxconn factories. Guns are illegal in China. The only people that could be allowed to be carrying guns would be the military. He talks about sharing coffee at a Starbucks with underground union members. Factory workers in Shenzhen aren't going to be able to afford even the most modestly priced item at Starbucks. That seemed a little strange to me. The whole thing was full of exaggerations and things that just didn't seem right. I Googled the translator's name, the only other person in this story, and the only person who could verify it. She said her name was Cathy. I Googled "Cathy" and "translator" and "Shenzhen." And immediately, I didn't even have to click on the link, you saw her phone number. I called her. When we got to the part where I was asking her about what she and Mike had seen, she was very uncomfortable with how he had portrayed the trip and made it clear that these things did not happen.*

Schmitz contacted *This American Life* and, in collaboration with the program, did a piece revealing that much of Daisey's account was not true. In an unprecedented response, *This American Life* and its host, the highly respected Ira Glass, retracted the original story.

Rob Schmitz, *Marketplace*

After it aired, there were hundreds of emails sent my way and to This American's Life. *Most of them praised the retraction and the work that we had done. There were also emails saying, "This can't be right. The translator must have lied to you. She lives in this terrible Communist country. They would've hurt her if she would've told the truth that Mike Daisey was telling." Hearing that was a little disappointing, because I had spent days with her, and she was just a normal Chinese translator who had gone to these factories every single day. She would have no reason to lie about these things. She was really upset that Daisey had spent all his time with her and then made a monologue, including her as a character without asking her for her permission, and lied about the things that he saw.*

It was a sobering example of how stereotypes of conditions in China had seeped into mainstream American consciousness, underscoring the challenges facing reporters trying to convey the many shades of a complex, rapidly changing society.

17

POISON

At the beginning of 2012, Bo Xilai was Communist Party chief in the huge metropolis of Chongqing in southwestern China. The son of Bo Yibo, a venerated Communist Party elder, and previously mayor of the thriving northeastern port of Dalian, and then minister of commerce, where he gained international attention for promoting trade with China, Bo Xilai was a rising star. In Chongqing, he had presided over rapid economic growth, a ruthless and highly publicized crackdown on crime in which thousands of people were arrested, and a revival of Cultural Revolution–style mass rallies. For foreign correspondents, the flamboyant Bo was a refreshing change from the stiff and colorless figures who dominated the Chinese leadership.

Evan Osnos, *New Yorker*

Bo Xilai was a presence like nothing I'd ever seen in Chinese politics. He was electric. He was this charismatic figure. He was tall, a backslapper. He was impressive in that way. Later, it became clear that the same kind of charisma that made him magnetic and attractive to foreign visitors also made him a threat to his peers. They saw him as somebody who didn't follow the same conventions of Chinese politics and was more comfortable putting himself out front than they were, and that bothered them.

Bo was widely seen as openly campaigning for a top position in Beijing, but there had already been a whiff of scandal around him.

Austin Ramzy, *Time*

There were serious problems, and this whole crackdown on organized crime, there were certainly abuses of the most basic rights. You could see it clearly when not only accused crime bosses were being arrested, but their lawyers were being arrested as well.

The questions extended to Bo's family—especially his attention-seeking son, Bo Guagua.

Jeremy Page, *Wall Street Journal*

Bo Guagua had the highest media profile, so when I started looking into the children of the Politburo members, he was the most visible. Those who stayed in China, they were shielded by state media controls, but what you often found was that the ones who were overseas were using social media a lot. And that was what Bo Guagua [then a student at Oxford University in England] was doing, putting out information about himself. You could see a lot about the kind of lifestyle he was leading. There was a series of miniscandals to do with photographs he posted at some ball in Oxford.

The photos showed Bo Guagua with a young English woman on each arm, lipstick on his mouth and shirt unbuttoned.

Jeremy Page, *Wall Street Journal*

For the son of a Politburo member to be in that environment, and for that to be spreading through social media, played into the disconnect between the Party and society. The fact he was doing that suggested to me only two possible explanations. One is that his father was fully aware, and thought it was fine, which implies almost an arrogance—that our children can be seen behaving like this in public, and no one's going to question where the money comes from, and how they managed to get into the school. Or, his father didn't know about it, in which case, it was more interesting that the kid was kind of AWOL doing his own thing, and that risked embarrassing Bo Xilai.

MURDER AND INTRIGUE

Then, in late February 2012, the most sensational scandal to rock China in years exploded.

Evan Osnos, *New Yorker*

The Bo Xilai scandal was so spectacular in its particulars. I mean, truly spectacular in the sense of the word, that it was beyond anything you could have written with a straight face as fiction.

It began when Chongqing's former police chief, Wang Lijun, sought refuge at the U.S. consulate in Chengdu. Wang Lijun had just been sacked by Bo Xilai. To the astonished American diplomats, Wang made a stunning claim about Bo's wife, Gu Kailai, whose combination of looks, family background (her father had been a former general and senior Party official), and education had earned her the nickname of the "Jackie Kennedy of China." The *Wall Street Journal's* Jeremy Page broke the first story.

Jeremy Page, *Wall Street Journal*

I heard that there was a British man who'd been killed in mysterious circumstances in Chongqing, and this might have been something that Wang Lijun had mentioned at the consulate. The most important allegation was that Gu Kailai had been involved in the murder of this British citizen, and that had been a source of dispute between Wang Lijun and Bo Xilai, and that's why Wang now feared for his life.

Evan Osnos, *New Yorker*

The police chief—his signature detail was that he'd been celebrated in the Chinese police press for having innovated important new ways to remove the organs from executed prisoners—fled into the embrace of the U.S. consulate in Chengdu. The U.S. consulate of course didn't want anything to do with him, so they sent him back out. But in the process, he has spilled the beans on his boss, and his boss's wife, for killing this British businessman. The businessman, by the way, satisfied all the expectations one could possibly want of somebody in that position, which is to say, he wore a linen suit, and drove a Jaguar with a

007 license plate. Seriously? This was our story? It was like Thanksgiving dinner day after day after day.

Jeremy Page, *Wall Street Journal*

I had never met the British businessman, but I had heard there was this British guy who was very close to the Bo family. I found out his name [Neil Heywood]. That gave me a huge advantage early on, because the way this story broke, it was sort of complex, with multiple sources. You had U.S. government officials on one side, who obviously knew about what Wang Lijun had said inside the consulate, and then you had British officials, who were aware of the death of this British guy in Chongqing, and then you had various Chinese individuals. It was very tricky. It was multiple sources, scraps of information. There was no single source you could sit down with and just get a read-out. And often you get something from one source, and you couldn't then go back and check. And the electronic surveillance environment here made everything doubly hard because people were becoming much more aware of that, so setting up meetings was incredibly difficult. No one wanted a text message coming from me to them saying, "Can we meet?" It involved some elaborate planning to be able to get access to people.

Page and his *Wall Street Journal* colleagues were more than a little nervous running his exclusive report claiming that businessman Heywood had been poisoned by Bo's wife.

Andrew Browne, *Wall Street Journal*

We were going after a potential member of the Politburo Standing Committee. It wasn't at all clear at that point that Bo was going to go down, and we were exposing corruption, appalling abuse of power, including murder, at the highest level of the Chinese government. It was electric reporting. I think we were the first news organization to open that window into the secretive world of the elite in China and we tapped into that enormous sense of resentment and anger about the way that Chinese society and politics have developed. The unity that exists between money, wealth, and power in China, and how it's manipulated by a small group of privileged families, the elite. Bo Xilai was very much representative of that trend.

Jeremy Page, *Wall Street Journal*

It was one of those stories where you press the button, metaphorically speaking, and then you see ripples going out around the world. It was a controversial allegation to make—that the wife of a serving Politburo member had been accused of murder, which presents, obviously, all sorts of legal difficulties. There was period where we were having to hold off and check with lawyers, and I was also in contact with the British government, trying to get them to make a statement. They kept saying, "We'll get back to you." Finally, they went public with their statement, on a Sunday. It was very brief, just saying they were investigating the death of a British citizen in Chongqing. Once they made that announcement, I could unload all the other stuff that I'd by now dug up, and could, most importantly, print the allegation that Wang Lijun had made in the consulate.

In the wake of Page's story, reporters dug further, unearthing more details of the murder. Heywood, a forty-one-year-old business consultant, had been in China since the 1990s, acting as a fixer and middleman for the Bo family with foreign officials and businesspeople, while helping Bo's son Guagua get into Harrow, the elite British private school he had also attended. Throughout 2011, however, tensions had developed in Heywood's relationship with the Bo family, largely over money, but likely exacerbated by the fact that, as a member of their inner circle, he knew so much about the couple's private affairs. On November 14, 2011, Gu Kailai summoned Heywood to Chongqing. After plying him with so much whiskey he began to vomit, she poured poison into his mouth, and scattered pills around the room to make it look like he had died of a drug overdose. When Heywood was found two days later, local police attributed his death to excessive drinking, and his body was quickly cremated with no autopsy. The episode would have remained largely unnoticed had Wang Lijun not sought refuge at the U.S. consulate in Chengdu three months later.

By now, though, the entire Beijing press corps was chasing the story, not only because the details of Heywood's death seemed like a plot for a B-grade spy movie, but because the scale of the scandal surrounding Bo, triggered by his own ambitions and his wife's ruthlessness, highlighted the broader power struggle underway with the Chinese Communist Party. One result was that many reporters were getting leaks from Chinese sources.

Keith Richburg, *Washington Post*

The Chinese Communist Party information apparatus lost control of the narrative because there were so many sources talking. Not all the information turned out to be accurate. There were all kinds of wild rumors, but a lot of it was accurate. And a lot of it was because of factions within the Party, because Bo Xilai had a lot of enemies, so a lot of people were willing to talk openly about his transgressions.

Edward Wong, *New York Times*

What we discovered while reporting on Bo Xilai was that when there's a break within the top ranks of the Party, when we have Party officials going after one of their own, people are more willing to leak information to foreign journalists. A lot of people started coming out of the woodwork and telling stories about Bo—people who wanted to tell the nature of Bo's rule in Chongqing, and how he had used the security apparatus to suppress things. Eventually, through talking to these people, you get more contacts that then tell you what they were seeing in Chongqing with the Bo family, and with the police chief. You start hearing things about Bo's wife, about the police chief, about their business tycoon partners, and through this, following up on all these threads, you start painting a picture of what's going on with this family.

Using the tools of investigative reporting, the journalists came up with one exposé after another: how Bo Xilai had wiretapped senior leaders from Beijing; how he had received millions of dollars from a Chinese tycoon; how Gu Kailai had transferred millions of dollars abroad; how her brother, under an assumed name, had served as the head of a company that controlled a major Chinese bank.

Jeremy Page, *Wall Street Journal*

I then worked with some colleagues in the U.S., who did a great job tracking down some U.S. individuals who had had dealings with Gu Kailai when she was a lawyer in Dalian. And I did some work in the UK. We found her name in some public documents. It was sort of a scribbled signature, and she was using an alias, "Horus Kai." [It turned out Gu had chosen "Horus" for her English name, after the ancient Egyptian god of war, sun, and sky.] We confronted an issue we often face—people using aliases. I know a lot of elite Chinese fami-lies do use different names to do business in Hong Kong and in the West. But we were fortunate, in that her date of birth was on the document. We also found her registration as a lawyer on one of the official websites in Beijing, which had her date of birth. And we also knew some people who had done business with her in Dalian who recognized this name, "Horus Kai," and said, "Yes, that was the name that she'd used."

Stan Grant, CNN

That was an extraordinary story. Here a princeling, at one point touted as a potential president himself, about to be welcomed into the inner sanctum, and then to see this fall apart so spectacularly. This was a story that ticked all the boxes—Communist Party intrigue and infighting, the rich and powerful in China, a murder mystery, the West meets the East. It had every possible ele-ment. I remember watching it all play out. The veil of the inner workings of the Party was being lifted. We were seeing the dirty laundry being aired. It was a spectacular story to watch unfold.

In April 2012, Bo Xilai was removed from all his posts. He was eventually tried and sentenced to life in prison. His wife was charged with murdering Neil Heywood and received a suspended death sentence. Wang Lijun, the for-mer police chief, was charged with defecting to a foreign power, and given fifteen years in jail.

THE CASE OF MELISSA CHAN

Also that April, the Chinese authorities refused to renew the visa for Al Jazeera's Melissa Chan—accusing her of unspecified violations of Chinese law. Chan had repeatedly angered the Chinese with her tough reporting, espe-cially her exposé of what were known as "black jails," a network of secret detention centers.

Melissa Chan, Al Jazeera English

Black jails are basically extralegal detention centers. They're created by a sys-tem where anyone in China with a grievance can go to Beijing. This is a centuries-old tradition. If you have a grievance in your home village, you can

travel to Beijing and petition. What was happening was that as these petition-
ers would appear in Beijing, local authorities would whisk them away and hold
them in these makeshift detention centers. I was really interested in this story,
because the authorities in Beijing always said, "We don't have control over what
some of these middling officials are doing, and what they're doing is against
the law, but in Beijing this kind of thing shouldn't be happening." But black
jails were being set up forty minutes from Tiananmen Square. I felt that it was
a really powerful story. It either showed the central authority's inability to con-
trol the periphery, or the central authority knew about these human rights
violations, and didn't care. So our team tried to capture these things on video.

We got a call from one of the petitioners who said, "My daughter's being
held." We went to this place. There was a guy guarding the door. We shoved
our way in. These are often cheap motels guarded at the front by a local thug
and the people are locked into rooms. We went in. There was a lot of evidence
it had been used as a black jail, because of the signage in the hallway about
times to eat, and rules and so on, but there weren't any prisoners. They had
been cleared the night before. The police were called in. We filmed the entire
incident—a local official from some province denying that this was a black jail
and yet trying to stop us. The woman had gone with us. Her daughter had gone
missing, so she was in tears. I'm sure Beijing authorities knew about our pres-
ence there. That obviously did not make them happy. I should've behaved myself
and I didn't. I just said, "Screw it." I lost my patience with them. Maybe I played
right into their hands. I'm not sure. But it was just like, "Screw you guys. I will
go and do these stories." They just probably had it with me.

Peter Ford, *Christian Science Monitor*

Melissa did particularly get in their face with the sorts of stories that she did,
and sometimes with the way that she related to the policemen who were sent to
try and rein her in. Melissa is not easily reined in by policemen or anybody else.

Melissa Chan, Al Jazeera English

After my departure, they decided [to] go on character-assassinating me, for lack
of a better word, saying that I had broken laws, which I've never been able to
figure out what exactly they meant. They really focused on the fact that I'm
supposedly very aggressive, and I upset police officers in China.

Her departure was a chilling message to the foreign press corps.

Melissa Chan, Al Jazeera English

I kept thinking of that Chinese proverb where you kill the chicken to scare the monkeys, and I was the proverbial chicken.

The Chinese authorities even warned the Beijing Foreign Correspondents Club not to publicize the pressure against journalists.

Peter Ford, *Christian Science Monitor*

We came under pressure not to put our statements up on our website, not to publicize the sort of violations that we do publicize, not to do anything which the government would regard as an attempt to put political pressure on them.

THE BLIND LAWYER SEEKS REFUGE

At the end of April, the blind dissident lawyer Chen Guangcheng, who'd been confined to his home in Shandong province, managed to elude his captors.

Edward Wong, *New York Times*

One of my colleagues heard a tip that Chen Guangcheng had made his way to the U.S. embassy in Beijing. We found this totally incredible. But the next morning, the AP broke the news that Chen was in the embassy. We were kicking ourselves for not having really dug into that tip. The reason is because I called a person at the embassy and said, "I heard that Chen Guangcheng is in the embassy." He was totally flabbergasted and said, "I can tell you that that's absolutely untrue." He later apologized to me and told me that he hadn't been lying to me. He just hadn't been briefed on what had happened and didn't know that Chen was there.

Austin Ramzy, *Time*

It was a huge deal because Secretary of State Hillary Clinton was coming to town, and suddenly all the things they were going to talk about were sidelined by the presence of this activist in the U.S. embassy. It was a story that changed very dramatically several times.

Chen soon left the embassy for a Beijing hospital.

Keith Richburg, *Washington Post*

I actually got the first phone call from Chen when he was heading to the hospital. It was Gary Locke, the U.S. ambassador. He said, "I have someone here who wants to talk to you." And he passed the phone over to Chen. Given our twenty-four-hour hyper news cycle, I immediately put it on Twitter. By Tweeting, I let all the other journalists know that Chen's on his way to the hospital, get over there now. I was later told by some colleagues from NBC and elsewhere, thanks for the Tweet. That's how we knew where we should go to set up our cameras. That actually showed how we were starting to use social networking as a news dissemination tool.

Outside the hospital, Chinese police were predictably obstructive.

Peter Ford, *Christian Science Monitor*

People were told that if they tried to report from that hospital, they would be in violation of their visa conditions and be liable to expulsion. They went anyway, and people got their stories, and nobody, during that incident, was expelled for anything they did in the way of reporting.

Keith Richburg, *Washington Post*

The interesting thing is, as much as the Chinese government tried to keep the lid on what was going on, we, the journalists, and the dissident community were all trading information via social networking sites about what was going on with Chen. The Chinese lost control of the narrative. They weren't able to control the flow of information. We had ways to get in touch with people. There was a friend of Chen's who was a dissident, who had been giving us information about Chen's condition at the hospital. This dissident was all of a sudden going to be detained. She started putting out on Weibo, "Help, journalists. There are cars outside my house. I think I'm going to be taken now." As the plainclothes police were coming to her door, she was tweeting out every instant, "OK, they're at the door now. I think they're going to take me away." We were putting this out in real time, that so-and-so dissident is being taken away by police, she's reported on her Weibo account. It was live reporting. I think that was something that the Chinese government wasn't ready for.

Eventually, after complex negotiations conducted by Secretary of State Clinton, Chen was allowed to leave for the United States.

18

FOLLOW THE MONEY

At the Bloomberg News bureau in Beijing, Michael Forsythe and his colleagues watched the *Wall Street Journal*'s groundbreaking coverage of the Bo Xilai story in the first few months of 2012 with thinly disguised professional jealousy.

Michael Forsythe, Bloomberg News

The Journal *was really leading the coverage, running circles around us and everybody else. I thought, "I'm really falling behind as a reporter." The worst moment came April 10, 2012, when Xinhua made an announcement about Bo Xilai being suspended from the Politburo, confirming pretty much everything the* Journal *had been saying.*

Ben Richardson was an editor at Bloomberg's Asian headquarters in Hong Kong.

Ben Richardson, Bloomberg News

We felt we were getting our heads handed to us on a plate. So Mike Forsythe said, "Why don't we do what we're good at, which is numbers, facts, data, and start looking at assets, building a spreadsheet." We just started digging around.

Playing catch-up, Forsythe researched a piece about the finances of Bo's wife, Gu Kailai, showing that she and her sisters controlled a web of businesses from Beijing to Hong Kong to the Caribbean worth at least $126 million.

Michael Forsythe, Bloomberg News

It was really from open-source documents. We didn't think it was all that great, but we liked looking at documents. There was a wealth of information. We published the story, and everybody was just agog. All of a sudden Bloomberg was on the map. We got very excited, and one story begat another story. And the story did begin to shift then, away from the Bo story towards wider issues.

At the same time, Ben Richardson was having coffee in Hong Kong with the son of a Chinese dissident. The conversation turned to the flood of leaks about Bo Xilai.

Ben Richardson, Bloomberg News

He turned and said, "Why are you writing stories that the Communist Party wants you to write?" We'd all been feeling a little uneasy about this anyway. I think Mike was already feeling the same. So he and I got together. It was almost impossible to tell what was being fed by the state and what was genuine news. We agreed—let's start focusing where people don't want us to focus. We started looking at the whole of the Politburo. We narrowed it down quite quickly to the top four members of the Politburo.

Michael Forsythe, Bloomberg News

We made these family trees [of all the members of the Politburo standing committee] and started Googling their names and came up with something from a stock prospectus. It was a company announcement that listed the assets of Xi Jinping's older sister in one company in Shenzhen. This was May 10, 2012. I will never forget the day. We realized at that moment that we had our story, and it was a big one. We stopped whatever else [we] were doing, and for the next forty-five days, we focused on building out this story.

Forsythe and a team of reporters and editors in Beijing and Hong Kong scoured documents and records, assembling a picture of how the relatives of

Vice President Xi Jinping, the man tipped to become China's next leader in the fall of 2012, had made millions of dollars in a host of businesses.

Michael Forsythe, Bloomberg News

I learned about these State Administration of Industry and Commerce (SAIC) records. We started pulling some of those, and gradually the assets expanded, and we had to document everything.

Ben Richardson, Bloomberg News

Anything we couldn't back up with a document came out. But the fact that we finally managed to say—this is a public document tied to that person. And we know that person is who they are because we got their Hong Kong ID card number, and we checked against the Chinese ID, and we've looked at the photograph on the Chinese ID, because you can get that from the search system. It's all there. And that was useful for Xi Jinping's niece, because she was using different names in mainland China, but once you're in Hong Kong, same name and same ID number. Now we're able to identify real estate assets.

Michael Forsythe, Bloomberg

A lot of times the paper would lead us to an address in Beijing, and we'd go knock on doors. We were trying to prove that the ownership of this telecoms company in Guangzhou was linked to the other sister of Xi Jinping and her family. In the SAIC documents, it listed this woman in Beijing who lived on the ninth floor of one of these old apartments built in the seventies and eighties. I went and knocked on the door. This old woman answered. I asked if this certain woman was there, and she said, "Oh that's my daughter. She's not home." "Can I contact her?" Well, she pointed to the wall, and said, "There's her cell phone number." I wrote it down, thanked her, went back to the office, called this woman, and I asked her who's the real head of this company, why are you holding the shares for this company, and she answered all the questions. She said, "Actually, the real head of the company is the brother-in-law of Xi Jinping. And I don't really know anything about the company"—she was the owner—"I don't really know anything about the company. I just do whatever they tell me." My colleagues and I just looked at each other and were just agog. We had just basically on record sourced the fact that Xi Jinping's brother-in-law was hiding ownership through very distant relatives.

Forsythe and his colleagues knew they were dealing with explosive material.

Ben Richardson, Bloomberg News

There was quite a bit of healthy paranoia. So, for example, you never take your mobile phone into the conference room, you switch it off, you cover the cameras on your phone or mobile devices. For the mainland Chinese staff who worked on it, there were extra layers. They were not allowed to do anything outside what a news assistant can do, like research. No one could work from home. If you had to have a conference call, you would use the internal Bloomberg apparatus. We had code names, so people weren't mentioned by name. "Teletubby" was Wen Jiabao. Xi Jinping was "Yoojin."

INVESTIGATING THE PRIME MINISTER

At the same time, the *New York Times*'s David Barboza had been pursuing his own investigation, which had begun more than a year earlier. He had originally intended to look at the business activities of the children of senior leaders, but soon began to focus on the family of Premier Wen Jiabao.

David Barboza, *New York Times*

I ended up on Wen simply because he's the one that I heard the most about. I had been going to dinners and meetings. I would go home, and write down notes, especially if they said anything about princelings or important people. I had hundreds of pages of these little notes, dated, and the name that came up the most was Wen.

Barboza initially focused on an insurance company called Ping An.

David Barboza, *New York Times*

It's Hong Kong–listed. I pulled the Hong Kong prospectus of Ping An and went through it. It had the thirty largest shareholders of Ping An in 2004, when it went public. I went through that list. I saw Morgan Stanley. I saw Goldman Sachs. I saw the Shenzhen government. And then I saw a bunch of Chinese companies that I had never heard of. I said, "OK, so what is Taihong? And what is Baohua?" They're obviously in the money in 2004. I need to figure out who these companies are.

Like Forsythe, Barboza made use of publicly available records in China's State Administration of Industry and Commerce.

David Barboza, *New York Times*

This is the goldmine. When I got them, I didn't know how to read them, so I had to get them translated. Sometimes they have four hundred pages per company. With all the Ping An companies, I wanted to chart who owned it. And any companies affiliated with these companies, I wanted a chart. Within that first month, I had found maybe a couple hundred million dollars related to the Wen family. And their names started to show up pretty clearly on some of the documents.

Barboza discovered one of the names was of an eighty-nine-year-old woman who turned out to be the mother of Wen Jiabao—and who held an astonishing one hundred million shares in a company called Taihong.

David Barboza, *New York Times*

One of Taihong's shareholders, which means one of Ping An's shareholders, was a smaller company that had, like, two shareholders. One of the shareholders was eighty-nine years old. By the ID card number, you can tell where they're from in China. You can tell their birthday. From the ID card, I knew this woman, who's holding one hundred million shares through Taihong, is from Tianjin, she's eighty-nine, and she's in the money. This eighty-nine-year-old woman gets shares of Ping An through Taihong. She got in before the IPO. That was very suspicious. So, of course, we looked up the name of this woman, thinking it had to be a relative of Wen. Our first run-through found that it wasn't the name of the prime minister's mother, but then on further research it turned out the prime minister's mother had changed her name, and this was the original name. It's not the name she's using now.

I think the light bulb moment was sort of like [an] "I was scared" moment. I was excited and scared at the same time when I found that, because I knew just by looking at the document that, if the government knew, they would be very concerned that I had that document. I was both scared and excited. A lot of people were warning me. They didn't even know what I was doing exactly, but

---

they were warning me, "If you do anyone related to princelings, you're going to be in big trouble." I was worried about who I had translating, what I was finding, so it was a light bulb moment to see, "Wow. This is the prime minister's mother."

Edward Wong, *New York Times*

China has a type of economy that's driven by the state, not an economy based on private enterprise or entrepreneurship. Because it's driven by the state, the reach of the top Party officials is everywhere. You have sons and daughters of top Party officials running state enterprises, or they have their own businesses that benefit from the rise of the Chinese economy. They know what companies to invest in. They know where to put their money. They get inside information on what companies might be successful, what companies might list when IPOs take place. In the States, it's what we might consider insider trading. In China, it's an entrenched part of the system.

SETTING OFF A BOMB

In mid-June, Michael Forsythe's team at Bloomberg asked the Chinese government for comment on their Xi Jinping story prior to publication.

Michael Forsythe, Bloomberg News

We sent letters to the Foreign Ministry and the State Council Information Office information office saying that "We are looking into the assets of Xi Jinping's relatives. We would really like to talk to Vice President Xi or anybody, about what this means." Some of the people at Bloomberg thought that they wouldn't take this that seriously. Others, including myself, thought that this would set off a bomb.

Ben Richardson, Bloomberg News

As soon as the letters went in, the pressure starts. And it ratcheted up and ratcheted up.

Michael Forsythe, Bloomberg News

In Beijing they started meeting with the Bloomberg News management: "You need to stop this story. The eighteenth Party Congress is coming up. This is a very sensitive time. This story crosses a red line. This will affect social stability in China." These kinds of arguments. Of course, to foreign journalists, we call that a news peg. The Chinese ambassador to the U.S., Zhang Yesui, had a meeting with the Bloomberg management in Washington. It didn't go too well. He wanted to kill the story. That didn't happen. Then he went to New York to talk to senior management at Bloomberg and pretty much got the same answer. To their credit, they were very firm about the need to publish the story.

They had sent us all to Hong Kong in June, at great expense—all the reporters, the Chinese news assistants, everybody, to work on this. We thought it would be safer there. We were all together at the Marriott Hotel, putting the story together. Most of the time, the last few weeks, reporting was done in Hong Kong. We just all felt we needed to be in the same place, and for safety reasons, we needed to be outside the mainland.

On June 29, Ben Richardson put the story online. The headline was "Xi Jinping Millionaire Relations Reveal Fortunes of Elite."

Ben Richardson, Bloomberg News

Quite frankly, pushing the button on a story of that magnitude after no sleep when it's five thousand words long, and it's incredibly complex—it was—I wouldn't call it terrifying. I was too tired—but it was up there. Mind-numbing. Mind-numbingly scary.

Michael Forsythe, Bloomberg News

The first thing that happened was a few days later, I had just gone back to Beijing, and it was July 4. I got a call from the managing editor in Hong Kong, and he said, "There's this weird message that people are trying to pass to you, that you shouldn't go back to China. You may be in danger." We just happened to have a vacation planned anyway. We were leaving the next day to go to Europe, a family vacation, so we moved into a hotel—my family, my wife and two children. And the next day we took off for Europe. Then it started getting really weird.

Evan Osnos, New Yorker

My wife got a phone call from one of her professional contacts—a woman who had a lot of connections to the leadership—and she asked to meet for coffee.

The woman said to Sarabeth, "Are you friends with Mike Forsythe?" Sarabeth said, "Yes, he's a friend." The woman said, "Well, then you need to tell him that it's no longer safe for him and his family in China, and they need to leave." Sarabeth wasn't sure what to make of this. She asked another question, "What does that mean?" The woman said, "Something will happen, and it'll look like an accident, but he'll be dead."

China scholar Leta Hong Fincher was Forsythe's wife.

Leta Hong Fincher, China Scholar

There were specific warnings about how Mike would have a terrible accident and be found dead, and nobody would ever know what had happened to him. There was a reference to Mike's wife and children. It was very frightening. I was particularly concerned about the safety of my children. I'm not going to name her, and to be honest, I'm still quite afraid of the consequences of talking about it. It was clearly designed to frighten us, and what was particularly frightening is because it came from this woman who represented a relative of the Chinese president. It was very worrying.

Michael Forsythe, Bloomberg News

It was two channels, really. One was Evan Osnos's wife. One was through a Columbia University professor. It was the same person who was transmitting the threats, but she was transmitting through two different outlets. But the message was pretty much the same—if I go back to China, I might get killed.

In further retaliation, the Chinese blocked the Bloomberg website and stopped giving visas to Bloomberg reporters. Of even greater concern, sales in China of Bloomberg terminals—a lucrative part of the company's business—were badly affected.

Curiously, though, the initial threats to Forsythe's life subsided.

Michael Forsythe, Bloomberg News

Bloomberg started doing a big security review, hired some people, did an assessment, started asking questions. A few days later, the husband of this person who had been transmitting these threats went through the Columbia University channel, and the message was, "He's not going to be killed, but he should really leave China in due course." And I think the Bloomberg management at the time and myself thought the odds are things will be okay if we go back to China.

Leta Hong Fincher, China Scholar

I was more rattled that he was. But we decided to just go back to Beijing. It was still quite traumatic. I was still very nervous about what had happened, but then we didn't really hear anything more.

Still, to be safe, in 2013, Forsythe and his family moved to Hong Kong.

By the summer of 2012, David Barboza was working full-time on Wen Jiabao and his wealthy relatives. Joseph Kahn was by now the *New York Times* foreign editor.

Joseph Kahn, *New York Times*

We had not seen many people show in a carefully documented way how this wasn't just petty corruption at a local level, that there were ways for the family and relatives of the Politburo elite to insert themselves into the business picture and enrich themselves. That was not very easy to demonstrate. And David set about to use China's own corporate records and securities listings to document that.

David Barboza, *New York Times*

I was working around the clock. I found every time we requested a company, we found ten more. If you can imagine this big chart, behind Ping An are thirty companies, and then behind those—any company you look at is like one hundred companies. I continued to map out a strategy of how to do it without setting off alarm bells, without letting people know, thinking about who was going to be translating, what I could show people. Also to go to lawyers, accountants, bankers, and test some of the theories without giving them what I was doing, because that was too sensitive. I told some bankers I was interested in writing about princelings in private equity, but I didn't tell anyone that I had a target. That was too dangerous for me to even mention.

As the story neared completion, Barboza became increasingly nervous.

David Barboza, *New York Times*

I was worried about my wife's safety—she's a Chinese citizen—about my own safety. I told my editors, "I'm not so sure I can finish in China. There's lots of pressure. I think they'll be able to capture anything I'm doing." They said, "You and your wife fly back to New York. Just finish here." We left with a huge suitcase full of documents. Very scary moment. If they captured that suitcase, what would happen? I had to photocopy everything I had and hide it in China, and then have the suitcase, and if it was lost, I had a backup. I was also emailing large document files to New York just in case I couldn't get out. But I got out.

Barboza felt the story had some loose ends, however; so in the autumn, he returned to China.

David Barboza, *New York Times*

I spent several weeks in New York writing and talking to editors and lawyers. One of the editors said to me, "Who can prove this other than you?" I said, "No one." He said words that I came to love, which were, "We need to hire an independent auditor to back you up." I was like, "Thank goodness." I was under so much pressure by that point I wanted the Times *to say, "We don't completely trust you. We want to make sure you're protected, and we're protected, by getting someone independent to look at these documents and verify they're real."*

After that month, we decided I needed to go back to China and do more reporting. There were still a lot of holes. There were still a lot of key people I didn't know their identities. And I hadn't visited Ping An. My editors asked, "Do you feel it's safe?" I said, "Well, I've written much of the story now and I have this huge document file in New York, so why don't I go back? Go to Ping An, find these other people." We also had an idea from that draft what we needed to get. I came back and sprinted from August until early October around China. Every good contact I had, I called and said, "Can you help me with this tidbit?" Not showing anyone the bigger picture. I showed some people my charts—I didn't put the names—and said, "Does this make sense? How does this work?" My main concern was, we've got to make sure it's right. I've got to have every document lined up. I've got to be prepared for a lawsuit. I've got to be prepared that, if we go to court, I can prove every single line.

In October, as we get close to publication, I started to have trouble with my computer. I felt people were following me. I called the editors and said, "I don't think I can edit from here. I feel people are going to burst in one day and everything's going to be taken." They said, "Why don't you come to New York or go to Hong Kong or Japan?" We thought Hong Kong may be not completely safe. A lot of people I was writing about were based in Hong Kong. The Chinese government wasn't going to be my problem. It was going to be the businessmen I was exposing, and that they would hire someone to handle us. So my wife and I decided to go to Japan.

Joseph Kahn, *New York Times*

He really did have this story nailed in a way that few investigative stories can ever be nailed—real numbers, documented evidence of a couple billion dollars in wealth held by the extended family of the prime minister. We went through a process of due diligence which we would for any story—consulting with the various parties that were directly involved in those transactions but also giving top levels of the Party, Wen Jiabao's own office, as well as the foreign ministries a chance to comment.

"YOU CANNOT PUBLISH THIS STORY"

When the Chinese authorities learned what the *Times* was planning, they went ballistic.

David Barboza, *New York Times*

The government got very angry. They were like, "Are you crazy? You cannot publish this story." I said, "Well. It's coming out Sunday." The government demanded that I come to Beijing immediately. I said, "I'm not in China." They said, "What do you mean you're not in China? Where are you? You have to come to Beijing." I eventually told them I'm in Japan. They argued with me and said they needed to see me. I said, "That's not going to happen. You have forty-eight hours to respond."

Joseph Kahn, *New York Times*

Rather than commenting, they went into something of a crisis mode where they began a full-scale campaign to keep us from publishing this story. China's ambassador to the U.S. visited top editors in New York to persuade us this was a politically sensitive story. They said it had inaccuracies, although they declined to be specific about what those were. They said it would be considered interference in their affairs and would disrupt the upcoming eighteenth Congress of the Communist Party. It was a very strong direct warning that we don't really hear very often. The New York Times *will pay a very heavy price. There will be serious consequences if you publish this. The threat was not especially subtle. It was pretty direct. We knew there would be a high price to pay.*

David Barboza, New York Times

We're planning to publish in Sunday's paper. From Thursday to Saturday, I'm living in the Tokyo bureau. I'm getting calls from the Wen family. I'm getting calls from friends of the Wen family who found out about the story who are lobbying on their behalf. I'm getting calls from the government, I'm getting calls from my editors, I'm getting calls from mysterious figures. It was nuts. It was one of the most difficult periods of my life. On Saturday morning, as we are maybe five hours from publication, the editors calmly say, "Would you consider going back to Beijing to meet the government and us not publishing on Sunday?" I said, "Are you joking?" They said, "We think the government really wants to talk to you. It's a huge story. It would only show them that we really do want to be as fair as possible. Give them the opportunity to speak, give them a chance. Since it's already written, it'll be published. Why not at least give them some face?" I talked to my wife, who was against me flying back. But in the end, I thought, the story's done. I should go back. At least we'd be able to say, "We gave you the chance." Who knows? Maybe they'll say something. We finally decided I'd go back for twenty-four hours. They would hold the story Sunday.

They pulled it out of Sunday's paper. I flew Monday. The idea was I'll meet the government and the Wen family and others on Monday and fly back early Tuesday with a report to New York about what they said. So they held the story, I met the government. They said, "Come alone. Make sure you're alone." They were pushing not to publish it. They said, "How did you come upon this story?" I told them the truth. There's no conspiracy. I never got any documents from anyone. This is how it really happened. Then they gave me their statement to give to the editors about how we'd better not publish, and about what that would mean for me personally if we published. I thought these statements and these arguments they were giving me were for the story. But, in the end, they said this is only for your editors. This is all off the record.

As the *Times* prepared to publish the story, Barboza was consumed by anxiety.

David Barboza, *New York Times*

I was torn, "Can we publish this story? What are the consequences? What does it mean for this family? What are these other billionaires going to do to us? What if I'm wrong? What will happen to the New York Times?" *I would say the next twenty-four hours were the scariest moments of my life.*

As soon as the story was published, with the headline "Billions in Hidden Riches for Family of Chinese Leader," Beijing's blocked the *Times* website, including a Chinese-language one that had just been launched.

Edward Wong, *New York Times*

The traffic within China to both sites in a China instantly dropped—a huge drop, and advertisers started getting skittish.

Joseph Kahn, *New York Times*

Then we faced a ban on new visas for New York Times *journalists. We had the visas of the reporters that we'd hired and tried to transfer from other organizations to ours rejected—Chris Buckley and Austin Ramzy, people who were working in China for other organizations came to work for the* New York Times *but were never allowed to be accredited as* New York Times *reporters, so had to leave.*

Chris Buckley, *New York Times*

I think it was unhappiness with the Times's *coverage, especially with the Wen Jiabao story, and I was collateral damage.*

Austin Ramzy, *New York Times*

The message is—don't cover the finances of the Chinese leadership and their families. And if you continue doing this, we'll just continue making it harder and harder for you to report. We'll make it impossible for you to add new people, and eventually you could be left with no one in China to cover the country.

Denied journalist visas for the *Times* in Beijing, Buckley rebased in Hong Kong, Ramzy in Taiwan and then later in Hong Kong.

To almost everyone's surprise, however, David Barboza's journalist's visa was renewed.

Austin Ramzy, *New York Times*

They were very careful about not kicking out a New York Times correspondent who they had previously credentialed. So, they didn't go for David. The only people blocked from receiving journalist visas were new hires, people who had been credentialed with other news organizations, so they could say, "We haven't kicked out any New York Times correspondent," because they didn't recognize me as a New York Times correspondent. I don't know if that distinction makes a lot of difference to the rest of the world, but I think in their minds it makes a distinction. They're trying to finesse it in a way that's a little hard to see on the outside.

Despite lingering worries about his safety, Barboza decided to remain in Shanghai.

David Barboza, *New York Times*

I started to think, "If we left China, am I really that much safer in New York? If people have billions of dollars, can they not get me in New York? Can they not get me in Europe? Can they not get me in Japan? There's nowhere I'm safe. I don't think I'm any safer in New York than in China In fact, I could be even safer in China because of the uncertainty of the thing. I felt people have treated me really well. I really love the country, I love the people, I love my job. When am I ever going to have a job like this?"

In 2013, Barboza was awarded the Pulitzer Prize.

"WHAT ARE THEY, THE COMMUNIST PARTY?"

When the expose of Wen Jiabao and his relatives came out, the *Times* also published a note from the editor detailing how the Chinese government had pressured the paper to kill the story. Bloomberg News, however, facing the loss of income from the cutoff of terminal sales in China, decided not to publicize the pressure tactics it had faced over Michael Forsythe's story about Xi Jinping's relatives.

Leta Hong Fincher, China Scholar

When the death threats were made, Bloomberg said we weren't allowed to tell anybody. Since I'm Mike's wife, I thought, "Okay, I won't go public." I'm very active on Twitter, so I decided I'm not going to Tweet about it. But then, a few months later, the New York Times *came out with their exposé of Wen Jiabao's family wealth and this long editorial talking about how the Chinese government placed a lot of pressure on the* Times *not to publish, and that they had received threats. I thought, "If the* New York Times *is going public about that, then of course Bloomberg should, and I'm going to tweet about it." So, I tweeted, "We received death threats following the publication of the story on Xi Jinping's family wealth." As soon as I tweeted that, Mike got a phone call from an executive at Bloomberg telling him, "Get your wife to delete her Tweet!" I started thinking, "What are they, the Communist Party? They don't have the power to censor people. I don't even work for them!" So, I did not delete the tweet, and it was retweeted hundreds and hundreds of times. But it still had a chilling effect because I didn't want Mike to lose his job, so I didn't tweet about it anymore. But the whole way Bloomberg handled the situation was extremely opaque. They didn't want anybody talking about what had happened. They didn't want to go into the fact that the Chinese government had strongly pressured them not to publish the story. They didn't want to talk about the repercussions of publishing the story. To me, that pressure coming from the Chinese government is just as important, if not more important, than the actual assets owned by the family of the Chinese president. But Bloomberg didn't want to talk about it.*

Meanwhile, Forsythe, Ben Richardson, and their colleagues had begun working on another investigative piece, this one looking at Wang Jianlin, the head of the giant Dalian Wanda corporation and China's richest man.

Ben Richardson, Bloomberg News

Wang Jianlin had just made the biggest overseas acquisition, which is effectively to take 2.6 billion dollars out of a country that has capital controls and stick it into America. His company was expanding all over the place. They invested in the highest residential hotel projects in Europe, being built right next the U.S. and Chinese embassies at the south bank of the Thames in London. The wife is going off to have dinner with Prince Charles at Windsor Castle. This stuff is very, very interesting. How do these people get to be that wealthy and powerful? It was an important story to show how he did it, and who he carried along with him.

Michael Forsythe, Bloomberg News

This one was almost a made-to-order Bloomberg story, about how this company rose up and how so many of the families were invested in this company. The learning curve about these things is steep. It took a year to put this story together.

Ben Richardson, Bloomberg News

Mike was the primary reporter. We started off with that lead that Mike had, which was, if you looked at Dalian Wanda's Chinese company filings, there was the name of a company that we knew to be Xi Jinping's family, because we'd already proved that fact in the Xi Jinping story. There was Jia Qinglin, who was a member of the Standing Committee, widely rumored to be very corrupt. We found his son-in-law had received a very juicy stake for Dalian Wanda for no apparent reason. We found a door to knock on through the Hong Kong filings. These Chinese leaders, who are able to hide all sorts of things from their citizens, when they go overseas, they seem to get a bit sloppy or arrogant or careless. They put their names down with the same ID cards, and lo and behold, the same ID cards show up in other filings. And it allows you to say with certainty that that is the person.

By late 2013, the story was ready to go.

Michael Forsythe, Bloomberg News

Fully edited, fully fact-checked, had been vetted by a lawyer, and generally praised by pretty senior people at Bloomberg—and then all of a sudden it was not. A 180-degree turn. And that led to a cascading series of events which got me fired.

Ben Richardson, Bloomberg News

You've now got senior- and mid-level management from both global management and regional management on a call to discuss what's supposed to be minor editorial tweaks to get the story ready for the final push. They said that "we've got bad news for you. Story's not going to run."

Officially, the reason was the story needed additional work. But in the same call, Bloomberg's top editor Matthew Winkler provided what appeared to be the real reason.

Ben Richardson, Bloomberg News

He said, "The Chinese Communist Party, they're Nazis. I've been thinking about how AP did it under the Third Reich, and how we can survive to fight another day." He said, "They will kick us out. We will lose our business in China. So let's do what we're good at! Let's write stories that are really surprising. No one's surprised that there's corruption in the Communist Party. Why don't we write about the stock market?" Then he turned to the story, where he basically said, "Story's not ready." I kept on saying, "We're not children. As adults in the room, you can tell us what's really going on. This story's clearly being spiked for political reasons." For some reason, the richest news organization in the world wants to kowtow to the Chinese government.

Forsythe shared the news with his wife, Leta.

Leta Hong Fincher, China Scholar

Mike had been working really hard on this. He'd been really excited and I had heard from him about how enthusiastic a lot of the senior editors were. I read the draft of the story. I saw that it had been fully fact-checked. It had extensive footnotes. It was like an academic paper, and I know that the lawyers checked every single fact. It was all ready to go. It was obvious that it was a business decision to kill the story.

In Beijing, the *New York Times*'s Edward Wong heard rumors about trouble at Bloomberg.

Edward Wong, *New York Times*

They had been working on that story for most of the year. Then we heard that top editors at Bloomberg told them that they couldn't run the story. There was a very heated conference call that took place with Matt Winkler, who was then the top editor at Bloomberg News, who mentioned a metaphor between Nazi Germany and China, saying how they have to approach reporting in China in a similar way to how reporters in Nazi Germany had approached reporting there—meaning trying to maintain access while still doing real journalism. The press corps in China, whether it's in Beijing or Hong Kong, is a very tight knit place. When there's grumbling, you start hearing about it, even if you don't know those reporters personally. I wasn't close with any of the Bloomberg reporters, but you start hearing this talk that Bloomberg reporters are unhappy, a story had been killed, and then you start following. And you find out it leads to decisions that are being made at the very top level at Bloomberg.

WITCH HUNT

On November 9, Edward Wong's story with the headline "Bloomberg News Is Said to Curb Articles That Might Anger China" appeared in the *New York Times*.

Ben Richardson, Bloomberg News

Then there was a witch hunt. When there's a witch hunt, no one ever survives.

At Bloomberg headquarters in central Hong Kong, Richardson, Forsythe, and others involved in the story were grilled by Bloomberg lawyers and HR managers furious that someone had talked to the *Times*. Forsythe was blamed for the leak and fired.

Michael Forsythe, Bloomberg News

After a grilling, I was walked out. It was a terrible time for me.

Leta Hong Fincher, China Scholar

To be perfectly honest, I did not know that he was going to talk to the New York Times *about what had happened. I was really upset with him at first because I knew that he would be fired. But I knew that he did the right thing. Somebody had to speak out about it.*

Bloomberg also used a confidentiality clause in the fine print of his contract to impose a gag order on Forsythe barring him from discussing details of his departure.

Michael Forsythe, Bloomberg News

I do have limits on that. Pretty painful. It's very awkward for me.

Leta Hong Fincher, China Scholar

But what happened afterwards was even more infuriating. Bloomberg not only threatened legal action against Mike, but also threatened legal action against me. I was simply Mike's wife. But they were trying to coerce me legally into signing a gag order so that I would never speak about what had happened. Mike already had a lawyer representing him, but it soon became clear that Bloomberg wanted just as much to silence me. It was particularly galling because Bloomberg insisted publicly that the story had not been killed, that it was a bad story, and that they were simply putting it on hold because it wasn't ready for publication. That was a blatant lie. Now Mike had signed a confidentiality agreement when he joined the company, so they said he had violated that agreement, and so that's why they were going after him legally. But they had no legal grounds whatsoever to pursue me. I ended up hiring my own attorney, and after a few letters back and forth, Bloomberg dropped their demand that I sign the gag order. I get nervous talking about it because I'm still worried that maybe Bloomberg will come after me and threaten legal action again. I feel very firmly that we do need to be up front about what happened, but at the same time, this is a very powerful media corporation, so it's not easy to defy them.

Within months, Ben Richardson quit Bloomberg in protest.

Ben Richardson, Bloomberg News

I was gone. I was toast from that conference call. There's no way you can work there. I got a letter from them the day I left saying you must sign this form, which said, "I agree to give you access to my home computer." They're still trying this game, all these threats. It's just nonsensical.

Bloomberg's Matthew Winkler and a company spokesman declined my requests for on-the record interviews. In early 2014, Michael Bloomberg stepped down as mayor of New York and again took charge of the organization bearing his name. At a meeting with employees, he was challenged about what had happened, and gave an awkward, rambling response, stammering that "when it comes to doing business around the world, the world is complex. And American values aren't the values of everybody."

Michael Forsythe, Bloomberg News

I feel very strongly that it's our responsibility as foreign reporters to report and document the wealth of Chinese leaders. Chinese reporters cannot do this. If they do, they'll go to jail. To me, the idea of a world where China is the biggest economy in the world, and it's forbidden to write about the wealth of the leaders is just dystopian. I don't want to live in that kind of world. I don't want my children to live in that kind of a world.

Within weeks of being fired, Forsythe was hired by the *New York Times* in Hong Kong. Bloomberg, meanwhile, having rid itself of Forsythe, made strenuous efforts to mend fences with Beijing. By 2015, the Chinese were granting the company new visas, and even let a Bloomberg reporter ask a question at a press conference during the annual meeting of the Chinese parliament.

David Barboza, *New York Times*

I hate to say it, but it looks like that part of their campaign was effective, which is to scare. So all of the journalists are worried about what they do in China.

Indeed, the *Times* Beijing bureau remained under pressure, with no new residence visas and continued blocking of the English- and Chinese-language websites.

David Barboza, *New York Times*

The Times suffered millions of dollars in losses by having the website blocked, having this Chinese-language team there that can't do anything, can't get ads, we can't get visas. There was a lot of pressure.

Ironically, however, at the same time, China's new leader, Xi Jinping, embarked on a sweeping campaign against corruption.

Josh Chin, who was half-Chinese and who had grown up in Utah, perfected his Mandarin at Tsinghua University, and received a journalism degree from UC Berkeley, was now a reporter in the *Wall Street Journal*'s Beijing bureau.

Josh Chin, *Wall Street Journal*

There was a legitimate problem with corruption in China. In the Hu Jintao era, there was a real problem. Literally every aspect of life in China was sullied by corruption. Parents used to have to bribe teachers to get their kids into school. It was just pervasive. There were all these scandals of officials who were really hurting the Communist Party's image. I think the corruption campaign was partly a response to that. In that sense it was legitimate.

Indeed, many of the senior officials who were targeted were involved in activities not much different from what Barboza, Forsythe, and their colleagues had documented.

David Barboza, *New York Times*

I am not convinced that the government was uniformly against my story, because people in government talked to me privately and said, "Congratulations." A lot of them said, "We can't say that publicly, but a lot of people love what you did. You actually helped Xi Jinping's anticorruption campaign." Everyone knew Wen and his family [were] doing this and it was outrageous. So almost no one attacked me.

Meanwhile, the *Times* continued to push the limits with its coverage.

Austin Ramzy, *New York Times*

There's a clash of two very stubborn institutions, the New York Times *and the Chinese Communist Party.*

But the *Times* was virtually alone in its willingness to pursue this kind of reporting.

Michael Forsythe, *New York Times*

There's a lot of reasons for that. One is that there's just not enough reporters. There are so many stories in China. You really have to have a pretty big news organization to actually give people the time to do these stories. The New York Times *is certainly one of them. Bloomberg was one of them. You also have to have people who are inclined to do these stories. I could spend all day going through documents and not talking to a human being and I'd be in cloud nine. That's just me. I think that might be David too, although David's sourcing and his human intelligence is second to none. The third reason is the sanctions, the crap that will come down on your company if you do this is very well known now. If you're another news organization in China and you're thinking about doing these stories, you know what's going to happen to you. Because you know what happened to the* New York Times, *and you know what happened to Bloomberg, so do you really want to do that?*

In mid-2015, after over a year of fresh reporting, Michael Forsythe's story about Chinese tycoon Wang Jianlin—the story that Bloomberg refused to publish, and that led to his dismissal—was published in the *New York Times.* The headline was "A Billionaire at the Intersection of Business and Power in China."

19

THE SURVEILLANCE STATE

Soon after becoming president and Communist Party chief in 2012, Xi Jinping launched the anticorruption campaign that would become a critical tool in his efforts to consolidate power. The numbers were staggering. By 2017, the authorities had investigated nearly 2.7 million officials and punished more than 1.5 million people, including high-ranking generals and several dozen members of the Communist Party's Central Committee.[1]

Josh Chin, *Wall Street Journal*

As a journalist, the interesting thing about the corruption campaign is that when it started off there were these really detailed accounts of all the terrible stuff people had been doing, which was enlightening in terms of the level of corruption inside the Party.

Among ordinary Chinese, the targeting of corrupt officials proved to be popular.

Chris Buckley, *New York Times*

Catching up with friends I'd made in the countryside years earlier, saying, "How are things going?" They would be happy to see the crackdown on corruption. The general complaint was that not enough people were being arrested, in particular local Party officials, who should be strung up as well. People welcomed this change.

But most striking was the way Xi used the campaign to topple his rivals. Apart from Bo Xilai, the most prominent victim was Zhou Yongkang, a member of the Politburo's nine-man Standing Committee, the former chief of domestic security, and a potential challenger to Xi. In 2015, Zhou was convicted of abuse of power, accepting bribes, and revealing state secrets, and sentenced to life in prison. It was a display of brute political strength.

Josh Chin, *Wall Street Journal*

When Zhou Yongkang went down, that was tectonic. Because there's this idea that former Standing Committee people are immune. To keep everything on an even keel at the top of the Party, those people were immune. For Xi to go after someone like that was really shocking. It was a huge, huge story, and a real signal that all of those guys—everyone at that echelon—are corrupt, so Xi was clearly making choices about who he was pursuing.

CRACKING DOWN ON CIVIL SOCIETY

As the anticorruption drive intensified, the Communist Party also increased pressure on what little remained of civil society.

Josh Chin, *Wall Street Journal*

There was Document Number 9, this leaked Communist Party directive listing seven topics the Party needed to look out for. It was a laundry list of liberal values—freedom of the press, constitutional government, separation of powers, all that stuff. It was like this warning of an ideological battle and the Party needed to eradicate all of this. The activists or scholars who started to get detained were working on issues in this document. The arrests matched up perfectly. It was clear something new was happening. It was a systematic turn against Western ideology. They weren't messing around.

Ian Johnson was now reporting for the *New York Times*. Johnson had a long-standing interest in religion in China. By 2016, much of his energy was taken up chronicling an aggressive crackdown on Christianity, highlighted by a government push to remove crosses from churches in the coastal province of Zhejiang, where Xi Jinping had previously been Party chief.

Ian Johnson, *New York Times*

You could see the tide was turning. They were targeting the churches as being too foreign.

For Johnson and the *Times*'s local researcher, Kiki Zhao, reporting the story became a game of cat and mouse to avoid police surveillance.

Ian Johnson, *New York Times*

I visited this outspoken pastor in Hangzhou. He was being followed, and then I got tailed. We got a van with dark windows. I sat in the back, and we drove up to the church. Kiki went out and saw the pastor and explained the situation and said, "Can we come in and interview you?" If the Pastor said yes, then I got out of the car and went in, and we interviewed him together. It was not really enjoyable sitting in the damn car, but it was the safest way for avoiding trouble.

UNCOVERING THE SURVEILLANCE STATE

Surveillance had been a fact of life for foreign correspondents in China for decades. Under Xi, however, the government was dramatically expanding the use of artificial intelligence and other cutting-edge technology to monitor the population with the goal of making the country the world's first digital totalitarian state.

Josh Chin, *Wall Street Journal*

Any reporter who has spent time in China is constantly worried about whether you might be under surveillance. The main thing I realized is that it actually works psychologically. You don't want surveillance to have an undue influence on your reporting, to limit the type of stories you are going to do, or the people you are going to talk to. But it is real, and you don't want to put sources at risk.

Even as reporters struggled to evade increasingly intrusive monitoring, they also sought to understand how the emerging Chinese surveillance state operated. Paul Mozur, a Dartmouth graduate, had started out as a journalist with local English-language publications in Hong Kong, and then covered technology in Taiwan and Beijing for the *Wall Street Journal* before joining the *New York Times*.

Paul Mozur, *New York Times*

One of the biggest things you noticed was cameras everywhere. You found your-self staring at these contraptions, wondering, "What the hell is going on with this stuff? Where is that data going? What is this new surveillance build-out, and what does it all mean?"

In late 2016, Josh Chin and his Shanghai-based *Wall Street Journal* col-league Singaporean Liza Lin visited the Beijing office of a new Chinese arti-ficial intelligence startup called Sense Time.

Josh Chin, *Wall Street Journal*

We went into their offices near Tsinghua University. It was like stepping into a sci-fi movie. They had this camera that scanned your face to let you in and cam-eras trained on the street categorizing every car and pedestrian and bicycle. It was unimaginable. We interviewed the executive. It turned out they were sell-ing a lot of this stuff to the police. There were other startups also selling to the police. And police departments all over China were using this technology. That was our entry point into the story. We spent most of an entire year basically reporting on surveillance.

Tech in China was already an important beat for many news organiza-tions, not least because of the emergence of immensely influential compa-nies like Huawei, Baidu, Tencent, and its fellow e-commerce giant Alibaba, and its charismatic founder, Jack Ma.

Paul Mozur, *New York Times*

I always think of Jack Ma in terms of Bill Clinton—this deeply charismatic man who should have been an American-style politician. Because you couldn't really do that, he went into the next best thing, which was business. If you really think about the heart of Alibaba, it's convincing poor Chinese people they can be just like him if they try to start a business and throw money at online advertising.

Jack was incredibly effective at that. He also couldn't help himself. He is a talker. These moments where he knew he should shut up and he just couldn't.

Meanwhile, Tencent, whose chief executive, Ma Huateng, also known as Pony Ma, was as reclusive as Jack Ma was garrulous, had developed an app that would become central to the lives of most Chinese—WeChat. Combining payments, e-commerce, and social media, the app enabled users to post photos, swap stories, buy things, pay bills, order take-out food, and get news. Moreover, its data, purchasing information, and chat logs were easily available to the government.

Josh Chin, *Wall Street Journal*

If you look at a company like WeChat, that has got to be the most valuable data that any company has. In one place you have data of people, who people's friends are, what they spend their money on, where they go, what they say. It's insane. No other company on Earth has that.

Shan Li, who was born in Beijing but grew up in Texas, also covered tech for the *Wall Street Journal*.

Shan Li, *Wall Street Journal*

Given how all encompassing it is in Chinese society and in people's lives, I think WeChat was very innovative. But the big tech companies like Tencent and Alibaba were also selling censorship software to other companies that didn't have the bandwidth to do it themselves.

Yet documenting the collaboration between the tech giants and the security apparatus was a major challenge.

Josh Chin, *Wall Street Journal*

Alibaba and Tencent are savvy, and very sensitive to questions about data. They were aware that privacy was a thing Western societies and media were interested in, so they did not want to talk. Trying to figure out how they shared their data with the government was the hardest story we did. We had to troll through all sorts of documents and talk to all kinds of people. Liza Lin, my coworker, reached out to local police in Hangzhou through social media and managed to

*convince them to talk to her and tell her how Alibaba was sharing informa-
tion with them.*

*When we started this story, Alibaba hired Sard [Sard Verbinnen & Co.], the
crisis PR firm. One of Sard's employees was a former Journal reporter based
in Hong Kong. He knew exactly how the Journal worked, how to navigate our
editorial process, and who to talk to to push Alibaba's view. We had quite a
long back and forth with them before the story went out. Interestingly, the process ended up confirming the key thing, which was that Alibaba had an office
on its campus where the police could go and work to directly access user data
for investigations. We had that from the police, but we didn't have it from Alibaba. In the process of going back and forth with them, they basically acknowledged its existence. In the end, it made us even more confident about the story.*

In their report, headlined "China's Tech Giants Have a Second Job: Helping Beijing Spy on Its People," Chin and Lin cited "people familiar with the
operation" who confirmed the existence of the police office on the Alibaba
campus and its role in "tapping into the trove of information the tech giant
collects through its e-commerce and financial-payment networks."[2]

In his own research on the surveillance state, Paul Mozur made an interesting discovery.

Paul Mozur, *New York Times*

*A lot of data is left out on the open Internet. Chinese police departments will
run tests on the software, or just start using the software, and won't lock down
the databases where it is being stored. What you can do if you know how is go
online and start pinging thousands of databases that have been left open and
grab a snapshot and see if there is anything of interest. We built a search engine
and started digging into what is effectively the back closet of the Chinese
Internet—through patent databases and procurement documents. You'd also
have all these incredible caches of data that showed the answers to a lot of the
questions about how the surveillance state was being run: what kind of facial
recognition algorithms were running, what the cameras were looking for, how
many alerts were being sent—all that kind of stuff.*

After months of research, Mozur producer a major article. The opening
sentence was "China is ramping up its ability to spy on its nearly 1.4 billion
people to new and disturbing levels, giving the world a blueprint for how to
build a digital totalitarian state."[3]

BLENDING IN

For all the harassment and monitoring, Mozur, Josh Chin, and Liza Lin were covering aspects of the system the Communist Party had long sought to keep hidden. Interestingly, they were not alone. A new generation of China correspondents was displaying a striking ability to penetrate below the surface of Chinese society. One key reason was that a growing proportion of the U.S. press corps comprised ethnic Chinese. Some, like the *Wall Street Journal*'s Shan Li and Chao Deng, had emigrated from China, become American citizens, and then returned to cover the country of their birth. Others, like Gerry Shih of the Associated Press (who in 2018 would join the *Washington Post*), Amy Qin of the *New York Times*, Alice Su of the *Los Angeles Times*, and the half-Chinese Josh Chin, had been born and raised in the United States. The *Wall Street Journal*'s Jonathan Cheng was Chinese Canadian. Their ethnic background and language skills enabled them to act less as outsiders and more as part of the society they were covering. They blended in and were more instinctively aware of cultural sensitivities.

Gerry Shih, Associated Press, *Washington Post*

It was hugely helpful. As things became so difficult, I basically just packed a pair of socks and an extra set of underwear in my backpack, and I was off. I do whatever I can to blend in.

Chao Deng, *Wall Street Journal*

I think it definitely benefited me to look Chinese and speak Chinese without a Western accent, and I tried to take advantage of that. There were definitely occasions where it was easy to be very discreet and just linger and get color and all of that.

One such occasion was a trip to Sandu county in impoverished Guizhou province. Chao Deng had read an online blog post by a broker who had marketed an infrastructure investment scheme in Sandu. When the county's Communist Party secretary was removed in a corruption scandal, the scheme collapsed. It was a classic example of local authorities in China running up vast amounts of debt for wildly ambitious construction projects. The broker was taking a group of angry investors to Sandu and allowed Chao to accompany them.

Chao Deng, *Wall Street Journal*

I tagged along with these investors trying to get their money back. There was this lady who was dressed very well and clearly wasn't from Guizhou. She was a broker of investment products, and I just latched onto her and followed her around. I felt like I was in the bear's lair with these investors inside a government building. But I wasn't kicked out. I disclosed I was a reporter, but for some reason it didn't click with them that I wasn't separate from the group of investors.

"AN AMAZING BEAT"

Amy Qin's parents had immigrated to the United States in the 1980s. They were among the more than fifty thousand Chinese, mostly students, who were allowed by the Bush administration to remain following the Tiananmen Square crackdown in 1989. Qin grew up in California and majored in Chinese studies at Berkeley. While doing a graduate degree at Oxford in 2012, she was contacted by Edward Wong of the *New York Times*, who was covering the Bo Xilai story. Bo's son, Guagua, was studying at Oxford, and Wong was looking for someone who could do some research there. That led to an internship in the *Times* Beijing bureau, and, eventually, a job as a reporter. Her focus was on arts and culture.

Amy Qin, *New York Times*

I always thought doing arts and culture stories could help round out the image of China that people were often getting through the media. It was an amazing beat. No one was really covering this stuff because most news organizations did not have the resources or the interest to do it. I didn't have any competition at all. It was great.

Qin's first *Times* story was about Liu Cixin, China's most popular science fiction writer. His novel *The Three-Body Problem*, which chronicled humanity's attempt to fend off an alien invasion, had become a global hit. Later, she profiled a Chinese rap group in Chengdu called the Higher Brothers and discovered that, even with Party censors banning the kind of topics associated with rap (sex, drugs, politics, and explicit language), the group still reflected the desire of many Chinese young people to assert their individuality.

Amy Qin, *New York Times*

They were pretty open. They were every bit the rappers you might expect.

She was also able to profile a Tibetan filmmaker, Pema Tseden. With his movies shot almost entirely with Tibetan actors and crew members, and often in the Tibetan language, as she noted in her story, Tseden was someone who "has managed to work within the censorship-heavy system while still producing films and stories that resonate with audiences far beyond the system's confines."[4]

Amy Qin, *New York Times*

He was worried about getting into trouble, although his films get released in Chinese theaters, so he is not exactly a rebel figure. But he is very careful when he talks. At that time, you were still able to skirt the line a little bit, and speak in this kind of coded language, where we all understand what people are saying—but they are not saying it outright. I was really interested in censorship and how people have become so skilled in saying things without actually saying them. I thought his films were just so different. You could see immediately that it was from a different perspective that did not exoticize Tibetans. Just in the way he was presenting that subject matter, he was pushing against the government line that you normally see about Tibet.

Qin did more than just cover the arts, however, and repeatedly found that being ethnic Chinese was a major advantage. This turned out to be particularly true in a story she reported about Pakistani women being trafficked as brides for Chinese men—a consequence of the imbalance between men and women resulting from China's one-child policy and long-standing cultural preference for boys.

Amy Qin, *New York Times*

A Pakistani woman was trafficked by a rural Chinese farmer in Shandong. She had escaped and talked to our reporter in Pakistan. They wanted me to find the farmer. I showed up in this village with my researcher, and both of us are, like, young Chinese girls. They're so suspicious of outsiders. We didn't tell the villagers we were journalists. We wanted to find the farmer first. I think they thought we were potential brides for the villagers. Then we called the guy, and he came and picked us up. We told him we were journalists and did a whole interview with him, which was great, but I can't imagine what would have happened had I not been ethnic Chinese.

Yet even apparently innocuous stories led to pressure on those Qin was covering, as she discovered when she went to Sichuan to interview Fan Jian-chuan, a wealthy property developer who had built the largest private museum complex in China.

Amy Qin, *New York Times*

He was an avid memorabilia collector. He had thirty museums, each dedicated to a different topic. He had one completely devoted to bound-feet shoes, one on the Flying Tigers from World War II, and one on sent-down youth from the Cultural Revolution. To balance out some of the more sensitive Cultural Revolution ones, he had one on the anti-Japanese war. I met with him and did all the interviews. He posted on Weibo that I was interviewing him. The authorities asked what I had been doing, and he asked me, "Please don't write this story because I am going to get into big trouble." I had already done the work, but I didn't want his museum to get shut down, so I decided not to do it.

EASING UP

Still, in a reflection of the contradictions that often characterized developments in China, during that same period, the Chinese authorities actually eased some of the restrictions on foreign journalists imposed in the wake of the investigate reporting of David Barboza and Michael Forsythe. A new visa was granted to Chris Buckley of the *New York Times*, who had been frozen out of China for nearly three years. Others would follow.

The policy shift came in the wake of a remarkable exchange between Xi Jinping and Mark Landler, the *New York Times* White House correspondent, during a visit to Beijing by President Barack Obama in November 2014. At a joint press conference following Obama's talks with Xi, Landler pressed the

Chinese leader on whether Beijing would ease visa restrictions for foreign journalists—an issue Obama had raised.

"Media outlets need to obey China's laws and regulations," Xi said. "In Chinese, we have a saying: The party which has created the problem, should be the one to help resolve it."[5]

Xi's blunt response—in effect blaming the journalists for their own predicament—appeared to signal little flexibility. But less than ten months later, as Xi prepared for his own state visit to Washington, the Chinese government suddenly lifted its ban on Buckley, and soon after gave visas to other journalists who had been waiting.

Austin Ramzy, *New York Times*

I think there was this fear in Beijing that Xi Jinping was going to be put on the spot, conceivably multiple times, over this, and it would be this embarrassment during this important visit. I think the timing fits that explanation.

Whatever the reason, China's door again opened for American and other foreign reporters.

Ian Johnson, *New York Times*

Things eased up. By 2020, the numbers were at or close to an all-time high. We might have had a dozen or fourteen people accredited. We all had J-1 journalist visas.

Chris Buckley, *New York Times*

My first impression returning was relief to get back in, but also a sense of unfamiliarity. In those brief few years, a lot had happened under Xi Jinping. The rules had changed. Figuring out who you could approach, who was willing to talk, who was now keeping a distance, how you could coax people to talk—all of that took me a little while. Generally, the paper was relieved to get back in. The Foreign Ministry and the State Council Information Office seemed to be, if not friendly, at least open to conversation. But at the same time, purges and arrests that had started up in 2013 had expanded, so people I knew, or had interviewed, had disappeared, been arrested, or were no longer speaking to their foreign friends.

At the same time, in its first digital media accreditation, Beijing even allowed American Megha Rajagopalan, who had been a China correspondent for Reuters from 2012 to 2016, to open a bureau for the online news website *Buzzfeed*.

Megha Rajagopalan, *Buzzfeed*

I think they saw some benefit in us coming. There was an elaborate courtship where the Chinese consulate in New York sent a bunch of officials to the Buzzfeed office there, and they took pictures together and stuff like that.

Rajagopalan had a luxury denied many reporters for daily media outlets.

Megha Rajagopalan, *Buzzfeed*

I was very lucky in that the ask for me was never to cover all the news in China. The philosophy at Buzzfeed was that we want to do things that move the needle, so we wanted to focus exclusively on scoops and investigations. I was working for a place where I could carve something out that everyone else wasn't already doing. There was a lot of talk about zagging when everyone else was zigging. I looked for stuff that wasn't being covered a lot.

This led to stories in *Buzzfeed* about the Chinese authorities forcing people to download an app designed to delete "dangerous" photos, the struggles of small American businesses to stay afloat against a sea of fake Chinese products, and Chinese investors being wooed by President Donald Trump's son-in-law, Jared Kushner.

Meanwhile, Steven Lee Myers had joined the *New York Times* Beijing bureau in 2017 after stints in Moscow, Baghdad, and Washington.

Steven Lee Myers, *New York Times*

There was a kind of—I wouldn't call [it] a golden period—but things had kind of calmed down. There had been some return to normal. But that didn't last very long.

20

EMPEROR FOR LIFE

In March 2018, Xi Jinping rocked the Chinese political system by ramming through a constitutional amendment allowing him to stay in office indefinitely. With no advance notice, he abolished the limit of two consecutive terms for the presidency introduced by Deng Xiaoping—a step Deng had taken to ensure that China would never again be subjected to a crushing dictatorship like that of Chairman Mao.

Chris Buckley, *New York Times*

Nobody ever anticipated that there would be an abolition of term limits. That was certainly a turning point—Xi Jinping throwing away the rule book and the reemergence of ideology that was much more explicitly about loyalty to Xi Jinping's ideas.

Jane Perlez, a veteran foreign correspondent with assignments in Africa, Eastern Europe, South Asia, and Southeast Asia, had been the *New York Times* Beijing bureau chief since 2012.

Jane Perlez, *New York Times*

As soon as I heard, I got on the phone to a nationalistically inclined prominent academic to ask his reaction. I remember so clearly. He said, "I can't talk about it, Jane. I can't talk about it. I'm shocked." And he hung up. That was it. I knew from that that this was a big deal, and that even Xi's supporters were taken aback. They didn't see it coming. The Chinese elite didn't see Xi pronouncing himself emperor for life.

Steven Lee Myers, *New York Times*

That was the moment when you felt something turn in China, politically speaking. People were taken aback by the audacity of his move. The system itself seemed to freeze. I think there was a greater sense of fear of where he was going and of what the consequences were of challenging that.

In one stroke, Xi had shattered the Communist Party's fragile norms around the sharing and transfer of power. The Party's history had long been marked by destabilizing succession battles—from Chairman Mao purging his rivals during the Cultural Revolution, to the toppling of the Gang of Four after Mao's death in 1976, to the sidelining of Mao's designated heir, Hua Guofeng, by Deng Xiaoping, to the ouster in the late 1980s of the two men chosen by Deng to succeed him, Hu Yaobang and Zhao Ziyang. While he unquestionably dominated the Chinese political system and had no obvious challenger, Xi also had no clear successor.

Chris Buckley, *New York Times*

Xi Jinping, as healthy and well cared for as he may be, is not immortal. What happens if he falls ill or worse? One of the difficult issues is that he has been building a lot of those institutions around himself. If Xi Jinping in theory wants to hand on power, how does that work? Is Xi, as a semiretired figure behind the scenes, going to be comfortable with that? That is going to be tricky. Any successor will have to build up their own authority. What if you have a 1980s scenario again, in which the leader says, "I'll take this one, thank you." And then, "You're not working out, and I'll change again. And then I'll change again." You have the makings of a real crisis there, as we saw in the 1980s.

For the American press corps, the immediate impact of Xi's power grab was to make covering China even harder.

Eunice Yoon had left CNN for CNBC, and had now been in Beijing for eight years.

Eunice Yoon, CNBC

With Xi Jinping, I feel the environment got tighter. I had so many more inter-
views canceled, or there was this questioning about you being an American or
being a journalist. There was one week where I had three interviews in a row
canceled.

Steven Lee Myers, *New York Times*

You definitely felt the change in attitude after the Xi maneuver. That changed
something in the system that made people much more wary of speaking out.
Pretty soon, people we used to talk to—scholars at universities, people that we
used to quote all the time—were saying, "I've been told by friends not to talk
to the foreign media."

Anna Fifield, a New Zealander who had previously been based in Seoul
for the *Financial Times* and then in Tokyo for the *Washington Post*, and who
had won acclaim for her coverage of North Korea, arrived in Beijing in 2018
as the *Post*'s new bureau chief.

Anna Fifield, *Washington Post*

When I arrived, there were experts and professors who would decline to talk.
They said they were not authorized to talk to the foreign media anymore. It
was difficult to tell how much of it was a direct instruction, and how much of
it was these people reading the winds.

TRUMP AND TRADE

The hostility to the American press corps was exacerbated by the sharp down-
turn in relations between China and the United States after Donald Trump
became president in 2017 and initiated a trade war. Aimed at forcing Beijing to
change what Trump saw as unfair trade practices, such as intellectual policy
theft and protectionist measures that put American companies at a disadvan-
tage, and to lower its trade deficit with the United States, Trump imposed
tariffs and other barriers, often announcing them via Twitter. China not surprisingly retaliated. Economic and political relations sharply deteriorated.

Initially, some reporters found that they shared with the few Chinese sources who would talk to them a common bewilderment over what to make of Trump

Chao Deng, *Wall Street Journal*

I remember when you went to meet Chinese sources, a lot of times, we would just sigh and say, "Yeah, we agree Trump is nuts." They would be complaining about how random and unpredictable this guy is.

Eunice Yoon, CNBC

Trump was so erratic. Talking to the folks at the Foreign Ministry, we would joke a bit. There were ways that we were drawn together in certain respects. We were all waking up at four or five in the morning, looking at our phones, seeing that he had tweeted. For me, it meant knowing I had to contact them for a statement, and I knew that the Foreign Ministry had to prepare something. There was a little bit of camaraderie, in an odd way. We were all having to deal with the same thing.

Initially, Yoon found that Chinese awareness of Trump's addiction to cable television boosted her access.

Eunice Yoon, CNBC

In the early stages of the trade negotiations, there was more of a willingness to talk to CNBC. They caught on that he was watching TV news, that he liked one CNBC anchor in the morning, and I was on that show quite a bit. In a way, it was quite helpful. It was seen as a way of communicating with President Trump.

But in general, China's long-standing suspicion of the foreign press left most correspondents frozen out as they struggled to cover the trade war.

Anna Fifield, *Washington Post*

There were experts who would decline to talk because it was politicized. I would watch CGTN [the English-language international service of China Central Television] and see who was authorized to talk in English about the Chinese

perspective on the trade war. This was a way to get some Chinese perspectives into my stories. By the end of 2018, beginning of 2019, those people all said they were not authorized to talk to the foreign media anymore. Even if they were saying the same things as Xinhua or the Foreign Ministry briefing, they would still not repeat it, nor would they repeat what they said on CGTN. It wasn't so much what they were saying, but the idea of being associated with American media at such a tense time. So as a journalist, that created a real problem, because I didn't want to write stories about the Chinese perspective on the trade war without quoting any Chinese people.

The journalists' dealings with the Trump administration weren't much better.

Chao Deng, *Wall Street Journal*

I don't think the Americans were very press-friendly. I don't recall them holding many press conferences when they were in Beijing.

Eunice Yoon, CNBC

The Obama administration would give us access to pressers or tell us what was happening in briefings. But with the Trump administration, the U.S. embassy went quiet. They wouldn't be pushing the Chinese side to have the American press there. They wouldn't be lobbying for us. And the Chinese were perfectly happy. If you don't want any journalists there, or if you only want to do an interview with Fox News, that's fine. It was just really hard to get access.

"SUDDENLY, NO ONE WOULD TALK TO YOU"

As U.S.-China relations deteriorated, so did the broader treatment of the American press corps.

Steven Lee Myers, *New York Times*

Access dried up. It became more and more tense, and relations got worse. It partly reflected where China was going politically, but also a sense that China felt like it was getting stronger and getting a bit more of a chip on its shoulder and felt like it was being unfairly treated by foreign journalists. Then, suddenly, it was, like, no one would talk to you.

Gerry Shih, *Washington Post*

The Chinese have become more and more antagonistic to foreign reporters. This trope that the foreign media is out to smear China and the Chinese people—that trickled down. All the time, you encounter cynicism and distrust out in the field.

But in March 2019, when Shih went to Jiangsu province to cover a chemical explosion, he discovered not all ordinary people bought into the Party line.

Gerry Shih, *Washington Post*

I was talking to villagers railing about the corrupt local officials, corrupt businesspeople, and how they were always dumping chemicals. Suddenly one of the locals asks, "Where did you say you are from?" I said, "I'm an American reporter with the Washington Post.*" They said, "If you're from the U.S. media, you are just going to make us look bad, right?" I was like, "No, I just want to tell the story of what's happening, and what you guys are saying." Others in the circle were starting to say, "Yes, she's right. We shouldn't be talking to this guy." Then I said, "Look, you're so frustrated, and you're talking to me. Are there local reporters you can talk to? Are they writing about this stuff?" They said, "No they're not. They're censored." I said, "What you want to do is talk to the press so that you can get your message out, specifically to Xi Jinping, because you believe Xi is one of the good guys. It's the local guys who are the bad guys. If you talk to me, I would be able to write that—not Chinese media." They were like, "Yeah, yeah, yeah, you're absolutely right. We should talk to this guy." Suddenly the mood changed. I thought these people were going to turn me in, but after that it was, like, you can sleep in our place for the night. We'll take care of you. There were actually plainclothes police who had heard I was there and were looking for me. They would come and give me a heads-up. I was never found during two or three days of being there.*

A few months later, however, Alice Su of the *Los Angeles Times* had a chillingly different experience when she visited Inner Mongolia to chronicle a campaign to impose Mandarin Chinese on Mongolian speakers. As she interviewed grandparents taking children to school, she was detained by police.

Alice Su, *Los Angeles Times*

They took me to a back room behind the police station. Inside was a cell with bars and a locked door. It was covered with soft padding so you couldn't hear anything. The man speaking to me was very confrontational. I told him I was a journalist and a foreigner, and I wanted to contact my embassy. He was yelling at me. I kept saying I wanted to make a call. He kept saying I couldn't. I was thinking I need to let someone know I'm here. When I reached for my phone, he placed his hands on my neck and pushed me into the cell and locked it. I was thinking this has veered off the script. You get detained and they might hold you for a few hours and then they let you go. It was quite scary. After an hour, they took me to another room with a tiger chair—the chair that has metal to secure your arms and legs. I'd heard a lot of people talk about it in interviews. Then he said, "I'm going to give you your human rights. You do not have to sit in that chair." Some people came and said they wanted to search me and take my jewelry, my watch, and my bra. I pushed back. They said you can't have any metal on you where you are going. At that point I was worried. I said no. I want to see your leader. They didn't take my undergarments, but they took my wedding ring and my watch.

After a couple of hours, they put me in a normal room and gave me water. I think someone in the station realized she really is a foreigner and a journalist, and we shouldn't be treating her this way. Finally, the Foreign Affairs people came and said, "We'll give you a ride to the train station," and put me on the train to Beijing. I do think being ethnic Chinese was a factor in my experience. It was a huge advantage to have a Chinese face, because in the first half of the day no one noticed me. I talked to people and got a really good story. On the other hand, I had a taste of being treated as a Chinese person. That was very unpleasant.

Alice Su's experience was extreme, but journalists traveling outside Beijing were encountering increasingly heavy-handed tactics—random wake-ups in the middle of the night for "visa checks," being followed, pushed, shoved, having equipment seized, or being detained. Visas were also held up or issued for shorter durations than the standard year, and threats were made not to renew visas at all unless journalists toned down their reporting.

WOLF WARRIORS

The most vivid symbol of China's more belligerent approach became the "Wolf Warrior," an assertive, often confrontational style inspired by two jingoistic Chinese action movies and adopted by Chinese officials.

Gerry Shih, *Washington Post*

The Wolf Warrior diplomacy was the central theme. You could see it in terms of foreign policy or China on the world stage. You see [it in] Xi's global aspirations. In terms of Chinese external propaganda, it became much more triumphant.

Steven Lee Myers, *New York Times*

I think it is the nationalistic bent of Xi, and the society more broadly. It's also [that] the sense of grievance that China is not being allowed to have its place in the world has led to this idea that China needs to be more assertive. We are not on our knees asking for help anymore. We're not begging journalists to come and cover our side of the story. We are going to tell our side of the story. We are going to tell other countries what to do. We are not going to seek compromise. And you see that over and over in almost every aspect of their foreign and national security policy.

That trend had become evident early on in Xi Jinping's tenure. In September 2013, Jane Perlez had traveled to Astana, the capital of Kazakhstan, to cover a speech by Xi at Nazarbayev University, founded by the president of Kazakhstan, Nursultan Nazarbayev.

Jane Perlez, *New York Times*

At the university lecture theatre, he made this speech saying we are going to build all these projects around the world and knit Central Asia closer to China. The subliminal message was, "Watch out United States." That was the start. It was pretty clear from that speech that Xi was going to forge a different path and try to put China, as fast as he possibly could, as the leader of the globe. The Chinese have thought for a long time that's their rightful position.

The speech in Kazakhstan was the first major public announcement of what became known as the "Belt and Road," a multibillion-dollar program to expand China's global influence through a vast program of infrastructure-building in the country's neighboring regions. In the following years, under the aegis of the Belt and Road, Chinese banks and companies financed and built everything from power plants, railways, and highways to ports and telecommunications infrastructure. The Belt and Road became Xi's signature foreign policy initiative, and a symbol of China's new global assertiveness.

In another move to reshape the international order, Beijing began more aggressively contesting the maritime territorial claims of the Philippines, Malaysia, Vietnam, Taiwan, and Brunei in the South China Sea, a strategic waterway through which one-third of the world's shipping flows. Claiming nearly the entire South China Sea as China's territorial waters, the Chinese government began harassing fishing vessels from rival countries and constructed a series of artificial islands that became the site of military bases, despite strong opposition both within the region and from the United States. At the same time, Chinese assertiveness led to heightened tensions with Taiwan, as well as with Japan, Australia, India, the European Union, and other nations, while relations with the United States continued to fray.

Also emblematic of China's ambitions was the "Made in China 2025" initiative. The program, designed to enable China to catch up, and then surpass, Western prowess in high tech, became a central feature of Xi's campaign for the "rejuvenation of the Chinese nation."

Jane Perlez, *New York Times*

I found "Made in China 2025" very interesting. This is China announcing we're taking on the West. We're going to be the preeminent power in semiconductors, in artificial intelligence, in a list of ten things in the tech world, by 2025. And we're going to put a lot of resources into this. And people in the West went tut-tut-tut. It's state-supported industry. This isn't playing by the rules. Well, guess what? The United States is now belatedly trying to catch up.

The Wolf Warrior mentality—overconfidence bordering on hubris, coupled with deep-seated fears and heightened hostility to foreign reporters—was a recipe for ever-greater confrontation with the Western media. And it would play out most intensely as journalists attempted to cover Beijing's brutal crackdown targeting millions of Muslim Uighurs in the northwestern province of Xinjiang.

21

"REEDUCATION" IN XINJIANG

Since the 2009 riots in Urumqi, discontent had continued to simmer in Xinjiang, as the region's large Uighur Muslim minority chafed at the continued migration of ethnic Han Chinese to the province and the steadily tightening controls imposed by the Communist Party.

A small minority of Uighurs turned to terrorism. In the fall of 2013, Uighurs were blamed for an incident in Beijing in which a car plowed into a crowd in Tiananmen Square, leaving five people dead. In 2014, a group of knife-wielding attackers slashed their way through a train station in Kunming, the capital of Yunnan province, killing twenty-nine people, while a series of other incidents in Xinjiang itself left dozens more dead. The episodes shook a Chinese leadership already deeply suspicious about the loyalty of the Uighur population.

As a Beijing-based reporter for Reuters, Megha Rajagopalan had covered these incidents. By mid-2017, as the newly accredited correspondent for *Buzzfeed*, she began to hear reports of camps where large numbers of Uighurs were being held for "reeducation."

Megha Rajagopalan, *Buzzfeed*

I was at drinks with a colleague from one of the wire services. He and a photographer had just taken a trip there and had hired a Uighur driver. At the end of this trip, their driver had come to them and said, "I am happy to have worked with you, but I may not see you again." They said, "Why?" And he said, "Well, I've been told I'm going to a reeducation center." And I'm like, "Well, what's that?" Then we started to hear from Uighur exile activists that things were starting to get a lot tighter. So, what I wanted to do was figure out what this reeducation thing was.

To learn more, Rajagopalan flew to Turkey, a country with which the Uighurs share linguistic, religious, and cultural similarities, and which, since the 1950s, had been the destination of choice for Uighurs fleeing China. As the home of the largest Uighur diaspora in the world—by some accounts numbering close to fifty thousand—it was easy for her to meet numerous Uighur exiles, who told her of camps in Xinjiang where friends and relatives were being detained.

Megha Rajagopalan, *Buzzfeed*

I asked everyone, "Do you know what these reeducation camps are?" Then I met a Uighur activist who said, "There's a place like that very near to where I used to live in Kashgar." He explained where it was in relation to the hotel or the street, and so then I went to find it.

Kashgar, once an oasis town on the Silk Road, and long the cultural heart of Uighur society, was in southern Xinjiang. Barely thirty minutes after checking into her hotel there, Rajagopalan had a visit from the police.

Megha Rajagopalan, *Buzzfeed*

The first thing they asked was, "Do you work for the New York Times?" I said no. They're like, "Well where do you work?" I said I work for this place called Buzzfeed, and I pulled out Buzzfeed.com on my phone. And, of course, it was a bunch of cat listicles and stuff like that. So they were like, "This seems fine. What are you going to report on?" And I said, "The everyday lives of people in Kashgar and Uighur people." And they said, "Well, this seems OK."

Nonetheless, Rajagopalan took no chances. Slipping out of her hotel before dawn to avoid surveillance and following the directions she had been given in Turkey, she was able to locate the camp she'd been told about, which was officially called the "Kashgar Professional Skills Education and Training Center."

Megha Rajagopalan, *Buzzfeed*

It was this huge compound with very high walls. They had propaganda posters like, "Cherish ethnic unity as if you cherish your own eyes." They had big gates, and there was a little police kiosk. The place was labeled something along the lines of "transformation through education." I took a picture and got chewed out by the police guard. I asked the guard what it was and went around to some of the local businesses. They sort of confirmed that it was what I thought it was.

Despite omnipresent surveillance, she found some local residents willing to talk. Said one Uighur, "People disappear into that place. So many people—many of my friends."[1]

Rajagopalan's long October 2017 *Buzzfeed* piece had the headline "This Is What a 21st Century Police State Really Looks Like." It contained her on-the-ground reporting in Xinjiang, as well as the accounts of the many Uighur exiles she had interviewed in Turkey—people who were afraid to have their names used, but talked about relatives disappearing into camps, or having to stop making phone calls home for fear of getting family members in Xinjiang into trouble.

The piece was the first major journalistic report on Beijing's intensified crackdown on the Uighurs, and the first one to confirm the existence of the detention camps. In the years that followed, the crackdown would become a staple of news coverage, as well as a source of growing tension between China and much of the rest of the world.

THE MISSING STUDENT

Soon after Rajagopalan's story came out, the AP's Gerry Shih also traveled to Turkey to investigate reports—which turned out to be true—that some Uighurs were joining radical Islamic guerrilla groups in Syria. Most of the Uighur exiles he met, however, were not militants. From them, he heard that growing numbers of Uighurs studying abroad were being summoned back to China—and then disappearing.

Gerry Shih, Associated Press

While I was in Turkey, the Uighur community there said a bunch of students had been called back to China. They said check this out. It is starting to become very worrying. Students are being told by officials to travel back and nobody is hearing from them. You need to find out what is happening.

From this, we got the first inklings of this massive network of reeducation camps. We didn't really know the extent. It was very difficult to travel inside Xinjiang. Communication was monitored between the people inside Xinjiang and the people outside. There was this cone of silence. People are scared to use WeChat and talk over the phone. You only get snippets of the full picture. So the Uighur diaspora wasn't sure what was happening. We knew that people overseas were being called back and disappearing. We also knew that people outside were telling us that their relatives were beginning to disappear to these reeducation centers.

As I was doing the militancy story in Turkey, I met students who had fled from Al-Azhar University in Cairo, because the Egyptians were helping the Chinese grab these people and deport them back to China. One family wanted to know about their brother, who was studying in Cairo, had been sent back, and never heard from again. They had heard from a relative in Urumqi that this kid may have died inside one of the centers, but they had no idea, and could not contact the mother. They asked me to go to Korla in southern Xinjiang, where the family is from. Because of this cone of silence, they had no way to call their mother and ask what happened to him.

The exiled relatives gave Shih the name and address of the mother of the missing student, and he traveled to Xinjiang to find her. Shih located the woman in a small village. She broke down as she told him she did not know if her son was dead or alive.

Gerry Shih, Associated Press

It was a traditional Uighur village with painted sun-bleached walls and tree-lined streets. We made sure there was nobody following us. We finally find the mother. Because of the danger, we didn't bring a translator. Her Chinese was pretty poor, so I had to have a Uighur in Turkey translate for me over the phone to ask about her son. She's like, "Yes, yes he did come back and then they came and took him away and I haven't seen him for months. Is he dead?" She was extremely worried. I had to tell her we had heard from other relatives that maybe he is, but I really don't know, and I'm sorry. She breaks down. I didn't really know what to do. I think it speaks to the complete murkiness in those days of what was going on with these people who had disappeared. What were their fates? Their families didn't know.

Later that day, Shih was detained by police, interrogated for an entire night, ordered to delete all his photographs, and followed by carloads of security agents until he left Xinjiang for Beijing. He never learned the fate of the missing student.

A COUNTERINSURGENCY WITHOUT AN INSURGENCY

During their visits, both Rajagopalan and Shih had been struck by the scale and intrusiveness of the surveillance. In addition to police on almost every street in Kashgar stopping people to ask for identification and, sometimes, inspect their cell phones, Rajagopalan wrote that "other equipment, like high-resolution cameras and facial recognition technology, is ubiquitous. In some parts of the region, Uighurs have been made to download an app to their phones that monitors their messages."[2] Shih too saw numerous police checkpoints and cameras and was briefly stopped outside a hotel by a police officer who said the public security bureau had been remotely tracking his movements by watching surveillance camera footage.

Spurred especially by Rajagopalan's reporting, the *Wall Street Journal*'s Josh Chin also decided to go to Xinjiang.

Josh Chin, *Wall Street Journal*

We were sort of racing Megha at the time to write the big Xinjiang surveillance story. We were worried about surveillance flying into Urumqi, so we ended up renting a car and driving in from [the neighboring province of] Gansu. As soon as you crossed into Xinjiang, you felt the difference. They had a security checkpoint at the border, and they pulled us out. There are security gates that everyone is supposed to go through, and they scan their ID card and their face. Tons of security—armed police with assault rifles. It felt like a counterinsurgency operation. From that moment on, I could hear my heart beating. There was so much tension. I don't think I have ever been more on edge reporting a story in China.

Along the highway to Urumqi, every few minutes you would pass surveillance cameras. We were constantly stopped. It was like nothing I had ever experienced before. Multiple times a day, being stopped, asked what we are doing. We concluded that as long as we kept moving, we wouldn't have any problems, because in China the police and security forces in any given area care a lot about what happens in their area, but don't really care outside of that. So we managed to get away with evading major problems by saying, "We're only here right now. We are on our way out of town."

At one point, we took a wrong turn and ended up on this dirt road. Out of nowhere, this SUV speeds past us, screeches to a halt, and blocks our way. Another car comes up behind us and blocks us in. We had twelve cops surrounding our car. They pulled us out and checked our documents. We were like, "What is this about? How did you find us?" They were, like, "Oh, a license plate scanner down the road noticed that you guys have an out-of-province license plate, and it sent an alarm to us, so we decided to investigate." It was quite effective. We had no idea where they came from and no indication we were being followed.

Chin's story in late December 2017 was headlined, "Twelve Days in Xinjiang: How China's Surveillance State Overwhelms Daily Life."

As these early reports emerged, Beijing said little about the camps, portraying its policy in Xinjiang as a reasonable response to the threat of terrorism. But the journalistic accounts clearly touched a raw nerve. At the end of 2017, Rajagopalan was called in by an official from the Beijing Public Security Department.

Megha Rajagopalan, *Buzzfeed*

He basically said, "We think some of your reports on human rights are wrong." I said, "If you have some specific things you want to correct, we are very open to that." He was like, "There is nothing in particular but you are wrong nonetheless."

Soon after, the government refused to renew her journalist's visa, effectively expelling her. In the summer of 2018, Rajagopalan left China, and moved to London.

By that point, China had become much more vigorous in pushing back against the intensifying international scrutiny and criticism. "There is no such thing as re-education centers," a Chinese official told a UN panel in Geneva. "There is no torture, persecution or disappearance of repatriated personnel."[3]

But journalists continued to dig. As the Chinese government was issuing its blanket denial, Josh Chin returned to Xinjiang, adopting a new strategy to avoid police detection.

Josh Chin, *Wall Street Journal*

Being half-Chinese, I have been mistaken for a Uighur before in Beijing. On this trip, I went by myself. I didn't take anything with me. I just walked around and used my iPhone. Just trying to blend in as much as possible. I ended up being able to move around without getting stopped. I even had a few Uighurs speak Uighur to me, assuming I was Uighur, which is a sign that it was working.

At the oasis city of Turpan, the site of an ancient Silk Road settlement, Chin was able to identify an internment camp. On one of its main buildings was a large sign in red Chinese characters, "Sense the Party's kindness, obey the Party's words, follow the Party's lead." Guards shouted at Chin to leave the area. Meanwhile, Chin's colleague, Jeremy Page, traveled to Almaty in neighboring Kazakhstan, where he interviewed Uighurs who had been detained and then fled China after being released, as well as others with relatives still being held. At the same time, Chin, Page, and fellow correspondent Eva Dou established contact with Planet Earth, a professional satellite company, and with Shawn Zhang, a law student in Vancouver, Canada, who had begun scouring Google Earth to locate images of camps in Xinjiang.

Josh Chin, *Wall Street Journal*

I worked with them to identify some of the camps, including one we had seen in our first story, which, when we checked it out on the satellite, had basically doubled in size in a year. None of us really knew that this open-source reporting, which has become a huge part of the Xinjiang story, was available. For China reporters, we never had a need to do this kind of reporting. You were always able to move around with relative freedom and relative safety, but in Xinjiang, because it was a sort of counterinsurgency without an insurgency, we had to use those methods.

On August 17, 2018, their story, with the headline "China's Uighur Camps Swell as Beijing Widens the Dragnet," was published. At the same time, Chris

Buckley was also working on the Xinjiang story. Like other reporters, he traveled to Turkey to interview Uighur refugees.

Chris Buckley, *New York Times*

Quite a lot of the Uighurs who had managed to flee were just too scared to have their names used. Given the amount of money it takes to essentially bribe your way out of Xinjiang, most of them were businesspeople, academics, doctors, professionals—people who had been a part of Xinjiang Chinese society as well and could speak Chinese and knew their way around the system. When you met them in Turkey, you could tell they were just terrified at speaking out about what they and their families had been going through.

Buckley then returned to China and made his way to Hotan, a town in Xinjiang on the edge of the Taklamakan Desert, where he found more evidence that the goal of Beijing's campaign was to erase any sense of Islamic identity among the Uighurs.

Chris Buckley, *New York Times*

They are trying to achieve a profound, even revolutionary, social transformation, so that in just a matter of a few years, they want to turn the Uighurs and other Muslim minorities into model minorities obedient to the central government, whose primary attachment and identification and ultimately language and values are with what is seen as the greater Chinese nation. It is a vast program of demographic, social, and political engineering.

Hotan felt like it was under martial law, with security and police outposts and checkpoints everywhere. In Hotan, nearly all the taxi drivers are Uighur. I used one driver to take me to the outskirts of the city, so I could go past some locations I wanted to see to get a sense of where they were and how I might get there. When we were coming back, we had to go through one of those big intimidating checkpoints, where they have security officers with guns walking on ramps above the checkpoints. He was taken away for about forty-five minutes. I waited in the taxi. I didn't want to leave him there. When he came out, it was like he'd seen a ghost. He looked terrified. I knew then that inadvertently, without going anywhere sensitive with him, I had brought him under intense pressure.

After that, even getting taxis, although it might be unavoidable some-times, was something I would do sparingly. I spent a lot of time walking around and going on buses. They used to hate it when you went on buses, because they never knew when you were going to get off. Catching buses became part of my technique. You get to go past checkpoints, see how people were treated. They would always send some worried-looking plainclothes security officers on the bus to watch you. But nonetheless, you could keep an eye on what was happening, and jump off when you wanted. I had spoken to Uighurs who pointed me where to look for detention sites, and I figured out how to get to this industrial zone on the edge of Hotan, where the pictures in the story are from.

TURNING A CITY INTO A PRISON

A month after Buckley's story, headlined "China Is Detaining Muslims in Vast Numbers. The Goal: 'Transformation,'" came out, he and Paul Mozur returned to Xinjiang. With his focus on technology, as he scoured the Chinese Internet, Mozur had discovered the existence of a facial recognition system specifically targeting Uighurs.

Paul Mozur, *New York Times*

We discovered this system that was automatically looking for Uighurs, no mat-ter where you are in the country. We are seeing it in Shanghai, in Hangzhou, in Henan. There's a facial recognition algorithm that is trying to identify the person, but then it tries to get characteristics. Is the person a Uighur? It says, "rec Uighur," and it just blows your mind, because they have literally automated racial profiling. They have put up these cameras, and any time a Uighur walks by, it's registering it. To plug in a single ethnicity at that level is disturbing.

Mozur and Buckley decided the focus of the story would be to see what it was like to live under such an intrusive surveillance system. This time, they made no effort to disguise their presence.

Paul Mozur, *New York Times*

People had talked about the surveillance state in Xinjiang, but nobody had really gotten into great depth about how it worked and what it was doing. We set out to understand that, and chronicle what it felt like. Chris and I went out in October of 2018. You land. They pick you up. Probably somebody comes and asks you who you are. When you get to your hotel, there's usually a PSB [Public Security Bureau] official there, sitting, waiting to talk to you. You realize you can't do anything. You can't interview a single person, because any time you buy a vegetable from somebody in the streets, they get that person's ID and record it to have a debrief with them about what you said and what you were doing. The idea that it was worth risking it to try to talk to someone, when we knew that so many hundreds of thousands of people were disappearing into the camps, was crazy.

What we did mostly was walking, trying to either video or photograph different elements of the security state—propaganda in the mosques, mosques closed, businesses abandoned. Checkpoints were everywhere, and they would delete all your photos. What I would do is run to these gross public bathrooms. They would come in with me in the stall next to me, or in the urinal. I would download the data and try to send some back and put in a bunch of USB drives and hide them, and then go walk into a checkpoint and get stuff deleted and do it again. That was how we collected enough information and photos and videos to do a proper multimedia piece about what it looked like and what it felt like.

Chris Buckley, *New York Times*

Not talking to people makes it sound very unrewarding. But it's sort of like being an anthropologist in a place where you didn't know the language. Even if we were very cautious about talking to people, there was a lot to be learned simply by looking at how security worked, how people interacted with each other, how they interacted with the police, how the police treated them, how the checkpoints worked, how much security there was around schools, hospitals, and other public buildings.

In addition to their on-the-ground reporting, the *Times* correspondents also conducted additional research online, some of it in collaboration with Victor Gevers, a Dutch security researcher. Gevers discovered an unsecured database stored online by SenseNets, a Chinese surveillance company, which he shared with the *Times*. It contained striking details about the scale of the monitoring in Xinjiang, including facial recognition records and ID scans for 2.5 million of Urumqi's 3.5 million people.

Paul Mozur, *New York Times*

Gevers is a white hat hacker. He looks for open databases, and if he sees something risky, he puts it out there to warn the world. He started looking at China. Seeing what he was finding, it was like, we need to do this—finding patents, digging through patent databases and procurement documents and sourcing, and triangulating to put together the whole story.

The months of research led, in the spring of 2019, to two powerful stories. One was a deep dive into the companies and technology that created and operated the Xinjiang surveillance system. The second was a multimedia piece, using photos and video clips Mozur and Buckley had surreptitiously taken on their travels to document, as the headline put it, "How China Turned a City Into a Prison."[4] As one example, it included a photo of a stretch of a street in which twenty surveillance cameras could be seen, and another photo of Uighurs passing through a security checkpoint to enter a mosque, where they prayed under police security cameras mounted on a wall.

Chris Buckley, *New York Times*

This was just a small insight into the momentousness of what people are going through out there.

Indeed, despite Beijing's strident denials, the reporting on Xinjiang was making it clear that China's campaign against the Uighurs—combining the most sophisticated technology and the crudest forms of repression—had created a human rights crisis the world was finding increasingly difficult to ignore.

22

"I STARTED TO CRY"

Continuing media coverage of the mass detentions and the effort to wipe out the Uighurs' cultural heritage turned Chinese policy in Xinjiang into a controversial international issue. Ironically, many Muslim nations, often those receiving major investments as part of the Belt and Road initiative or otherwise leery of offending Beijing, remained silent. But in the West, there was a growing chorus of condemnation. Many international companies doing business in China found themselves caught in the crossfire.

The *Wall Street Journal*'s Chao Deng and Eva Dou traveled to Xinjiang to explore the business angle.

Chao Deng, *Wall Street Journal*

Xinjiang was a huge producer of cotton and garments. We were trying to trace the suppliers of Western companies. We narrowed it down to this town called Aksu in southern Xinjiang because there were a bunch of suppliers and a textile industry/campus there.

Like other reporters, Deng and Dou found it difficult to talk to people. Officials frequently interrupted interviews. In one case, a young Uighur woman admitted that she had been in a "vocational training program," and that, "before, I used to have extremist thoughts, but now they're all gone." Officials abruptly took the woman into an adjoining room. When she returned, she told Deng and Dou that she had been reprimanded for revealing a secret. "Even speaking of it [the camp] is not allowed," she said.[1]

Deng's attempt to take photographs in Aksu led to even greater problems.

Chao Deng, *Wall Street Journal*

I had taken this photo of a building with a slogan. My minder said I couldn't take photos of this building. I continued to do so. I think I pushed a little bit too far, and he said it was a military building. They accused me of taking photos of a military compound. For a whole night, Eva and I were in an office being videotaped, and having to apologize and write a confession. My original statement was something like, "I accidentally took a photo of a military building, and I promise not to endanger China's national security." But they wouldn't allow me to inject the word "accidentally," so I had to rewrite my statement and take it out. It was very nerve-wracking. We were just worried that we weren't going to be able to get out of there. I was basically just writing what I was told.

Still, Deng and Dou were able to document that supply chains originating in Xinjiang were providing products to companies including Adidas, Gap, and H & M. In addition, they discovered that the Hong Kong–based Esquel Group, the world's largest contract shirt maker, whose customers included Calvin Klein, Tommy Hilfiger, Nike, and Patagonia, had set up spinning mills in Xinjiang near the region's cotton fields.

Chao Deng, *Wall Street Journal*

It was the first comprehensive piece about sourcing from Xinjiang. Eva and I broke the fact that some of these bigger names were connected to Xinjiang. Western companies only started looking into their supply chains when we started calling them asking for comment, so they were basically forced to say we will look into this.

THE DAUGHTER AND THE CHILDREN

But the repression continued, with the authorities particularly targeting Uighurs with overseas connections. In September 2019, exiled Uighurs living in Australia and Sweden told *Washington Post* bureau chief Anna Fifield the story of Mayila Yakufu. After sending money from her parents' savings—the product of years running a trading business in Xinjiang before emigrating to Australia in 2007—Mayila had been detained and accused of "financing terrorism."

Anna Fifield, *Washington Post*

The story was about the family of a woman who had been imprisoned for "terrorist financing" for sending money to family members in Australia so they could buy a house. But all the reporting was done on the phone with family members in Australia and Sweden, and experts and exiles. Then I went to Yining. The family gave me a list of places they had liked to go to, so I just went and got atmosphere and color and took some photos. I didn't actually do any reporting. It is a very strange situation. Usually as a foreign correspondent, you go places to talk to people. But when I went by myself on these trips to Xinjiang, I was actively not talking to people for fear of putting them in danger.

Meanwhile, as reporting on Xinjiang became increasingly difficult, the Chinese Internet remained a valuable resource. Amy Qin of the *New York Times* found a diary online written by a Han Chinese teacher sent to Xinjiang to teach Uighur children. The diary noted that some of his students did not have families because their parents were in detention. Of one first-grader, he wrote, "The most heartbreaking thing is that the girl is often slumped over the table alone and crying. When I asked around, I learned it was because she missed her mother."[2]

To avoid surveillance, Qin booked a ticket to Xinjiang at the last minute, hid her cell phone in a bag that blocked the signal, carried multiple USB sticks to save her photos, and tried to do most of her reporting on her first day, before checking into a hotel, which would report her presence to the police.

Amy Qin, *New York Times*

The way you prepare for going to Xinjiang is like you feel that you're—I don't know what it's like to be a spy, but I feel like maybe that's what it's like. The idea is that you have to do all your reporting on the first day. Hopefully you can do it before they are onto you.

Qin found a school that matched the description she had read online.

Amy Qin, *New York Times*

There was a sightseeing spot nearby, so we asked the driver to take us there. Of course, the police were following us. We decided we were not going to talk to anyone. We went to the school. It matched everything that we learned from the Internet. So we got confirmation that the school exists. We saw the dormitories. They were very little kids, like five, six years old.

Using the teacher's diary, her own observations, and government documents she found online, she filed a report about the nearly half-million Uighur students separated from their families and undergoing education and indoctrination at Party-run schools.

FERKAT'S MOTHER

Throughout 2019, Paul Mozur maintained contact with Ferkat Jawdat, a Uighur who had moved to the United States in 2011 to join his father, who had emigrated in 2006. However, his mother, Minewer Tursun, had remained in China, unable to get permission to leave. Ferkat became an American citizen, and, after his mother was detained, one of the most outspoken critics of Chinese behavior in Xinjiang. On a trip to the United States in early 2019, Mozur got in touch with Ferkat about doing an episode of the *New York Times* podcast *The Daily* on the Uighurs and his mother's plight.

Paul Mozur, *New York Times*

He was willing to go on the record. I met with him. He chain-smokes as he is talking. It is clearly incredibly traumatic. We put the episode out. Days after, his mother is let out of the camps. She calls him and talks to him on WeChat but is praising the Communist Party all the time. She has to play up this stuff to be allowed out, and there are people watching her. Eventually Ferkat gets this call from a PSB [Public Security Bureau] officer on WeChat saying, "If you just stop speaking out, if you don't go to these public events anymore, maybe we can get her out for you, but you need to put in some good faith here and shut the fuck up." Ferkat kind of debates this for a little while, and of course I am having him record it all. He gives me everything, and we do an episode about it. But he decides that it's not worth it. We decide finally, "Why don't I try to visit her?"

On a WeChat call with his mother, Ferkat held up a piece of paper on which he had written, "Mom, I'm sending someone to you to talk to you." She put her finger to her mouth and shook her head to signal her agreement, despite the risks. In August 2019, Mozur, now back in China, flew to Urumqi, and then to Yili in northern Xinjiang.

Paul Mozur, *New York Times*

At this point, I have a good understanding of how the surveillance system works. The main way they know you are in a place is hotel registration and transportation because both of those are registered in national databases. So I knew to buy tickets literally hours before the flight, because nobody is going to be awake to check this stuff until the morning, when they get in. I take a 5 AM flight out of Urumqi, get out of the plane, and there is nobody here. I buy two umbrellas— it's a big rain—pull up my collar, pull down my hat, get into a cab and I'm off. There was nobody following me. I stroll right into his mother's house. I sat next to her for two hours interviewing her with Ferkat on the line to translate from Uighur into English. We got testimony out of her about the camps, how terrible they were. While she is doing this, I am hiding recordings, running three recordings on three different phones, and stopping and saving them and dumping them into different USBs, with the idea that the police will eventually show up.

Indeed, at 9 AM, local Communist Party officials did arrive, and Mozur left immediately. But he made it back to Beijing with the interview, which aired on another episode of *The Daily* in early December.

Paul Mozur, *New York Times*

After we ran that final episode, she was put under a new level of surveillance, where she can't be in the living room of her house with her family without secret police being there. She can't meet with a friend without police sitting with her in the café. Her Internet service has been mostly cut. Her TV has been cut. It's almost "death by surveillance," where you are ostracized in the community because everybody knows that they are going to have to deal with the police when she is around, although she is able to communicate with her son to some degree. Later Ferkat would share with me that somebody he knew, basically an intermediary, sent a threat from the head of the Public Security bureau in

Yili saying, "If this guy [Mozur] comes back again, we will basically nongsi your mother." It isn't exactly, "Go out and murder her," but it is like, "Let her die. We'll find a way for her to die."

THE XINJIANG PAPERS

In late 2019, Chris Buckley and Austin Ramzy came into possession of over four hundred pages of internal Chinese government documents that outlined specific policies for repressing Xinjiang's Uighur population. It was what the *Times* described as "one of the most significant leaks of government papers from inside the Communist Party in decades,"[3] and provided an unprecedented inside view of the crackdown. The documents included the text of a secret speech Xi Jinping gave after visiting Xinjiang in which he told officials to show "absolutely no mercy," as well as directives and reports about the surveillance and control of the Uighur population.

Austin Ramzy, *New York Times*

One of the big things the documents told us was how focused Xi was on the question of Xinjiang. Those documents don't have him saying "build these camps." What they have is him traveling through Xinjiang and saying there is a problem, you need to do more to take care of this problem of terrorism, separatism, of religious extremism. Then you see local officials using Xi's speech to justify their plans and the effort that eventually led to this mass incarceration campaign.

A few of those documents talk about the camps in detail. At first the existence of the camps was denied by Beijing. Then they were described as 'vocational programs' essentially for those who might otherwise go astray—to teach them Chinese and basic skills. But these documents make it pretty clear this is punishment. This is not about training or anything.

Chris Buckley, *New York Times*

It is a very partial but revealing look into how decision-making happened in Xinjiang, so that over a period of two years, you had this extraordinary buildup of mass detentions. It's not the full story by any means, but it shows policy-making at different levels, and it shows thinking at Xi Jinping's level.

The Chinese reacted with fury. The Foreign Ministry did not deny the authenticity of the documents, but said the report was "a clumsy patchwork of selective interpretation" that was "deaf and blind to the facts."[4] China's ambassador to Britain, Liu Xiaoming, told journalists, "I would say there's no so-called labor camps. These are vocational, educational, and training centers. They are there for the prevention of a terrorist. What we are doing is nothing to do with eradication of ethnic groups, religious. In Xinjiang, religious freedom is fully respected."[5]

Barely a week later came another leak—twenty-four pages of Xinjiang internal government documents from 2017 that detailed measures needed for stricter security at internment camps. The documents were provided by Uighurs outside China to the International Consortium of Investigative Journalists, a Washington-based nonprofit that brought together multiple news organizations, including the *New York Times*, to examine them. The documents undermined Chinese claims that its policy toward the Uighurs was benign. The headline in the story written by Ramzy and Buckley was "Leaked China Files Show Internment Camps Are Ruled by Secrecy and Spying."

Austin Ramzy, *New York Times*

The leak just said to me there are people [in the Communist Party] who objected to what was happening in Xinjiang to such a strong degree that they were willing to risk their personal safety.

THE GENOCIDE DEBATE

The scale of repression in Xinjiang led a growing number of governments, analysts, and human rights activists to accuse Beijing of committing genocide against the Uighurs. For journalists, the charge of genocide—defined in international law as the commission of specified acts "with intent to destroy, in whole or in part, a national, ethnical, racial or religious group"[6]—raised complex questions about how to characterize events in Xinjiang in their coverage.

Josh Chin, *Wall Street Journal*

The Journal *as an institution is really careful about that stuff. We even had this debate about whether we could call the camps "concentration camps" or not. We ended up calling them "internment camps." We felt that calling them "concentration camps," even though that is how they are referred to in Chinese—if you directly translate from Chinese, they use the word "concentrated"—was inevitably going to evoke the Nazi comparison. And we weren't really sure what the camps were, and what was happening in them, so it might have taken the story in a direction that we weren't really prepared for it to go. So we conservatively decided to go with "internment camps" at the time.*

With "genocide," we have been attributing it. The challenge is that it's new. We have never really seen this before. Of course, elements of what is happening in Xinjiang have happened before, obviously. That is probably why the story is so powerful, because of the historical parallels. But at the same time, there's never been a regime that did what China is trying to do in Xinjiang, using the tools that China is using. I think everyone is struggling with this. Everyone is reaching for these twentieth-century terms because that's all we have. But they don't really fit.

Austin Ramzy, *New York Times*

I don't think what's happening in Xinjiang is at all a genocide in the sense of a mass extermination. But I do think there is an effort to restrict population, to restrict culture and language, and things like that. If there were to be a formal designation of genocide it would be along those lines. But with the U.S. declaration [that China was committing genocide] it became seen as a very political thing, which I think complicates the issue even more.

Megha Rajagopalan, *Buzzfeed*

It is important to distinguish between terms like "genocide" and a term like "ethnic cleansing." The reason is that "ethnic cleansing" is a term that has no legal definition. It means different things to different people. We can argue about whether something is "ethnic cleansing" or not. "Genocide," on the other hand, has a precise definition in international law. There have been, to me, compelling arguments that this fits that definition. The attributes that can make a particular situation a genocide go well beyond mass state-sponsored killing. For that reason, the debate actually matters. I don't think it is just about semantics, because if a government labels something as a "genocide" it carries certain responsibilities and can also persuade policy actors.

Chris Buckley, *New York Times*

I think it's a mistake to become overinvested in the genocide label. Whatever is happening in Xinjiang, there are many crimes against humanity that could be leveled at what's been happening there. So to become so politically and emotionally invested in the idea that we have to call it "genocide" is probably a mistake of political tactics. I think it just distracts from taking in the enormity of what's happening there.

Steven Lee Myers, *New York Times*

You can debate that legally, and people do, but there is no debating what is happening there and what its goal is. It is to make people obedient subjects of a one-party state.

UNCOVERING THE CAMPS

After her expulsion, *Buzzfeed*'s Megha Rajagopalan moved to London, but continued to follow developments in Xinjiang. At a workshop about online investigative reporting in Berlin in 2018, she met Alison Killing, a British architect who used maps and data to look at human rights issues.

Megha Rajagopalan, *Buzzfeed*

I had gotten attached to the story and wanted to continue doing it. Alison got really interested. As an architect her thoughts were about the structure of the camps, and all the spatial questions around understanding the Xinjiang issue. We started to talk about whether we can use satellite imagery to find more of the camps.

They began by looking at maps on the Chinese search engine Baidu. When they zoomed in on the location of a known camp—one that had previously been visited or identified by journalists—a light grey tile would mask the details.

Megha Rajagopalan, *Buzzfeed*

At that time there were a number of camp locations that were known. Alison pulled up a couple. She noticed there were these gray squares saying the image cannot be produced. She was like "huh?" It's possible that Baidu didn't have the image. It was cloudy that day, or something when they took the photo. But there is actually a different kind of grey square that appears when that is the case. Immediately, we thought this is probably censorship. We did a test of a few of them, and it turned out all the known camps had these grey squares. Then we thought, "What if we find all of the gray squares and that gives a clue as to where the camps might be?"

But the process wasn't so simple.

Alison Killing, Architect

We ended up with an absolutely crazy number of masked locations. What they were censoring was anything of strategic value—industrial estates, wind farms, solar farms, power lines, military bases, military training areas, and the camps. The way we decided to get this number down was by focusing along major infrastructure routes—roads, cities, and towns and the areas around them. For camps, you are going to need gas and electricity, water, and Internet. It's easier to connect to municipalities than dig a channel three hundred kilometers out into the desert. You need to get materials and people there. People work there. They need to live somewhere. It makes sense that these places are near infrastructure and large settlements.

They enlisted the help of an Austrian computer programmer, Christo Buschek.

Alison Killing, Architect

Christo built a tool that overlaid the locations of masked tiles on Google Maps. There would be a pinpoint over the location where there was a masked tile, and then I would go through them one by one. We could see where the censorship was in Baidu, and then go and look at a platform where there was no censorship like Google Earth and check what was actually there. I had a moment of, "Oh my God, they are trying to hide all these places, and in doing so, they've revealed the entire network. And we can use their attempts at concealing this to probably find all of it." That felt kind of unbelievable.

Since around seventy of these places had already been found, we had pretty good clues as to what they looked like. There are two sorts of camps. There are camps from early on the program, which were built in late 2016, early 2017. They were former schools and hospitals and even apartment buildings converted into camps. In those places, you would see weird things, like blue-roofed industrial sheds built in the spaces between the apartment buildings. You would see walls that had been built around the compound walling off part of the compound. And you would see barbed-wire passageways leading between buildings, and barbed-wire pens up against the buildings. We knew that they were camps. Based on those, we could say what the characteristics were of this sort of camp. So that gave us a rubric that we could use.

Then, starting in about 2017, they began building these more permanent camps. Those for the most part looked like prisons elsewhere in China. They would have a perimeter wall that would be one and a half or two meters thick, guard towers at the corners and a few places along the wall. Then multiple levels of barbed-wire fencing on either side of the wall. So very clearly very heavily fortified places. So that's what we did with satellite imagery.

To corroborate their findings, Rajagopalan interviewed two dozen former prisoners who had fled Xinjiang. They told her of torture, hunger, overcrowding, solitary confinement, forced birth control, and other abuses, as well as providing invaluable details about the location and physical layout of camps where they had been held.

Megha Rajagopalan, *Buzzfeed*

All of this stuff is irrelevant if you don't have a sense of the human beings that are being harmed. That why it is important to talk to exiles. The other thing is that exiles can tell you things you can't see in a satellite image. In a satellite image you cannot see that there are lines painted on the hallway floor, for instance, that mark patterns where they have to walk, the surveillance cameras on the sides of the bathrooms, or stuff like that. There are a lot of things for which you need people to put together. So, we spent a lot of time basically trying to match exiles to particular campsites.

I struggled emotionally. The worst moment was—we had done this six-hour interview with a Uighur woman in Kazakhstan, and the Kazakh government was threatening to deport her back to China, where she was likely to be sent to a camp again. She had had the most harrowing experience in this camp. She told us about it at length, and she was coughing the entire time because she was sick. We were so tired and so hungry, and it was such a difficult story, that my interpreter and I walked out, and it started to snow, and we literally sat at a restaurant for an hour and didn't say anything. It was moments like that. I remember getting back to London from a trip. It was such a disconnect after talking to all these camp survivors seeing normal people that I just started to cry in the taxi. I couldn't deal with it.

Ultimately, they were able to confirm the existence of 268 newly built camps, some big enough to house more than ten thousand people. Their six-part series appeared in *Buzzfeed* during the autumn of 2020. In 2021, Rajagopalan, Killing, and Buschek were awarded the Pulitzer Prize in International Reporting "for a series of clear and compelling stories that used satellite imagery and architectural expertise, as well as interviews with two dozen former prisoners, to identify a vast new infrastructure built by the Chinese government for the mass detention of Muslims." It was *Buzzfeed*'s first Pulitzer Prize.

23

EPIDEMIC

In early January 2020, reports emerged of a mysterious pneumonia-like illness in Wuhan, the largest city in central China. With a population of over eleven million, it was the capital of Hubei province and a major transportation hub, with river, highway, high-speed rail, and air links to the rest of China. The local authorities initially downplayed the outbreak, saying little, and insisting there was no evidence of human-to-human transmission. In Beijing, however, CNBC bureau chief Eunice Yoon wasn't so sure. As a Singapore-based correspondent, she had covered the SARS outbreak of 2003.

Eunice Yoon, CNBC

The government at the time [January 2020] was saying it's not such a big deal. It's only transmitting through animals. But because of my SARS experience, I was thinking this could be a big thing.

On January 8, the *Wall Street Journal* became the first major publication to report that Chinese scientists had discovered a new strain of coronavirus through genetic sequencing of samples from pneumonia patients in Wuhan. Natasha Khan, who had been born and raised in Hong Kong and had covered science and health for six years for Bloomberg News before joining the *Journal*, broke the story.

Natasha Khan, *Wall Street Journal*

I had gotten the confirmation from several people. I was very confident that it was accurate. I think the significant part of the story was that they had sequenced the strain and had found it was a coronavirus that had never been seen or discovered before. The story was published at 8:30 PM local time here. It was picked up by ProMED-Mail. It is sort of this alert service for the infectious disease community.

The report embarrassed Chinese officials, who had been forbidden by the government from publishing any details. The next day, state media revealed the discovery, and, the following day, announced the first known death. COVID-19 was about to sweep the People's Republic, engulf the world—and provide the American press corps in China with the story of a lifetime.

For the next week, as Wuhan hosted a major Communist Party provincial congress, the authorities remained largely silent.

Eunice Yoon, CNBC

But then, we started hearing through hospital workers in Beijing who knew doctors in Wuhan who were saying it was spreading from human to human. I got scared because I thought there is too much chatter now in the medical community about the problems in Wuhan. There was definitely something there, and it was spreading.

One of the earliest whistleblowers was a Wuhan doctor named Li Wenliang. He had raised the alarm on Chinese social media in late December, sending a message on WeChat to a group of his medical school classmates about the mysterious SARS-like infection, only to be reprimanded by police for "spreading rumors." But on January 20, China's most prominent epidemiologist, Zhong Nanshan, who had won praise for his role in combating the SARS epidemic, confirmed the existence of human-to-human transmission.

Reporters headed to Wuhan.

Shan Li, *Wall Street Journal*

We were going to just bring surgical masks, and then a colleague of mine in the Beijing bureau pushed three N-95 masks at me and she said, "You have to take it and wear it." I said, "Is this really necessary?" She said, "Please, do it for me." I took the three N-95 masks, and off we went. Wuhan was completely quiet. There was basically no one on the streets. We went to the main COVID hospital that had been designated to treat patients. It was just packed with relatives handing over food and stuff.

FIRST REPORTS

Ramy Inocencio, who had been a Peace Corps volunteer in China before working for CNN and the *Wall Street Journal* in Hong Kong, and then for Bloomberg TV in New York, had become the CBS News Beijing correspondent in mid-2019. Arriving in Wuhan on January 20, he and his camera crew immediately headed for the Huanan Seafood Wholesale Market. In addition to seafood, the market also sold exotic wildlife, including hedgehogs, badgers, salamanders, snakes, and civets, which were believed to have triggered the SARS outbreak in 2003. The fact that some of those initially diagnosed with the new disease had worked at the market added to the speculation that it might have been a location where the virus jumped from animals to humans.

Ramy Inocencio, CBS News

We needed to get video of the market and do a piece to camera there. We did the stand-up outside one of the gates. Then a guy started walking quickly towards me shouting, "Don't film here. Don't film here." Before he got too close, I stopped filming. We jumped in the van and drove off.

Outside the Jinyintan Hospital, as ambulances were driving in, Inocencio interviewed several people. One man, whose wife was a patient, refused to go on camera.

Ramy Inocencio, CBS News

He was really upset. He said the government couldn't be trusted but didn't want to get in trouble for saying that.

With enough elements for a story, the CBS team headed back to Beijing to file.

Ramy Inocencio, CBS News

We didn't think we need to be there anymore. We thought we could fly down again if we need to. Got to the Wuhan airport, and it was packed. Everyone was wearing a mask. It was clear that everyone was trying to get the hell out of there. I thought, "Shit. This is SARS all over again."

Meanwhile, David Culver, a Cuban American who had just been hired as CNN's Beijing correspondent after working in local TV news in the United States, arrived in Wuhan with a camera crew.

David Culver, CNN

We took the train from Beijing. By the time we arrived, it was an eerie ghost town. I wondered, "What are we walking into?" On January 22, we gathered a fair amount of video. At the market, we did a drive-by to get video, and then we pulled up to jump out. It was just a few seconds, and they were on us, and said, "You have to go." At the hospital, they did have security outside. We were able to do standups in front of it, but that was the extent of it.

Shan Li spent that day visiting hospitals, where she saw throngs of relatives waiting to deliver food to patients.

Shan Li, *Wall Street Journal*

Mostly what I remember from that day is this air of mystery. Everyone we talked to had different theories about, how transmissible is it? My brother's cousin's business partner caught it and died. Did he have anything to do with the market? Did he live near the market? No one basically had a clue what was going on.

LOCKDOWN

At 3 AM the next morning, Shan Li was awakened in her hotel room by a phone call from bureau chief Jonathan Cheng.

Shan Li, *Wall Street Journal*

Jon said, "Wuhan is going under lockdown. What do you want to do?" My first thought was, "This is fake news. Where did you get that idea? You can't do that to a city this big." Then Jon said, "No, no, no. The government announced it. This is happening. What do you want to do?" My instinct was I wanted to stay.

Jonathan Cheng, *Wall Street Journal*

I remember that night very well because I hardly slept. One of my deputy editors was Yoko Kubota. She was very, very concerned. Shan is on one end of the spectrum. Yoko is on the other. Yoko kept arguing, "We need to pull her out. I can't live with the possibility that she gets sick." Shan was like, "No, I'm here. I'm good."

Shan Li, *Wall Street Journal*

I went to the train station to do reporting, because I figured there would be a ton of people trying to get out. I got there about 5 or 5:30. Completely empty. I realized it was Chinese New Year. Everyone would be at home because it's a holiday. Then I talked things over with our security guy in Hong Kong. He said, "How many N-95 masks do you have?" I told him I have three. He said, "You have to leave. That's not enough masks. We don't know whether we will be able to get any to you during lockdown, because we have never seen a lockdown like this before." Luckily, when I got to the train station, I had bought a ticket to Beijing just in case. It was the last train before the lockdown. Then, things started getting really manic because people had woken up and were just running to the station. By then, all the tickets had been sold out. It was mayhem. Everyone was confused. There was a lot of screaming. They brought in police and military guys. I was running around and interviewing people. And people were just stunned at what was happening. At that point, I decided to leave.

Jonathan Cheng, *Wall Street Journal*

Shan wrote a great story about being at the train station with all this panic all around her. And no sooner did she get back to Beijing than she said, "We need to go back to Wuhan."

CNN's David Culver had also received a 3 AM call from a colleague in Beijing.

David Culver, CNN

He said the city is going on lockdown. We need to get you guys out of there. I called my photographer and producer. What stood out to me in that moment was not our safety, because you are on an adrenaline high. But then I looked around the train station. I saw moms and dads handing off their kids to grand-parents or other relatives, and they were crying. I also looked at my photographer and producer. They were starting to think, "Should we leave? Should we even be getting on this train?" There was a moment of saying, "Are we leaving the story behind?" But our desire was countered by folks who saw the bigger picture, and said, "Let's keep telling the story. We don't know if they will shut down Internet or if they will block you being able to report." In hindsight, it was the right decision, but it really weighed on us.

At the same time, we had a producer in New York from Go There *[a recently launched CNN show focusing on a single topic that was streamed on Facebook]. She said, "Can you start doing selfies? Just record little things here and there." And I did, about the madness of it all. They ended up stringing that together, and it became one of the first indicators that this was a story people were interested in, because it is still the most watched news video ever on Facebook.*

INSIDE A CLOSED CITY

But as journalists and many residents were fleeing, Chris Buckley of the *New York Times* was arriving.

Chris Buckley, *New York Times*

I got on a train the morning the lockdown was announced. I'm thinking to myself, "Somebody is going to say, 'Hey, turn around, you have to go back.'" It doesn't happen. Eventually, we get to Wuhan. I had this image of the train station lined with police officers telling people to stay out of the city, and certainly keeping out reporters. But the station essentially had no security at all. I thought, "What's happened?" I stepped outside, and there's not much security either.

I found a driver and started going round to the hospitals. You see lots of people, especially older people, waiting to be tested. I did lots of interviews outside hospitals. I did get a sense that a lot of people have flu-like symptoms, or pneumonia-like symptoms. You could tell it was getting serious because people were being wheeled into hospitals, or ambulances arriving all the time. You could see inside overcrowded reception areas trying to deal with far too many people.

The next morning, as he left his hotel, Buckley noticed that he was being followed.

Chris Buckley, *New York Times*

I am always very wary to see if I am being followed. I noticed the telltale SUV. I take a mental note of the number plate. I note that when we turn a corner, we are still being followed. I asked my driver to drop me off about a kilometer from one of the major hospitals. The SUV stopped about seventy yards behind us. One of the guys gets out and starts following me. I waited until he was close and then turned around and basically told him to piss off. "The city is in crisis. People are dying. Why are you wasting your time following me?" and told him to fuck off. He just jumped out of his skin and started walking off. For the rest of that day, I was followed, but at a distance and not intruding on interviews. For the rest of the time in Wuhan, I really wasn't followed at all.

Like Buckley, Amy Qin of the *Times* and Chao Deng of the *Wall Street Journal* also discovered that even though no one was allowed to leave, trains were still stopping in Wuhan.

Amy Qin, *New York Times*

You could talk to the conductor and ask them to let you off there. I was pretty scared, because at that point we had no idea what the situation was, or how dangerous it was. We didn't know was how tight the lockdown was going to be, or how difficult it would be to get out. We did not realize until once we were there. Then it kind of dawned on us that if any of us get sick, and all the hospitals are very overwhelmed right now, what would happen? We couldn't get medivaced out.

As the disease took hold, the reporters discovered, to their surprise, that they were generally able to operate without the usual harassment and interference.

Chao Deng, *Wall Street Journal*

It was bizarre. I did two weeks of unhindered reporting. The first week, it almost felt like I had walked into this place where access was almost unfettered, which is very strange in China. I remember going inside some of the field hospitals that were still under construction. I took this bus into this construction site with a bunch of Chinese construction workers. I was in PPE gear, and no one asked me any questions.

Amy Qin, New York Times

At that point we didn't know how transmissible the virus was. People were getting turned away from hospitals and going home and then infecting other family members. We went to this one hospital. In the emergency area, people were sitting around in this courtyard getting IV drips, because the hospital was so full. We met a family. They told us almost the entire family was sick except for the father, and one person had already died. That was so striking. This whole family got sick, so we decided to write a story. We didn't know how easily transmissible it was, and we also didn't know about asymptomatic spread. I don't know that that story was the trigger point where people were able to realize that, but looking back, several of the family members were sick right in front of us and had tested positive but had no symptoms at all.

THE HORROR STORIES MULTIPLY

Because of the risk, the logistical problems, or the small number of staff in China, many news organizations chose not to send reporters to Wuhan, covering the story from Beijing.

Anna Fifield, *Washington Post*

Because we were only a two-person bureau, we could not go to Wuhan because we could not risk one of us getting stuck there. So neither Gerry Shih nor I went.

Many Wuhan citizens were using WeChat and other Chinese social media to describe their plight. This became an invaluable source of information for correspondents not in the city.

Alice Su, *Los Angeles Times*

It was great for reporting, because people were posting phone numbers online and saying, "Please help me because my parents are dying. I can't get them into

*the hospital." Nobody was helping them. I just called these numbers and peo-
ple were talking because something devastating was happening.*

Meanwhile, the situation in Wuhan was steadily getting worse.

Chris Buckley, *New York Times*

*The horror stories really multiplied about a week in. That first week, it was cer-
tainly serious and getting more serious. Given the exponential spread of the
virus, it multiplied so much more over the following week or two and began to
appear as a much more serious crisis.*

Journalists reacted to the risks of covering the outbreak in different ways.
Alice Su had covered the Middle East before moving to Beijing.

Alice Su, *Los Angeles Times*

*I spent a lot of time in Iraq and Gaza and the West Bank. I was more scared
with COVID than I had been in hostile environments in the Middle East. All
we knew was that cases kept increasing. We knew so little about the disease
and we didn't know what was going to happen. I do think if it was [a] conflict
zone I wouldn't hesitate to go. But this ... there was just such a sense that
there was so much that we don't know. I chose not to go to Wuhan at that time.*

Chao Deng, *Wall Street Journal*

*I don't remember being scared so much as having a lot of adrenaline go through
me. Just tried to focus on what I need to do.*

Shan Li, *Wall Street Journal*

*We really didn't know that much, and it was a great story. I just have a science
fiction interest in infectious diseases, and I really wanted to see it for myself. It
was just too good to turn down.*

Gerry Shih, *Washington Post*

*It was scary. It's invisible. I guess that is probably the difference. In a conflict,
I suppose you more or less know where the threat is coming from, and who is*

on what side. With the virus, everybody is vulnerable. It could be anywhere. It does sort of make you feel a bit freaked out.

Chris Buckley, *New York Times*

If you told me now you were putting me in a time machine and sending me back there, I'd probably be a lot more anxious. But at the time, I didn't grasp how infectious it might be, and the idea of asymptomatic spread wasn't an established fact then. Things like that would have probably made me a lot more anxious if I had thought about them. The other thing—it's got nothing to do with heroics, but this is a great story, and I'm here, and there aren't very many other journalists here, and I have got to make this work. There is an excitement to it.

Initially, the authorities were so distracted by the exploding outbreak that local Chinese journalists suddenly discovered they had more space to cover the story without the usual tight controls.

David Culver, CNN

My producer started following very closely these Chinese local journalists who broke a lot of this early on. They had this brief window of freedom to independently report things. In that window, there was incredible, incredible detail of the stories coming out. Even on CCTV you saw images of people in tears, and it validated a lot of what we were seeing online. It also gave us, for that moment, the contacts of people who were speaking out and putting their name on record with the local Chinese journalists. So we said, "Let's contact some of them."

Chris Buckley, *New York Times*

We owe an enormous thanks to our colleagues in the Chinese media, who began revealing these stories and began pressing against censorship and exposing information.

THE DEATH OF LI WENLIANG

By the end of January, whistleblower Dr. Li Wenliang, who had treated infected patients, was himself seriously ill with COVID. In Beijing, David

Culver and his local producer managed to reach him on the phone. In between coughing fits, he described what was happening.

David Culver, CNN

He was being very candid about being punished for speaking out. He told us the timeline of when he initially reported it to his friends. He said he had got called in because someone had screenshot it and sent it out. So his name was tied to it. When that happened, he was told to sign a paper by the local police that said, "I will stop spreading rumors and lies." He signed it. He went back to work and contracted the virus.

It was Li Wenliang's only broadcast interview. But the doctor had been exchanging online messages with Chris Buckley. "If the officials had disclosed information about the epidemic earlier," he told Buckley, "I think it would have been a lot better. There should be more openness and transparency." Of his treatment by the police, he said, "I felt I was wronged, but I had to accept it. Obviously, I had been acting out of good will. I have felt very sad seeing so many people losing their loved ones."[1]

On February 7, Li Wenliang died. His death triggered an outpouring of grief on Chinese social media.

Chris Buckley, *New York Times*

There was this enormous, overwhelming wave of emotion on the Chinese Internet.

Anna Fifield, *Washington Post*

I remember seeing all my WeChat moments and all the candles. This public outpouring of grief and anger over the fact that the government had tried to silence criticism and this brave one had died. I think the government must have been very worried.

Chris Buckley, *New York Times*

In terms of the government's handling of public opinion, that was the real crisis point for them.

David Culver, CNN

I think that was a night when, if we thought there was going to be a turning point for this country in one direction or another, that was it. You started to feel the uncertainty of social stability. It was rocking. There was an uneasiness in the air. It felt like something could shift.

New York Times tech correspondent Paul Mozur had been tracking how the government was using surveillance tools as the outbreak worsened. Some months later, a hacker group calling itself C.C.P. Unmasked provided him with massive amounts of data they had retrieved from the Cyberspace Administration of China, including details on how the authorities reasserted control over the Internet in the wake of Li Wenliang's death. Working with two other New York Times colleagues and a reporter from Pro Publica, which had also been given the data, Mozur cowrote a long story with the headline "No 'Negative' News: How China Censored the Corona Virus."[2]

Paul Mozur, *New York Times*

We banded together with Pro Publica, and start this email exchange with the hackers, where we are slowly going through all the stuff they have, and they are providing more source code and proof to verify what they did. In the process, we realized that one of the companies they hacked was responsible for storing the day-to-day forums and communications of the Cyberspace Administration of China in Hangzhou. We have on a very, very local level, and on a city level, the day-to-day content management rules. You could basically see how the bureaucracy was run in a way we had never seen before.

Xi Jinping had created the Cyberspace Administration of China in 2014 to centralize the management of Internet censorship and propaganda. Li Wenliang's death produced its most serious crisis yet.

Paul Mozur, *New York Times*

When Li Wenliang died, they are told at first, "Don't do everything. Just get a part of it. Take down the severe ones, things that are calling for action, things that are over the top." And then like a week later they come back, and they are like, "OK, people are mourning, but we need to go back and take down more. Look for candles. Look for other things that would be indicating respect for Li

Wenliang." We see this order to basically pull Li from any trending topics and bury articles about him in the archives. At that point, within an hour, you can literally see—because people wrote about it—how he basically just drops off the trending category.

There's this kind of half-step that they do, which I don't think people understand, which is that you can allow space for people to talk about something without actually letting it go viral. You can let people shout into the wind, and other people won't see what they are saying. It won't go viral or be on any lists, but it will still be out there. Then later you come back and delete that stuff. You kind of let the shouting happen, but you put people in different rooms, so they are shouting by themselves almost. Then you go back and delete the shouts a week later. That's basically what happened.

This was the moment that Xi has been building for. When it came, they were able to effectively surf it and manage it in a way that was shockingly powerful. They pulled down everything, and people who tried to archive stuff got arrested. After a month or two, with enough propaganda about the world bringing viruses in and how China beat the virus and the world didn't, things turned.

David Culver, CNN

The way they got it under control was two-part. One was censorship: to remove as many of the posts as possible, and to start suppressing as quickly as possible. The other was a recrafting of the narrative: to portray Li as, yes, this man has died, but he is one of the front-line heroes that we have—a doctor who tried to do what he could, but the adversary that he faced was the local government. So it was all just local, local, local. Not the central government. The central government is the one who came in and recognized him as a martyr and recognized that the local government had been bad to him.

THE PARTY VS. THE VIRUS

At the same time, the Communist Party finally began to put its immense organizational clout to work to try to bring the outbreak under control.

Eunice Yoon, CNBC

It was incredible how China mobilized to get on top of the pandemic. It was almost like a light switch just flipped. They realized how serious it was, and they wanted to get on top of it. If I didn't wear a mask, even if I was outside or just walking by myself, I would get scolded. And that was nothing compared to the stories we were seeing on social media of authorities making sure that people would comply. What was so impressive was all the resources being coordinated, and groups of medical workers being flown in to wherever needed the help. And all the masks and the manufacturing being done. That was so impressive.

Chris Buckley, *New York Times*

The Party apparatus starts to shake itself into activity. They are starting to send officials from city government offices across Wuhan into neighborhoods and saying, "Organize these people. Find retired officials, Party members. If they don't want to come out, you tell them, 'This is your job. If you are not coming out now, there are going to be consequences.'" This process of mobilizing at the grassroots. And that began to make a difference.

THE "SICK MAN OF ASIA"

Four days before Li Wenliang's death, the *Wall Street Journal* had published an opinion piece by Bard College professor and foreign affairs commentator Walter Russell Mead titled "China Is the Real Sick Man of Asia." The term had often been used to describe China at a time of extreme weakness and foreign domination in the late nineteenth century, a period described in Chinese history books as a "century of humiliation." The headline sparked a furious response in China and generated intense unease among *Journal* staffers.

Josh Chin, *Wall Street Journal*

When the headline hit, it immediately struck me as tasteless. I remember thinking this might be a problem. We had reporters and researchers who kept encountering sources who would bring it up. In some cases, they were encountering a lot of real anger. Then the Global Times wrote about it and stirred up more anger. Then the Foreign Ministry started bringing it up. It was clear there was some kind of campaign to use this to pressure us. I think a lot of the anger was real. It's not hard to understand why people would find the headline offensive in the middle of a pandemic.

In a sign of Beijing's anger at the American press, when Jonathan Cheng had arrived to become bureau chief in August 2019, he had only been given a six-month visa. That same month, the Foreign Ministry refused to renew the visa of *Journal* reporter Chun Han Wong, a Singapore national who had angered the authorities with an article in July detailing an Australian investigation into alleged links between a cousin of Xi Jinping and money laundering and suspected organized crime. As February 19, 2020, the last day of Cheng's visa, approached, he was concerned he would suffer the same fate.

Jonathan Cheng, *Wall Street Journal*

The way they did it with Chun Han was they allowed his visa to lapse on his expiry date. When we woke up on D-day, I had my suitcase open, and I started to put stuff in it. My wife and I booked plane tickets to leave. Keep in mind, on February 19, 2020, there weren't a whole lot of tickets left, because this was right in the thick of the Wuhan lockdown, and nobody wanted Chinese planes landing in their country. I was thinking I would be the shortest-tenured bureau chief in Wall Street Journal *history. At 1:30, the Foreign Ministry said we need you to come in at 2:30. We are at the height of COVID. We have the whole sick man thing brewing. We have reporters in Wuhan. We have a million things going on. I'm thinking I'm going to get kicked out. I've hardly dealt with MOFA [the Ministry of Foreign Affairs] because they have been stiff-arming me since I arrived. Josh Chin, who is the deputy bureau chief and has been in China a lot longer, asked me, "Do you want me to come along to MOFA?" I said, "Yes, please, because I don't know what's going to go down, and I may need to scramble after this to get to the airport."*

Josh Chin, *Wall Street Journal*

At that point, I was the longest-tenured member of the bureau. But I was late. I got stuck in traffic. Jon had already gone into the meeting. I tried to go in, and they wouldn't let me. I was in the waiting area of the international press center.

Cheng arrived at the meeting to be told that his visa was going to be renewed for six months. But the Foreign Ministry then dropped a bombshell.

Jonathan Cheng, *Wall Street Journal*

They tell me, "Here's your visa. But we are immediately expelling Josh Chin, Chao Deng, and Philip Wen [an Australian who had reported with Chun Han Wong on the investigation of Xi Jinping's cousin]." My jaw dropped. I was like, "Why them? What have they got to do with this?" I said to them, "You realize this is going to be a really big deal?" And they said, "We know." And they said, "It's done."

Josh Chin, *Wall Street Journal*

Jon walked out. His face was white. I was like, "Oh shit. They kicked you out." He's like, "No. They kicked you out—and Phil, and Chao." It was not something that I had ever considered possible. I must have been so shocked that my face didn't register. Jon looked at me and said, "You look remarkably calm." In my mind, I was, "Oh, my God." But my face didn't have time to register.

It was the first time China had simultaneously expelled multiple journalists from one news organization in decades. But Beijing had timed its move carefully. The day before, the Trump administration had designated five major Chinese news organizations with staff in the United States, including the *People's Daily*, the Xinhua News Agency, and CGTN, as foreign government functionaries, rather than journalistic entities, imposing limitations on their movements. So in addition to playing the nationalism card—in announcing the expulsions the Chinese Foreign Ministry spokesman declared that "the Chinese people do not welcome media that publish racist statements and smear China with malicious attacks"—Beijing was also able to portray its move as retaliation for a Trump administration decision.

Jonathan Cheng, *Wall Street Journal*

Then we had to break the news to Phil and Chao. At the time, Chao was in Wuhan and confined to her hotel until the lockdown was lifted. She was barred from reporting. She was effectively expelled, but physically they allowed her to stay in Wuhan until the lockdown was lifted.

Chao Deng, *Wall Street Journal*

I remember that moment. It was very painful. I was really upset. I was coming back from this amazing interview that my researcher and I got with this lady who live near Huanan Market. She was one of the earliest known COVID patients. Josh called me. I was still sort of giddy from my interview with this woman. You know how it is. A reporter tells their editor what they've got. At the time we were all worried about Jonathan Cheng's visa not getting approved. Then Josh broke the news. I remember he said, "They dropped a nuclear bomb on us." I said, "What do you mean?" Then he told us. I was just in shock. I couldn't really process it. Fortunately, I was with a veteran researcher at the time, and she helped me get through that moment. We were thinking if we go back to the hotel room that that was it. So we actually went on to do one more interview, because we figured that it would take a bit of time before Beijing told Wuhan authorities that we shouldn't be out reporting, so we figured we do one more interview and then go back to our room.

The next day, fifty-three *Journal* reporters, based in China, Hong Kong, and elsewhere, including the three who had been ordered to leave, signed a letter to the paper's management describing the headline as "derogatory" and urging the paper to apologize.

"This is not about editorial independence or the sanctity of the divide between news and opinion," the letter said. "It is not about the content of Dr. Mead's article. It is about the mistaken choice of a headline that was deeply offensive to many people, not just in China. We find the argument that no offense was intended to be unconvincing: Someone should have known that it would cause widespread offense. If they didn't know, they made a bad mistake, and should correct it and apologize."[3]

Chao Deng, *Wall Street Journal*

I felt very committed to be part of that effort. When the letter was drafted, and people put their names on it, we wholeheartedly believed what was in that letter and hoped that senior management would take it very seriously.

The paper's management expressed understanding but insisted that the news and the largely conservative opinion departments remained separate. There was no apology.

Josh Chin, *Wall Street Journal*

I had five days to get my stuff together. I ended up in Japan, because it was one of the only countries that had open borders in Asia. I was incredibly numb

through most of the process, until there was a moment where someone men-
tioned Yunnan food to me. You can't get good Yunnan food outside of China.
For whatever reason, that was the moment where it suddenly hit me. I'm not
going back. Then the floodgates opened. I was thinking about all the people I
wasn't going to be able to see, all the places I wanted to go that I couldn't, and
all the aspects of the story I wasn't going to be able to tell anymore.

Meanwhile, with sweeping lockdowns and harsh controls, China gradually began to bring the outbreak under control. But the American press corps
was about to face a devastating new blow.

24

EXPULSION

When he left Beijing for Wuhan on January 23, Chris Buckley expected to be there for a week or two.

Chris Buckley, *New York Times*

Our bureau in Beijing had been vigilant enough that they had collected a few masks. As a precaution, I had taken a few home, so I threw those in my bag, and a shirt and some underwear and socks. That's essentially what I traveled with, thinking I would be there for a week or so.

But as the weeks passed, the lockdown deepened, and COVID spread, Buckley was determined to stay on.

Chris Buckley, *New York Times*

One of the big burdens for me was dealing with people who were much more worried about me than I was about myself, including my wife and daughter back in Beijing, who were freaking out. But my wife calmed down pretty quickly. And then my parents back home, and people like that. I reassured them, "Look, I'm taking good care of myself, being careful. I have all these masks. Don't worry." They were much more anxious than me, and I was keeping busy with work.

The Chinese authorities, however, began urging him to leave.

Chris Buckley, *New York Times*

This woman from the Wuhan Foreign Affairs Office called a few days into the lockdown saying, "Hi. We know you are here. We would really like you to leave. If you want to leave, we can get you back to Beijing." The woman kept calling me. We were good friends by the end. She was always both friendly and fretful at the same time. I guess one interpretation of it was they wanted to get press out of the city. And they were worried about foreigners dying on their watch. She would call up with this anxious tone in her voice saying, "It's time to leave. This is your very last chance. I can help you get out of the city today, but after this, you are here. You can't get out."

EVACUATION FLIGHTS

The United States, Australia, Japan, and other foreign governments had begun organizing evacuation flights for their nationals trapped in Wuhan. Amy Qin decided to go. One reason was that in January, just before the lockdown, she had renewed her journalist's visa, but was granted only two months. Concerned that she would be stuck in Wuhan as her visa expired, Qin got on an evacuation flight, did two weeks of quarantine in the United States, and then, with about a month left on her visa, returned to Beijing.

Shan Li had been lobbying her editors at the *Wall Street Journal* to send her back to Wuhan from the moment she stepped off the last train out of the city on the day of the lockdown.

With a colleague, Shan managed to reach the city of Xiangyang, the second largest in Hubei province, a three-hour drive from Wuhan.

Shan Li, *Wall Street Journal*

We got stuck in Xiangyang. The entire city was in lockdown. No one was allowed to leave the hotel. The local Foreign Affairs liaison officer was very nice. He said, "Look, the Americans are having one last evacuation flight today. If you guys aren't on it, you are going to be stuck in this hotel." I called Jon Cheng, and we decided to get on the flight. It was early afternoon. It was a mad scramble to get seats. We got in a car that the hotel arranged. That was a surreal trip because the highway to Wuhan was completely empty. It was a cargo plane that the State Department had converted, and they had crammed in as many seats as possible and put in some lavatories in the back. There was a part in the back sectioned off with plastic sheets for anyone they thought might have COVID like a makeshift quarantine area.

After a two-week quarantine in the United States, Shan, like Amy Qin, flew back to Beijing.

"YOU'VE HAD YOUR FUN"

Meanwhile, the Chinese Foreign Ministry was again pressing Chris Buckley to leave.

Chris Buckley, *New York Times*

The Ministry of Foreign Affairs people in Beijing began calling, with the message "Time to get out. You've had your fun." The fellow at the Chinese Foreign Ministry who called me regularly was a very nice guy. We always had a good professional relationship. He would deliver these warnings to me, but it was never enemy sort of style. He was getting more and more anxious about me being there. I could tell. He was getting worried, not just about the consequences of having a foreigner fall ill in Wuhan, but also me in particular. I think we were close enough to think of each other as friends. He was quite tearful on some of those calls. Essentially, I said, "I'm here. I'm keeping myself safe. I can't leave the story. It's my responsibility to be here now. I couldn't forgive myself if I got on one of those flights. Thank you very much. I understand you truly are worried about my personal well-being. I really appreciate that, but please understand that I want to stay here. And I'd send him these very long WeChat messages explaining that in Chinese, and he would send me an emoticon of somebody crying."

Buckley persevered, producing increasingly hard-hitting reports, including a detailed reconstruction, reported with Paul Mozur, of how the government's initial handling of the epidemic allowed the virus to take hold. In a piece headlined "As New Coronavirus Spread, China's Old Habits Delayed Fight," they wrote that "the authorities silenced doctors and others for raising red flags. They played down the dangers to the public, leaving the city's 11 million residents unaware they should protect themselves. Even as cases climbed, officials declared repeatedly that there had likely been no more infections. By not moving aggressively to warn the public and medical professionals, public health experts say, the Chinese government lost one of its best chances to keep the disease from becoming an epidemic."[1]

Chris Buckley, *New York Times*

Those investigative pieces took a lot of work, just going through documents on procedures for reporting on SARS-like corona cases, and what you should do, and figuring out what the system was, and why it had failed. Full credit both to the domestic Chinese press, which uncovered some of these problems early on, but also to our researchers in Beijing, Shanghai, and Hong Kong, who were doing mighty work as well.

The authorities were furious. In mid-February, the state-run *Global Times* denounced Buckley in a commentary with the headline "*The New York Times* and Chris Buckley Misrepresent China's Efforts to Defeat the Coronavirus."[2]

Chris Buckley, *New York Times*

At that point, it was like, "Whatever. Say what you like." The criticisms they mounted were so fragile. The fact is that so many of the things we had reported had been reported by parts of the Chinese media as well. I just thought, "Who cares? If they are criticizing me for coronavirus coverage, that is a hard mes-sage to sell to the wider Chinese public." I thought they just tripped themselves up again.

THE SECURITY STATE FIGHTS THE VIRUS

For his part, Mozur was traveling to as many cities as he could to chart how the surveillance system was working during the pandemic, and how it was being used to further strengthen the Party's authoritarian rule.

Paul Mozur, *New York Times*

I was looking at the way they were changing their technical policies—whether any of the contact tracing was working, how health codes started to appear,

what the health codes were doing. The result was that we were able to method-
ically figure out how many people were under what kind of lockdown. It was
literally several hundred million people who weren't allowed to leave their
apartments except for once every three days under a sort of passport system.
And another four hundred or five hundred million were on a pretty close ver-
sion of that. So effectively, seven hundred or eight hundred million people were
under some kind of house arrest.

And then to see these health codes come out. We broke down the code of the
Alibaba health code, and the first line of code says, "Send data to police." You
see also how the security state is in full action here and in a pandemic situa-
tion is as important a part of their response as any public health institution. I
felt like that said a lot about where we were and what the efforts to build out
the surveillance state meant for the broader political outlook.

The health code itself was fascinating too, because it was a system put together
in a matter of weeks at the behest of the public security bureau by Ant Finan-
cial that immediately controlled whether people could go out of their houses or
not. People were given no explanation. People would just have red codes, and
that meant they couldn't go anywhere. We went to Hangzhou, trying to see what
it felt like. We were hanging out with one of the old ladies who runs a metal
detector at the subway station. And there's a whole fever alarm system set up
already as well. This guy comes down and he has a red code, and she says, "You
can't take the subway." He says, "I have a note from the head of my local Party
committee that says I have quarantined for two weeks since I got back from
Spring Festival, so I should be able to go." He shows it to her, and she says,
"Sorry, I can't accept this. I need a green code." And he says, "OK," and he leaves.
This poor bastard can't take the subway even though he's been back more than
two weeks. So this crappy product immediately had say over everybody's entire
mobility.

Eunice Yoon, CNBC

Even on Chang An Avenue, right outside our Beijing office, one of the shoot-
ers was taking video of the protocols at the subway station, people starting
to wear masks and goggles and stuff like that. He caught some guy who was
having his temperature taken. And he had a fever. This guy started running.
All these police chased him down and grabbed him and threw him in the
back of the van. It was just that level of scary. You didn't want that to hap-
pen to you.

TIT FOR TAT

Despite its distaste for the mainstream U.S. media, the Trump administration, which had adopted an increasingly harsh line toward Beijing as COVID spread and the November 2020 U.S. presidential election approached, had denounced the expulsion of the three *Wall Street Journal* correspondents in February and threatened retaliation. Soon after, the administration announced that it would reduce from 160 to 100 the number of visas for Chinese journalists allowed to work in the United States for state-run Chinese news organizations like the *People's Daily*, Xinhua, and CGTN, forcing sixty Chinese to leave. In mid-March, Beijing retaliated.

Amy Qin, *New York Times*

I had fallen asleep on the couch that night, and I woke up and had a ton of text messages, and I looked, and it was like, "Oh fuck."

Qin discovered she was one of more than a dozen reporters from the *New York Times*, *Washington Post*, and *Wall Street Journal* who were being expelled. It was the Chinese government's most sweeping attempt in years to intimidate international media, punish those whose reporting the Communist Party disliked, and ensure that the Party would control the narrative—both at home and abroad.

The Chinese announcement said that all U.S. citizens working for the three papers whose credentials expired in 2020 would have to turn in their press cards and leave. Moreover, they were barred from going to Hong Kong, long a base for watching China outside the mainland.

Steven Lee Myers, *New York Times*

I had no sense it was coming. My partner had checked her phone and woke me up. I was like, "Shit. This means I have ten days to leave China." It was in the middle of a pandemic, and it was right when all the borders started to close everywhere.

Gerry Shih, *Washington Post*

It definitely came as a shock. I remember staying up all night on my porch drinking whiskey and smoking cigarettes with my partner, trying to figure out what we were going to do next.

Among those expelled were Shan Li and five other reporters for the *Wall Street Journal*, and Paul Mozur, Ian Johnson (who happened to be out of China when the decision was announced), and two others from the *New York Times*. Those ordered to leave were among the most aggressive in covering both Xinjiang and the COVID outbreak. More than half were ethnic Chinese. Many of them felt the Trump administration's crudely confrontational approach had provided Beijing with an excuse to do something it had long wanted to do.

Ian Johnson, *New York Times*

It was one of the Trump administration's own goals. The Chinese can say, "Look, you kicked out sixty of ours. We're just kicking out a small number of yours. We are being reasonable." And yet they managed in one fell swoop to just about obliterate the sort of deep reporting that could be done in China.

Indeed, the primary targets of the expulsions were the three U.S. media organizations with the reporters and the money to do real investigative journalism in China. While other bureaus contained first-class journalists, the pressures of daily news coverage meant that in general only the *Journal*, the *Times*, and, to a lesser extent, the *Post* had the resources and staff to go beyond the headlines and devote weeks, even months, to a single story.

Gerry Shih, *Washington Post*

They got the better part of the deal in terms of getting rid of a bunch of pesky reporters who just did more revelatory stuff, potentially embarrassing stuff, than the Chinese journalists in America.

Josh Chin, *Wall Street Journal*

It's an old debate about reciprocity—whether the U.S. government should take a harder line towards all these Chinese journalists in the U.S., given the way the Chinese Communist Party restricts foreign reporters in China. For the longest time, the prevailing argument was that the U.S. has freedom of speech. How do you justify restricting Chinese journalists if one of your core principles is freedom of speech? Until Trump, that argument ended up prevailing. The argument that it was an own goal makes sense. It really hurt the foreign press corps. I am sure that the Party is happy not to have all of us there.

Chris Buckley, *New York Times*

Like a lot of my colleagues, my reaction was both shock, and what a colossal miscalculation by the Trump administration. You think you are going to play hardball with the Chinese government without China playing hardball back. But I had not anticipated it would be this hardball.

To make matters worse, along with the expulsions, many local assistants working for U.S. news bureaus were forced by the Foreign Ministry's Diplomatic Service Bureau, which handled local staffing for foreign media outlets, to quit their jobs.

Steven Lee Myers, *New York Times*

The Diplomatic Service Bureau suddenly called in one of our researchers and she was told to resign and don't tell them anything. Then they called in another one and said the same thing. Of course, by this time I knew about it. And we were raising hell with the Foreign Ministry and the Diplomatic Service Bureau. The DSB just stopped responding to us. Then they fired our office manager, who was not involved in journalism at all. Her job was to manage the bureau budget and expenses. So we lost three of our Chinese staff at the same time. It was obviously all part of an orchestrated campaign against us.

During the ten days I had to get out, I was dealing with the Foreign Ministry for all of us. In one of my meetings, this guy just looked at me and said, "I feel like sometimes there are journalists in the West who simply do not like Communists." And I felt like I was in 1950 again. How do you even argue with that? It's not our job to like you or not. A lot of Chinese are great people. We don't hate China, but they think we do. They think it's like a bias that we carry with us almost genetically. It's fed by the chip on the shoulder, the sense of grievance they have had for 150 years of colonial oppression.

Interestingly, Beijing did not expel reporters for the American TV networks like CNN's David Culver, Eunice Yoon of CNBC, and Ramy Inocencio of CBS.

Ramy Inocencio, CBS News

We questioned why that was so. The investigative resources that the New York Times *and* Wall Street Journal *have, with their ability to dive superdeep and do these long-form things I think made them bigger targets than CBS or ABC or NPR. If they were going to target folks, it would be the people who were the biggest thorns in their sides.*

THE LAST STORY

Before leaving China, Paul Mozur decided to make one more reporting trip to Anhui province.

Paul Mozur, *New York Times*

We were trying to talk to people about a positive story—how China beat COVID, what it feels like to have done two months of hard lockdown and reengage again. But there are ten secret police following us around, deliberately disrupting our interviews. Every time we go to talk to a shopkeeper or a person in a restaurant, police would walk up and immediately whisper in their ear, and they say, "Oh, sorry, it's not convenient for me to talk." So the last bit of my reporting trip was spent kind of messing with the police, using the tricks I had learned— like hop on the subway, go one station, hop off, and get on the train going the other way. Each time they lose half their people because they have to have one person on and one person off—or jump off and jump back on. So mess with them to the point where we had like one person following us. We tried to lose them in a park but failed. But it didn't matter because what the hell were we going to do anyway? So that was the final reporting trip for me.

By now, Chris Buckley had been in Wuhan for more than two months. His visa had expired in late February. Although unable to leave the city because of the lockdown, he was told by the authorities to stop working.

Chris Buckley, *New York Times*

I actually did keep working. It's just that my name didn't appear on stories. I was keeping busy, partly for mental therapy, because, apart from anything else, people know that if you are quarantined, you go nuts if you don't have anything to do. I was happy to keep working. I was keeping an eye on the city. I should say I was still allowed to go out every day, unlike some of the other journalists, who were literally trapped in their hotels. I did take advantage of that to go for walks by the Yangtze River, go to the bank occasionally to find an ATM that actually worked. Or when shops and pharmacies were still open, I could go buy a few things. I became more aware of having a responsibility to the people at the Westin Hotel who kept the place running, heroically. During those first weeks, nobody had any effective masks or anything like that. I did share some of the gear to the hotel staff because I wanted them to be safe.

Despite the expulsions, Buckley continued to hope he might be allowed to remain in China.

Chris Buckley, *New York Times*

If I had been a cold-headed rationalist about my chances of staying in China at that point, I knew they were pretty slim. But I always was hopeful that the Chinese Foreign Ministry would see the error of its ways and let me stay. I was still thinking, "If I can get back to Beijing, work it a little—we have had our bad patches over the past year or two, but we can get past that. Just give me a couple of months." That was my thinking. I was colossally delusional. At that point, someone at the Foreign Ministry called me and said, "Here is what is going to happen. Cases are going down in Wuhan. They are going to start opening the city. When it does, you are going to leave. You are going to go into a quarantine in Beijing. You are going to have a few days to prepare, and then you have to leave."

In mid-April, after seventy-six days under lockdown, Chris Buckley returned to Beijing. In early May, with his wife and daughter, he left China for Australia. The day before his departure, he did an interview with Bill Birtles, the Beijing correspondent for Australian TV. Four men followed and filmed him as he headed to the interview. When Buckley tried to talk to them, they ran away.

25

THE DOOR CLOSES

With the American press corps decimated, China's campaign against foreign journalists escalated. In September 2020, as relations between China and Australia frayed over Canberra's call for an international inquiry into the origins of COVID, TV correspondent Bill Birtles and a Shanghai-based colleague, Mike Smith of the *Australian Financial Review*, felt compelled to seek refuge at Australia's embassy in Beijing and consulate in Shanghai. The two were being sought by Chinese police, who wanted to question them about Cheng Lei, an Australian-Chinese anchor for the government-controlled English-language CGTN, who had just been detained on vague national security grounds. They feared an exit ban or worse. After several days of high tension, Australian diplomats negotiated their safe departure from China, while Cheng Lei remained in custody. At the end of 2020, Haze Fan, a Chinese national working as a news assistant for Bloomberg, was detained for "endangering national security." And in March 2021, BBC correspondent John Sudworth, who had been in China for nine years and had angered the authorities with his reporting about Xinjiang, left on short notice in the face of a growing campaign of intimidation in the state-run Chinese media, as well as threats of legal action.

By 2021, the size of the Western press corps in China had shrunk dramatically, with no Australians and just a handful of Americans. Using COVID as a convenient excuse, the Chinese authorities told the few American reporters still on the ground that if they left the country for any reason, they would not be permitted to return. Indeed, the COVID outbreak accelerated a broader pattern of China shutting itself off from the rest of the world. Visitors were sharply limited, along with students and tourists, as well family members of those with valid working visas. Some journalists went a year or longer without being able to see their families, who were stuck outside China. Meanwhile, the government, again citing COVID as the reason, effectively stopped issuing new passports and exit permits for most of its own citizens.

Alice Su of the *Los Angeles Times* was one of the few American reporters not expelled.

Alice Su, *Los Angeles Times*

I think COVID is the real reason for these moves. But it also fits in with this broader trend of China turning inwards, becoming more insular—that we don't want or need so much outside contact or influence.

At the same time, there were growing signs that Xi Jinping had abandoned many of the features that had helped produce the remarkable progress of previous decades. Having crushed his domestic enemies, silenced internal dissent, and reimposed ideological orthodoxy, Xi began to reorder the Chinese economy. As market-oriented reforms stalled, the climate for foreign investors became increasingly inhospitable, with the state tightening its grip over the economy. Money and resources flowed to notoriously bloated and inefficient government enterprises, as far more nimble and creative private firms faced growing pressure. One sign of this trend was the Communist Party's assault on one of the most vibrant parts of the economy—the tech sector. In November 2020, the government abruptly blocked what would have been a record-breaking IPO in Hong Kong of the Ant financial group. Soon thereafter, Jack Ma, the chairman of Ant's parent company, Alibaba, and the most famous and popular tech entrepreneur in China, was forced to take a dramatically lower public profile. Ma had criticized government oversight of the finance industry, and the decision to pull the IPO was reportedly made by Xi Jinping himself.

Josh Chin, *Wall Street Journal*

I've always wondered how Xi Jinping felt about someone like Jack, who is kind of like a rival in some ways, in terms of representing China. He is this charming guy, totally at home at Davos, in New York. He can fly all around the world and talk to all sorts of people and charms them. He speaks English really well. He does represent China in a way, in some ways more successfully than Xi does, because Xi is so awkward and uncomfortable outside of the Chinese context.

In mid-2021, Didi, the Uber of China, listed on the New York Stock Exchange. Days later, Chinese regulators ordered the company to stop signing up new users and pulled it from Chinese app stores.

Paul Mozur, *New York Times*

More and more and more, we see the government is wading into the tech industry and changing it fundamentally.

Josh Chin, *Wall Street Journal*

We've seen this huge antitrust campaign against all tech companies in China. The data piece of it in particular is a major factor. Just in covering surveillance, you realize how important it is to the Party, but also that the best data is not in the CCP's hands. It's controlled by Alibaba and Tencent. This data is immensely powerful and useful, and it's central to the way the CCP is thinking about governance. The Party always felt a little nervous about that. But it has been fascinating to see them take this strong of a move. It's a bit of a paradox, because if they limit these companies, then they also limit the sorts of data they can collect.

In addition to tightening the Party's control over China's domestic tech giants, such intervention in the private economy, which wiped hundreds of billions of dollars off share prices, was also clearly intended to discourage Chinese tech companies from listing their stocks in the United States. It became another illustration of movement toward a Sino-American economic decoupling, driven as much by an increasingly inward-looking China as a United States increasingly skeptical of engagement.

SHAPING THE NARRATIVE

Meanwhile, with China's borders almost entirely closed, the Communist Party gained even more control over both the people and the information allowed into the country. And the dramatic reduction in the presence of American and other foreign journalists fit into a broader effort by Beijing to shape the narrative about China not only at home, but around the world.

Anna Fifield was not expelled, but in mid-2020 she left Beijing and the *Washington Post* to become the editor of the *Dominion Post*, a newspaper in her native New Zealand.

Anna Fifield, *Washington Post*

I was sad to leave, but I didn't realize at the time just how relieved I was to be outside—what a weight it was off me to not be there anymore. I think the Chinese feel they don't need foreign correspondents. When they were reforming and opening up and attracting investment, it was necessary to have foreign correspondents. But now they have CGTN and various propaganda outlets, and Wolf Warriors and Twitter. I think they feel they can get their message out without having to go through pesky foreign media, who also write stories they don't like. This is very much a shift from the Chinese Communist Party, in that they see us as all risk and no gain.

Ian Johnson eventually relocated to Germany and then New York.

Ian Johnson, *New York Times*

They used to accept foreign journalists as part of the cost of doing business in the modern world. You've got to take your lumps. You have to allow those pesky foreign journalists in. You've got to let them write what they want. That's all begun to end. They just began to not accept critical reporting.

Gerry Shih initially rebased in Taiwan.

Gerry Shih, *Washington Post*

The tit for tat with the U.S. was the obvious surface reason, but the deeper cause was that domestically, they had gotten so good at quashing media that people just weren't used to having muckraking reporters. If you are a Chinese politician or official, you are used to a world where you don't really have to contend with anybody ever questioning anything. And you start looking abroad and saying, "Why are these guys able to do it? How dare they?" Because they are not used to it, anybody who challenges you stands out even more. They had successfully dispatched the local reporters, and so they were left with us. We became more appalling to their sensitivities the longer we were around.

From the Communist victory in 1949 until the United States and China established diplomatic relations three decades later, generations of China watchers had sat, mostly in Hong Kong, peering across a closed border, relying on refugees, the official media, and rare, tightly controlled visits to figure out what was happening in mainland China. Ironically, more than half a century later, the wave of expulsions created a strange sense of history repeating itself.

Steven Lee Myers, *New York Times*

It really feels to me like the door is closing on China. There was once a time long ago when the door was closed and we were kind of peeking in windows and looking over the fence. We essentially covered China from outside. In my case, that's what I'm doing again.

TAIWAN—THE NEW LISTENING POST

But Myers was not doing so in Hong Kong. In the wake of China's imposition of a draconian national security law in July 2020, following months of prodemocracy protests in 2019, and Beijing's decision not to allow any of the expelled reporters to move there, Hong Kong's role as a hub for journalism in Asia and a center for observing China was badly damaged. Myers rebased in Seoul, and soon after, the *New York Times* moved its entire Asian digital headquarters to the South Korean capital, leaving only Austin Ramzy and a small number of other editorial staff based in the former British colony.

Steven Lee Myers, *Washington Post*

On one level, there are stories that you do the same here in Seoul as if you were sitting in Beijing—the kind of stories you are able to do by covering official statements and talking to experts outside China. And that's true on a lot of stuff that I do, especially diplomatic stuff.

For many of the expelled reporters, including Gerry Shih, Chao Deng and Josh Chin of the *Wall Street Journal*, and Amy Qin and Paul Mozur of the *New York Times*, Taiwan became the preferred destination.

Amy Qin, *New York Times*

People in Taiwan have the language and the whole island is oriented towards China. That's the main axis of politics. I think Taiwan is a more interesting story now, so being able to report both on the Taiwan story and China is useful. But I think there are just a lot fewer mainlanders in Taiwan than in Hong Kong, so you don't get the same really good sources and information as you get in Hong Kong. And getting people on the phone in China is very challenging. Everything just takes multiple steps even for a very simple story. It is very frustrating. But the glimmers from the Chinese Internet are very helpful, and there are still people in China you can talk to.

Gerry Shih, *Washington Post*

I look at the Chinese press and Chinese social media every day. You're having Zoom calls with Chinese academics. Back in the day, you would talk to a businessman who had traveled to China. Today what I do is the same thing. I know when American businessmen are having Zoom calls with their Chinese counterparts, and then I have a Zoom call with them afterwards. Basically the same thing, except it's all done over Zoom. But in terms of elite politics, it's harder, because in China what people are willing to say face-to-face and what they're willing to say over the phone is way different.

"THE HUMAN INTEREST STORIES ARE THE FIRST VICTIM"

Ironically, though, in some ways being barred from China proved to be less of a drawback than it had been. As a global economic powerhouse, Chinese companies, and the relatives and allies of the elite who ran them, operated openly in a variety of international business centers. This, coupled with the broader expansion of China's international role, was providing new opportunities for important journalistic work. With access to the mainland reduced, a new kind of China watcher was emerging, skilled not only in reading the tea leaves of Chinese propaganda, but also in deciphering balance sheets and corporate reports, making use of the Internet and Chinese social media, and following China's activities beyond its borders. But after so many years of trying, against difficult odds, to travel, dig beneath the surface, develop contacts, and gain a deeper understanding of the texture of Chinese society—the color and human interest stories beyond the high-level politics and diplomacy—being frozen out of the mainland carried a cost.

Josh Chin, *Wall Street Journal*

There is this risk that coverage of China is going to become more polarized and less nuanced, because you have fewer people to tell the human story about China. It's become almost impossible to write a story about China that is about people. Now, everyone is stuck outside of China doing stories that are much more driven by political and economic conflict, because those are the stories you can write.

Gerry Shih, *Washington Post*

What you're left with are the stories about Wolf Warrior diplomacy and China's foreign policy travails. All the essentially positive stories about slices of life, that's all gone out the window. I can't describe what life is like in China from Taiwan. I can tell from my own reporting that it is going to be this increasingly negative cycle of diplomacy and confrontation with the world.

Steve Lee Myers, *New York Times*

There's that feeling of being there that you only get by being there. You can't fake it.

Chao Deng, *Wall Street Journal*

I never thought I would be in Taiwan. I just took it as a given that I would cover China from inside China. I would love to do more narrative-driven stuff and get more into the people stories in China. Now, having to try to do it abroad, I am so pessimistic and worried that our readers are going to get a very narrow, one-dimensional view of China.

Anna Fifield, *Washington Post*

The human stories are the first victim of this trend. It hurts China because it turns them into this two-dimensional boogieman. You don't get any of their humanity and the things we have in common.

Jane Perlez, *New York Times*

It is going to be terrible for those who are trying to understand China from out-side of China. But I think it will be equally terrible for China itself, because China is huge, complex, riveting, fascinating—the most important country in the world. The United States and China are now having at it. And we need to understand, to use the cliché, who our competitor is.

Steven Lee Myers, *New York Times*

I think the Chinese just don't care. I don't think they feel they are losing any-thing by not having reporters there. I don't think they want us to see the nuance of China. They don't want to put up with us asking what their own reporters won't ask.

"HE DOESN'T DO LOVEABLE"

July 2021 marked the hundredth anniversary of the founding of the Chinese Communist Party. In the run-up to the centenary, Xi Jinping gave a speech to senior Party officials in which he said it was important to present the world with an image of a "credible, loveable, and responsible China."[1] Some com-mentators suggested that Xi was acknowledging that China's Wolf Warrior diplomacy had not been well received. Indeed, Beijing's muscular assertive-ness, from the South China Sea, its crackdown in Hong Kong, and menacing moves toward Taiwan, to continued tensions along the Sino-Indian border and bullying behavior toward Australia, Canada, the Philippines, Lithuania, the European Union, and other countries, as well as its heightened hostility toward the United States, had triggered an international backlash. It was arguably the harshest external environment China had faced since the Mao years. Moreover, the Biden administration was continuing the tough Amer-ican approach toward China, albeit without Donald Trump's incoherence, racism, and bombast. Meanwhile, efforts to ratify an investment agreement with the European Union, which had taken seven years to negotiate, stalled after a series of sanctions and countersanctions over Xinjiang, while tensions with other governments continued to simmer.

Beijing, however, sought to frame international pushback as evidence that China was being surrounded and besieged by enemies determined to block its legitimate rise, tapping into the deep strain of nationalism the Party had fostered. At home, particularly with the centenary, it led to a strident kind of triumphalism, promoting Xi as the indispensable leader guiding China to greatness. Yet the triumphalism was also marked by an obsession with propaganda, control, and security that, underneath the surface, suggested to some a lack of confidence. Shortly before the giant July 1 celebration, for example, Eunice Yoon and her crew visited a Beijing museum to film one of the many exhibitions being staged to promote the Party's past glories.

Eunice Yoon, CNBC

There were quite a few people who were very proud of the government. The Party has done a lot. It makes sense. But the security lockdown was just so ridiculous. They are just so scared. Even for this exhibition, it was total lockdown. Police everywhere. They were going to allow people to go in, but only in monitored groups. Everything has to be so controlled. In another country, you could just have a party. Yeah, there would be security. But that is totally not allowed here. And it just makes me feel like, "Why are they always so scared?"

Indeed, apart from growing international pushback, in the medium term, the Communist Party faced serious internal challenges—an ageing population, a weak social security system, a shrinking workforce, a sluggish economy (including curbs on its most innovative sector), a potential succession crisis when Xi leaves the scene, and a political system with deep questions about its ability to manage such a daunting collection of problems.

Against this backdrop, it was perhaps not surprising that Xi's comments about making China more "loveable" sparked considerable international interest, and even speculation that they might presage, if not a change in substance, at least one of tone. But on July 1, wearing a gray Mao suit and speaking to tens of thousands of people in Tiananmen Square, Xi declared that "The Chinese people will never allow foreign forces to bully, oppress or enslave us. Whoever nurses delusions of doing that will crack their heads and spill blood on the Great Wall of steel built from the flesh and blood of 1.4 billion Chinese people."[2]

Eunice Yoon, CNBC

He said we should have China tell its own narrative and make it more loveable. But then he does this. You're not making yourself loveable. He doesn't do loveable.

Later in July, Alice Su and Mathias Boelinger, a correspondent from the German TV network Deutsche Welle, went to Zhengzhou in Henan province to report on devastating floods that left dozens dead.

Alice Su, *Los Angeles Times*

One woman came up to us and wanted to talk about an underground market that had been flooded. She was saying the government wasn't helping them to drain the waters, so her company was spending money to drain the water themselves. They were upset. As we were talking, two other women pulled her away and got really angry. Later in the day, she sent me a lot of distressed messages. She was threatened by her supervisor, who told her that the police were going to question her. I stopped contacting her after that.

Meanwhile, Su and Boelinger were surrounded by a group of agitated onlookers.

Alice Su, *Los Angeles Times*

The crowd was angry. They were shouting, "You are smearing China. You are spreading rumors." And at one point, a man pulled out his cell phone, and he had this image of a white man. I didn't know who it was. And then he started saying, "This is him. This is him." I took a look at the phone, and it clearly wasn't him.

It turned out that many in the crowd mistakenly believed the German was actually BBC journalist Robin Brant. Angry at Brant's coverage, especially a report questioning the effectiveness of the city's multibillion-dollar flood control efforts, the Henan Communist Party Youth League had posted a call on the social media network Weibo, where it had a million followers, to track and confront Brant.

Alice Su, *Los Angeles Times*

In some ways, it was quite comical. There's a manhunt going on, and these people couldn't tell the difference between two tall, foreign men. But then Mathias and I thought, "We've got to clarify and say what actually happened." When we both wrote about it on Twitter, we also became targets of this campaign. I got thousands and thousands of messages on Weibo, on Twitter, Facebook, email, really hateful messages, saying, "You are a Han traitor." Some of them were very sexually violent. There were death threats. Some said, "Beat them. Kill them. Let's find their families." Really vicious stuff.

Their experience highlighted a new risk facing American and other foreign reporters in China—not from police or officials, but from an increasingly nationalistic populace inflamed by vituperative doses of antiforeign and antimedia propaganda.

Alice Su, *Los Angeles Times*

There is a qualitative change. Everyone here has been ingesting this constant propaganda stream that the U.S. and foreigners and foreign media are evil. They see this every single day on the news, and from the Ministry of Foreign Affairs, and the kind of toxic stuff that comes out, and their social media is full of it. I know what people are consuming. The truth is that the propaganda has been successful. There is growing hostility among regular people towards foreign journalists—just for existing. You work really hard and people hate you for it. It makes the pressure a lot higher. I just keep reminding myself that it's still not everyone. And the work is still important. Even if the majority of Chinese are hostile to foreigners, what's the point of pulling your punches? If you're going to be here doing this job, it should be doing [it] to make it worthwhile, and I should be getting the stories they don't want told.

Josh Chin, *Wall Street Journal*

It's not at the North Korea level yet, and hopefully it doesn't ever get there, but it feels like it is going in that direction.

Indeed, the Communist Party's moves to largely seal the country's borders because of COVID had become almost a physical extension of an increasingly inward-looking mindset, from top leaders to many ordinary people. With international flights limited, the flow of tourists, academics, and businesspeople down to a trickle, and few Chinese traveling overseas, the country—for all its economic and political clout—was more cut off from the rest of the world than at any time since the Cultural Revolution. The government's efforts to drum up a narrow-minded form of nationalism to counter the "Western values" it so despised only accentuated this trend.

For the tiny handful of American journalists still on the ground, conditions therefore remained extremely challenging, although every so often came moments that lifted their spirits, as Alice Su discovered in the wake of her reports on the Henan floods in the summer of 2021.

Alice Su, *Los Angeles Times*

Among the thousands of messages I got were some that were really encouraging— messages from Chinese people I know, and from strangers, saying, "This doesn't represent all of China. Thank you for being here. You must report the truth."

Indeed, for all their travails, most journalists today—like those who came before them—maintained a deep interest in and an abiding affection for China and its people and recognized the importance of trying to understand and convey the "truth" of the country as they saw it. Although influenced to varying degrees by the political currents of their times, throughout the decades, they also brought with them the enduring values of the best of Western journalism—seeking to witness and accurately record history as it happened, to challenge those in power by chronicling the consequences of their actions, to provide a voice for the voiceless. Often, they did so under difficult, stressful, and sometimes dangerous conditions and, given the opportunity, would undoubtedly do so again.

After his expulsion, Chris Buckley, widely viewed as the dean of contemporary China correspondents, rebased in Sydney. But he was still reporting on the country where he had lived and worked for nearly thirty years, and which he sorely missed.

Chris Buckley, *New York Times*

I like working in Beijing. I like working in China, I like getting out on the ground in China. The heart in me wants to go back, and I would go back straightaway.

NOTES

1. THE CHINESE CIVIL WAR

1. John Roderick, interviewed by James Lagier, July 17, 1998. AP20.1, AP Corporate Archives, New York.
2. Stephen R. MacKinnon and Oris Friesen, *China Reporting: An Oral History of American Journalism in the 1930s and 1940s* (Berkeley: University of California Press, 1990), 81.
3. John Roderick interview, July 17, 1998.
4. Roderick, July 17, 1998.
5. Roderick, July 17, 1998.
6. Seymour Topping, "Covering the Chinese Civil War," in *Covering China*, ed. Robert Giles, Robert W. Snyder, and Lisa DeLisle (New Brunswick, NJ: Transaction, 2001), 19.
7. Roderick, July 17, 1998.
8. Roderick, July 17, 1998, p. 149.
9. "Fall of Mukden: Eyewitnesses Record Last Hours of Key City in Battle for China," *Life*, November 8, 1948, 35.

2. CHINA WATCHING

1. John Roderick, interviewed by James Lagier, July 17, 1998. AP20.1, AP Corporate Archives, New York.
2. Roderick, July 17, 1998.
3. Roderick, July 17, 1998.
4. Roderick, July 17, 1998.

3. "A STRUGGLE OF SEA MONSTERS"

1. John Roderick, interviewed by James Lagier, July 17, 1998. AP20.1, AP Corporate Archives, New York.
2. ABC News, Listening Post East, 1960.
3. The Roots of Madness, documentary, 1967.
4. John Roderick, interviewed by James Lagier, July 17, 1998. AP20.1, AP Corporate Archives, New York.

4. THE WEEK THAT CHANGED THE WORLD

1. Tom Jarriel, telegram to ABC News, February 21, 1972.
2. Cited in Alistair Horne, *Kissinger, 1973: The Crucial Year* (New York: Simon and Schuster, 2009), 81.

5. END OF AN ERA

1. *The People of People's China*, ABC News documentary, December 1, 1973.
2. John Burns, "John Burns, June 28, 1971—June 23, 1975," *Toronto Globe and Mail*, October 2, 2009.
3. Joseph Lelyveld, "Kissinger Gives Pledge in Beijing," *New York Times*, November 29, 1974.
4. Robert Elegant, "People's China: The Third Epoch," *Quadrant* 40, no. 5 (May 1996): 19–25.
5. Ford Library, National Security Adviser, Trip Briefing Books and Cables for President Ford, Presidential Trips File, Box 19, 11/28–12/7/75, Far East, Briefing Book, Peking, Meeting with Chairman Mao, President's copy (3). Secret; Sensitive.
6. "Memorandum of Conversation, President Ford meeting with Chairman Mao," December 2, 1975, https://digitalarchive.wilsoncenter.org/document/118073.pdf?v=0 f38601b9897b13df36f467ec82b83eb.
7. *Doonesbury*, syndicated comic strip, May 9, 1976.
8. Fox Butterfield, "The Intriguing Matter of Mao's Successor," *New York Times*, April 1, 1976.

6. OPENING UP

1. John Roderick, interviewed by James Lagier, July 17, 1998. AP20.1, AP Corporate Archives, New York.
2. Roderick, July 17, 1998.
3. Roderick, July 17, 1998.
4. Roderick, July 17, 1998.
5. Richard Bernstein, "Human Rights in China: A Journey of Conscience," *New York Times Magazine*, April 16, 1989.
6. Bernstein, "Human Rights in China."
7. Fox Butterfield, "Love and Sex in China," *New York Times Magazine*, January 13, 1980.

7. "YOU WERE WRITING WHAT WE WERE THINKING"

1. Michael Weisskopf, "China's Birth Control Policy Drives Some to Kill Baby Girls," *Washington Post*, January 8, 1985.

8. TESTING THE LIMITS

1. Cited in Richard Baum, *Burying Mao* (Princeton: Princeton University Press, 1994), 200.

13. THE NEW MILLENNIUM

1. Joseph Kahn, "Party of the Rich; China's Congress of Crony Capitalists," *New York Times*, November 10, 2002.

19. THE SURVEILLANCE STATE

1. "Strict Party Self-Discipline to Continue," *Global Times*, October 19, 2017.
2. Liza Lin and Josh Chin, "China's Tech Giants Have a Second Job: Helping Beijing Spy on Its People," *Wall Street Journal*, November 30, 2017.
3. Paul Mozur, "A Surveillance Net Blankets China's Cities, Giving Police Vast Powers," *New York Times*, December 17, 2019.
4. Amy Qin, "From a Tibetan Filmmaker, an Unvarnished View of His Land," *New York Times*, June 21, 2019.
5. Mark Landler, "Fruitful Visit by Obama Ends with a Lecture from Xi," *New York Times*, November 12, 2014.

21. "REEDUCATION" IN XINJIANG

1. Megha Rajagopalan, "This Is What a 21st-Century Police State Really Looks Like," *Buzzfeed*, October 17, 2017.
2. Rajagopalan.
3. Nick Cummings-Bruce, "No Such Thing: China Denies UN Report of Uighur Detention Camps," *New York Times*, August 13, 2018.
4. Chris Buckley and Paul Mozur, "How China Uses High Tech to Subdue Minorities," *New York Times*, May 22, 2019; Chris Buckley, Paul Mozur, and Austin Ramzy, "How China Turned a City Into a Prison," *New York Times*, April 4, 2019.

22. "I STARTED TO CRY"

1. Eva Dou and Chao Deng, "Western Companies Get Tangled in China's Muslim Clampdown," *Wall Street Journal*, May 16, 2019.
2. Amy Qin, "In China's Crackdown on Muslims, Children Have Not Been Spared," *New York Times*, December 28, 2019.

3. Chris Buckley and Austin Ramzy, "'Absolutely No Mercy': Leaked Files Exposed How China Organized Mass Detentions of Muslims," *New York Times*, November 16, 2019.
4. Reuters, "Leaked Chinese Documents Show Details of Xinjiang Clampdown," Reuters, November 19, 2019.
5. CNN Newsroom, transcript, November 19, 2019, https://transcripts.cnn.com/show /cnr/date/2019-11-19/segment/20.
6. Convention on the Prevention and Punishment of the Crime of Genocide, article 2, United Nations, December 9, 1948.

23. EPIDEMIC

1. Chris Buckley and Paul Mozur, "A New Martyr Puts a Face on China's Deepening Coronavirus Crisis," *New York Times*, February 7, 2020.
2. Paul Mozur, Raymond Zhong, Jeff Kao, and Aaron Krolik, "No 'Negative' News: How China Censored the Coronavirus," *New York Times*, December 19, 2020.
3. Cited in Paul Farhi, "Wall Street Journal Reporters Protest 'Sick Man' Headline in Wall Street Journal," *Washington Post*, February 23, 2020.

24. EXPULSION

1. Chris Buckley and Paul Mozur, "As New Coronavirus Spread, China's Old Habits Delayed Fight," *New York Times*, February 1, 2020.
2. "*The New York Times* and Chris Buckley Misrepresent China's Effort to Defeat the Coronavirus," *Global Times*, February 14, 2020.

25. THE DOOR CLOSES

1. Steven Lee Myers and Keith Bradsher, "China's Leader Wants a 'Loveable' Country. That Doesn't Mean He's Making Nice," *New York Times*, June 8, 2021.
2. Chris Buckley and Keith Bradsher, "Marking Party's Centennial, Xi Warns That China Will Not Be Bullied," *New York Times*, July 1, 2021.

SUGGESTED READING

PRE-1949

Bernstein, Richard. *1945: Mao's Revolution and America's Fateful Choice*. New York: Vintage, 2015.

French, Paul. *Through the Looking Glass: China's Foreign Journalists from Opium Wars to Mao*. Hong Kong: Hong Kong University Press, 2009.

MacKinnon, Stephen, and Oris Friesen. *China Reporting: An Oral History of American Journalism in the 1930s and 1940s*. Berkeley: University of California Press, 1987.

Peck, Graham. *Two Kinds of Time*. Seattle: University of Washington Press, 2008.

Rand, Peter. *China Hands*. New York: Simon and Schuster, 1995.

Rowan, Roy. *Chasing the Dragon: A Veteran Journalist's First-Hand Account of the 1949 Chinese Revolution*. Guilford, CT: Lyons, 2004.

Snow, Edgar. *Red Star Over China*. Rev. ed. New York: Grove, 1969.

Topping, Seymour. *On the Front Lines of the Cold War: An American Correspondent's Journal from the Chinese Civil War to the Cuban Missile Crisis and Vietnam*. Baton Rouge, LA: LSU Press, 2010.

White, Theodore, and Annalee Jacoby. *Thunder Out of China*. n.p.: Andesite, 2015.

1950S AND 1960S

Dikotter, Frank. *The Cultural Revolution: A People's History, 1962–1976*. London: Bloomsbury, 2016.

——. *Mao's Great Famine: The History of China's Most Devastating Catastrophe, 1958–1962*. New York: Bloomsbury, 2011.

Elegant, Robert. *China's Red Masters*. Westport, CT: Greenwood, 1971.

Hinton, William. *Fanshen: A Documentary of Revolution in a Chinese Village*. Berkeley: University of California Press, 1997.

Karnow, Stanley. *Mao and China: Inside China's Revolution*. New York: Penguin, 1984.

MacFarquhar, Roderick, and Michael Schoenals. *Mao's Last Revolution*. Cambridge, MA: Belknap Press of Harvard University Press, 2008.

Spence, Jonathan. *Mao Zedong: A Life*. New York: Penguin, 2006.

1970S AND 1980S

Baum, Richard. *Burying Mao: Chinese Politics in the Age of Deng Xiaoping*. Princeton: Princeton University Press, 2018.

Bernstein, Richard. *From the Center of the Earth: The Search for the Truth About China*. Boston: Little, Brown, 1982.

Butterfield, Fox. *China: Alive in the Bitter Sea*. New York: Bantam, 1983.

Garside, Roger. *Coming Alive: China After Mao*. New York: McGraw-Hill, 1981.

Leys, Simon. *Chinese Shadows*. New York: Penguin, 1978.

Lilley, James, with Jeffrey Lilley. *China Hands: Nine Decades of Adventure, Espionage and Diplomacy in Asia*. New York: Public Affairs, 2004.

MacMillan, Margaret. *Nixon and Mao: The Week That Changed the World*. New York: Random House, 2008.

Mann, James. *About Face: A History of America's Curious Relationship with China from Nixon to Clinton*. New York: Vintage, 2000.

——. *Beijing Jeep: A Case Study of Western Business in China*. New York: Routledge, 2018.

Mathews, Jay, and Linda Mathews. *One Billion: A China Chronicle*. New York: Random House, 1983.

Platt, Nicholas. *China Boys: How U.S. Relations with the PRC Began and Grew*. Washington DC: New Academia Publishing/Vellum, 2010.

Pomfret, John. *Chinese Lessons: Five Classmates and the Story of the New China*. New York: Holt, 2007.

Schell, Orville. *Discos and Democracy: China in the Throes of Reform*. New York: Anchor, 1989.

Tyler, Patrick. *A Great Wall: Six Presidents and China*. New York: Public Affairs, 1999.

TIANANMEN AND THE 1990S

Calhoun, Craig. *Neither Gods nor Emperors: Students and the Struggle for Democracy in China*. Berkeley: University of California Press, 1997.

Chinoy, Mike. *China Live: People Power and the Television Revolution*. Lanham, MD: Rowman and Littlefield, 1999.

Ignatius, Adi, Bao Pu, Renee Chiang, and Roderick MacFarquar. *Prisoner of the State: The Secret Journal of Premier Zhao Ziyang*. New York: Simon and Schuster, 2009.

Kristof, Nicholas, and Sheryl WuDunn. *China Wakes: The Struggle for the Soul of a Rising Power*. New York: Vintage, 1995.

Lampton, David. *Same Bed, Different Dreams: Managing U.S.-China Relations, 1989–2000*. Berkeley: University of California Press, 2002.

Lim, Louisa. *The People's Republic of Amnesia: Tiananmen Revisited*. Oxford: Oxford University Press, 2014.

Schell, Orville. *Mandate of Heaven: The Legacy of Tiananmen Square and the Next Generation of China's Leaders*. New York: Simon and Schuster, 1995.

THE EARLY 2000S

Abraham, Thomas. *Twenty-First Century Plague: The Story of SARS*. Baltimore: Johns Hopkins University Press, 2004.
Chang, Leslie. *Factory Girls: From Village to City in a Changing China*. New York: Random House, 2008.
Hessler, Peter. *Country Driving: A Journey Through China from Farm to Factory*. New York: HarperCollins, 2010.
——. *River Town*. New York: Harper Perennial, 2006.
Johnson, Ian. *Wild Grass: Three Portraits of Change in Modern China*. New York: Vintage, 2005.
McGregor, James. *One Billion Customers: Lessons from the Front Lines of Doing Business in China, New York*. New York: Free Press, 2007.
Pan, Philip. *Out of Mao's Shadow: The Struggle for the Soul of a New China*. New York: Simon and Schuster, 2009.
Schmitz, Rob. *Street of Eternal Happiness*. New York: Broadway, 2016.

THE RISE OF CHINA

Chin, Josh, and Liza Lin. *Surveillance State: Inside China's Quest to Launch a New Era of Social Control*. New York: St. Martin's, 2022.
Demick, Barbara. *Eat the Buddha: Life and Death in a Tibetan Town*. New York: Random House, 2020.
Economy, Elizabeth C. *The River Runs Black: The Environmental Challenge to China's Future*. Ithaca: Cornell University Press, 2010.
——. *The Third Revolution: Xi Jinping and the New Chinese State*. New York: Oxford University Press, 2018.
Fincher, Leta Hong. *Betraying Big Brother: The Feminist Awakening in China*. London: Verso, 2018.
Garnault, John. *The Rise and Fall of the House of Bo*. London: Penguin, 2012.
Kroeber, Arthur. *China's Economy: What Everyone Needs to Know*. New York: Oxford University Press, 2016.
Kynge, James. *China Shakes the World: A Titan's Rise and Troubled Future—and the Challenge for America*. New York: Houghton Mifflin Harcourt, 2006.
Mann, James. *The China Fantasy: Why Capitalism Will Not Bring Democracy to China*. New York: Penguin, 2007.
McGregor, Richard. *The Party: The Secret World of China's Communist Rulers*. New York: Harper Perennial, 2010.
Osnos, Evan. *Age of Ambition: Chasing Fortune, Truth, and Faith in the New China*. New York: Farrar, Straus and Giroux, 2015.
Schell, Orville, and John DeLury. *Wealth and Power: China's Long March to the Twenty-First Century*. New York: Random House, 2013.

Sheridan, Michael. *The Gate to China: A New History of the People's Republic and Hong Kong*. New York: Oxford University Press, 2021.

Shirk, Susan. *China: Fragile Superpower*. Oxford: Oxford University Press, 2008.

Wasserstrom, Jeffrey, and Maura Elizabeth Cunningham. *China in the 21st Century: What Everyone Needs to Know*. New York: Oxford University Press, 2018.

Watts, Jonathan. *When a Billion Chinese Jump: How China Will Save Mankind—or Destroy It*. New York: Scribner, 2010.

Wei, Lingling, and Bob David. *Superpower Showdown: How the Battle Between Trump and Xi Threatens a New Cold War*. New York: Harper Business, 2020.

INDEX